South Korea's Democracy in Crisis

SOUTH KOREA'S DEMOCRACY IN CRISIS

The Threats of Illiberalism, Populism, and Polarization

Edited by Gi-Wook Shin and Ho-Ki Kim

Stanford | Walter H. Shorenstein
Asia-Pacific Research Center
Freeman Spogli Institute

ROWMAN & LITTLEFIELD
Lanham • Boulder • New York • London

Shorenstein APARC addresses critical issues affecting the countries of Asia, their regional and global affairs, and U.S.-Asia relations. As Stanford University's hub for the interdisciplinary study of contemporary Asia, we produce policy-relevant research, provide education and training to students, scholars, and practitioners, and strengthen dialogue and cooperation between counterparts in the Asia-Pacific and the United States.

The Walter H. Shorenstein Asia-Pacific Research Center
Freeman Spogli Institute for International Studies
Stanford University
Encina Hall
Stanford, CA 94305-6055
http://aparc.fsi.stanford.edu

Walter H. Shorenstein Asia-Pacific Research Center, 2023.

Published by Rowman & Littlefield
An imprint of The Rowman & Littlefield Publishing Group, Inc.
4501 Forbes Boulevard, Lanham, MD 20706
www.rowman.com

86–90 Paul Street, London EC2A 4NE, United Kingdom

First printing, 2023
ISBN 978-1-5381-7781-5 (paper)
ISBN 978-1-5381-7780-8 (cloth)
ISBN 978-1-9313-6871-1 (electronic)

Library of Congress Control Number: 2022932495

Contents

Tables and Figures

Tables

Figures

Abbreviations

CCEJ	Citizens' Coalition for Economic Justice
CSAT	College Scholastic Ability Test
CSO	civil society organization
DPK	Democratic Party of Korea
FOIP	Free and Open Indo-Pacific
GRDP	gross regional domestic product
GRI	gross regional income
IHRLSG	International Human Rights Law Study Group
IMF	International Monetary Fund
KFEM	Korea Federation for Environmental Movements
KGSS	Korea General Social Survey
KIEP	Korea Institute for International Economic Policy
KTU	Korean Teachers and Education Workers Union
LDS	Lawyers for a Democratic Society (*Minbyeon*)
MMP	mixed-member proportional
NGO	nongovernmental organization
NKDB	Database Center for North Korean Human Rights
NSL	National Security Law
PISA	Program for International Student Assessment
POEA	Public Officials Election Act
PR	proportional representation
PSE	private supplementary education (*sa-gyo-yook*)

PSPD	People's Solidarity for Participatory Democracy
SMD	single-member district
USKI	U.S.-Korea Institute
WSG	*Wooribeop* Study Group
WVS	World Values Survey

Contributors

BYONGJIN AHN is a professor at Kyung Hee University, where he was also the former rector of the Global Academy for Future Civilizations. Ahn holds a PhD from the New School for Social Research, where he received the Hannah Arendt Award for his doctoral dissertation, "Learning to Speak American: The Use of Values Appeals in the 1984 and 1996 Presidential Elections." Ahn is currently a columnist for *Joongang Daily* and guest commentator on the Korea Broadcasting System. His fields of interest are the American presidency and Korean politics.

VICTOR CHA is a professor of government and holds the D.S. Song-KF Chair in the Department of Government and School of Foreign Service (SFS), and serves as vice dean for faculty and graduate affairs in SFS at Georgetown University. He left the White House in 2007 after serving since 2004 as director for Asian affairs at the National Security Council (NSC). At the White House, he was responsible primarily for Japan, the Korean Peninsula, Australia/New Zealand, and Pacific Island nation affairs. Cha was also the deputy head of delegation for the United States at the Six-Party Talks in Beijing and received two outstanding service commendations during his tenure at the NSC. He was appointed to the Defense Policy Board for the Biden administration in 2021 and serves as a Senior Fellow for Human Freedom (non-resident) at the George W. Bush Institute in Dallas, Texas.

Cha is the author of five books, including the award-winning *Alignment Despite Antagonism: The United States-Korea-Japan Security Triangle* (Stanford University Press, 1999, winner of the 2000 Ohira Book Prize) and *The Impossible State: North Korea, Past and Future*

(Harper Collins Ecco, 2012), which was selected by *Foreign Affairs* as a "Best Book on the Asia-Pacific for 2012." His latest works include *Powerplay: Origins of the American Alliance System in Asia* (Princeton University Press, 2016) and a forthcoming book on the study of North Korea through data. He is also co-authoring a new book on the modern history of Korea. He has published articles on international relations and East Asia in journals, including *Foreign Affairs*, *Foreign Policy*, *International Security*, *Political Science Quarterly*, *Survival*, *International Studies Quarterly*, *International Journal of the History of Sport*, and *Asian Survey*.

SEONGSOO CHOI is an associate professor of sociology at Yonsei University, Korea. His research interests include the sociology of education, social stratification and mobility, family demography, and quantitative research methods. His recent research has been published in *American Sociological Review*, *Demography*, and the *Korean Journal of Sociology*.

LARRY DIAMOND is a senior fellow at the Hoover Institution and the Mosbacher Senior Fellow in Global Democracy at the Freeman Spogli Institute for International Studies (FSI) at Stanford University. He is also professor, by courtesy, of political science and sociology and a Bass University Fellow in Undergraduate Education at Stanford. He co-leads the Hoover Institution's programs on China's Global Sharp Power and on Taiwan in the Indo-Pacific Region. At FSI, he leads the Program on Arab Reform and Democracy, based at the Center on Democracy, Development, and the Rule of Law, which he directed for more than six years. He also co-leads FSI's Global Digital Policy Incubator. He served for thirty-two years as the founding coeditor of the *Journal of Democracy* and is a senior consultant at the International Forum for Democratic Studies of the National Endowment for Democracy.

Diamond's research focuses on democratic trends and conditions around the world and on policies and reforms to defend and advance democracy. His latest books are *Ill Winds: Saving Democracy from Russian Rage, Chinese Ambition, and American Complacency* (Penguin Press, 2019) and *China's Influence and American Interests*, coedited with Orville Schell (Hoover Press, 2019). He offers a massive open online course on Comparative Democratic Development through the edX platform.

SEONGWOOK HEO is a professor of public law at Seoul National University (SNU) Law School. He teaches administrative law, environmental law, and law and economics. He received his PhD in law and LLM degree from SNU Graduate School of Law, and his bachelor's degree in economics from SNU. His recent research and teaching are focused on laws concerning climate change, energy, AI and privacy, and legal policy on the judicial system.

Heo was a participant in the process of framing the Green Growth Act and the Emission Trade Act in Korea. Prior to joining SNU Law School in 2006, he served as a judge of Seoul's Central District Court. He was a presiding judge on a specialized panel for intellectual property law cases in the Seoul Central District Court from 2005 to 2006.

Heo is currently a board member of the Korean Public Law Association, the Korean Environmental Law Association, the Korean Law and Economics Association, and the Korean Regulation Law Association.

ARAM HUR is an assistant professor of political science at the University of Missouri, where she also serves as codirector for the MU Institute for Korean Studies. She is the 2021 Sherman Emerging Scholar Awardee of the Korea Society and a 2018–19 U.S.-Korea NextGen Scholar, selected by the Center for Strategic and International Studies as "the next generation of Korea specialists in the United States." Her research focuses on national politics and democracy, with a focus on issues of national identity change, integration, and democratic quality in East Asia.

Hur's work is published in academic journals such as the *British Journal of Political Science*, *Comparative Politics*, and the *Journal of East Asian Studies*, and has been cited in media outlets such as the *New York Times*, *Washington Post*, and *Foreign Policy*. Her first book, *Narratives of Civic Duty: How National Stories Shape Democracy in Asia*, is forthcoming from Cornell University Press in November 2022. Hur holds a PhD from Princeton University, MPP from the Harvard Kennedy School, and BA with honors from Stanford University.

JUN HO JEONG is a professor in the Department of Real Estate, Kangwon National University. He holds a DPhil in economic geography from Oxford University. Previously, Jeong worked at the Korea Institute for Industrial Economics and Trade as a research associate and the director of the institute's economic survey and forecasting division. His current research interests include issues of income and wealth inequality, and industrial policies in Korea.

HO-KI KIM is a professor of sociology at Yonsei University. He received his PhD from Bielefeld University in Germany. He was the Korea Program's 2021 Koret Fellow at Stanford University's Shorenstein Asia-Pacific Research Center. Kim's major research interests include political sociology and modern social theories. He is the author of *Contemporary Capitalism and Korean Society* (in Korean, 1995), *Modernity and Social Change in Korea* (in Korean, 1999), *Reflections on the Civil Society in Korea* (in Korean, 2007), *Zeitgesit and Intellectuals* (in Korean, 2012), *Adventures of Intellectuals in Modern Korea* (in Korean, 2020), and "Change of Ideological Terrain and Political Consciousness in South Korea" (2005).

IL-YOUNG LEE is an economist and a professor at Hanshin University. He has authored several books in Korean, including *Korean Peninsula Economy in the New Normal Era* (2019), *Innovator Economics* (2015), *Korean Peninsula Economy: New Progressive Alternative* (2009), *Chinese Agriculture: Compression to East Asia* (2007), *North Korea's Agriculture: Situation and Prospect* (2004), and *China's Agrarian Reform and Economic Development* (1997).

KWANHU LEE has been a secretary for public communication messaging to South Korea's prime minister since June 2021. He received his PhD in political science from University College London. Prior to pursuing his PhD, Lee served as legal advisory staff to a member of South Korea's National Assembly for six years (2003–08). Before joining the government, Lee worked at the Institute for Social Science at Sogang University (2013–19), and pursued his interests in local democracy and public policy as a research fellow at Gyeongnam Research Institute for two years (2019–21). Lee's research interests include political legitimacy, representation, and party politics.

YONG SUK LEE is an assistant professor of technology, economy, and global affairs at the Keough School of Global Affairs at the University of Notre Dame. Lee's research focuses on new technologies, such as artificial intelligence and robotics in relation to labor economics, entrepreneurship, and urban economics. His current research focuses on how artificial intelligence and robotics affect labor, and the governance and ethical issues related to these new technologies. Lee also focuses on the application of machine learning to examine socioeconomic questions, such as bias, urban inequality and change, and the demand for skill. In addition, Lee's research examines aspects of technology education and entrepreneurship, e.g., education and mobility, and entrepreneurship and economic growth.

Prior to joining the University of Notre Dame, Lee was on the faculty at Stanford University as the SK Center Fellow at the Freeman Spogli Institute for International Studies. Prior to Stanford, he was assistant professor of economics at Williams College. He received his PhD in economics from Brown University, a MPP from Duke University, and bachelor's and master's degrees in architecture from Seoul National University. Lee also worked as a real estate development consultant and architecture designer as he transitioned from architecture to economics.

MYOUNG-HO PARK is a professor of political science at Dongguk University in Seoul. He is vice president of the Korean Political Science Association and president of the Korean Association of Democratic Civic Education. Park's research interests are in comparative political processes and Korean electoral and party politics, and he has published several articles and book chapters on the latter. He has served as the president of Korean Association of Party Studies. Park received a PhD in political science from Michigan State University.

GI-WOOK SHIN is the William J. Perry Professor of Contemporary Korea in sociology and a senior fellow at the Freeman Spogli Institute for International Studies at Stanford University. He established Stanford's Korea Program in 2001, and has been directing the Walter H. Shorenstein Asia-Pacific Research Center at Stanford since 2005. As a historical-comparative and political sociologist, his research concentrates on social movements, nationalism, development, and international relations, with focus on Korea and broader Asia. Shin is the author/editor of over twenty books and numerous articles. His books include *The North Korean Conundrum* (2021), *Strategic, Policy, and Social Innovation for a Post-Industrial Korea: Beyond the Miracle* (2018); *Divergent Memories: Opinion Leaders and the Asia-Pacific War* (2016); *Global Talent* (2015); *New Challenges for*

Maturing Democracies in Korea and Taiwan (2014); and *One Alliance, Two Lenses: U.S.-Korea Relations in a New Era* (2010). Shin is currently writing a book seeking to explain the rise of four Asia-Pacifc giants (Japan, China, India, and Australia) through a talent development lens.

Preface

In April 2020, I published an article, "Korean Democracy is Sinking Under the Guise of the Rule of Law," in the South Korean monthly magazine *Shindonga*. Three months later, I published its revised version, "South Korea's Democratic Decay," in the *Journal of Democracy*. To my surprise, the two pieces sparked a great deal of attention in both South Korea and the United States, and many of my friends and colleagues urged me to organize an academic conference to further assess the current state of Korean democracy and to discuss its future. Fortunately, Professor Ho-Ki Kim at Yonsei University in Seoul, my longtime friend and collaborator, was willing to work with me on this project during his quarter as a Koret fellow here at the Shorenstein Asia-Pacific Research Center's (APARC) Korea Program.

In November of 2020, we held a conference—virtually, due to COVID-19—that addressed the question: "Is Korea's Democracy in Crisis?" Its papers, representing the perspectives of participants from both Korea and the United States, are collected here in this volume. This was American academia's first serious collaborative effort to assess the status of Korean democracy and its implications for Korean society and politics. Seeking to be non-partisan in our discussions, we invited experts that hail from both progressive and conservative leanings. In fact, several of this volume's Korean authors are former activists who fought for democracy in the 1980s but have become increasingly concerned with the recent backsliding of Korean democracy. Besides the chapter authors, a number of experts served as paper discussants and provided valuable input to conference discussions. They included Joan Cho (Wesleyan University), Jacob Reidhead (KIMEP University), Tom

Ginsburg (University of Chicago), Yumi Moon (Stanford University), Sungsup Ra (Asian Development Bank), Misook Lee (*Munhwa Ilbo*), Hannah Kim (University of Nebraska, Omaha), Paul Chang (Harvard University), Joon-woo Park (former South Korean ambassador to the European Union and Singapore), and Won-Taek Kang (Seoul National University).

This conference and book are part of an initiative I lead called the "New Asia Project." The project is a cluster of multi-year studies focused on new societal issues and challenges faced by Korea and its neighboring countries. I am grateful to Chairman Chang Won Chey for his generous gift to the New Asia Project, and to the Korea Foundation for its intermediary support: both have made this conference and publication possible. I would also like to extend thanks to Heather Ahn and Joyce Lee for helping to organize the conference, and to Raymond Ha for translating several of the chapters from Korean to English. I thank Haley Gordon and Kelsi Caywood for their help in editing the book chapters, and to George Krompacky for preparing the finalized volume.

This book will be released shortly after the 2022 Korean presidential election, and it is my hope that these chapters will help illuminate a brighter way forward for South Korea's democracy. At time of writing, we are currently working on translating this volume into Korean.

Gi-Wook Shin
Director
Shorenstein APARC and Korea Program

South Korea's Democracy in Crisis

INTRODUCTION

Korea's Democratic Decay

Worrisome Trends and Pressing Challenges

Gi-Wook Shin and Ho-Ki Kim

South Korea's democratic development since 1987 has been lauded as an exemplary case of the "third wave" of global democratization.[1] Even the turmoil around the scandal-plagued presidency of Park Geun-Hye (2013–17), whose impeachment was demanded by the "candlelight protests" of 2016–17, was widely seen as a positive sign of a maturing democracy, replete with ordinary Korean citizens taking an active part in their country's political affairs.[2] In *The People vs. Democracy*, Yascha Mounk claims that Korea successfully defended liberal democracy from sliding back to authoritarianism through nationwide protests, safeguarding a democracy built on popular sovereignty.[3]

Many observers both in Korea and abroad, including both of us, had high expectations for the new administration of Moon Jae-in, who was elected in May 2017 following the Candlelight Movement. President Moon, a former human rights lawyer and a friend and adviser to the late Roh Moo-Hyun, the last progressive president, promised to create a new nation in which "the opportunities are equal, the process is fair, and the result is just." Vowing to swiftly move away from old

---

1 For brevity, we refer to "South Korea" as "Korea" throughout this book unless otherwise specified in the text.

2 Gi-Wook Shin and Rennie Moon, "South Korea after Impeachment," *Journal of Democracy* 28, no. 4 (October 2017): 117–31; Kim Ho-Ki, "Out of the Shadows: The Collapse of Park Geun-Hye and the Future of South Korea," *Global Asia* 11, no. 4 (2016): 80–85.

3 Yascha Mounk, *The People vs. Democracy* (Cambridge: Harvard University Press, 2018).

political legacies and achieve national unity, his administration took encouraging steps to realize the spirit of participatory and deliberative democracy that was embodied by the candlelight protests. The public applauded his efforts; his approval ratings reached over 80 percent during his first year in office.[4]

However, it did not take long for warning signs to appear in various corners of Korean society. Many intellectuals, including leading progressive scholars such as Choi Jang-Jip and Chin Jung-Kwon, grew increasingly concerned by illiberal trends in Korea's politics. To be fair, democratic backsliding did not begin with the Moon government. Still, it is troubling to observe that it has continued under and even been accelerated by the current regime, since it is staffed with former democracy activists who came to power after Park was impeached for her violation of democratic rules. Recent trends in Korea toward illiberalism and populism look similar to what has been happening in many other democracies, both old and new. This book examines aspects of Korean democracy that resemble or differ from those found elsewhere. In doing so, we seek to identify factors that accelerate or delay Korea's advance toward political tolerance, social justice, and other democratic values, and discuss how Korea can reverse the current retreat of democracy.

Democracy under Global Attack

Democracy did not develop without struggles. At two critical junctures in the twentieth century, democracy had to withstand totalitarian assaults from both the right and left.[5] Liberal democracy survived fascism in World War II, and it also won the competition against communism, which concluded with the downfall of the Soviet Union. Observing this triumphant march of Western democracy, Francis Fukuyama declared that humanity had arrived at liberal democracy as the "end of history."[6] Samuel Huntington similarly expressed an optimistic view of the future of democracy when he proclaimed the "Third Wave of

4 Shin and Moon, "South Korea after Impeachment."

5 Hannah Arendt, *The Origins of Totalitarianism* (Berlin, Germany: Schocken Books, 1951); Michael Mann, *Fascists* (Cambridge: Cambridge University Press, 2004).

6 Francis Fukuyama, *The End of History and the Last Man* (New York: Free Press, 2006).

democratization, during which nearly thirty countries, including Korea, made the democratic transition between 1974 and 1990."[7]

However, democracy has entered a period of regression in the past decade. As Larry Diamond observes in chapter 10, the ratio of countries gaining to those declining in freedom was at parity in 2006 and then fell to a deficit thereafter. A 2018 Freedom House report notes that seventy-one countries suffered a decline in civil liberties and political rights during the previous year, representing the twelfth consecutive year of a net global decline in democracy. The report concludes, "Democracy is in crisis. The values it embodies are under assault and in retreat globally."[8] As Diamond also warns in *Ill Winds: Saving Democracy from Russian Rage, Chinese Ambition, and American Complacency*, autocrats supported by China and Russia are rising, but democracy's advocates are on the defense.[9] Mature democracies are becoming extremely polarized and dysfunctional, he observes, while emerging democracies are growing more corrupt. Even the United States and the United Kingdom, which saved liberal democracy from fascist and communist assaults in the last century, are not immune from this global tide of democratic depression.

In *Healing the Heart of Democracy*, social activist Parker Palmer laments that the politics of our era have caused grief and sorrow instead of freedom, equality, and happiness. When politics—which must provide the norms and structures that uphold our communities—can no longer be a source of hope, we feel pain. Palmer sharply criticizes the politics of our era for failing to achieve the essential goal of contributing to democracy and the public good. Those with different views are demonized, while decisions are made based on convenience, not a consideration of pressing human needs. *Healing the Heart of Democracy* provides an unvarnished portrait of democracy in the twenty-first century.[10]

---

7 Samuel Huntington, *The Third Wave: Democratization in the Late Twentieth Century* (Norman, OK: University of Oklahoma Press, 1991).

8 Michael Abramowitz, "Freedom in the World 2018: Democracy in Crisis," accessed November 30, 2021, https://freedomhouse.org/report/freedom-world/2018/democracy-crisis.

9 Larry Diamond, *Ill Winds: Saving Democracy from Russian Rage, Chinese Ambition, and American Complacency* (New York: Penguin Press, 2019).

10 Parker Palmer, *Healing the Heart of Democracy: The Courage to Create a Politics Worthy of the Human Spirit* (Hoboken: John Wiley & Sons, 2011).

Now, at the beginning of a new decade, there is greater pessimism than optimism about democracy across the world. In particular, the global upsurge of populism, as seen in the ascendance of far-right political parties, lies at the core of this pessimism.

Democracy and Populism

Populism is not new, but its twenty-first-century version reveals how democracy and populism are two sides of the same coin. Populism draws fervent support from citizens for its anti-elitist orientation, but it also endangers democracy with its anti-pluralist values. By emphasizing popular sovereignty and the primacy of the people against the establishment, it denounces elitism and the incompetence of politicians, while simultaneously threatening democracy by rejecting political pluralism. Contemporary populism challenges the established political order in two ways: anti-elitism and anti-pluralism.

Numerous observers have already pointed to populism as the most influential political trend across the world in the 2010s. As seen in the rise of Donald Trump and Bernie Sanders (United States), the National Front (France), Alternative for Germany, the UK Independence Party, the Five Star Movement (Italy), Syriza (Greece), and Podemos (Spain), populism has caused a political earthquake in Western countries, with reverberations reaching into civil society as well. As described by John Judis, populism, whether leftist or rightist, places the confrontation between the people and the elite at the center of its political narrative.[11] Right-wing populism further adds a divide between the national ingroup and the outgroup. In the U.S. and European context, the outgroup includes immigrants, refugees, social and religious minorities, and sexual minorities.

The origins of populism can be traced to the Narodniks (Russia) and the People's Party (United States) in the late nineteenth century. The latter had a decisive influence on the development of populism. It advocated for the regulation of industries and private enterprises, as well as the adoption of a progressive tax code to alleviate inequality. There was a resurgence of populism in Latin America in the 1940s and 1950s, as can be seen from the appearance of Peronism, the Argentinian movement that gained momentum in light of perceived government failure to

11 John Judis, *The Populist Explosion: How the Great Recession Transformed American and European Politics* (New York: Columbia Global Reports, 2016).

address the needs of the working class. Populism returned to the scene in Western Europe in the 1990s with the National Front in France and the Northern League in Italy. It also made a comeback in Latin America in the 2000s under the Hugo Chávez regime in Venezuela.

Mounk argues that democracy has reached a new "populist moment." This is the third such moment, following its struggle against fascism and communism. Mounk focuses on the crisis of liberal democracy, which has been the dominant political paradigm since the 1990s. This crisis takes two forms. The first is "democracy without rights," wherein "authoritarian strongmen" rely on populist forces to march toward dictatorial rule. The second is "rights without democracy," in which technocratic institutions overwhelm democratic politics. A hatred of political elites, the intensification of political tribalism through social media, and the growing prevalence of fake news—these are all tangible signs of a democracy in danger.[12]

Steven Levitsky and Daniel Ziblatt also analyze the contemporary crisis of liberal democracy in *How Democracies Die*. They observe that the erosion and downfall of democracies since the post–Cold War era has been caused not by military coups or social revolutions, but rather through the actions of democratically elected leaders. This has occurred not only in Venezuela under Chávez and the United States under Trump, but also in Georgia, Hungary, Nicaragua, Peru, the Philippines, Poland, Russia, Sri Lanka, Turkey, and Ukraine. In other words, democracy is being overturned at the ballot box, not by guns or uprisings.[13]

In their view, symptoms of a democracy in crisis emerge when established political parties and politicians join forces with populists. The ruling party brands the opposition as a treasonous, unpatriotic enemy. The party that loses an election refuses to accept the results and deploys conspiracy theories. The president circumvents the legislature and overuses executive orders. The legislature uses its constitutional authority over the budget to throw the executive branch into crisis, or it pursues impeachment on questionable grounds. The government silences critics through libel suits or other means. These are all commonly observed phenomena in countries where populists are in power.[14]

---

12 Mounk, *The People vs. Democracy*.

13 Steven Levitsky and Daniel Ziblatt, *How Democracies Die* (New York: Crown, 2018).

14 Levitsky and Ziblatt, *How Democracies Die*.

There are three defining characteristics to twenty-first-century populism. First, it is not constrained by ideology. Trumpism is a right-wing version, while Podemos has a left-wing orientation. As Cas Mudde and Cristóbal Rovira Kaltwasser point out, it is a "thin-centered ideology" that can be easily fused with liberalism or socialism.[15] Second, populism divides society into a "corrupt elite" and the "pure people." It holds that politics should express the "general will" of the people. To populists, the primary objective of politics is to reclaim popular sovereignty by fighting against the elite. Third, as Jan-Werner Müller emphasizes, it opposes political pluralism or distrusts institutional representation. According to populists, only their supporters belong to "the people."[16]

Three factors have been critical to the recent upsurge of populism. The first is the hardening of structural inequalities. Since the dawn of the neoliberal era in the 1980s, socioeconomic inequalities have steadily increased. In 1980, the share of total income accounted for by the nation's top 10 percent of earners was 34.2 percent in the United States, 29.9 percent in Western Europe, 36.5 percent in Japan, and 32.8 percent in Korea. By 2019, the share increased to 45.5 percent in the United States, 34.8 percent in Western Europe, 44.9 percent in Japan, and 46.5 percent in Korea.[17] According to the French economist Thomas Piketty, this had to do with the emergence of "inheritance-based capitalism." In his best-selling book *Capital in the Twenty-First Century*, he argues that in an economy where the rate of return on capital outstrips the rate of growth, inherited wealth will always grow faster than earned wealth.[18] That is what we face today. Citizens called upon politicians to address these inequalities, but established politicians—both on the left and the right—were largely ineffectual.

The second is the continued progress of globalization. There was a large wave of immigration to Western countries when globalization began in earnest around the 1970s and 80s.[19] The number of international migrants tripled between 1970 and 2019, from 85 million to

15 Cas Mudde and Cristóbal Rovira Kaltwasser, *Populism: A Very Short Introduction* (New York: Oxford University Press, 2017).
16 Jan-Werner Müller, *What Is Populism?* (Philadelphia: University of Pennsylvania Press, 2016).
17 World Inequality Database, https://wid.world/data, accessed December 1, 2021.
18 Thomas Piketty, *Capital in the Twenty-First Century* (Cambridge: Harvard University Press, 2017).
19 David Held et al., *Global Transformations: Politics, Economics and Culture* (Stanford: Stanford University Press, 1999).

272 million, more than half of whom now reside in Europe and North America.[20] In recent years, there has been a large influx of Muslim refugees into Western European countries. There was high tolerance for foreign workers and immigrants during periods of economic prosperity, but immigration and refugee policy became a fiercely debated "hot potato" after the 2008 financial crisis and the 2015 refugee crisis. We have recently seen the rise of anti-immigrant sentiment sweeping the West, providing fertile ground for populism. Populist leaders of several EU member states, such as Hungary, Italy, and Austria, took a hardline approach to migration and refugee issues to instigate fear and to garner electoral support. According to the spring 2016 Global Attitudes Survey by the Pew Research Center, a median of 59 percent across ten EU countries expressed concern that the influx of refugees would increase the likelihood of terrorism and a median of 50 percent believed that refugees imposed a burden on their countries. In countries like Italy, Hungary, Greece, Poland, Germany, and the Netherlands, a much larger proportion of people responded that diversity made their country a worse place to live than those who believed diversity made their country a better place to live.[21]

The third is the development of the information society. Whereas the internet and smartphones enabled social movements to swiftly mobilize the general public, social media platforms such as Facebook and Twitter opened a direct channel of communication between citizens and politicians.[22] A considerable number of citizens viewed existing forums of public dialogue, including the press and media outlets, as part of the elite establishment. As a result, citizens began to bypass these traditional forums and met face-to-face with politicians on social media. In addition, social media can provide a fertile ground for populism by amplifying the salience of political polarization (see chapter 8).

In sum, inequality, globalization, and an information society all combined to create an uncertain transitional period during which citizens

20 International Organization for Migration, *World Migration Report 2020* (Geneva, Switzerland: IOM, 2019).

21 Richard Wike, Bruce Stokes, and Katie Simmons, "Europeans Fear Wave of Refugees Will Mean More Terrorism, Fewer Jobs," Pew Research Center, July 11, 2016, https://www.pewresearch.org/global/wp-content/uploads/sites/2/2016/07/Pew-Research-Center-EU-Refugees-and-National-Identity-Report-FINAL-July-11-2016.pdf.

22 Christian Fuchs, *Social Media: A Critical Introduction* (London: Sage Publications, 2017).

became increasingly dissatisfied with the political establishment, which was seen as failing to address pressing issues. Populism thrives in this atmosphere of discontent, and thus began the era of populism.

What, then, is the outlook for populism in the coming decade? Given current social and political realities, it is not unlikely that populism will gain traction as a political alternative that reaches beyond right- or left-wing ideologies. Judis saw the emergence of populism as reflecting a demand to overhaul the prevailing political paradigm.[23] Despite the only recent emergence of scholarly concern, populist forces are already starting to replace the established political class in many parts of the world. This is not to say that populism only has negative consequences. It can provide an external shock to established and often corrupt political actors and push them toward meaningful reforms. However, those who study populism warn that its anti-pluralist values will threaten liberal democracy. Populism creates a politics of division, not unity. It creates hatred, not tolerance. Although it advocates popular sovereignty, its binary distinction of the people versus the elite raises the specter of "two nations in one country."

Taken together, it is likely that populist forces will continue to gain political power in the 2020s. If socioeconomic inequalities are not alleviated and citizens' trust in the competence of establishment politicians remains low, then voters may elect populists into office. The way politics is consumed and shared by the public has also substantially changed. One of the reasons that populism draws the public's attention is that it focuses on the political charisma of individual politicians. This leads to the personalization of political authority. Both "traditional" print media and "new" online media play a decisive role in this process. Such phenomena are already an integral part of the era that we are living in.

It is difficult to predict to what extent the institutions of representative democracy will be able to overcome the limitations of the political establishment in the 2020s. If the political class remains mired in elitism, then populism—with its emphasis on popular sovereignty—will gain ground, and the era of populism is very likely to continue. It is also very important to consider the context in which the current upsurge of populism has taken place. In every country, the primary cause has been the deepening of inequalities and the incompetence of politicians. If establishment politicians are unable to effectively alleviate

---

23 Judis, *The Populist Explosion.*

socioeconomic inequalities, populism will continue to grow as democracy withers away.

Korea's Democratic Regression

Korea is following global trends in its slide toward a democratic regression. As noted above, both liberal-democratic norms and institutions are under attack across the world. The symptoms of democratic decline are increasingly hard to miss in Korea. They are appearing in many corners of Korean society—the hallmarks of zero-sum politics in which opponents are demonized, democratic norms are eroded, and political life grows ever more polarized. To be sure, it might be premature to declare that Korea's democracy is in crisis, but we believe that it is showing clear warning signs, as outlined below.[24]

The politics of "deep-rooted evil"

When those in power begin to demonize the opposition, it is a sign that things may be going wrong for democracy. The Moon administration's campaign of "eradicating deep-rooted evil" from Korean society and politics is one example. The new power elite triumphantly proclaimed a mission of eradicating "deep-rooted evil perpetrated by those in authority" and changing the mainstream of Korean society.[25] In practice, however, this has meant two things: bureaucratic purges and political prosecution. There is nothing novel in Korean politics about a new administration seeking to set itself apart from its predecessor or going after lingering corruption. However, justifying such actions with dualistic logic—attacking the other side as a "great evil" and "reactionary"—has been less typical since democratization.[26] Such rhetoric opens the door to attacks on democratic norms.

---

24 This is drawn from Gi-Wook Shin, "South Korea's Democratic Decay," *Journal of Democracy* 31, no. 3 (July 2020): 100–14.

25 "Opening Remarks by President Moon Jae-In at New Year Press Conference," Cheong Wa Dae, January 10, 2019, https://english1.president.go.kr/BriefingSpeeches/Speeches/106.

26 Similar actions occurred during the Kim Young-Sam administration (1993–98). As the first civilian government in more than three decades, the Kim administration sought to remove the legacies of military-authoritarian regimes through such logic. The authoritarian-democratic divide was obvious at that time, but today's context is very different.

Besides convicting former president Lee Myung-Bak and former supreme court chief justice Yang Seung-Tae, the bureaucratic purges have seen officials who were in charge of policy implementation—not policy formulation or decision—grilled as if they had more authority than they did, resulting in excessive punishments.[27] These include special investigations of the Ministry of Foreign Affairs' 2015 "comfort women" agreement with Japan, the Ministry of Unification's 2016 decision to close the Kaesong Industrial Complex, and the Ministry of Education's 2015 reinstatement of government-published history textbooks for secondary education. These investigations led to the punishment of numerous government officials (both at the executive and working levels) involved in policy implementation.[28] Policy reviews are common practice for any new administration, but such ideologically driven investigations and punishments as those by the Moon government are rare in liberal democracies. By the end of 2017, thirty-nine special task forces and committees, largely consisting of pro-government experts (including many from progressive civic and labor organizations), were formed under twenty-nine ministries and government agencies with a clear objective to eradicate the "deep-rooted evil" of previous conservative governments. The legality of such actions and the activities of these ad hoc groups have been questioned by many, stirring much controversy in and out of the ministries and government agencies that were called upon.

Contrary to Moon's promise to foster national unity, this all-out campaign has sharpened polarization, accompanied by tense mobilizations on both the right and the left. On the right, there is the so-called *Taegukgi* Brigade, named after the Korean national flag that its adherents wave during protests to demonstrate their patriotism. On the left, there are the zealous presidential supporters known as *Moon-ppa* (a

27 Some 40 percent of the prosecutorial resources at the Seoul Central District Prosecutors' Office were devoted to this task—an exceptionally large-scale investigation compared to any democratic administration in Korea. During the investigations, at least five individuals who were labeled as perpetrators from past conservative regimes committed suicide.

28 For example, the special investigation committee in the Ministry of Education requested an investigation of seventeen individuals and ordered disciplinary punishment for six working-level public officials for their involvement in the government-published history textbook project during the Park Geun-Hye administration. See "Ministry of Education to Request Prosecution Investigation of Seventeen for Carrying Forward the Government Textbook Project" [in Korean], *Yonhap News*, June 8, 2018, https://www.yna.co.kr/view/AKR20180606040700004.

neologism that stands for "Moon's fanatics"). Protests against Moon are held just a few blocks from the Blue House, while pro-Moon protests occur about a dozen kilometers and a world away, on the far (southern) side of the Han River. This geographic separation reflects a deeply divided society, where anger and resentment are crowding out tolerance and a willingness to compromise.

Under Moon, Korean society has rapidly fragmented amidst a pervasive atmosphere of mistrust and conflict between individuals, groups, and generations. There is now a greater likelihood that conservatives, who scored a landslide victory in two mayoral by-elections for Seoul and Busan in April 2021, will launch their own campaign to "eradicate [new] deep-rooted evils" if they regain power in the upcoming presidential election in March 2022. Demands by the political opposition to impeach the president may become the new norm. A descent into a cycle of provocation and revenge, reminiscent of Greek tragedies or the "literati purges" in late-fifteenth- and sixteenth-century Korea under the Joseon dynasty (1392–1910), is a real possibility for Korean politics.

Interfering with the courts

Separation of powers is fundamental to liberal democracy. The courts are the last line of defense for the rule of law. From the outset, however, the Moon government has abused its administrative powers to undermine this basic principle and politicize the courts. As Seongwook Heo discusses in chapter 5, a judge who had been the head of a progressive lawyers' group was appointed as the secretary of legal affairs in the Blue House. Another recently retired judge with a similar résumé was subsequently named as his successor. These two judge-turned-officials have reportedly spearheaded the effort to "eradicate deep-rooted evil" in the judiciary, culminating in the arrest of several senior judges. This includes former chief justice Yang Seung-Tae, who was detained in January 2019 on a raft of charges related to scandals surrounding former president Park.

The naming of officers of the law, such as prosecutors, to high-level jobs at the Blue House has long been a controversial issue in Korea. It led to a March 2017 amendment of the Korean Prosecutors' Act by the Moon administration, which stipulated at least one year of retirement before an ex-prosecutor could assume a Blue House post. Nonetheless, the appointment of former judges proceeded on the grounds that there were no laws forbidding it. Yet this practice was even more troubling, since judges are supposed to be politically independent. The legal loophole was closed in February 2020 with an amendment to the Court Organization Act. However, the Moon government's deliberate exploitation of this loophole prior to the amendment blurred the lines between the judicial and executive branches. As such, it was an ominous attack on the constitutional principle of separation of powers (see chapter 5).

Furthermore, there has been a trend of jurists immediately plunging into partisan politics after resigning or retiring. In the April 2020 election, three judges left the court to run for the National Assembly, all as members of the ruling Democratic Party, and won seats while echoing the Moon administration's rhetoric to "eradicate deep-rooted evil." They were nominated by the party because they shared the same political views. After being elected, they led the initiative to impeach a senior judge, even though a court had already found that he was not guilty. The danger is apparent: if judges with particular ideological views start jumping into politics, it could turn legal rulings into the equivalent of campaign appeals and undermine faith in the fairness and impartiality of the courts.[29]

Such acts are not only problematic but also highly dangerous, as President Moon has the time and power to reshape the courts during his tenure. Korea, like France and Germany, has both a Supreme Court and a Constitutional Court. Justices on these bodies serve six-year terms, while the president has a single five-year term. The one-year difference is intentional. It ensures that judicial power is not fully subordinated to executive authority. However, due to the impeachment of President Park, President Moon has a rare opportunity to reshape both courts. During his term, he has named thirteen justices (including the chief justice) of the fourteen-member Supreme Court and eight of the nine justices on the Constitutional Court, six of whom are progressively

---

29 An example of a controversial decision would be the Supreme Court's November 2018 ruling that two Japanese corporations owed compensation for the thirty-five years of forced labor to which Koreans were subjected during Japan's 1910–45 occupation of the Korean Peninsula. An example of a hot issue would be the Supreme Court "blacklist" scandal. On these matters, see, respectively, "Japan May Take South Korea Wartime Labor Dispute to International Court of Justice: NHK," Reuters, July 17, 2019, http://www.reuters.com/article/us-southkorea-japan-laborers-idUSKCN1UD02Z; and He-Suk Choi, "Supreme Court in Hot Water over Blacklist, Political Bias Allegations," *Korea Herald*, January 24, 2018, http://www.koreaherald.com/view.php?ud=20180124000861.

inclined. With the ruling bloc now in charge of all three branches of government, the danger of undermining legal principles looms larger than ever. Liberal democracy cannot survive without checks and balances, which cannot be applied without independent courts.

Changing the rules of the game, holding double standards

Election laws are "rules of the game" that are essential to upholding democracy. If powerful actors unilaterally change these rules to their own advantage, it is hard for others to accept the results that follow. In 2019, the ruling Democrats bypassed the main opposition party and worked with three smaller parties to enact a new electoral system that introduced a number of seats filled according to mixed-member proportional (MMP) representation. The National Assembly has 253 seats elected from single-member districts (SMDs). The remaining forty-seven seats were filled through proportional representation (PR) from closed party lists. Before 2019, all PR seats were distributed based on parties' respective vote percentage. The changes that were passed in December 2019, however, left only seventeen of the PR seats to be distributed in the old manner. The other thirty seats were now to be distributed according to a quasi-MMP formula that was expected to favor small parties, which is why the smaller opposition parties had backed this shift in the first place.

The stated goal was valid: giving minority parties a larger voice in the legislature. The manner in which this rule change passed the National Assembly may have been within the letter of the law as well. Even so, changing the rules of the game against the will of the main opposition party violates the spirit of liberal, constitutional democracy. Powerless to stop the change, the main opposition party adapted by forming a novel "satellite" party that ran only for PR seats while the parent party ran only for SMD seats—all to maximize the combined number of seats.

At first, the Democrats attacked the idea of a satellite party as an underhanded political trick. Later, however, they formed one of their own, claiming that "popular militias" were rising up to defend the progressive cause. The original intent of adding an MMP element to the system slid rapidly into irrelevancy as all actors outdid each other in finding ways to circumvent the rules. The April 2020 election results showed that these tricks worked well. The two major parties together captured thirty-six of the forty-seven PR seats, leaving smaller parties out in the cold. This was all done within the letter of the law, but both the ruling party and its opponents left democratic norms and the liberal-democratic spirit bruised and battered. The satellite party of the ruling bloc merged with its parent party soon after the elections, despite public outcry.

There is also the matter of double standards. The Moon administration claims solidarity with the weak and the disadvantaged as proof that it is uniquely qualified to reform society. Yet the row over former justice minister Cho Kuk showed in no uncertain terms that the president and his party would not hesitate to behave like any other power elite when crossed. Cho was a Seoul National University law professor who had been one of President Moon's first key appointments, serving at the Blue House as senior secretary for civil affairs. Widely known as an outspoken progressive intellectual, he had also been active in civil society and often stressed the need to reform Korea's legal system.

In the second half of 2019, during Cho's confirmation hearings at the National Assembly for the Justice Ministry post, a plethora of corruption allegations against him emerged in the press. The Supreme Prosecutor's Office under Yoon Seok-Youl investigated and later indicted Cho and his family on charges that included bribery and document fraud. The Blue House, the Democratic Party, and their supporters reacted with fury, denouncing the investigation and the subsequent legal proceedings as a reactionary plot. A Democratic legislator who had dared to criticize Cho's appointment was excoriated as "anti-reform" because he had been a prosecutor before entering politics. None of this was enough to save Cho, who resigned under public pressure after only thirty-five days as justice minister and is now undergoing trial alongside his wife.[30]

This imbroglio made the Moon administration's double standards painfully apparent. A government that had shown no qualms about wielding prosecutorial power against its political opponents could not stand seeing a friend such as Cho become the target of a criminal investigation. Suddenly, prosecutors needed to be held in check. Choo Mi-Ae, who from 2016 to 2018 led the Democratic Party and served as the justice minister after Cho, imposed restrictions on public disclosures of indictments and added an additional layer of decision-making

30 Chung Kyung-shim, his wife, was sentenced to prison in December 2020 for four years; Cho Kuk's trial is still underway as of this writing.

to separate the bringing of charges from the investigation itself. In defending these changes, she cited the importance of "the right to a fair trial."[31] That is at least creditable in principle, even if the administration showed no interest in such reforms until one of its own found himself in the hot seat. Choo's moves to tie Prosecutor General Yoon's hands by demoting key prosecutors in charge of sensitive investigations are less creditable. These maneuvers were within her legal authority, but deeply troubling. Prosecutors are not merely executive agents. They are officers of the judicial system as well, and concerns about the separation of powers also apply in this instance.

The double standard that the Moon administration applied during the Cho Kuk affair represents a failure to respect the spirit of the candlelight protests. Regard for law above party would also impel stepping aside to let prosecutors thoroughly investigate matters such as the Blue House's alleged interference in the June 2018 Ulsan mayoral election. Thirteen individuals, including senior secretaries to the president, have been indicted for extensive illegal efforts to ensure that a close friend of the president would triumph in his bid to become the mayor of Ulsan, a key industrial city.[32] In the National Assembly, Democratic Party lawmakers openly called for Prosecutor General Yoon's resignation and even threatened to designate him as the first case of the newly established Corruption Investigation Office for High-ranking Officials, which began its work on July 1, 2020.[33] Once considered a key ally, Yoon came to be feared and reviled as someone whose office may follow the Ulsan investigation wherever it leads, including to the president himself. The Moon administration refused to show forbearance in its exercise of power and complained because not all the results were to its liking. Yoon ultimately resigned from his position and has become a symbol of the anti-Moon opposition. He is now running for the presidency as the candidate of the main opposition party.

---

31 Kim Se-Jeong, "Justice Minister Defends Decision to Block Indictment Disclosure," *Korea Times*, February 12, 2020, http://www.koreatimes.co.kr/www/nation/2020/02/251_283304.html.

32 The efforts included an abusive police investigation that may have been engineered from the Blue House. See Myong-Sik Kim, "Blue House and 2018 Ulsan Mayoral Election Conspiracy," *Korea Herald*, February 12, 2020, http://www.koreaherald.com/view.php?ud=20200211000862.

33 "Shameful Distractions," *JoongAng Daily*, April 20, 2020, https://koreajoongangdaily.joins.com/news/article/article.aspx?aid=3076281.

Politicizing civil society, infringing on free speech

Civil society was an active and important player in Korea's journey toward democracy.[34] In 1960, student-led protests forced Korea's first authoritarian president, Syngman Rhee, out of office. In 1979, public protests created schisms inside the ruling bloc, leading to the assassination of general-turned-president Park Chung-Hee. In 1987, large-scale demonstrations pressured the Chun Doo-Hwan dictatorship into accepting the reforms that marked Korea's transition to democracy. The 2016–17 candlelight protests likewise built on broad civic participation to galvanize Korean politics. Civil society has also provided manpower to political society. Many leaders of student movements in the 1970s and 1980s entered politics and the so-called 386 activists (who were in their thirties when the term was coined in the 1990s, attended college in the 1980s, and were born in the 1960s) hold key posts in the Moon administration. Several high-ranking officials were also key members of a leading civic organization called the People's Solidarity for Participatory Democracy, including Cho Kuk and the first three policy chiefs in the Blue House. Many other ministers, senior presidential secretaries, and National Assembly members were leading student or civic activists. In short, yesterday's protesters have become the props of today's power structure.

The political prominence of Korean civil society is not altogether a heartening sign for democracy, however. As Kwanhu Lee argues in chapter 3, civil society looms as large as it does because Korea has an unstable party system that struggles to produce policies that are responsive to social demands. Active civic participation in politics is encouraging, but when institutions such as parties are immature and dysfunctional, as Myoung-Ho Park points out in chapter 4, this may leave society politicized and polarized to an unhealthy degree. If the vagaries of a mercurial "street democracy" come to outweigh representative, constitutional institutions, it does not bode well for democratic stability.

Adding to this foreboding has been the spectacle offered by many former democratic activists, now ensconced in office, who are leading

34 Gi-Wook Shin and Paul Y. Chang, eds., *South Korean Social Movements: From Democracy to Civil Society* (London and New York: Routledge, 2011).

the charge against fundamental democratic rules and norms.[35] As the noted political scientist Choi Jang-Jip observes, these new elites are running the government as if they are still fighting against authoritarianism. Instead of appreciating democratic rules and standards that promote tolerance and compromise, they seem intent on living in the past and reprising their glory days as bold, young activists.[36] They still seem to think they are "fighting the power" when, in fact, they *are* the power. Korea's politicized civil society is stunting, not advancing, liberal democracy.

One worrying sign is the rising trend of infringements on the freedom of speech. In late 2018, the Moon government declared a "war on fake news," encouraging state agencies to report false or misleading news accounts, especially videos on conservative YouTube channels, to law enforcement. There was pushback as opposition lawmakers and conservative intellectuals denounced the "war" as an attempt to silence critical voices.[37] In February 2020, the Democratic Party went so far as to sue a professor for her newspaper op-ed asking readers to vote for "any party but the Democratic Party" in April. Staffers at think tanks dependent on government funding are under pressure not to write or say anything that will upset the administration. As Victor Cha laments in chapter 9, the Johns Hopkins University–affiliated U.S.-Korea Institute—a leading Washington, D.C. think tank that focused exclusively on the Korean Peninsula—lost its funding from Seoul and had to close in 2018 when it rejected a Blue House demand to fire its director and assistant director. The Moon administration reportedly objected to these individuals on the grounds that they were too conservative.[38]

---

35 See Lee Cheol-Seung, *The Generation of Inequality* [in Korean] (Seoul, Korea: Munhak-gwa Chiseong-sa, 2019).

36 Choi Jang-Jip, "The Crisis and Consolidation of Korea's Democracy, and Alternatives for a New Political Order" [in Korean], paper presented at *Kim Dae-Jung and Democracy: Thought and Practice* at Kim Dae-Jung Library, Yonsei University, December 9, 2019.

37 Choe Sang-Hun, "South Korea Declares War on 'Fake News,' Worrying Government Critics," *New York Times*, October 2, 2018, http://www.nytimes.com/2018/10/02/world/asia/south-korea-fake-news.html.

38 Anna Fifield, "Korea Think Tank at U.S. University to Close after Seoul Withdraws Funding," *Washington Post*, April 11, 2018, https://www.washingtonpost.com/world/asia_pacific/korea-think-tank-at-us-university-to-close-after-seoul-withdraws-funding/2018/04/11/87adc3a8-3d64-11e8-912d-16c9e9b37800_story.html.

The aggressive behavior and even fanaticism of the *Moon-ppa* had a substantial political impact. In addition to holding street demonstrations, they are not above harassing individuals and groups whose views they dislike, barraging targets with text messages and malicious online comments.[39] When a judge issued a ruling they opposed, they doxed him, posting his personal information on the internet. A merchant who voiced concern about the "godawful" economy when the president visited his store was targeted with personal harassment, receiving verbal abuse and threats of violence. National Assembly members, intellectuals, and journalists with "unacceptable" views find themselves inundated by tsunamis of angry, threatening texts and other forms of cyberbullying. As confrontation worsens and extreme supporters grow increasingly strident, Korean intellectuals are choosing to engage in self-censorship. Voices of reason and conscience—which every free and democratic society must have—are being muffled, if not silenced altogether.

Chauvinistic populism

The fusion of political polarization and populism, which is drawing explosive popular support, is an important feature of the global democratic depression. The chauvinistic populism that has emerged in Korea is akin to what we are witnessing elsewhere. Whereas populism in the United States and Europe comes mainly from the right, Korea's populism resembles Latin American left-wing populism. Moon's is a government of the left, but its leftism has not stopped it from trafficking in nationalist appeals. Moon himself has praised Admiral Yi Sun-Sin, a national hero known for fighting the Japanese in the late sixteenth century, in at least one speech. In 2017, the Blue House took a petty swipe at Japan by serving prawns caught near the islet group known as Dokdo—long the subject of a territory dispute between Seoul and Tokyo—at a state banquet for President Trump.[40] Calls to boycott Jap-

39 Kwon Kyong-Ae, a progressive lawyer who once supported the Moon government but became a leading critic after the Cho Kuk controversy, calls this "*Moon-ppa* fascism." See her new book, *Time of Lawlessness* [in Korean] (Seoul: Chonnyon-ui sangsang, 2021).

40 Yi Sun-Sin is famed for his victories during the Imjin War (1592–98), including one in which he used a mere dozen ships to defeat a much larger Japanese fleet, marking a critical turning point in the war. On the Dokdo prawns, see Justin McCurry, "Japan Anger over South Korea's Shrimp Surprise for Donald Trump," *The Guardian*, November 9, 2017.

anese goods are recurring events in Korea; there was such a boycott campaign in mid-2019.

It is an old story: politicians are wrapping themselves in the flag to distract the public from something else. Behind references to Admiral Yi and other such patriotic mainstays as the Tonghak Peasant Rebellion of 1894 and the National Debt Repayment Movement of 1907 is the Moon administration's eagerness to boost approval ratings while avoiding responsibility for ongoing economic difficulties and the neglect of bilateral relations with Japan. In 2019, the Democratic Party's think tank even issued a report on how Seoul-Tokyo frictions could help the party's candidates at the polls in 2020.

It should hardly need explaining, one would hope, that inflaming diplomatic tensions by deploying small seafood in even smaller political stunts—to say nothing of trying to split Koreans into hostile factions with charges of "traitor" being hurled around—is no way for the high officials of a democratic republic to live up to their duties and responsibilities. Cheap chauvinistic gambits are unbecoming of those tasked with leading a country that belongs to the G20, wields serious military power in one of the world's most strategic regions, boasts the globe's twelfth-largest economy, exerts worldwide cultural influence (through K-Pop, among other exports), and has been a competitive democracy for decades. Such behavior seeps into Korea's external affairs: as Victor Cha argues in chapter 9, "Democratic erosion is evident in foreign policy when a state no longer privileges such [liberal] values in its diplomacy." The Moon administration, he concludes, "does not externalize norms of compromise and negotiation in its relations with other states."

When populism is on the rise, political logic and emotional appeals take center stage. Professionalism and expert opinions are dismissed, and it becomes difficult to hold rational debates. For example, when the administration said that it would act on a campaign pledge to raise the minimum wage (a common populist policy), many economists advised incremental increases over time, since a large chunk of Korean employment comes from self-employed individuals who hire temporary workers.[41] Moon and his advisers dismissed these economists as mouthpieces for a "privileged few" and raised the minimum

41 Jungmin Lee, remarks at a seminar on "Minimum Wage and Employment Dynamics in Korea," Walter H. Shorenstein Asia-Pacific Research Center, Stanford University, February 7, 2020. See also "Fallout from Minimum Wage Hike

wage 16.4 percent in 2018 and another 10.9 percent in 2019.[42] These steep hikes have caused small employers vast difficulties and cost many temporary workers their jobs. The tragic irony of workers losing their jobs due to policies that were billed as helping them is not one that the administration wishes to acknowledge, much less fix. Contrary to government expectations, as Jun Ho Jeong and Il-Young Lee well document in chapter 6, economic disparities have increased, providing fertile ground for the rise of populism.

Rescuing Korean Democracy from Further Regression

These trends can be readily understood within the conceptual framework of populism outlined above. The progressive political scientist Choi Jang-Jip drew public attention by characterizing the current state of Korea's democracy as one of "political polarization, an attack on representative democracy, and the emergence of a radical populism that prioritizes direct democracy."[43] Given that these aggressive and illiberal measures are the work of a leftist government in Korea, they are taken in the name of the people, but are hostile to the spirit and sometimes the letter of constitutional democracy. Disturbingly, the key figures in Korea's democratic backsliding are former pro-democracy activists—including President Moon himself, a human rights lawyer—who have now risen to power. They are preening themselves on their own moral superiority as they stress ideological purity and embrace a politics of confrontation, resentment, and even hatred.

The key question is why such populist phenomena are appearing at this political moment. To answer this question, we need to understand larger, structural forces, especially how weak political parties and the public's distrust in establishment politicians, as well as growing economic disparities, contributed to the rise of populism in Korea (see chapters 3 and 6). Furthermore, as Park points out in chapter 4, civil society, which played an instrumental role in Korea's march toward

Spreading," *Korea Herald*, July 31, 2017, http://www.koreaherald.com/view.php?ud=20170731000686.

42 In comparison, the average annual rate of increase from 2010 to 2017 was 5.3%.

43 Choi, "The Crisis and Consolidation of Korea's Democracy."

democracy, became highly politicized and powerful, adding fuel to the fire of populism. Cha argues in chapter 9 that illiberal populism has even spilled over into foreign policy. On the other hand, Byongjin Ahn offers a different perspective in chapter 1, noting that Korea's progressive power elite is not populist enough in the sense that they have failed to address popular demands. Rather, they are just incompetent illiberal actors.

Because populism emphasizes the restoration of popular sovereignty, it will always remain inseparable from democracy. However, populism is also an unwelcome guest in that it debilitates institutionalized politics and representative democracy. This is particularly so for a country like Korea, which does not have robust party politics and still suffers from "the politics of the vortex."[44] As noted above, the crux of the problem is that populism is highly likely to threaten democracy due to its illiberal, anti-pluralist tendencies. Socioeconomic inequalities provide fertile soil for the ascendance of populism too. In other words, if trust in politicians remains low and structural inequalities are not alleviated, it is likely that both new and existing political actors will deploy populism as a central part of their message ahead of the March 2022 presidential election.

The progress of democracy is anything but inevitable, and this is certainly true in Korea. Democracy can further retreat in Korea, despite all the achievements that have been made since 1987. While Korea still maintains the procedural rule of law, the core democratic norms of mutual tolerance and forbearance are being increasingly undermined, and society is rapidly being polarized. Even the court and civil society, which must defend democratic ideals against abuses of political power, have become highly politicized. As Korea enters a new decade, it must deeply reflect upon how it will protect and sustain democracy. This should be a priority for the new administration that will come into power in May 2022.

There are no simple solutions for rescuing a democracy in trouble. Still, concerted efforts should be made to improve the structural conditions that led to societal polarization and political populism by implementing proactive employment, tax, and welfare policies. Economic democratization, which bolsters social equality, should be a primary objective. Representative institutions should be strengthened, including

44 Gregory Henderson, *Korea: The Politics of the Vortex* (Cambridge: Harvard University Press, 1968).

political parties, and the independence of the judiciary should be protected.

Yet, it is no less important to foster and adhere to the two norms that Levitsky and Ziblatt articulate: "mutual toleration" and "institutional forbearance." Democracy cannot be upheld with institutions alone. As they emphasize, political actors must acknowledge each other as legitimate competitors, and they must be prudent and fair-minded in exercising their institutional prerogatives. Mutual toleration and institutional forbearance provide the procedural foundation upon which the democratic ideal of pluralism can be realized. If this foundation decays, democracy will eventually fall into decline.

This Book

This book is based on a (virtual) conference convened in November 2020 by the Walter H. Shorenstein Asia-Pacific Research Center at Stanford University. The chapters compiled herein address a wide range of issues relating to the past, present, and future of Korea's democracy. In particular, the following interrelated topics are closely examined, as they are central to Korea's democratic decay: illiberalism, political polarization, party politics, politicization of the judicial system and civil society, nationalism and social media, economic inequalities, education, and foreign policy. This book, scheduled to be published right before the inauguration of the new administration in May 2022, can be expected to stimulate constructive discussions on how to restore Korea's democratic norms and institutions.

We begin with an examination of sources of illiberalism in Korean democracy in the first two chapters. In chapter 1, Byongjin Ahn traces illiberal tendencies among Korean progressives to the fact that the ruling elite of the Moon administration, many of them former fighters for democracy, did not have a chance to learn or experience a political order characterized by liberal values or institutions. Their values and modus operandi were forged in a struggle against a military-authoritarian regime during their formative years. As a result, they "have little interest in liberal values, such as respect for legal procedures and checks and balances." At best, the Moon administration practices majoritarian, if not authoritarian, rule: Ahn views Korea's political order as "a hybrid regime, in which majoritarian impulses and liberal constitutional democracy coexist." Ahn, a former democratic activist in the 1980s who was imprisoned by the authoritarian regime, laments the lack of appreciation for liberal values among his former colleagues and argues that "they are lacking in the characteristics needed to be a transformative political force and ended up becoming the new establishment" in Korea.

In chapter 2, political scientist Aram Hur tackles the question of illiberalism by focusing on a structural aspect of Korea's democratization. In her view, Korea's democratization was not just an anti-regime or anti-authoritarian struggle, but fundamentally a nationalist conflict between progressive and conservative forces over identity. Instead of alleviating this conflict, Korea's pathway to democratization entrenched it, as competing nationalist factions refashioned themselves as competing political parties under the new electoral system. Nationalist polarization poses a fundamental risk, as it views democratic competition as a zero-sum race for ownership over the state, considering "the political opposition . . . [as] an existential threat to 'our' nationalist vision that must be eliminated." The illiberal norm of "win at all costs" was embedded into Korea's party system early on, undermining democratic norms of mutual tolerance and forbearance. Although the roots of Korea's illiberalism were planted long before democratization, nationalist polarization and illiberal forms of competition have been persistent, if worsening, features of Korean democracy that pervade both progressive and conservative parties.

In chapter 3, Kwanhu Lee, a political scientist working at the Prime Minister's Office of Korea, explains the persistence of political polarization by examining party politics. In his assessment, Korea's party system, even in today's post-2017 era, still lacks the capacity to resolve the simultaneous eruption of conflicting issues that have accumulated throughout the authoritarian and democratization eras. While there exists severe conflict between the two leading political parties, the main problem "is not ideological polarization, but rather political polarization and the radicalization of political behavior amplified by social media." In the past, the key axis of party conflict was regionalism, but now intergenerational divides have further complicated the battle lines. In his view, the major challenges facing Korean parties are twofold: addressing socioeconomic inequalities and increasing diversity in political representation. In particular, he points to the urgency of concerted efforts to incorporate the "invisible" voices of the majority into the political arena. Otherwise, ordinary citizens will find that "the most common way to make their voices heard is through mass public opinion" rather than through their representatives, increasing the danger of political populism.

Chapters 4 and 5 discuss the politicization of two of the once most trusted institutions in Korea—civil society and the courts. In a 2001 survey of "most trusted groups in Korea," they ranked second and fourth, respectively.[45] As political scientist Myoung-Ho Park points out in chapter 4, civil society gained the public's trust by making decisive contributions in purging the legacies of authoritarian rule, addressing issues ranging from political corruption to real estate speculation to environmental protection and human rights. However, as its political influence grew, Korea's civil society has become highly politicized and partisan. A large number of civic activists entered institutional politics (government and the legislature), and such "politicization of personnel from civil society . . . leads to the politicization of policy." Civil society is no longer the defender of democracy that it once was, Park laments, but rather has become "a means of mobilizing ordinary citizens in a divisive, partisan politics of confrontation and stalemate." As a result, the Korean public's trust in civil society plunged over the years: 22.4 percent of respondents in 2014 stated that they trusted civil society, but this fell to 10.9 percent in 2018 and further declined to 10.1 percent in 2019.

Likewise, the Korean judiciary has become highly politicized, undermining its integrity. In chapter 5, Seongwook Heo—a judge-turned-academic—points out that President Moon, who had a chance to reshape the court by nominating thirteen of fourteen Supreme Court justices during his term, including the chief justice, heavily recruited his appointees from two groups: the *Wooribeop* Study Group (WSG) and Lawyers for a Democratic Society (LDS), both of which are well known for their liberal views. Analyzing several recent cases, he then shows how the ideologically tilted composition of the court has led to controversial decisions. In addition, Heo brings attention to the problematic nature of appointing a judge to a senior position in the Blue House to lead the campaign to "eradicate deep-rooted evil" in the judiciary, a campaign that resulted in the conviction of the former chief justice and former justices of the Supreme Court. He also notes with concern the behavior of three judges who took leading roles in

45 "Online Public Opinion Survey: What Institution Is Most Trusted in Korean Society?" [in Korean], *Monthly Chosun*, September 2001, https://monthly.chosun.com/client/news/viw.asp?nNewsNumb=200109100025.

attacking the former chief justice to get elected as members of the National Assembly. Heo argues that this is "unprecedented, and . . . could easily lead to the politicization of the judiciary and even an erosion of the separation of powers." He warns that the public has begun to lose faith in the judiciary system, which is increasingly seen "as just another field for fighting dirty political battles."

Chapters 6 to 8 discuss how economic inequalities, education, and social media have produced and amplified political polarization and conflict in Korea. In chapter 6, leading progressive economists Jun-Ho Jeong and Il-Young Lee examine how regional and generational disparities have developed over time and how they have affected and will affect democracy in Korea. Using several economic and social indicators, they show that regional (the capital region versus the rest of the country) and generational ("baby boomers" versus youth) disparities have continued to deepen since democratization, leading to the emergence of a new group of individuals who strongly feel that they have been "left to die." In their analysis, the Park Geun-Hye administration "crumbled as it ignored and neglected this new group," despite its campaign pledge of "economic democratization." "Intent on avoiding the path taken by its predecessor, the Moon administration declared 'people first'" as its policy priority but has not taken proactive steps to deal with the worsening trends of the two divergences. On the contrary, the sharp rise in housing prices in Seoul since 2017 has become a source of despair for those outside Seoul and among the younger generation. Warning that "Korea's economic divergences could once again throw its democracy into chaos," Jeong and Lee urge the nation to take up "the vital task of connecting and uniting disparate regions and generations" before it is too late.

Chapter 7 discusses institutional characteristics of Korea's education system and how education can help foster mature democracy. Sociologist Seongsoo Choi first identifies areas of change and continuity in Korea's educational system from the authoritarian to the democratic era. For example, the extreme uniformity that was imposed by the authoritarian regime through militaristic discipline and totalitarian ideology has weakened since democratization. On the other hand, the institutional features of prioritizing college admissions and ranking students solely by standardized academic achievement for that purpose—which emerged as education was mobilized as an efficient means for economic development—have persisted and even strengthened in some respects. Choi believes that establishing the role of public education in cultivating mature democratic citizens and implementing this effectively are of paramount importance, but both have been largely overlooked due to the long shadow of authoritarian legacies. Accordingly, he argues that educational reform will be essential for developing a mature civic culture based on more inclusive norms and practices and embracing diversity as a critical social value, while maintaining the dynamic aspects of appreciating achievement and competition.

In chapter 8, economist Yong Suk Lee shows how social media can amplify the salience of political polarization. This is an extremely important topic for Korean democracy, as the nation is among the most wired in the world, and social media is regarded as a major means of political mobilization and polarization. Based on a number of survey results, Lee shows that Korea, laden with examples of political rivalry and factionalism, has not necessarily become more polarized. Instead, it is the *salience* of polarization that has increased. Lee argues that new online media technologies are the driving force behind this trend. Internet news and social media lower the barriers to entry, and nearly anyone who is willing can create and disseminate news. His analysis shows that social media users are more polarized in their viewpoints and are more likely to participate in political protests, amplifying societal divisions for political gain. In other words, the increasing salience of extreme and polarized political viewpoints on social media can undermine democracy by influencing public opinion and encouraging the political participation of individuals with extreme views. Lee concludes with suggestions to minimize the potential harms of polarization in today's balkanized media environment.

Chapter 9 addresses the impact of democratic decay on foreign policy, an important but largely unexplored topic in the study of democracy. Despite the limited scholarly attention, Professor Victor Cha, the Korea Chair at the Center for Strategic and International Studies, argues that "elements of illiberal foreign policy—in its objectives, tactics, and execution—ring truer than most would recognize." In the case of Korea, democratic erosion affects its foreign policy in three ways: (1) values-based diplomacy; (2) consensus-based diplomacy; and (3) polarized foreign policy. More specifically, Cha shows how the Moon administration "deprioritizes political freedom, civil liberties, and transparency in its diplomatic goals," as is most evident in the devaluing of human rights in policies related to North Korea and China. In addition, Cha argues, "the inability to externalize democratic norms of compromise and negotiation result in inflexible, zero-sum diplomacy and demonization of foreign interlocutors." This trait has been especially evident in Korea's policy toward Japan. A long-term impact of illiberalism on foreign policy can be consequential as Korea becomes increasingly estranged from its democratic partners in the Asia-Pacific region, leaving it vulnerable to Chinese influence and bullying. Even if it is not permanent, Cha warns, this backsliding "could have secondary and tertiary effects on the resilience of the U.S.-Korea alliance and long-lasting impacts on Korea's international reputation."

The final chapter looks at the Korean experience in comparative perspective. Larry Diamond, a leading expert on democracy, observes that democratic recession is not unique to Korea. After outlining broad global trends of democratic failures since 2006, he identifies domestic and international factors most responsible for such decay, which can be readily applied to the Korean case. He then discusses lessons from around the world on how to reverse democratic backsliding and how Korea can learn from and adapt them. Diamond makes several provocative but specific suggestions, such as "designing a more balanced mixed-member proportional system" to mitigate political polarization and extending the term of supreme court justices to fifteen years (from the current six years) to reduce politicization of the judiciary. Yet, he concludes, only so much can be accomplished through institutional reforms. We concur that the "question of how to build a new culture of commitment to democratic norms of tolerance and mutual respect and restraint among diverse political forces"—both at the elite and mass levels—"should be a leading one in Korean society today."

We firmly believe that liberal democracy is a necessity, not a choice. There are no other political institutions that uphold freedom and equality and empower citizens better than liberal democracy. We hope that the chapters included in this book can facilitate critical self-reflection and serious discussions among Koreans and other concerned individuals to save this hard-won democracy from further decay. The collective effort to protect and defend democracy has perhaps never been as critical as it is today.

Bibliography

Abramowitz, Michael. "Freedom in the World 2018: Democracy in Crisis." Accessed November 30, 2021. https://freedomhouse.org/report/freedom-world/2018/democracy-crisis.

Arendt, Hannah. *The Origins of Totalitarianism*. Berlin, Germany: Schocken Books, 1951.

Cheong Wa Dae. "Opening Remarks by President Moon Jae-In at New Year Press Conference." January 10, 2019. http://english1.president.go.kr/BriefingSpeeches/Policies/106.

Choe, Sang-Hun. "South Korea Declares War on 'Fake News,' Worrying Government Critics." *New York Times*, October 2, 2018. http://www.nytimes.com/2018/10/02/world/asia/south-korea-fake-news.html.

Choi, He-Suk. "Supreme Court in Hot Water over Blacklist, Political Bias Allegations." *Korea Herald*, January 24, 2018. http://www.koreaherald.com/view.php?ud=20180124000861.

Choi, Jang-Jip. "The Crisis and Consolidation of Korea's Democracy, and Alternatives for a New Political Order." [In Korean.] Paper presented at "Kim Dae-Jung and Democracy: Thought and Practice" at Kim Dae-Jung Library, Yonsei University, December 9, 2019.

Diamond, Larry. *Ill Winds: Saving Democracy from Russian Rage, Chinese Ambition, and American Complacency*. New York: Penguin Press, 2019.

"Fallout from Minimum Wage Hike Spreading." *Korea Herald*, July 31, 2017. http://www.koreaherald.com/view.php?ud=20170731000686.

Fifield, Anna. "Korea Think Tank at U.S. University to Close after Seoul Withdraws Funding." *Washington Post*, April 11, 2018. https://www.washingtonpost.com/world/asia_pacific/korea-think-tank-at-us-university-to-close-after-seoul-withdraws-funding/2018/04/11/87adc3a8-3d64-11e8-912d-16c9e9b37800_story.html.

Fukuyama, Francis. *The End of History and the Last Man*. New York: Free Press, 2006.

Held, David et al. *Global Transformations: Politics, Economics and Culture*. Stanford: Stanford University Press, 1999.

Henderson, Gregory. *Korea: The Politics of the Vortex*. Cambridge: Harvard University Press, 1968.

Huntington, Samuel. *The Third Wave: Democratization in the Late Twentieth Century*. Norman: University of Oklahoma Press, 1991.

International Organization for Migration. *World Migration Report 2020*. Geneva, Switzerland: IOM, 2019.

"Japan May Take South Korea Wartime Labor Dispute to International Court of Justice: NHK." Reuters, July 17, 2019. http://www.reuters.com/article/us-southkorea-japan-laborers-idUSKCN1UD02Z.

Judis, John. *The Populist Explosion: How the Great Recession Transformed American and European Politics*. New York: Columbia Global Reports, 2016.

Kim, Ho-Ki. "Out of the Shadows: The Collapse of Park Geun-hye and the Future of South Korea." *Global Asia* 11, no. 4 (2016): 80–85.

Kim, Myong-Sik. "Blue House and 2018 Ulsan Mayoral Election Conspiracy." *Korea Herald*, February 12, 2020. http://www.koreaherald.com/view.php?ud=20200211000862.

Kim, Se-Jeong. "Justice Minister Defends Decision to Block Indictment Disclosure." *Korea Times*, February 12, 2020. http://www.koreatimes.co.kr/www/nation/2020/02/251_283304.html.

Kwon, Kyong-Ae. *Time of Lawlessness*. [In Korean.] Seoul: Chonnyon-ui sangsang, 2021.

Lee, Cheol-Seung. *The Generation of Inequality* [In Korean.] Seoul: Munhak-gwa Chasseing's, 2019.

Lee, Jungmin. Remarks at a seminar on "Minimum Wage and Employment Dynamics in Korea." Walter H. Shorenstein Asia-Pacific Research Center at Stanford University, February 7, 2020.

Levitsky, Steven and Daniel Ziblatt. *How Democracies Die*. New York: Crown, 2018.

Mann, Michael. *Fascists*. Cambridge: Cambridge University Press, 2004.

McCurry, Justin. "Japan Anger over South Korea's Shrimp Surprise for Donald Trump." *The Guardian*, November 9, 2017.

"Ministry of Education to Request Prosecution Investigation of Seventeen for Carrying Forward the Government Textbook Project." [In Korean.] *Yonhap News*, June 8, 2018. https://www.yna.co.kr/view/AKR20180606040700004.

Mounk, Yascha. *The People vs. Democracy*. Cambridge: Harvard University Press, 2018.

Mudde, Cas, and Cristóbal Rovira Kaltwasser. *Populism: A Very Short Introduction*, New York: Oxford University Press, 2017.
Müller, Jan-Werner. *What is Populism?* Philadelphia: University of Pennsylvania Press, 2016.
"Online Public Opinion Survey: What Institution is Most Trusted in Korean Society?" [In Korean.] *Monthly Chosun*, September 2001. https://monthly.chosun.com/client/news/viw.asp?nNewsNumb=200109100025.
Palmer, Parker. *Healing the Heart of Democracy: The Courage to Create a Politics Worthy of the Human Spirit*. Hoboken: John Wiley & Sons, 2011.
Piketty, Thomas. *Capital in the Twenty-First Century*. Cambridge: Harvard University Press, 2017.
"Shameful Distractions." *JoongAng Daily*, April 20, 2020. https://koreajoongangdaily.joins.com/news/article/article.aspx?aid=3076281.
Shin, Gi-Wook, "South Korea's Democratic Decay." *Journal of Democracy* 31, no. 3 (July 2020): 100–14.
Shin, Gi-Wook, and Paul Y. Chang, eds. *South Korean Social Movements: From Democracy to Civil Society*. London and New York: Routledge, 2011.
Shin, Gi-Wook, and Rennie Moon. "South Korea After Impeachment." *Journal of Democracy* 28, no. 4 (October 2017): 117–31.
Wike, Richard, Bruce Stokes, and Katie Simmons. "Europeans Fear Wave of Refugees Will Mean More Terrorism, Fewer Jobs." Pew Research Center, July 11, 2016. https://www.pewresearch.org/global/wp-content/uploads/sites/2/2016/07/Pew-Research-Center-EU-Refugees-and-National-Identity-Report-FINAL-July-11-2016.pdf.
World Inequality Database. https://wid.world/data. Accessed December 1, 2021.

CHAPTER ONE

Why Is Korean Democracy Majoritarian but Not Liberal?

Byongjin Ahn

Korea has drawn attention across the world for its 2016 candlelight protests and effective handling of the COVID-19 pandemic without resorting to extreme measures such as a national lockdown. Indeed, considering the widespread emergence of right-wing populism across the globe, the rise of a progressive movement like the "Candlelight Revolution" is highly unusual. This movement was more than just a political event. It was also a cultural phenomenon that aligned with a wave of artists who embody a new set of values. For example, BTS, a music band that has attained global fame, represent the same zeitgeist as the protests following the *Sewol* ferry disaster and the broader candlelight movement.[1] Their songs and music videos not only express solidarity with the struggling and the vulnerable, but also affirm liberal values such as human dignity.

At the same time, President Moon Jae-In has received a great deal of criticism even from progressive circles for displaying less integrity and a more partisan attitude than previous progressive administrations. His administration appointed Cho Kuk, a fiercely partisan figure, as minister of justice; suspended Prosecutor General Yoon Seok-Youl; and criticized Choi Jae-Hyung, the chairman of the Board of Audit and Inspection.[2] For these actions, the Moon Jae-In administration has

---

1 The *Sewol* sank off Jindo Island, off the southern coast of Korea, on April 16, 2014, resulting in the death of 304 individuals—almost all of them high school students on a field trip. The captain of the ferry has been found guilty of gross negligence and was sentenced to thirty-six years in prison.

2 Yoon Seok-Youl, the former prosecutor general, indicted Cho Kuk and his wife on charges that included document fraud and bribery, but the Blue House and

suffered the dishonor of being labeled *naeronambul*—a government of "double standards."[3] Even progressive academics such as Choi Jang-Jip and Chin Jung-Kwon have gone so far as to portray the Moon administration as regressing toward totalitarianism. Renowned overseas scholars such as Gi-Wook Shin have also voiced concerns that Korean democracy is on a path toward decay.[4]

How can Korea's democracy receive such blistering criticism and exceeding praise at the same time? Is either the criticism or praise based on an incorrect diagnosis of the situation? Or if the two can meaningfully coexist, how can that be the case? This is a perplexing puzzle in Korean politics.

To understand this puzzle, Korea's current political order needs to be viewed as a hybrid regime, in which majoritarian impulses and liberal constitutional democracy coexist. Employing Ginsberg and Huq's definition, I define liberal constitutional democracy as rule of law and liberal forms of governance and practices. Instead of simply upholding the rule of the majority after a free and fair election, a liberal constitutional democracy also guarantees liberal rights and the integrity

---

the Democratic Party were adamant in defending Cho at any cost. The Korean Supreme Court eventually ruled in January 2022 that Cho's wife was guilty, a decision that will have a negative effect on Cho's own trial. Prosecutor General Yoon was intensely questioned for political motivation in the National Assembly's audit of state affairs in October 2020. Lastly, Choi Jae-Hyung, the chairman of the Board of Audit and Inspection (BAI), was harshly criticized by influential figures in the Democratic Party for investigating whether the Ministry of Trade, Industry and Energy engaged in improper practices in decommissioning a nuclear power plant much earlier than planned. (The BAI is a constitutionally mandated entity that acts as the inspector general for the entire executive branch in South Korea.) Moon admitted in a press conference in January 2021 that Choi's investigation was not politically motivated. Both Yoon and Choi became presidential candidates of the opposition People Power Party after these political adversities.

3 The phrase *naeronambul* is commonly used in Korea to refer to a double standard. Its literal meaning is connected to the phrase, "If they do it, it's a romance; if others do it, they call it an extramarital affair." According to a survey of 906 professors in Korea by *Kyosu Shinmun* (Professors' Daily), a majority pointed to "double standards" as the zeitgeist of 2020. See Park Kang-Soo, "I Am Right and You Are Wrong" [in Korean], *Kyosu Shinmun*, December 20, 2020, https://www.kyosu.net/news/articleView.html?idxno=59131.

4 Gi-Wook Shin, "South Korea's Democratic Decay," *Journal of Democracy* 31, no. 3 (2020): 100–14.

of the law and legal institutions.[5] While mainstream progressive elites in the Blue House and the ruling Democratic Party of Korea (DPK) clearly have majoritarian impulses, Korean society as a whole—due to its dynamic civil society—is on a chaotic and tortuous but gradual path toward a liberal political order.

In elaborating upon this argument, this chapter adopts a comparative perspective with the United States. The U.S. presidential system served as the prototype for Korea's own presidential system, and the fundamental limitations of the U.S. presidential system—including a "dysfunctional constitution," as described by Sanford Levinson—are issues of concern for all liberal democratic states that have a similar system of government.[6] As such, a comparison with the United States, which is currently making efforts to rebuild a durable liberal order in the post-Trump era, can yield a wealth of valuable insights into Korea's political situation. Conversely, Korea's political system could also provide a novel perspective for understanding American politics.[7]

The Complexities of Korea's Current Political Order

The most widely cited and controversial view among Korean scholars regarding the state of Korea's democracy after democratization is Choi Jang-Jip's theory of party politics. According to Choi, an eminent progressive political scientist, the quality of Korea's democracy has worsened since democratization in the late 1980s. Korea's democracy is riddled with populist behavior instead of showing a stable but dynamic expression and resolution of conflicts based around political parties. "The concentration of power around the president has increased, and the rule of law is in danger," Choi writes, further noting that "the fusion of civil society and civic movements into the state has emerged as an obstacle to the growth of a pluralistic society and the development of political parties." He even goes so far as to say that "the direct

5 Tom Ginsberg and Aziz Z. Huq, *How To Save A Constitutional Democracy* (Chicago: University of Chicago Press, 2018), 8–9.
6 Sanford Levinson and Jack M. Balkin, *Democracy and Dysfunction* (Chicago: University of Chicago Press, 2019).
7 This essay is based both on my sober reflection on experiences as a pro-democracy activist in Korean politics and my academic interest in American liberalism.

democracy advocated and used by progressive forces today is similar to totalitarianism."[8]

Choi's critique of the Moon administration is much harsher than his previous critique of the Roh Moo-Hyun administration (2003–08), but the underlying logic has remained consistent. In fact, Choi was highly critical of Roh's emergence as a presidential candidate through the "cut-off" round of the DPK primaries, characterizing the process as a populist movement that hindered the development of political parties.[9] Choi fundamentally attributes this type of populist behavior to a lack of understanding among progressive political elites, who instead rely on a theory of combative "movement" politics from the era of pro-democracy protests. Other progressive intellectuals, including Chin Jung-Kwon, interpret the Moon administration as part of the global rise of "soft authoritarianism," as embodied by figures such as Trump.[10] Choi served as a policy adviser to President Kim Dae-Jung, and Chin is a highly influential political commentator in both progressive circles and major media outlets.

However, it would be inappropriate to label this lack of liberal values as Western-style authoritarian populism. A close examination of Korea's progressives reveals that they do not share the clear and consistent desire of globally ascendant right-wing populists, including Trump, for authoritarianism or totalitarian rule. While they are shrewd in mobilizing their narrow base of fervent supporters, Korea's progressives are inept in wielding populism as a political tool. The weakness of the Roh administration in its later years, for example, originates from insufficient populist mobilization against conservative elites.[11] Normative assessments aside, the Roh administration lost political capital in its later years after attempting bipartisan, anti-populist governance through a "grand coalition." When the candlelight protests began, Moon—then the leader of the DPK—initially dragged his

---

8 Choi Jang-Jip, "Korean Democracy after Candlelight Movement-The Change of Ideological Terrain and The Desirable Role of Conservative Party" [in Korean], Colloquium Lecture at Seoul National University, November 27, 2020.

9 Choi Jang-Jip, *Democracy after Democratization* [in Korean] (Seoul, Korea: Humanitas, 2005).

10 Chin Jung-Kwon, *How Progressives Collapse* [in Korean] (Seoul, Korea: Chunnyuneusangsang, 2020).

11 Byongjin Ahn, *The Impeachment Politics of Roh and Clinton* [in Korean] (Seoul, Korea: Prungil, 2004).

feet.[12] Other than setting up an official Blue House petition website or going public with appeals to the pro-Moon base, there have not been any creative efforts to open a space for direct democracy.

Furthermore, the problem with the political elite of the Moon administration is not that they still hold an activist view of politics, as claimed by Choi Jang-Jip, but rather that they have lost it. The Moon administration has not shown political acumen in garnering public support or mobilizing populist sentiment against the elite on issues such as emergency disaster relief during the COVID-19 pandemic or *chaebol* reform. This is markedly different from, for instance, the progressive populism of Gyeonggi Province governor Lee Jae-Myung, who does not have a typical background in pro-democracy activism. The fundamental problem is not that Korea's progressives have excessively activist tendencies. Instead, it is that they are lacking in the characteristics needed to be a transformative political force and have ended up becoming the new establishment. The Moon administration has, in fact, bought into an old economic paradigm spearheaded by the Ministry of Economy and Finance. In doing so, it has compromised with the old establishment.

Another shortcoming of the Choi Jang-Jip and Chin Jung-Kwon critiques is that they fail to adequately acknowledge the progress that Korea's society has achieved, by focusing only on the limitations of progressive political actors. Despite the authoritarian tendencies and incompetence of progressive political actors, there has been continued social progress. Korea's vibrant civil society has ousted obsolete political forces at the ballot box. As intellectuals raised concerns about the tyranny of the majority after an overwhelming victory for the ruling party in the April 2020 parliamentary elections, some moderate citizens promptly withdrew their support. There has also been intense criticism from "new millennials" and younger generations regarding gender issues and other new sources of political cleavage. While the United States is locked in a two-party stalemate, the situation in Korea is very fluid. As noted by Jeong Young-Hoon and Park Sung-Won of the National Assembly Futures Institute, today's new millennials in Korea have extremely progressive attitudes toward issues such as pluralism

12 It was Ahn Cheol-Soo, the centrist and leader of the third-party People's Party, who made the first move to join the protests. Moon is not well versed in the populist mode of politics. He is committed to direct democracy only in rhetoric.

and climate change.[13] They belong to a global generation of new millennials, and they are the potential driving force behind the creation of a new political realignment.

Despite the ruling party's adamant defense of Cho Kuk and criticism of Yoon Seok-Youl and Choi Jae-Hyung, Moon surprisingly—albeit belatedly—admitted in a press conference in January 2021 that "Yoon is the prosecutor general of this administration" and insisted that both Yoon and Choi were not politically motivated. This abrupt change of course, which can be seen as a politically inclusive gesture, could be attributed to the checks enforced by the judicial branch (within a liberal constitutional order) and declining approval ratings.

The narrowly focused critique advanced by Choi Jang-Jip and others can lead to similarly narrow implications for the future of Korea's democracy. I do not believe that Korea's future will be defined mainly by authoritarian populism or totalitarian tendencies. There was a great deal of controversy when Lee Hae-Chan, the former leader of the DPK, expressed a desire that his party remain in power for several decades. However, Lee's goal is an impossible dream. Korea has a vibrant society that makes it difficult to build and sustain a majority coalition in the medium to long term.

If anything, the real problem is that the situation in Korea is too volatile to devise a consistent, well-defined plan for the future. In the United States, the Founding Fathers placed the responsibility for formulating such a plan with the Senate, but the Senate has degenerated into a short-sighted, highly partisan institution. Korea has never had a similar political institution, and its politics are anything but far-sighted. The most serious problem facing Korea's democracy is its inability to address long-term issues such as economic stagnation and the climate crisis, not a tyranny of the majority. The Moon administration was initially viewed as a "climate villain" on the international stage until Moon declared the goal of carbon neutrality by 2050. Nevertheless, the climate crisis has not been a defining issue for the administration because its destructive effects have so far been relatively mild on the Korean Peninsula.[14] When extreme catastrophes—including climate-

---

13 Jeong Young-Hoon and Park Sung-Won, "The People's Choice: Transitioning to a Sustainable, Equitable Society" [in Korean], *State Future Strategy Insight* 6 (November 19, 2020), https://www.nafi.re.kr/new/report.do?mode=view&articleNo=1732&article.offset=0&articleLimit=9.

14 In an address to the National Assembly in October 2020, Moon declared that Korea would be carbon neutral by 2050. His administration, however, has not yet

induced disasters and global pandemics—become far more frequent, both progressives and conservatives will be mired in political paralysis, regardless of who is in power. Neither end of the political spectrum has developed a new paradigm and specific roadmap to prepare for this impending crisis.

The difference in opinion between Choi Jang-Jip and myself can fundamentally be traced to varying interpretations of Schattschneider's work and the role of populism. Choi advocates for political development based on a stable yet dynamic conflict between two "responsible" political parties—a view based on Schattschneider's theory of party politics.[15] Thus, Choi is critical of bottom-up populist mobilization, as seen in the rise of Roh Moo-Hyun, because it undermines the stability of political parties. By contrast, I am highly critical of Schattschneider's theory of party politics. While the theory may serve as a template for political parties in mid-twentieth-century American politics, it is becoming an increasingly outdated model as "citizen politics" takes center stage. Building on the theoretical work of Russell Dalton, the current era is better characterized as one of political engagement based on citizen networks.[16] In this view, there is no objection to bottom-up populist mobilization per se. As John McCormick notes, a balance between representative democracy and populism is unavoidable in liberal politics.[17] An effort to entirely exclude populism from politics will, as Chantal Mouffe argues, give rise to radical populist forces outside the formal political sphere. I agree with Mouffe's theoretical view in that such external dynamism can act as a positive force if it is channeled in an appropriate fashion.[18] In this regard, I also agree with Zaretski, a professor at the New School for Social Research, in that a vital liberal center and its productive interactions with a vigorous left (i.e., left-wing populism) are critical for political development.[19]

In sum, the diagnosis of "authoritarian populism" or a "totalitarian tendency" fails to fully capture the complexities of Korea's current

provided a convincing and specific roadmap for accomplishing this goal.

15 E. E. Schattschneider, *The Semi-sovereign People: A Realist's View of Democracy in America* (San Diego: Harcourt Brace Jovanovich College Publishers, 1975).

16 Russell Dalton, *Citizen Politics: Public Opinion and Political Parties in Advanced Industrial Democracies* [in Korean] (Seoul, Korea: Arke, 2010).

17 John McCormick, *Machiavellian Democracy* (Cambridge: Cambridge University Press, 2011).

18 Chantal Mouffe, *The Return of the Political* (New York: Verso, 2006).

19 Eli Zaretski, *Why America Needs A Left* (New York: Polity, 2012).

political order. Relying on majoritarian rule but lacking a populist impulse, the Moon administration has neither succeeded in consolidating liberal institutional norms nor, conversely, hegemonic authoritarian populism. It is therefore necessary to adopt a more structural and comparative approach in assessing the limitations of progressive political forces in Korea. This stance is motivated by a particular interpretation of Korea's political system as a "dualist democracy." The following sections explore this concept by comparing Korea with the United States.

Korea's Dualist Democracy: A Comparison with the United States

The American political system, which served as the prototype for Korea's presidential system, can be characterized as a "dualist democracy." There is a formal political sphere that maintains a hegemony over political affairs, and an external impetus from the popular will that only manifests in a forceful manner during periods of crisis.

Proposed by Ackerman, the concept of a "dualist democracy" is based on the observation that the United States is a representative democracy where political elites respond to and are responsible toward citizens.[20] James Madison envisioned this novel system, in which the interest groups that best represent the people will achieve victory in elections. These interest groups compete with one another and seek to exert their influence, enabling the political system to be responsive to the people. If those in power are no longer responsive, then citizens cast—in Przeworski's words—"paper stones."

This represents the typical mode of operation for such a political system. However, every political order undergoes periods of crisis. When the institutions of representative democracy are severely lacking in responsiveness, there is a temporary yet enormous upsurge among "the people." Ackerman argues that the momentum from such a popular movement is then incorporated into the constitutional order, enabling the political order to recover its vitality. In the theoretical literature on popular constitutionalism, a constitution is understood in two ways—as a document that is formally enacted, and also as an open, constructive process resulting from "bottom-up" politics. Ackerman analyzes the history of American political development by distinguishing

20 Bruce Ackerman, *We the People*, vol. 1 (Boston: Belknap Press, 1993).

between periods of "normal politics" and "constitutional moments" in a dualist democracy. For example, Ackerman does not interpret political changes during the New Deal as an institutional battle among the three branches of government, but instead takes a broader view and analyzes how the people—in a forceful expression of their will during an extraordinary period—voted in a "plebiscitary presidency" that interacted with the judicial branch.

The characteristics of America's "dualist democracy" are evident in its liberal political order. During periods of "normal politics," the formal institutions of politics maintain a hegemony over the political order. Specifically, this "hegemony" consists of a constellation of institutional and cultural factors: a set of intricate institutions based on liberal values; a system for educating and cultivating talented individuals; institutional patriotism; a competitive two-party system and accompanying norms; the resilience of liberal actors (pluralism, responsiveness, governance skills); a pluralistic civil society; and a sufficient basis of material resources to maintain this system. By contrast, the external impetus from the popular will only manifests in a meaningful way during periods of crisis.

The political system in the United States has been structured around liberal values that are inherent to the founding constitutional order, which in turn have been supported by the institutional patriotism of internal and external actors. Institutional patriotism refers to a respect for the values and ethics embedded in a set of institutions, as well as a desire to preserve and protect the integrity of these institutions. External shocks, meanwhile, only have an effect to the extent that the two competing parties respond to the results of public opinion polls. The popular will does not threaten the hegemony of the formal political sphere. As a result, it is highly unlikely that the two major parties will undergo substantial realignment, as they frequently have in Korean party politics. Consider, for instance, the Tea Party movement, a powerful populist movement in the United States in recent years. It did not give rise to a new political party, but rather resulted in a qualitative change within the Republican Party. At the other end of the spectrum, radical, socialist forces have become a faction within the Democratic Party, which remains conservative by European standards.

It is, however, necessary to reexamine the resilience of the dualist democracy model in the United States and furthermore consider the classic question of why the U.S. presidential system has not been successfully exported to other contexts. Korea's success in achieving both democratization and industrialization has been widely praised. However, it is now time to weigh the costs and benefits of having adopted a U.S.-style presidential system. It appears that this model has reached a state of paralysis even in the United States due to a serious "bug" in the system. The challenge of transplanting a foreign institutional design, combined with its serious design flaws, has given rise to a variety of complications.

As noted above, American politics can be characterized as a dualist democracy. Korean politics can also be understood as a dualist democracy, but in the opposite sense. Specifically, the external impetus of the popular will is always the driving force in politics, and the formal political sphere does not possess hegemony. This observation is related to the concept of a "contentious society," proposed by Hagen Koo and others.[21]

Why does Korea display the opposite pattern, even though its political institutions are heavily influenced by those of the United States? Unlike the framers of the U.S. Constitution, the individuals who led the Constitutional Assembly in Korea did not firmly believe in liberal ideals or the importance of a republic. President Syngman Rhee studied liberal values during his time in the United States and played a key role in transplanting the U.S. presidential system to Korea. Because of his personal characteristics, however, President Rhee was most comfortable with a heavily authoritarian, charismatic style of leadership. The Founding Fathers of the United States, drawing on republican liberal values, designed a presidential system based on the separation of powers and led by legislative bodies. The Senate was intended as a forum for nonpartisan cooperation, and the House of Representatives was designed to respond to the people's will. By contrast, Rhee and his allies fused liberalism and authoritarian tendencies to create a presidential system with an extremely weak legislature. They institutionalized a highly centralized, unitary state ruled through plebiscitarian, charismatic leadership. In addition, extreme partisan politics was merely the modern manifestation of a long legacy of tribal politics dating back to the Joseon dynasty. Accordingly, Gregory Henderson, the Tocqueville of Korean politics, labeled this style of politics "the Politics of the Vortex."[22] His observation remains relevant today.

---

21 Hagen Koo, *State and Society in Contemporary Korea* (Ithaca: Cornell University Press, 1994).

22 Gregory Henderson, *Korean Politics of the Vortex* [in Korean] (Seoul, Korea: Hanwol, 2013).

Korea's institutions have departed from the U.S. presidential system. The authority of the legislature remains relatively weak. It is severely lacking in its ability to check a powerful presidency or other entities under the executive branch, including the Ministry of Justice and various intelligence agencies. On the other hand, the president wields immense power and has the plebiscitary authority to call a referendum on important issues. Political parties are structured along factional lines, and there is little space for lively, substantive debates. Henderson's observation regarding the extreme concentration of power in Seoul is still valid.

The events of 1987 were a "constitutional moment" in Korea that gave rise to a new political order, much like the New Deal era in the United States. Progressive political forces gained the opportunity to rise to power through competitive electoral politics, and the ability of state agencies to arbitrarily interfere in politics was substantially reduced. Therefore, 1987 is viewed as a watershed moment in the formation of a democratic political order in Korea. However, the limitations of this political order must be clearly recognized. The institutional arrangements discussed above can be systematically deployed to one's advantage if there is the political will to do so. Korean political scientists who expressed optimism after 1987 about the achievement of procedural democracy and the subsequent shift toward the task of "economic democratization" had to substantially revise their views after witnessing the arbitrary use of state authority during the Lee Myung-Bak (2008–13) and Park Geun-Hye (2013–17) administrations.

While overestimating the quality of Korea's democracy, some scholars also underestimated the weak influence of the formal political sphere and the relative strength of external, popular forces. The seemingly unbreakable authority of the Park Geun-Hye administration showed signs of instability before finally collapsing under the weight of the Candlelight Revolution. Despite the formal political elite's firmly held illusions, it was always the dynamic force of the popular will that acted as the final arbiter in Korean politics.

The Candlelight Revolution first seemed to be a transformational moment in the Korean politics that had grown out of the 1987 system. It was a victory for liberal politics within the framework of a U.S.-style dualist democracy. Bottom-up popular mobilization served as the impetus for an impeachment process that followed formal, constitutional procedures. Nevertheless, the candlelight movement possessed a distinctly new and revolutionary character. It was not a collectivist phenomenon like past social movements, but rather an open network of pluralistic individuals through which new millennials expanded their societal influence. This is why *nanum munhwa* (a "culture of sharing") defined the movement as a "revolution," sparking a new political order that will take shape over the next thirty years.[23]

In a different sense, however, the Candlelight Revolution is also a relic of the *ancien régime*. The basic institutional arrangements that were established in 1948 and maintained through the events of 1987 continue to structure political interactions today. Moreover, the deeper problem is that liberal political forces developed their present-day characteristics within this *ancien régime*. While there is now an opportunity to construct a new political order, the potential agent of that change is trapped within the old political order. Because progressive political actors took shape within the old order and were lacking in material resources, they did not have the opportunity to be instilled with liberal values. Given the constraints of a unitary system, they also lack access to a diverse pool of individuals to draw upon. There is no incentive to innovate through competition, with the political right growing increasingly obsolete. Having entered the political scene under these limitations, Korea's progressives are lacking in pluralism, responsiveness to the popular will, and governance skills compared to their counterparts in the United States.

Korean progressives now stand at the crossroads of their old limitations and a new and complex social situation. They have the unwavering support of the so-called *chin-Moon* ("pro-Moon") or *chin-Myong* (pro-Myong) bases, which hold fast to a combative view of democratic politics formed during the era of pro-democracy activism. Lacking in liberal values, they understand democracy in terms of a winner-take-all struggle against reactionary, authoritarian forces. This is related to the post-1987 shift from a "cadre" party to a broad-based "mass" party, as seen in the use of "cut-off" party primaries. Consequently, the party's core base of supporters wields greater influence. The history of political party development in the United States is repeating itself in Korea. There has been progress in the sense that "feudalistic" party leaders and activists now wield less power, but with the concomitant side effect of an excessively influential base of combative supporters and sound-bite-driven politics.

23 Kim Ye-Seul, *The Candlelight Revolution* [in Korean] (Seoul, Korea: Neuringuleum, 2017).

At the same time, progressives in Korea are faced with distinctly new social and political developments. Novel features of contemporary American politics—including a focus on self-expression, individual dignity, and a politics of pluralistic identities—have appeared in Korea as well, centered around new millennials and especially among women. It is precisely in this context that BTS, whose songs address the theme of individual dignity, in the context of the candlelight protests and the *Sewol* ferry disaster, can be understood as an artistic expression of the zeitgeist.[24] Taken together, the candlelight protests and BTS are part of a "1968-style" social phenomenon in Korea. Unlike the Korean protests of the past, however, there is an emphasis on self-expression. The progressive politicians who came of age in the pro-democracy protests were only one of many participants in the Candlelight Revolution. They have shown clear limitations in their ability to understand or represent this new zeitgeist. This applies not only to the DPK, but also to the Justice Party. Furthermore, the inter- and intra-generational cleavages—encompassing issues such as employment and the availability of quality jobs—present new challenges, as do various class-based issues.

So far, Korean progressives' response to this novel situation diverges from the reaction of their counterparts in the United States. Liberals in the United States share a common commitment to liberal values and institutional patriotism. There is internal disagreement mainly regarding how to fix the capitalist system: incremental reform or radical, structural change. Their opponent, the Republican Party, gradually changed into a combative political movement that disregards legal procedures and considers liberals to be the enemy of American civilization. The critical juncture in this transformation was Newt Gingrich's 1994 "Contract with America" and the legislative campaign that followed. Trump's emphasis on the "clash of civilizations" in both his domestic and foreign policy is not an aberration, but rather the culmination of this trend.[25]

By contrast, mainstream progressive forces in Korea, including the DPK and the Justice Party, struggled for survival in a hostile competition against the authoritarian right for many years. They are thus primarily

24 Byongjin Ahn, "Candlelight Revolution, BTS Revolution, and the Future of Liberalism," Paper presented for *BTS: A Global Interdisciplinary Conference Project*, Kingston, London (2019).

25 Byongjin Ahn, *The Changing Faces of America* (Seoul, Korea: Medici, 2016).

seeking to protect their interests and maintain a stable political base. They have little interest in liberal values, such as respect for legal procedures and checks and balances. Their political consciousness is lacking in a commitment to liberal values, unlike that of their counterparts in the United States. Their objective is not to construct a soft authoritarian or totalitarian regime, but rather to engage in a 1987-style political struggle between pro-democratic and anti-democratic factions. There is no evidence of a clear ideological commitment to soft authoritarianism. They are incompetently juggling various realities: their commitment to majoritarian values, the need to achieve political victory, and the dawn of a new political era.

With the changing of the times, the progressive political elite are becoming part of the top 20 percent of Korean society instead of leading the way in creating the post-candlelight political order. Among the citizens who support these elite, those who are facing economic insecurity due to the decline of the manufacturing sector—among other reasons—are finding their identity and social status under threat.[26] These individuals seek to have their identity affirmed in their support for democratic values and the struggle against "deep-rooted evils" as they encounter job insecurity and adjust to the greater social role played by women. The difference between American and Korean progressives is that among the latter, there are individuals with a strong patriarchal bias within both the DPK and the Justice Party. This was made clear in the hostile response among some supporters of these two parties to the allegations of sexual misconduct by Seoul mayor Park Won-Soon. For example, they unleashed blistering criticism against two young congresswomen for refusing to attend Park's funeral. Korean society has been thrown into chaos as it simultaneously confronts modern-era identity struggles, a process that the United States began decades ago, and postmodern issues such as the climate crisis.

The progressive elite, who now belong to the top 20 percent of Korean society, are much better off than they were before, but they still have a relatively weak base of material support. They still see themselves as outsiders. They seek to stay in power for several decades to complete the task of democratization and establish themselves as a stable political force. However, attempting to create and sustain a permanent majority coalition while lacking in liberal values is not the

26 Hong Sung-Kook, *The Contraction Society* (Seoul, Korea: Medici, 2019).

same as totalitarianism. A key characteristic of Korea's dualist democracy is that it promptly strikes down any attempts at such a regime, even if there are actors who wish to pursue such a path. One only needs to look at the downfall of the Park Geun-Hye administration, which had once appeared invincible, and the Democratic Party's resounding defeat in the April 2021 by-elections. If the opposition parties are able to turn themselves toward a more resilient liberal direction, the political landscape will be drastically transformed. Regardless of who wins the presidential election in 2022, Korea must undergo arduous change before it becomes a mature liberal democracy that is qualitatively different from its current form of dualist democracy. In many ways, Korea is suffering from the overdue side effects of "compressed" economic growth and rapid democratization.

The Decline of the Liberal Order and the Rise of the MZ Generation

How can we evaluate the legacy of Moon's administration? First and foremost, it is an administration that has failed to address the most pressing problem of the era: the consolidation of the liberal constitutional political order. The Candlelight Revolution reaped positive outcomes within the constitutional framework by impeaching President Park Geun-Hye for her arbitrary governance, thereby creating momentum for constitutionalism. Moon's administration could have built on this momentum to establish a more robust liberal constitutional order. However, lacking enthusiasm for liberal values, Moon's administration took a more regressive course than previous progressive administrations, leaving Korea's politics unstable and extremely polarized. It is by no means desirable for citizens' movements to confront one another, filling the streets of Seocho-dong (supporting former justice minister Cho Kuk) and Gwanghwamun (opposing Cho Kuk).

Second, the Moon administration's indifference to the ethical basis and values of liberalism triggered a backlash from the conservative camp, continuing the cycle of mutually hostile interactions. If the Moon administration had further consolidated the liberal constitutional order, South Korea's conservatives would have had no choice but to adapt to this order to try and restore their lost hegemony. However, the Moon administration's use of double standards and its arbitrary style of governance have lured the conservatives into a similar mode of politics. The so-called politics of "antagonistic interdependence" that has dominated Korean politics is still in action.

Daniel Galvin, an eminent theorist of party politics in the United States, has pointed out that the biggest driving force for sustainably innovating a party in the medium to long term is a situation in which the political leader and his or her party have lost the election and have become a minority party.[27] However, in Korea, even if one loses the election, it is sufficient to simply mobilize hostile political enthusiasm toward the other side instead of innovating. Ruling political parties have the tendency to disregard the popular mandate and engage in self-destructive actions without restraint. This creates negative perceptions of politics and provides fertile soil for the emergence of extreme populist forces that exploit these by relying on individual charisma.

Third, the Moon administration failed to seize the opportunity to rectify the flaws of Korea's dual democracy. In contrast to the United States, the nature of institutional politics in Korea—weak hegemony in everyday processes and the frequent appearance of movement politics—is highly likely to continue for some time. The strong influence of movement politics and the antagonistic interdependence of political forces are unlikely to foster productive competition among elites within the representative system. The frailty of the elites casts a dark shadow on Korean politics, which is on the brink of a grand transformation. In this era of "long-term emergencies" internationally—the climate crisis, the COVID-19 pandemic, the so-called new cold war between the United States and China—and domestic issues such as the stagnation of Korea's job market and an unbalanced model of economic growth centered on Seoul and large conglomerates, Korea's society requires political elites to have a deeper commitment to fundamental values and display competence in addressing policy challenges. However, the continuation of Korea's current dual democracy is highly likely to lead to frequent chaos and disaster during the "new normal" that is now beginning.

Although the Moon administration failed to consolidate Korea's liberal constitutional order, there were also aspects in which liberalism rose in society as a whole. In particular, regardless of the intentions of the ruling and opposition parties, the political awakening of the MZ

27 Daniel Galvin, *Presidential Party Building: Dwight Eisenhower to George W. Bush* (Princeton: Princeton University Press, 2010).

(Millennial and Z) generation has emerged as a critical issue during Moon's presidency.[28] In June 2021, the conservative party elected Lee Jun-Seok, a thirty-seven-year-old Trumpian politician, as its leader—the youngest party leader in Korea's modern history. This unprecedented anomaly cannot be simply explained by the aspirations of conservative voters for a transfer of power in the 2022 presidential election. Policies to address the lack of jobs and status anxiety among the younger generation have become core campaign themes of presidential candidates from both the ruling and opposition parties.

This has emerged in the context of widespread societal demands for a paradigm shift through the empowerment of the MZ generation. Witnessing the MZ generation's daring resistance to the longstanding practice of seniority, for instance, some corporations are moving to reform the seniority wage system, which many experts had regarded as impossible to eradicate in the short term. As companies respond to the MZ generation's preference for socially responsible consumption and their sensitivity to the climate crisis, there is an increasing emphasis on values in both product development and corporate management (e.g., environmental, social and corporate governance).

Moreover, the cultural power of Korea's MZ generation, embodied by groups such as BTS, has now become a global phenomenon. In addressing neighboring countries such as China and North Korea, this generation urges confidence and political equality and demands universal values such as human rights. Jeong Young-Hoon and Park Sung-Won of the National Assembly Futures Research Institute conclude that Korea's MZ generation, which places greater emphasis on individual freedom, holds an identity that is drastically different from that of previous generations.[29] The aforementioned values are precisely those on which contemporary liberalism focuses.

---

28 While these two generations are often lumped together because of certain similarities, Millennials and Generation Z have their own distinctive identity and internal cleavages. For instance, there is a wide gender gap in the appreciation of the climate crisis as a real threat among young women and men in their twenties. However, when it comes to rising political voices, they can be regarded as one generational unit. See Kim Da-Eun, "South Korea Climate Crisis Report in 2022" [in Korean], *Sisa In*, January 25, 2002, http://www.sisain.co.kr/news/articleView.html?dxno=46627.

29 Jeong and Park, "The People's Choice: Transitioning to a Sustainable, Equitable Society."

Although the Moon administration has shown a tendency toward liberal regression, Korean society as a whole is experiencing a strange lag during which the emergence of new values, including liberalism, coexists with nonliberalism. Korea's political order is thus passing through an age of "dualist power" in which the old order is gradually declining and a new order is slowly emerging.

The most urgent task facing Korean politics, I would argue, is the continual implementation of dual tasks. Specifically, these are to (1) continue progress toward the full realization of liberal constitutional ideals while (2) rearranging the political order to give a more central role to the future-oriented MZ generation. Modern liberalism, for all its great accomplishments, has so far been ineffective in addressing the issue of sustainable development. Its vision of democracy is mostly centered on the present, at the expense of future generations. A political regime that is incapable of implementing decisions critical for future inhabitants of the earth (both human and nonhuman) will stumble from crisis to crisis, as we are witnessing in the so-called Anthropocene and post-COVID eras. Those who seek to transform Korean politics face the daunting challenge of performing complex political acrobatics to simultaneously address these two seemingly impossible tasks.

Unlike those of the United States, the new agents of political change in Korea—including the new millennials—are weak in demographic, economic, and political terms. There is, however, no shortcut on the path ahead. There is no choice but to create the momentum for transformative change by tirelessly working to cultivate liberal ideals among the next generation of political actors and formulate a policy agenda that extends beyond those ideals.

The explosive momentum of Korean politics, coming from the rapid acceleration that drove the country's economic growth, has already swiftly turned once impossible tasks into a "new normal" with the unprecedented arrival of "disaster capitalism" during the pandemic. As Korea turns toward the challenges of the future, the important thing is to honestly face reality and exercise what the political philosopher Giorgio Agamben called "the courage of hopelessness."[30]

30 Slavoj Zizek, *Pandemic Panic: COVID-19 Shakes the World* [in Korean] (Seoul, Korea: Bookhouse, 2020).

Bibliography

Ackerman, Bruce. *We the People*, vol. 1. Boston: Belknap Press, 1993.

Ahn, Byongjin. *The Impeachment Politics of Roh and Clinton.* [In Korean]. Seoul, Korea: Prungil, 2004.

———. *The Changing Faces of America.* [In Korean.] Seoul, Korea: Medici, 2016.

———. "Candlelight Revolution, BTS Revolution, and the Future of Liberalism." Paper presented for BTS: A Global Interdisciplinary Conference Project. Kingston, London, 2019.

Chin, Jung-Kwon. *How Progressives Collapse.* [In Korean.] Seoul, Korea: Chunnyuneusangsang, 2020.

Choi, Jang-Jip. *Democracy after Democratization.* [In Korean.] Seoul, Korea: Humanitas, 2005.

———. "Korean Democracy after the Candlelight Movement—The Change of Ideological Terrain and the Desirable Role of the Conservative Party." [In Korean.] Colloquium Lecture at Seoul National University, November 27, 2020.

Dalton, Russell. *Citizen Politics: Public Opinion and Political Parties in Advanced Industrial Democracies.* [In Korean.] Seoul: Arke, 2010.

Galvin, Daniel. *Presidential Party Building: Dwight D. Eisenhower to George W. Bush*, Princeton: Princeton University Press, 2010.

Ginsberg, Tom, and Aziz Z. Huq. *How To Save A Constitutional Democracy*. Chicago: University of Chicago Press, 2018.

Henderson, Gregory. *Korean Politics of the Vortex.* [In Korean.] Seoul, Korea: Hanwol, 2013.

Hong, Sung-Kook. *The Contraction Society.* [In Korean.] Seoul, Korea: Medici, 2019.

Jeong, Young-Hoon, and Park Sung-Won. "The People's Choice: Transitioning to a Sustainable, Equitable Society." [In Korean.] *State Future Strategy Insight* 6 (November 19, 2020). https://www.nafi.re.kr/new/report.do?mode=view&articleNo=1732&article.offset=0&articleLimit=9.

Johnson, Charles, and Katherine E. Newcomer. *U.S. Inspectors General: Truth Tellers in Turbulent Times*. Washington D.C: Brookings Institution, 2019.

Kim Da-Eun. "South Korea Climate Crisis Report in 2022." [In Korean.] *Sisa In*, January 25, 2002. http://www.sisain.co.kr/news/articleView.html?dxno=46627.

Kim, Ye-Seul. *The Candlelight Revolution.* [In Korean.] Seoul, Korea: Neuringuleum, 2017.

Koo, Hagen. *State and Society in Contemporary Korea*. Ithaca: Cornell University Press, 1994.

Levinson, Sanford, and Jack M. Balkin. *Democracy and Dysfunction.* Chicago: University of Chicago Press, 2019.

McCormick, John. *Machiavellian Democracy*. Cambridge: Cambridge University Press, 2011.

Mouffe, Chantal. *The Return of the Political*. New York: Verso, 2006.

Norris, Pippa, and Ronald Inglehart. *Cultural Backlash: Trump, Brexit, and Authoritarian Populism*. Cambridge: Cambridge University Press, 2019.

Park, Kang-Soo. "I Am Right and You Are Wrong." [In Korean.] *Kyosu Shinmun*, December 20, 2020. https://www.kyosu.net/news/articleView.html?idxno=59131.

Schattschneider, E. E. *The Semi-sovereign People: A Realist's View of Democracy in America*. San Diego: Harcourt Brace Jovanovich College Publishers, 1975.

Shin, Gi-Wook. "South Korea's Democratic Decay." *Journal of Democracy* 31, no. 3 (2020): 100–14.

Zaretski, Eli. *Why America Needs a Left: A Historical Argument.* New York: Polity, 2012.

Zizek, Slavoj. *Pandemic Panic: COVID-19 Shakes the World.* [In Korean.] Seoul, Korea: Bookhouse, 2020.

CHAPTER TWO

Uses and Misuses of Nationalism in the Democratic Politics of Korea

Aram Hur

In a little over three decades, Korean democracy has made impressive strides. The fledgling democracy survived the devastating Asian financial crisis of the late 1990s and underwent a peaceful transfer of power to the opposition. Public support for democracy is widespread, national turnout rates are typically higher than those of many older Western democracies, and Korea routinely ranks high on most indices of democratic quality.[1] After the mass candlelight protests of 2016 that led to the peaceful impeachment of President Park Geun-Hye over corruption charges in 2017, international media even remarked that "South Korea just showed the world how to do democracy."[2]

Korea's image as a leading success story from the Third Wave of democratization has recently come under question, however. Observers have noted increasingly blatant use of illiberal tactics by recent administrations to suppress political competition.[3] These are not formal violations of the law, but subversion of existing laws to systematically target the opposition, be it the competing party or critical voices in civil society. Examples include cycles of retribution between parties through

1 In 2019 the Economist Intelligence Unit's Democracy Index ranked South Korea as the world's twenty-third-most democratic country, ahead of all other Asian democracies and the United States, which ranked twenty-fifth.

2 Ishaan Tharoor, "South Korea Just Showed the World How to Do Democracy," *Washington Post*, May 10, 2017, https://www.washingtonpost.com/news/world views/wp/2017/05/10/south-korea-just-showed-the-world-how-to-do-democracy/.

3 Andrew Yeo, "Has South Korean Democracy Hit a Glass Ceiling? Institutional-Cultural Factors and Limits to Democratic Progress," *Asian Politics & Policy* 12, no. 4 (2020): 539–58.

indictments, abuses of executive privilege to skew judiciary oversight, and curtailment of freedom of speech under the guise of neutrality. Such practices are not well captured by standard indices of democracy, which tend to focus on formal, institutional aspects of democratic rule. A closer look at Korea therefore reveals a consolidated democracy, but one riddled with illiberalism, and which Gi-Wook Shin recently described as on the path to "democratic decay."[4]

How accurate is this depiction of Korea's democratic trajectory? What explains the apparent tolerance for illiberalism in an otherwise vibrant democracy? This chapter addresses both questions. First, despite characterizations of Korea's illiberal slide as an undesirable legacy of the Moon Jae-In administration, I show through historical data that illiberal partisan competition has been a long-standing feature of Korean democracy. I trace the frequency of indictments under three controversial laws for all incumbent administrations dating back to 1987 and find that such illiberal tactics have been part of the political toolkit of *both* conservative and progressive parties since democratization. Illiberal practices have intensified in certain areas, but they are not new. As such, they should be seen as a worsening symptom, not cause, of Korea's stalled democratic quality.

The pervasiveness of illiberalism across the political spectrum raises the second puzzle. Why have illiberal practices persisted despite the rise of the progressives—the former pro-democracy activists? In the second part of this chapter, I argue that the answer lies in a key historical feature of Korea's democratization: nationalist polarization during the early phase of democratic transition. "Nationalist polarization" refers to a specific form of partisan polarization, where the parties are primarily divided on competing nationalist ideologies. Extreme polarization of any kind is detrimental to democracy, but nationalist polarization poses a fundamental risk, as nationalist claims are both state-seeking and existential. Nationalist polarization reframes the goal of democratic competition as a zero-sum race for ownership over the state. It also reframes the political opposition from a policy challenger that must be respected to an existential threat to "our" nationalist vision that must be eliminated. Both phenomena weaken what Steven

4 Gi-Wook Shin, "South Korea's Democratic Decay," *Journal of Democracy* 31, no. 3 (July 2020): 100–14. For Korea's democratic development in comparative perspective, see Aurel Croissant and Jeffrey Haynes, "Democratic Regression in Asia: Introduction," *Democratization* 28, no. 1 (2021): 1–21.

Levitsky and Daniel Ziblatt dub the informal guardrails of liberal democracy: forbearance and mutual tolerance.[5]

Using historical process-tracing, I show that Korea's democratization was not just an anti-regime or anti-authoritarian struggle, but fundamentally a nationalist conflict between elite factions from the Cold War. Instead of alleviating this conflict, Korea's pathway to democratization entrenched it, as competing nationalist factions refashioned themselves as competing political parties under the new electoral system. The nationalist roots of Korea's party system explain the curious poverty of liberalism among progressives. Modern-day progressives were forged not only as a reactionary force against authoritarianism, as Byongjin Ahn points out in chapter 1, but also as the underdog in an ongoing nationalist struggle to claim ownership over the state. As a result, political victory is prized over commitment to liberal values. The illiberal norm of "win at all costs" was embedded into Korea's party system from the start, the effects of which are manifesting more clearly as the progressives have gained political clout.

Yet illiberal party politics is sustainable only if the public tolerates it. Why would a democratic citizenry condone such transgressions by political elites? This is particularly puzzling in Korea, where, from the national gold drives during the Asian financial crisis to high voter turnout, citizens have often displayed impressive levels of civic duty in the name of nation.[6] A unifying ethnic national narrative (*danilminjok*), which bound Korean citizens and the democratic state as if one body, was long seen as a positive force behind Korea's democratic development.[7] What has changed?

I argue that the apparent tolerance for illiberalism among the Korean citizenry is driven at least in part by the fragmentation of the *danilminjok* narrative at the mass level. Several cross-cutting pressures have made the foundational narrative untenable. For one, Korea's economic liberalization since the late 1990s has widened the class gap to unprecedented levels. Korea now ranks second among countries of the Organisation for Economic Co-operation and Development (OECD)

5 Steven Levitsky and Daniel Ziblatt, *How Democracies Die* (New York: Crown Publishing, 2018).

6 Aram Hur, "Citizen Duty and the Ethical Power of Communities: Mixed-method Evidence from East Asia," *British Journal of Political Science* 50, no. 3 (2020): 1047–65.

7 Aram Hur, *Narratives of Civic Duty: How National Stories Shape Democracy in Asia* (Ithaca: Cornell University Press, forthcoming).

in income inequality. According to the World Inequality Database, as of 2021, 25 percent of the national wealth is concentrated among the top 1 percent of earners, whereas only 6 percent belongs to the bottom 50 percent of earners.[8] At the same time, Korea has the lowest birth rate among OECD countries. A dramatic decline in fertility has all but necessitated foreign labor and interracial marriage, literally changing the ethnic face of Korea and demanding state investments toward multiculturalism. Both developments have saddled a growing swath of the native citizenry—particularly the working class and those with ethnocentric views—with feelings of being written out of the national success they helped to build.

With the loss of an overarching metanarrative (*geodaedamron*) that reaffirms the idea of an inclusive nation based on *minjok*, the once robust national basis for civic duty is weakening. Instead, voters support parties or candidates who promise a narrow nationalist vision that protects "my" Korea from "the other." As more citizens act as "partisans first, democrats second" at the ballot box, civic duty gives way to partisan duty.[9] I show with three waves of data from the Asian Barometer Survey between 2006 and 2015 that national pride is increasingly associated with greater tolerance for illiberalism among both conservative and progressive supporters. It is the confluence of national fragmentation at the mass level and nationalist polarization at the party level that has offered illiberal democratic elites electoral impunity for their transgressions.

Is Korean democracy in a watershed moment? While the Moon administration is certainly not the cause of the illiberal slide, I argue that it nevertheless carries special weight given the critical juncture—the impeachment and moral repudiation of Park Geun-Hye—at which it came to power. The Moon administration's legacy as a potential reckoning for Korean democracy will critically depend on the public's reaction: whether most citizens will make a stand for democratic principles, before and even despite their group interests, or continue to fall prey to divisive identity politics at the cost of liberal values.

8 See "Korea," World Inequality Database, https://wid.world/country/korea/, accessed November 28, 2021.

9 Matthew Graham and Milan Svolik, "Democracy in America? Partisanship, Polarization, and the Robustness of Support for Democracy in the United States," *American Political Science Review* 114, no. 2 (2020): 392–409.

Patterns of Illiberalism in Korean Democracy

Illiberal practices of democratic elites can take different forms, but the kinds that cause alarm among scholars of democracy are those that violate the foundations of democratic competition: mutual tolerance and forbearance. Both are critical to upholding the "bounded uncertainty" that enables power sharing in a democracy. As Philippe Schmitter and Terry Karl argue in "What Democracy Is...and Is Not":

> In a democracy, representatives must at least informally agree that those who win greater electoral support or influence over policy will not use their temporary superiority to bar the losers from taking office or exerting influence in the future, and that in exchange for this opportunity to keep competing for power and place, momentary losers will respect the winners' right to make binding decisions.[10]

Once the possibility of a real oppositional challenge vanishes, democracies can quickly devolve into competitive authoritarianism.

The quality of a democracy is typically assessed based on topical categories (political, civil, freedom of press), but I focus on the actions of political actors. I define illiberalism as practices that aim to systematically minimize or even eliminate the political opposition. Building on an analysis conducted by Stephan Haggard and Jong-Sung You, I examine the historical pattern of three controversial laws in Korea that are often weaponized by incumbents: criminal defamation laws, national election laws, and the National Security Law.[11] Focusing on the same set of laws over time helps mitigate concerns about selection bias. Moreover, since all three laws have been in effect since or before formal democratization in 1987, I am able to provide a longer view of trends in illiberalism across all administrations, not just the most recent.

Criminal defamation laws

Criminal defamation laws are meant to protect individuals against reputational damage in cases of false information or slander. In practice,

10 Philippe C. Schmitter and Terry Lynn Karl, "What Democracy Is . . . and Is Not," *Journal of Democracy* 2, no. 3 (1991): 82.

11 Stephan Haggard and Jong-Sung You, "Freedom of Expression in South Korea," *Journal of Contemporary Asia* 45, no. 1 (2015): 167–79.

however, such laws can have a chilling effect when leveraged against the opposition or critics of the incumbent regime. Because reputational damage is subjectively defined and criminal sentences range from egregious fines to bans on holding public office and even jail time, defamation laws are easily weaponized by those in power. For such reasons, the United Nations Human Rights Committee declared the criminalization of libel as a violation of freedom of expression in a contentious case centered on the Philippines in 2012.[12] Most advanced democracies have followed suit by decriminalizing such laws.

Korea remains one of a handful of democracies to uphold criminalization, and incumbents have often invoked the law. Figure 2.1 shows that the frequency of defamation arrests and investigations has steadily increased since democratization in 1987, save for a temporary dip during the final years of the Park Geun-Hye administration following its apex in 2015. Notably, although the criminal defamation law is often seen as an authoritarian legacy of the conservatives, the rate of investigations and arrests continued to increase during the progressive Kim Dae-Jung (1998–2003) and Roh Moo-Hyun (2003–08) administrations. The rates peaked during the return of the conservatives under the Lee Myung-Bak (2008–13) and Park Geun-Hye (2013–17) administrations, but the early years of the Moon Jae-In administration also show an uptick, even as Moon campaigned on cleaning up the "deep-rooted irregularities accumulated over the past nine years."[13] These patterns challenge the common assumption that criminal defamation is uniquely part of the conservatives' political arsenal.

Election campaign laws

Korea has extremely stringent laws restricting the timing and content of campaigning for public office. Article 58 of the Public Officials Election Act (POEA) limits election campaign activity, which includes any action aimed at winning an election outside of usual party activities, preparations for the campaign, and the official intent-to-run statement,

12 Scott Griffen, "UN: Philippines Journalist Defamation Conviction a Violation of Free Speech," International Press Institute, February 2, 2012, https://ipi.media/un-philippines-journalist-defamation-conviction-a-violation-of-free-speech/.

13 "What Moon Jae-in Pledged to Do as President," *Korea Herald*, May 10, 2017, http://www.koreaherald.com/view.php?ud=20170509000521.

FIGURE 2.1 Investigations and arrests for defamation, by type and party of incumbent, 1987–2019

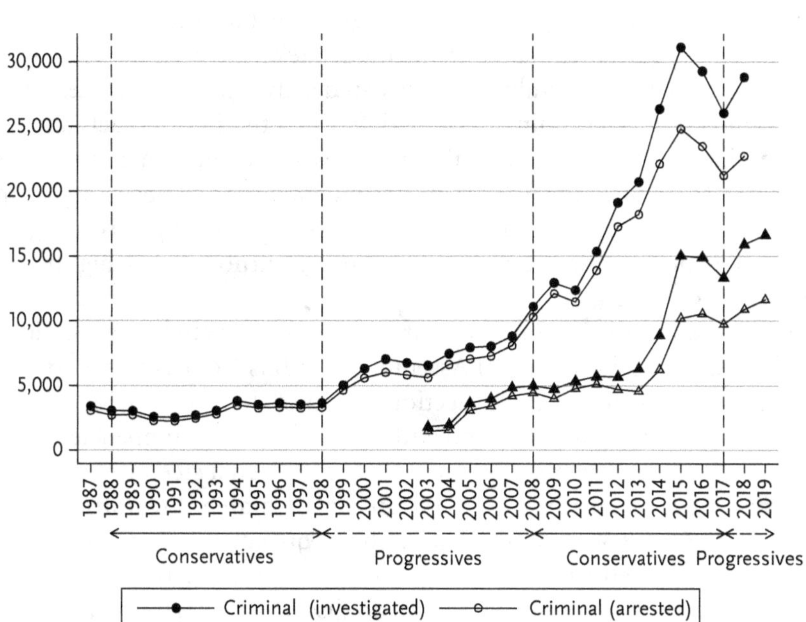

SOURCE: Republic of Korea Prosecution Service, *Prosecution Yearbook* [in Korean], https://www.spo.go.kr/site/spo/ex/board/List.do?cbIdx=1603.

to an officially designated "election period": a brief fourteen-day window for National Assembly and local elections and a twenty-three-day period for presidential elections. The POEA also outlines the following rules for "fair competition" in Article 7: "A political party and a candidate taking part in an election [. . .] shall not engage in any conduct detrimental to the good morals and social order in supporting, propagandizing, criticizing or opposing the platform and policy of a political party or the political views of a candidate." Article 8 extends such neutrality standards to campaign reporting by the media. These are not *pro forma* statutes. Individuals or civil society organizations charged with violations face multiyear imprisonment and exorbitant fines.

In principle, the POEA aims to level the playing field for candidates of all socioeconomic and political backgrounds. In practice, it can be subverted to construct what Haggard and You describe as an "enormous incumbent advantage" for the party in power.[14] The short campaign period prevents unestablished challengers from effectively promoting themselves, and the subjective language on what counts as negative campaigning suffers the same problems as the criminal defamation law. Under the guise of neutrality, the law can disadvantage candidates from the opposition. The timing of amendments to the POEA, each adding increasingly narrow language about permissible campaign materials or activities, is telling. Since 1987, most amendments have been added in the years 1997, 2004, and 2008: the years immediately preceding or following presidential elections when party turnover was highly expected or occurred.

Figure 2.2 shows the number of election-law-related investigations and indictments for National Assembly elections from 1988 to 2016. I focus on National Assembly elections because they occur with greater frequency (every four years) and within presidential incumbencies (five-year terms). Since democratization, there has been a steep rise through the first opposition turnover, with the only notable downturn occurring during the Roh administration. The frequency has been on the rise again with the return of the conservatives. In short, as is the case with the criminal defamation law, there is no discernable partisan pattern to how frequently election campaign law violations are invoked.[15]

National Security Law

The final analysis concerns indictments under the controversial National Security Law (NSL). The NSL, which has been in effect since

14 Perhaps despite such tactics, Korea's National Assembly still has high turnover rates due to a weak party system. While the conservative versus progressive factional divide is stable, the specific parties that comprise each faction are highly unstable and candidate centric, with parties rebranding or dissolving and new ones emerging with each election. This instability creates many "lame duck" incumbents and incentivizes misbehavior, rendering them vulnerable to turnover. See Marko Klasnja and Rocio Titiunik, "The Incumbency Curse: Weak Parties, Term Limits, and Unfulfilled Accountability," *American Political Science Review* 111, no. 1 (2017): 129–48.

15 Figure 2.2 shows the cumulative number of investigations and does not differentiate by type of charge. Some charges, like false propaganda, are examples of illiberal practice aimed at eliminating the opposition as defined in this study, whereas others, like money laundering, are not. In any given year, I find that the total count is roughly split between false propaganda, illegal gifting/money laundering, and miscellaneous violations.

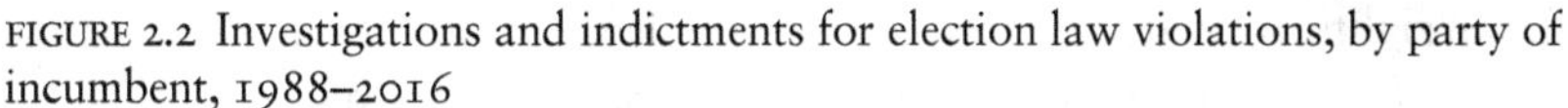

FIGURE 2.2 Investigations and indictments for election law violations, by party of incumbent, 1988–2016

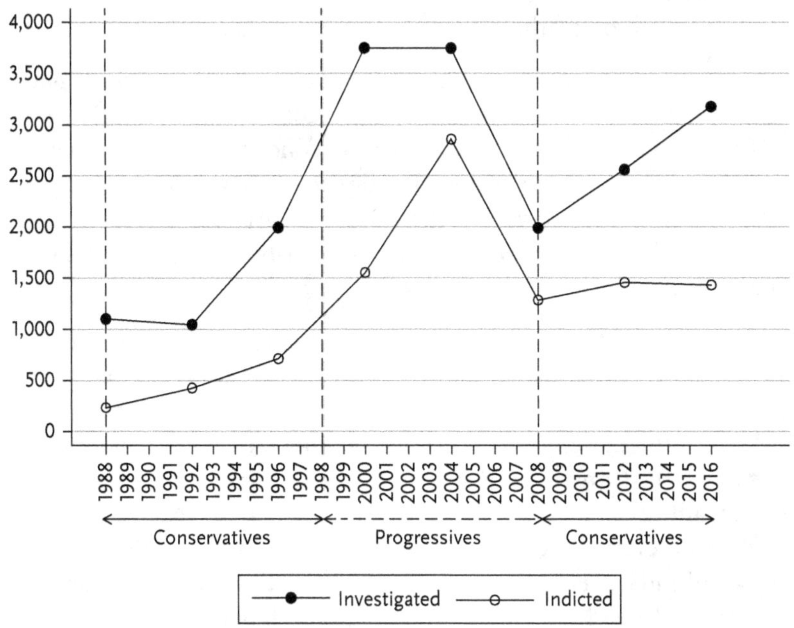

SOURCE: Republic of Korea Prosecution Service, *Prosecution Yearbook* (1992 onwards); archived news articles in *Joongang Ilbo* (1988 election).

1948, is a relic of Japan's public security law that was the primary tool for colonial repression. As stated in Article 1 of the law, the NSL aims to "secure the security of the State and the subsistence and freedom of nationals, by regulating any anticipated activities compromising the safety of the State."[16] In the aftermath of the Korean War, the NSL was seen as a necessary safeguard against communist infiltration from the North. During South Korea's authoritarian era, the NSL was aggressively invoked to eradicate any remaining pro-communist forces.

Following democratization in 1987, the NSL was amended to curtail potential abuses of the law. A 1991 amendment to Article 1 added that the law "shall not be permitted . . . to restrict unreasonably the fundamental

16 "National Security Act," Korea Legislation Research Institute, https://elaw.klri.re.kr/eng_service/lawView.do?hseq=26692&lang=ENG, accessed November 30, 2021.

human rights of citizens guaranteed by the Constitution." In that same year, Article 2(2), which designated all communist states as "anti-government organizations" was deleted, and the language of the controversial Article 7 was amended to add the italicized conditional clause:

> Any person who praises, incites, or propagates the activities of an anti-government organization, a member thereof or of the person who has received an order from it, or who acts in concert with it, or propagates or instigates a rebellion against the State *with the knowledge of the fact that it may endanger the existence and security of the State or democratic fundamental order* shall be punished by imprisonment for not more than seven years.[17]

Figure 2.3 plots the number of indictments under the NSL from 1985 to 2019. Indictments did not immediately decline after democratization: save for a temporary dip following major amendments in 1991, indictments climbed steadily, peaking at almost 700 cases in 1997. With the transfer of power to the progressives in 1998, there was a significant drop to fewer than fifty indictments per year. The Roh administration even made an unsuccessful attempt to repeal the law. The number of indictments nearly quadrupled by 2013 with the conservative return of Lee Myung-Bak and gradually faded after Moon Jae-In entered office in 2017.

A 2012 Amnesty International report cited the "worrying trend of increased arbitrary use of the NSL in the Republic of Korea since 2008," stating that while South Korea has special security concerns with respect to North Korea, "security concerns should never be used as an excuse to deny people the right to express different political views and to exercise fundamental human rights including the right to freedom of expression [. . .]."[18] Indeed, notable cases under the NSL have occurred in what appear to be politically opportune moments for the conservatives. For instance, after the *Cheonan* incident—the sinking of a South Korean Navy corvette during U.S.-Korea joint military exercises in March 2010—the Lee Myung-Bak administration swiftly blamed North Korea and silenced further media discussion in

17 "National Security Act," emphasis added.

18 Amnesty International, "The National Security Law: Curtailing Freedom of Expression and Association in the Name of Security in the Republic of South Korea," November 2012, https://www.amnestyusa.org/wp-content/uploads/2017/04/s_korea_nsl_report_embargo_2911_asa_25_006_2012.pdf.

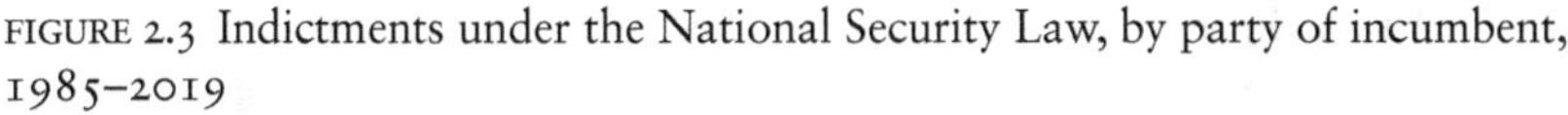

FIGURE 2.3 Indictments under the National Security Law, by party of incumbent, 1985–2019

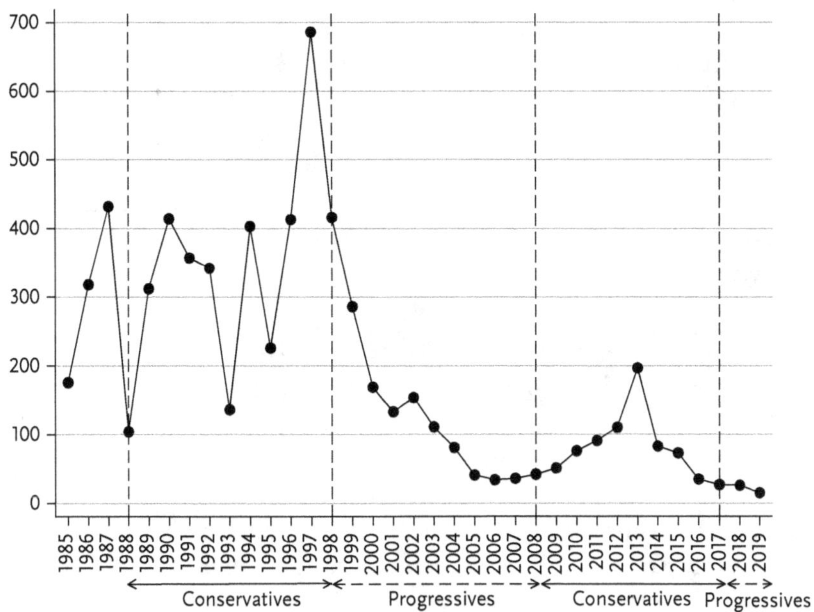

SOURCE: Republic of Korea Prosecution Service, *Prosecution Yearbook* [in Korean].

the name of national security, seemingly to galvanize conservative voters for the upcoming local elections in June.[19] Similarly, the post hoc charge against Kim Eun-Hye, who was indicted for espionage on an official visit to North Korea that had been approved by the previous progressive administration, raised questions about electoral opportunism ahead of the 2012 presidential election. Given its post–Cold War authoritarian roots, the NSL is most susceptible to partisan abuse by conservatives among the three laws examined here, and that is, in fact, what the data suggest. Seen together with the other laws, however, it is clearly the exception and still begs the question of why its use has persisted even after democratization.

The historical data in this section demonstrate two points. First, illiberalism has been a persistent feature of Korean democracy since

19 Jong-Sung You, "The 'Cheonan' Incident and the Declining Freedom of Expression in South Korea," *Asian Perspective* 38, no. 2 (2015): 195–219.

democratization in 1987. Second, illiberal practices are far from a partisan phenomenon. When seen over time, the invocation of controversial laws does not show a clear conservative or progressive bias, even as both sides accuse the other of being "illiberal." Criminal defamation investigations have steadily increased regardless of the party in power, whereas election law charges have peaked during progressive incumbencies and invocations of the NSL have peaked under the conservatives. In this context, the illiberal transgressions of the Moon administration are not an aberration, but a continuation of a long-standing pattern in Korean democracy. The problem with the quality of Korea's democracy is better characterized as a lack of progress, not one of regress.

Nationalist Polarization and Illiberal Democratic Elites

What is puzzling about the persistence of illiberalism in Korean democracy is why it was not uprooted with the rise of the progressives—the former pro-democracy activists. I argue that nationalist polarization in the early stages of Korea's democratization explains this conundrum. After explaining why nationalist polarization is particularly detrimental to the development of democratic norms, I use historical process-tracing to illustrate how the national politics of Korea's democratization sowed the seeds for illiberal partisan competition from the outset.

Nationalist polarization is a specific form of partisan polarization. Parties can be polarized on a variety of ideological dimensions. For instance, the left-right divide in most advanced democracies is typically based on ideological differences about redistribution. Nationalist polarization is when the parties are fundamentally divided on nationalist ideology. The differences can be definitional—about "who we are"—or directional—about "where we ought to go." What matters is that competing parties see each other as espousing *mutually exclusive* visions of the nation.

Extreme polarization of any kind can turn "pernicious" in democracies.[20] But nationalist polarization fundamentally reframes democratic competition as zero-sum. What distinguishes nationalist claims

20 Murat Somer and Jennifer McCoy, "Transformations through Polarization and Global Threats to Democratization," *Annals of the American Academy of Political and Social Sciences* 681, no. 1 (2019): 8–22.

from other identity-based claims, such as those focused on class or race, is that nationalism is inherently *state-seeking*. The nation is a political community that sees itself as deserving of its own territory and self-rule: ". . . nations are not just unified by culture; they are unified by a sense of purpose: controlling the territory that the members of the group believe to be theirs."[21] Achieving congruency between the nation and the state lies at the heart of any nationalist movement. Under nationalist polarization, elections are no longer about policy. They are about state capture.

When state ownership becomes the end of democratic competition, it also redefines the acceptable means to get there. Specifically, nationalist polarization incentivizes two kinds of illiberal behaviors by political elites. The first is treatment of the opposition as an existential threat. In social psychology, the "black sheep effect" refers to the phenomenon whereby deviant "in-group" members are judged more harshly than "out-group" members because they internally threaten the sense of group security.[22] When the political opposition espouses a mutually exclusive nationalist vision, the imperative of achieving nation-state congruency justifies the use of whatever means necessary—including illiberal tactics—to eliminate the opposition. This erodes one of the democratic guardrails identified by Levitsky and Ziblatt: mutual tolerance.

The second illiberal behavior is the prioritization of the party's nationalist agenda over democratic principles. In contexts of nationalist polarization, parties have a singular goal: to achieve nation-state congruency under "our" nationalist vision. In practice, this means throwing forbearance and procedural justice out the window to force through the party's nationalist agenda once in office. The first casualty in this process is typically the democratic principle of public consent. Indeed, both conservatives and progressives in Korea have subverted laws to clamp down on civil society in times of public opposition to the party's nationalist agenda, be it during mass protests against Kim Dae-Jung's Sunshine Policy or candlelight protests opposing U.S. beef

21 Lowell Barrington, "'Nation' and 'Nationalism': The Misuse of Key Concepts in Political Science," *PS: Political Science and Politics* 30, no. 4 (1997): 712. See also Ernest Gellner, *Nations and Nationalism* (Ithaca: Cornell University Press, 1983).

22 Jose Marques, Vincent Yzerbyt, and Jacques-Philippe Leyens, "The 'Black Sheep Effect': Extremity of Judgments toward Ingroup Members as a Function of Group Identification," *European Journal of Social Psychology* 18, no. 1 (1988): 1–16.

imports during Lee Myung-Bak's push to ratify the Korea-U.S. Free Trade Agreement.

When democracies are born into contexts of nationalist polarization, illiberal competition becomes ingrained as part of the institutional norm. As the incumbent party post-democratization establishes a blueprint and the opposition reciprocates in turn, illiberal practices are internalized into party politics. This is why Dankwart Rustow presciently stated in his seminal "Transitions toward Democracy" that national unity is a necessary condition to sustain democratic rule by temporary majorities:

> On matters of economic policy and social expenditures you can always split the difference. [. . .] But there is no middle position between Flemish and French as official languages, or between Calvinism, Catholicism, and secularism as principles of education. The best you can get here is an "inclusive compromise" [. . .] Yet it also entrenches the differences instead of removing them, and accordingly it may convert political conflict into a form of trench warfare.[23]

When Korea's democratization is seen through the lens of nationalist polarization, the reason for the persistence of illiberalism—even as the progressives, the former pro-democracy activists, have risen to power—becomes clear. Democratization did not alleviate preexisting nationalist tensions from the Cold War, but rather entrenched them into the electoral party system, setting the stage for the kind of partisan "trench warfare" Rustow warned about. To illustrate this, I trace the nationalist roots of the modern-day partisan divide in Korea.

Korea's nationally polarized democratization

Korea formally democratized in 1987, but to understand the nationally polarized context in which it did, it is necessary to look back to Japanese colonialism in the early twentieth century.[24] Korea's now popularized national narrative of a singular bloodline (*danilminjok*) was a survival response to Japanese colonialism: by sourcing the nation in the

---

23 Dankwart Rustow, "Transitions to Democracy: Toward a Dynamic Model," *Comparative Politics* 2, no. 3 (1970): 359–60.

24 Parts of this section draw on collaborative work in Aram Hur and Andrew Yeo, "The Long Shadow of Nationalist Polarization: Democratic Ceilings in East Asia" (conference paper, American Political Science Association, 2021).

people's bloodline, this narrative divorced the concept of a "nation" from political authority, allowing the Korean nation to maintain a continuous identity even during colonial rule.[25] Post-independence, even as Korea's elites became bitterly divided along the Cold War's ideological fault line, both sides framed their claims within the *minjok* narrative—as the best way to protect the autonomy of the Korean people.[26] The pro-communist northern faction aligned with the Soviet Union and the anti-communist southern faction aligned with the United States, leading to a civil war that resulted in the current division of the Korean Peninsula.

While most previous works about Korea's "nationalist division" focus on North versus South Korea, nationalist conflict continued *within* South Korea as well.[27] Over the three decades of authoritarian rule that followed in South Korea, the seeds of a nationally polarized democracy were planted. The Syngman Rhee, Park Chung-Hee, and Chun Doo-Hwan administrations saw the remaining pro-communist forces in South Korea as an impermissible threat to "our" Korea that had to be purged. Hundreds of accused dissidents were jailed, tortured, and even executed. Political rhetoric from this authoritarian era eerily echoes the Manichean frame used by contemporary progressives focused on "eradicating deep-rooted evils" (*jeok-pye-cheong-san*).[28] For instance, Chun Doo-Hwan invoked similar good-versus-evil rhetoric against the opposition in 1987, justifying his refusal of constitutional reform as a matter of national survival:

> We must not waste this important period when we must decide the destiny of the nation by continuing to be absorbed in counterproductive

25 Bruce Cumings, "The Legacy of Japanese Colonialism in Korea," in *The Japanese Colonial Empire*, eds. Ramon Myers and Mark Peattie (Princeton: Princeton University Press, 1984), 478–96; Michael Robinson, *Cultural Nationalism in Colonial Korea, 1920-1925* (Seattle: University of Washington Press, 1988).
26 Gi-Wook Shin, *Ethnic Nationalism in Korea: Genealogy, Politics, and Legacy* (Stanford: Stanford University Press, 2006); Sheila Miyoshi Jager, *Narratives of Nation Building in Korea* (New York: M.E. Sharpe, 2003).
27 As Shin notes in *Ethnic Nationalism in Korea*: "Contention over national identity was not confined to the inter-Korean state level. It also occurred between state and society" (167). See also Gi-Wook Shin, James Freda, and Gihong Yi, "The Politics of Ethnic Nationalism in Divided Korea," *Nations and Nationalism* 5, no. 4 (1999): 465–84.
28 Park Moo-Jong, "Eradication of Deep-rooted Evils," *Korea Times*, March 16, 2017, https://www.koreatimes.co.kr/www/opinion/2018/05/636_225839.html.

> conflict, confrontation, and antagonism. To do so would deepen our internal schisms and dissipate national resources, thereby endangering the very existence and survival of the nation.[29]

Despite efforts to eradicate pro-communist forces, a second pivot breathed new life into the opposition in South Korea. As authoritarian control peaked with Park Chung-Hee's implementation of the *Yusin* Constitution, political discontent grew among students, intellectuals, and laborers. This anti-regime force gained momentum through the late 1970s, blossoming into what became the Minjung Movement, united under the principles of the "three *mins*" (*minjung* ["people"], *minjok* ["nation"], and *minju* ["democracy"]). As it grew, it co-opted parts of the pro-communist faction under the shared belief that the true autonomy of the Korean people could not be achieved without reunification with the North.[30]

The Minjung Movement was more than just a pro-democracy movement. It stirred what historian Namhee Lee calls a new kind of "oppositional nationalism," which saw as its end not democracy per se, but a nationalist revival centered on restoring power to the people:

> . . . the rise of the *minjung* movement in South Korea was intimately tied to the critical reevaluation of modern Korean history; giving alternative and new meanings to past events was key to developing the notion of *minjung* in the *minjung* movement. Reworking history was a process of discursive contestation between officially sanctioned memory and counter-memory, between the state discourse of dominant nationalism and the *minjung* movement's oppositional nationalism.[31]

The intersectionality between "new" and "old" progressive forces under the banner of a *minjung* nationalist ideology set the stage for continued nationalist conflict in Korea's post-democratization era. The *minjung* movement's pro-democracy push culminated in the June Democratic Uprising of 1987, in reaction to Chun Doo-Hwan's unilateral announcement of Roh Tae-Woo as his successor—a final affront to the

29 Clyde Haberman, "President of South Korea Orders a Halt to Debate on Constitution," *New York Times*, April 13, 1987, https://www.nytimes.com/1987/04/13/world/president-of-south-korea-orders-a-halt-to-debate-on-constitution.html.

30 Paul Y. Chang, *Protest Dialectics: State Repression and South Korea's Democracy Movement, 1970–1979* (Stanford: Stanford University Press, 2015).

31 Namhee Lee, *The Making of Minjung: Democracy and the Politics of Representation in South Korea* (Ithaca: Cornell University Press, 2007), 24.

growing popular demand for direct presidential elections. The precise manner by which formal democratization occurred, however, did not serve as a real or even symbolic victory for the opposition.

Chun's choice to reinstate popular elections and civil liberties was a classic example of what Dan Slater and Joseph Wong describe as democratization through the "strength to concede."[32] Noticing a growing rift between the opposition's leaders, Kim Young-Sam and Kim Dae-Jung, which was partly symptomatic of the different forces that blended under the "new progressives," the conservatives predicted that Roh would still win in a popular election. Chun's final speech solidified this story of "democratization-from-above," framing liberalization not as a concession, but as part of the incumbent party's plan for "the best interest of the country and the people."[33] Indeed, as the two Kims split the opposition ticket, Roh handily won South Korea's first democratic election. With Kim Young-Sam unexpectedly merging with the conservative party to win the next presidential election, it would not be until 1998—a full decade after democratization—that the progressives would finally enter the Blue House under Kim Dae-Jung.

What this analysis illustrates is that Korea's democratization was not just an anti-regime or even pro-democracy struggle, but fundamentally a nationalist conflict between elite factions. Democratization simply institutionalized this conflict into the electoral system, in the form of competing political parties. Even as the specific parties have changed since democratization, mutually exclusive nationalist visions are still at the heart of the divide between conservative and progressive factions. At their core, conservatives are still defined by a staunchly anti-socialist, hardline stance against North Korea. In contrast, progressives are defined by a pro-socialist, engagement-oriented stance toward North Korea, backed by a hardline stance against any foreign intervention, particularly from the United States. This explains why South Korea's partisan divide often fails to follow a consistent ideological spectrum.[34] Party polarization in Korea is rooted not in ideology, but in identity.

---

32 Dan Slater and Joseph Wong, "The Strength to Concede: Ruling Parties and Democratization in Developmental Asia," *Perspectives on Politics* 11, no. 3 (2013): 717–33.

33 "Excerpts from Speech by South Korea President," *New York Times*, July 1, 1987, https://www.nytimes.com/1987/07/01/world/excerpts-from-speech-by-south-korea-president.html.

34 Russell J. Dalton and Aiji Tanaka, "The Patterns of Party Polarization in East Asia," *Journal of East Asian Studies* 7, no. 2 (2007): 203–23.

Seeing Korea's democratization through the lens of nationalist polarization sheds light on why illiberal practices such as oppositional purges, repression of civil society and the press, and Manichean rhetoric between competing parties have been long-standing features of its democracy. The seeds for such illiberalism, as I have traced above, were planted decades before even the prospect of democratization, the effects of which have manifested steadily and more clearly over time as the progressives have risen to power.[35]

One might still ask, however, whether the nationalist rhetoric is just a façade for what are illiberal desires for unchecked power, rather than its cause. In the beginning, the answer was probably both: a wedge in elite nationalist discourse opened a political opportunity for scheming entrepreneurs, who further fueled nationalist fragmentation in their efforts to consolidate power. Yet the illiberal ambition of a handful of would-be demagogues is unlikely to have yielded an entire institutional legacy of illiberalism without real and palpable nationalist tensions among elites. Even when certain progressive leaders tried to uphold liberal principles, such as when Roh Moo-Hyun sought to abolish the NSL, their own parties rallied to bring them back into the fold. Nationalist polarization may have started as a strategic tool, but it has gained a powerful force of its own in sustaining illiberalism in Korea's democracy.

National Fragmentation and Democratic Support

If nationalist polarization incentivizes illiberal competition among democratic elites, then the other side of the coin is why democratic citizens condone such behaviors. In a consolidated democracy, political elites can misbehave only to the extent that they expect impunity from voters. Often, lack of information about elite behavior is seen as a reason for electoral impunity, but this is unlikely to be the case in Korea. Not only is it one of the most digitally connected countries in the world, but every misstep from either party coalition is closely followed

35 Sook-Jong Lee, "Democratization and Polarization in Korean Society," *Asian Perspective* 29, no. 3 (2005): 99–125. "Dissidents and activists who were isolated during the authoritarian past now gained the legitimacy to challenge vested interests; they emerged as new elites. As they began competing with the older power centers, social division became almost inevitable" (102).

by partisan media.[36] Why would citizens knowingly vote for candidates and parties who violate democratic principles?

I argue that a fragmenting national narrative at the mass level explains such puzzling electoral support in Korea. What is interesting about nationalist politics in Korea is that even as elites in the post-1945 period were bitterly divided over the nationalist vision—the "where we ought to go"—both factions appealed to the same Korean *minjok* narrative at the mass level—the "who we are"—to legitimate their positions to the people.[37] The popularized narrative of an ethnic Korean nation remained durable because it was politically powerful: it homogenized identity not only across citizens, but also between citizens and the state, instilling strong beliefs of nation and state as a singular body. In prior work, I show that this nation-state linkage generated measurable benefits for Korean democracy in terms of strong civic duty and high levels of voluntary compliance from citizens.[38]

Yet cross-cutting socioeconomic pressures are fraying this once unifying national narrative. Following the Asian financial crisis of the late 1990s, income inequality in Korea has accelerated in ways that have exacerbated regional and generational disparities, as Jun Ho Jeong and Il-Young Lee show in chapter 6. As the state-directed development of the authoritarian era gave way to what Kwanhu Lee characterizes in chapter 3 as the "hasty liberalization" of markets, Korean workers were left unprotected from the volatility of the international economy. China's swift domination of low-cost manufacturing pushed many Korean laborers out of the global market. To remain economically competitive, the state instead focused on technological development, investing in creative talent among the top tier at the expense of labor, driving an enormous skew in the proportion of national wealth held by the upper versus lower classes.

At the same time, the fertility rate is rapidly declining. In 2020, the birth rate in Korea was 0.84: a Korean woman is more likely to remain childless than have at least one child in her lifetime.[39] Beyond its obvious

36 Matthew S. Winters and Rebecca Weitz-Shapiro, "Lacking Information or Condoning Corruption: When Do Voters Support Corrupt Politicians?," *Comparative Politics* 45, no. 4 (2013): 418–36.

37 Shin, *Ethnic Nationalism*, 166–82.

38 Hur, "Citizen Duty."

39 See Kim Soo-Young, "Tentative Birth and Death Statistics for 2020," February 24, 2021, accessed September 20, 2021. https://www.korea.kr/news/policy

effects on labor supply, the fertility decline has also inverted the usual triangle-shaped age distribution, creating an oversized elderly population supported by a diminishing younger one.[40] The welfare challenges have all but necessitated foreign labor and, importantly, marriage migrants. These foreign women, usually from Southeast Asian countries, come to Korea as brides for rural Korean men who have lost out on the marriage market. As of 2018, the Ministry of Gender Equality and Family estimated almost 343,800 marriage migrants in Korea, with over 237,000 mixed-race Korean children born from such unions.

In response to the changing ethnic face of Korea, the state has taken a dual-track approach, advocating for a multicultural (*damunhwa*) shift from native Koreans, while demanding participation in assimilationist training from foreign wives. The inconsistent nature of the state's response reflects Korea's fraying *minjok* narrative. In a 2015 survey about national identity conducted by the East Asia Institute, nearly half of Koreans (49.7 percent) supported a multicultural Korea, but 38.9 percent preferred an ethnically homogeneous one.[41] Perhaps most tellingly, the percentage of Koreans who were "unsure" of what kind of country Korea ought to be increased from 2 percent to almost 12 percent between 2010 and 2015.

Such national fragmentation comes with democratic costs. When a generalized, identity-based linkage to the democratic state erodes, citizens are more likely to revert to a tit-for-tat approach to democratic politics. For the lower class and organized labor, worsening income inequality with a weak social welfare system seeds feelings of being written out of the nation's economic success, for which they made tremendous sacrifices. For native Koreans who identify with the ethnic narrative, the state's increasing investment in multiculturalism—at the expense of native tax dollars—can yield similar feelings of being left

---

BriefingView.do?newsId=156438030 (in Korean). See also "South Korea's Fertility Rate Falls to a Record Low," *The Economist*, August 30, 2019. As of 2018, South Korea is the only OECD country with a fertility rate lower than 1.

40 Elizabeth Stephen, *South Korea's Demographic Divided: Echoes of the Past or Prologue to the Future?* (Washington, D.C.: Rowman & Littlefield / Center for Strategic and International Studies, 2019). Stephen reports that as of 2019, elderly South Koreans who are over sixty-five years of age outnumber youth under fifteen years of age by 1.2 million, and nearly half of the elderly population lives in poverty.

41 Nae-Young Lee and In-Jin Yoon, *South Korean Identity: Change and Continuity, 2005-2015* (Seoul, Korea: East Asia Institute and Asiatic Research Institute, 2016).

behind. Such citizens are likely to lean toward parties and candidates who promise to protect a nationalist vision of "us" against "them." This sets up a perfect storm for a growing proportion of Korean citizens to act as "partisans first, democrats second" at the ballot box. Voters are much more willing to compromise democratic principles and turn a blind eye to illiberal transgressions to support their preferred nationalist party or candidate, because what is at stake is their *sense of self* amidst a rapidly changing national story.

Both progressives and conservatives show signs of leveraging the growing nationalist division at the mass level as an electoral strategy. For instance, the Moon administration's instigations of nationalist conflicts with Japan, from the General Security of Military Information Agreement withdrawal to tensions over "comfort women" reparations, have coincided with either poor domestic performance or critical midterm elections. Likewise, conservatives have been known to invoke long-standing hostilities with North Korea at electorally opportune moments, such as the Lee Myung-Bak administration's swift blame of the *Cheonan* incident on North Korea prior to the local elections in 2010 or the post hoc indictment of Kim Eun-Hye for espionage leading up to the 2012 presidential election, when there were concerns about a turnover to the opposition. On both sides, the assumption appears to be that fanning nationalist sentiments historically associated with each faction casts a "misty veil" over voters, diverting their attention away from the policy failures or illiberal misbehaviors of partisan incumbents.[42]

Survey data suggest that such nationalist strategies are increasingly effective on partisan voters. The Asian Barometer Survey has recurrently asked questions on national pride and attitudes toward democratic norms for waves two, three, and four (years 2006, 2011, 2015, respectively). Using these time-series data, I plot how the relationship between national pride and tolerance for illiberalism has evolved over the past decade. Notably, the period between 2006 and 2015 also coincides with the window of rapid national fragmentation, during which income inequality skyrocketed and landmark policies on multiculturalism were passed.

Figure 2.4 examines citizen support for three specific kinds of illiberal practices: (a) "When judges decide important cases, they should

42 Frederick Solt, "Diversionary Nationalism: Economic Inequality and the Formation of National Pride," *Journal of Politics* 73, no. 3 (2011): 821–30.

FIGURE 2.4 Effect of national pride on tolerance of illiberal views for self-identified partisans, 2006–15

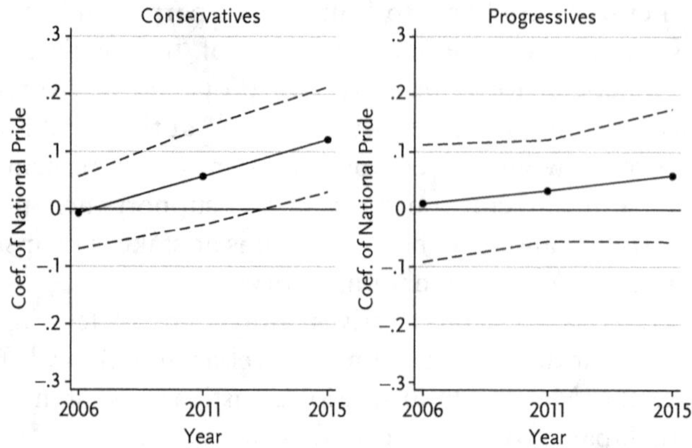

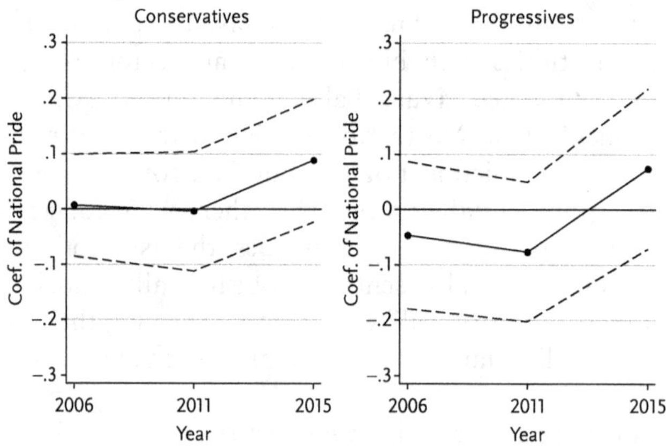

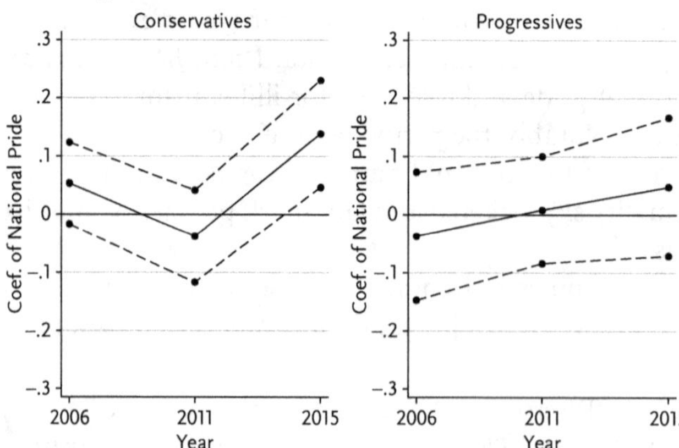

NOTE: OLS regressions with all variables rescaled 0–1.
SOURCE: Asian Barometer Survey waves 2–4.

accept the view of the executive branch"; (b) "If we have political leaders who are morally upright, we can let them decide everything"; and (c) "When the country is facing a difficult situation, it is OK for the government to disregard the law in order to deal with the situation." For each item, respondents were asked how strongly they agree or disagree. I focus on these items because they capture actual illiberal elite behaviors that have occurred in recent administrations. All figures plot the estimated effect of national pride on tolerance for illiberalism by party identification, controlling for age, education, income class, and gender.[43]

Before moving to the results, it is worth emphasizing how counterintuitive a positive relationship between national pride and tolerance for illiberalism should be in a consolidated democracy. In established democracies, there are typically strong injunctive norms *against* illiberal behaviors and in support of liberal and participatory behaviors. Then in nation-state democracies, we should expect stronger national identification to be associated with pro-democratic norms, as scholars have found for voting and participation in the United States.[44]

The figures, however, show the opposite pattern in Korea. Among self-identified partisans, there is an increasingly positive relationship between national pride and illiberal tolerance over time. For partisan voters, greater feelings of national pride are associated with stronger support for a non-independent judiciary, a unilaterally powered executive, and override of procedural justice—all foundational elements of illiberal rule. The trend is noticeable among conservative and progressive supporters alike through alternating partisan incumbencies between 2006 and 2015.

These figures are descriptive snapshots and do not tell us directly whether nationalist rhetoric causes partisan voters to ignore liberal principles at the ballot box. Nevertheless, there is a clear directional

---

43 All estimates are from ordinary least squares (OLS) regressions with variables rescaled 0 to 1, such that the coefficient can be interpreted as the estimated percentage point change in illiberal tolerance. The sample includes self-identified partisans only. Party names change very frequently in South Korea, so the "conservative" vs. "progressive" categorization was based on the ideological faction of the respondent's preferred party. Supporters of short-lived fringe or splinter parties were excluded.

44 Leonie Huddy and Nadia Khatib, "American Patriotism, National Identity, and Political Involvement," *American Journal of Political Science* 51, no. 1 (2007): 63–77.

trend. The pattern is consistent with nationalist fragmentation at the mass-level. As what it means to be Korean becomes ambiguous, voters have shifted their identity attachments away from the state at large and toward specific parties that offer a nationalist vision that best serves their interests. As partisan duty supplants civic duty, voters increasingly prioritize supporting "my" nationalist party over upholding liberal principles.

Korea's Democratic Trajectory

The recent intensification of illiberal practices under the guise of rule of law in Korea has worried observers of Korea and democracy alike. Long praised as a success story of Third Wave democratization, such signs of faltering in Korea have been met with alarmist narratives of democratic backsliding and erosion. Yet taking a historical view on invocations of three controversial laws by incumbents dating back to 1987, I show that illiberal forms of competition have been a persistent, if worsening, feature of Korean democracy that pervades both parties.

In the face of problems, a common reaction is to "kick the dog." Blame for Korea's intensifying bouts of illiberalism has shifted from targeting specific leaders, parties, and appointees to even bureaucrats. This chapter shows that the roots of Korea's illiberalism grew long before democratization even took place. What has enabled it to persist is the unfortunate confluence of long-standing nationalist polarization at the elite level and fragmentation of a once unifying national narrative at the mass level.

What is Korea's democratic trajectory going forward? In his model of democratic transitions, Rustow identified the final step as the "habituation phase," when democratic rulers and citizens gradually internalize democratic norms through a "joint learning experience."[45] A critical juncture in Korea's democratic habituation was undoubtedly the peaceful, procedure-bound impeachment of President Park Geun-Hye. This was a remarkable feat, especially given the symbolic baggage that she carried as the daughter of former military dictator Park Chung-Hee. The 2016 impeachment reified the power of democratic principles and procedure in a way unseen since perhaps the first democratic reforms

45 Rustow, "Transitions to Democracy."

following the June Democratic Uprising of 1987. It was a moment of reckoning in the Korean collective consciousness.

The Moon Jae-In administration's legacy is to serve as a durability test for this habituation among Korean citizens. The Moon administration was born out of this historical moment and therefore carried special moral responsibility to uphold the triumph of democratic principles and procedures. Yet in many instances, it has failed to abolish the same double-standard, illiberal tactics of the conservatives that it promised to purge. The corruption scandal surrounding the appointment of former justice minister Cho Kuk echoed traumas of procedural injustice from former administrations. The many confrontations with Japan and unprecedented engagement with North Korea were seen by many as the familiar electoral tactic of fanning nationalist sentiments at opportune moments.

Yet the Moon administration's legacy is defined not so much by what it did, but by what response it provoked in the public. That response has been swift. President Moon's approval rating, which began at over 80 percent at the start of his incumbency, more than halved to 39 percent in the aftermath of the Cho Kuk scandal, *despite* the boost from Korea's successful response to the first wave of the COVID-19 pandemic.[46] And if the conservative sweep of the 2021 by-elections were any indication, as V.O. Key, Jr., famously said, "voters are not fools."[47] The real threat to Korea's progressives is not winning or losing the next election, but failing to recognize that the Korean citizenry has passed a watershed moment in democratic habituation with Park's impeachment and is beginning to prize the intrinsic value of democratic process and procedures.

The illiberal shortcomings of Korean democracy are systemic and cannot be fixed with a single electoral turnover. The issue is not the moral character of a single leader, but a deeply embedded institutional norm. And while the underlying beliefs that sustain that norm may take longer to change, behaviors can be changed rather quickly by restructuring incentives. Stricter regulations to protect an independent judiciary, the abolishment of subversive laws, and stronger rules

46 Jihye Lee, "South Korea's Moon Sees Approval Rating Hit New Low Amid Scandal," *Bloomberg News*, October 17, 2019, https://www.bloomberg.com/news/articles/2019-10-18/south-korea-s-moon-sees-approval-rating-hit-new-low-amid-scandal.

47 V.O. Key, Jr., *The Responsible Electorate: Rationality in Presidential Voting, 1936–1960* (Cambridge: Harvard University Press: 1966).

around press freedom are important starts. But none of this can happen without electoral pressure from the public. The first step in improving Korea's democratic quality therefore lies with the same force that buttressed the country's early democracy against the odds: the people. The citizenry's willingness to once again stand for the self-determination of the Korean people—the core narrative that runs through *minjok*, *minjung*, populist, and even multicultural reinterpretations of Korean nationhood—despite the lures of class or ethnic tribalism, will be the key to supplying the new leadership with the political ammunition necessary to take the difficult steps toward institutional reform.

Bibliography

Amnesty International. "The National Security Law: Curtailing Freedom of Expression and Association in the Name of Security in the Republic of South Korea." November 2012. https://www.amnestyusa.org/wp-content/uploads/2017/04/s_korea_nsl_report_embargo_2911_asa_25_006_2012.pdf.

Barrington, Lowell. "'Nation' and 'Nationalism': The Misuse of Key Concepts in Political Science." *PS: Political Science and Politics* 30, no. 4 (1997): 712–16.

Chang, Paul Y. *Protest Dialectics: State Repression and South Korea's Democracy Movement, 1970–1979*. Stanford: Stanford University Press, 2015.

Croissant, Aurel, and Jeffrey Haynes. "Democratic Regression in Asia: Introduction." *Democratization* 28, no. 1 (2021): 1–21.

Cumings, Bruce. "The Legacy of Japanese Colonialism in Korea." In *The Japanese Colonial Empire*, edited by Ramon Myers and Mark Peattie, 478–96. Princeton: Princeton University Press, 1984.

Dalton, Russell J., and Aiji Tanaka. "The Patterns of Party Polarization in East Asia." *Journal of East Asian Studies* 7, no. 2 (2007): 203–23.

"Excerpts from Speech by South Korea President." *New York Times*, July 1, 1987. https://www.nytimes.com/1987/07/01/world/excerpts-from-speech-by-south-korea-president.html.

Gellner, Ernest. *Nations and Nationalism*. Ithaca: Cornell University Press, 1983.

Graham, Matthew, and Milan Svolik. "Democracy in America? Partisanship, Polarization, and the Robustness of Support for Democracy in the United States." *American Political Science Review* 114, no. 2 (2020): 392–409.

Griffen, Scott. "UN: Philippines Journalist Defamation Conviction a Violation of Free Speech." *International Press Institute*, February 2, 2012. https://ipi.media/un-philippines-journalist-defamation-conviction-a-violation-of-free-speech/.

Haberman, Clyde. "President of South Korea Orders a Halt to Debate on Constitution." *New York Times*, April 13, 1987. https://www.nytimes.com/1987/04/13/world/president-of-south-korea-orders-a-halt-to-debate-on-constitution.html.

Haggard, Stephan, and Jong-Sung You. "Freedom of Expression in South Korea." *Journal of Contemporary Asia* 45, no. 1 (2015): 167–79.

Huddy, Leonie, and Nadia Khatib. "American Patriotism, National Identity, and Political Involvement." *American Journal of Political Science* 51, no. 1 (2007): 63–77.

Hur, Aram. "Citizen Duty and the Ethical Power of Communities: Mixed-method Evidence from East Asia." *British Journal of Political Science* 50, no. 3 (2020): 1047–65.

———. *Narratives of Civic Duty: How National Stories Shape Democracy in Asia*. Ithaca: Cornell University Press, forthcoming.

Hur, Aram, and Andrew Yeo. "The Long Shadow of Nationalist Polarization: Democratic Ceilings in East Asia." Paper presented at the American Political Science Association conference, 2021.

Jager, Sheila Miyoshi. *Narratives of Nation Building in Korea*. New York: M.E. Sharpe, 2003.

Key, V.O. Jr. *The Responsible Electorate: Rationality in Presidential Voting, 1936-1960*. Cambridge: Harvard University Press: 1966.

Kim, Soo-Young. "Tentative Birth and Death Statistics for 2020" [in Korean]. February 24, 2021. Accessed September 20, 2021. https://www.korea.kr/news/policyBriefingView.do?newsId=156438030.

Klasnja, Marko, and Rocio Titiunik. "The Incumbency Curse: Weak Parties, Term Limits, and Unfulfilled Accountability." *American Political Science Review* 111, no. 1 (2017): 129–48.

Korea Legislation Research Institute. "National Security Act." https://elaw.klri.re.kr/eng_service/lawView.do?hseq=26692&lang=ENG. Accessed November 30, 2021.

Lee, Jihye. "South Korea's Moon Sees Approval Rating Hit New Low Amid Scandal." *Bloomberg News*, October 17, 2019. https://www.bloomberg.com/news/articles/2019-10-18/south-korea-s-moon-sees-approval-rating-hit-new-low-amid-scandal.

Lee, Nae-Young, and In-Jin Yoon. *South Korean Identity: Change and Continuity, 2005–2015*. Seoul, Korea: East Asia Institute and Asiatic Research Institute, 2016.

Lee, Namhee. *The Making of Minjung: Democracy and the Politics of Representation in South Korea*. Ithaca: Cornell University Press, 2007.

Lee, Sook-Jong. "Democratization and Polarization in Korean Society." *Asian Perspective* 29, no. 3 (2005): 99–125.

Levitsky, Steven, and Daniel Ziblatt. *How Democracies Die*. New York: Crown Publishing, 2018.

Marques, Jose, Vincent Yzerbyt, and Jacques-Philippe Leyens. "The 'Black Sheep Effect': Extremity of Judgments toward Ingroup Members as a Function of Group Identification." *European Journal of Social Psychology* 18, no. 1 (1988): 1–16.

Park, Moo-Jong. "Eradication of Deep-rooted Evils." *Korea Times*, March 16, 2017. https://www.koreatimes.co.kr/www/opinion/2018/05/636_225839.html.

Republic of Korea Prosecution Service. *Prosecution Yearbook* [in Korean]. https://www.spo.go.kr/site/spo/ex/board/List.do?cbIdx=1603.

Robinson, Michael. *Cultural Nationalism in Colonial Korea, 1920-1925*. Seattle: University of Washington Press, 1988.

Rustow, Dankwart. "Transitions to Democracy: Toward a Dynamic Model." *Comparative Politics* 2, no. 3 (1970): 337–63.

Schmitter, Philippe C., and Terry Lynn Karl. "What Democracy Is . . . and Is Not." *Journal of Democracy* 2, no. 3 (1991): 75–88.

Shin, Gi-Wook. *Ethnic Nationalism in Korea: Genealogy, Politics, and Legacy*. Stanford: Stanford University Press, 2006.

———. "South Korea's Democratic Decay." *Journal of Democracy* 31, no. 3 (July 2020): 100–14.

Shin, Gi-Wook, James Freda, and Gihong Yi. "The Politics of Ethnic Nationalism in Divided Korea." *Nations and Nationalism* 5, no. 4 (1999): 465–84.

Slater, Dan, and Joseph Wong. "The Strength to Concede: Ruling Parties and Democratization in Developmental Asia." *Perspectives on Politics* 11, no. 3 (2013): 717–33.

Solt, Frederick. "Diversionary Nationalism: Economic Inequality and the Formation of National Pride." *Journal of Politics* 73, no. 3 (2011): 821–30.

Somer, Murat, and Jennifer McCoy. "Transformations through Polarization and Global Threats to Democratization." *Annals of the American Academy of Political and Social Sciences* 681, no. 1 (2019): 8–22.

Stephen, Elizabeth. *South Korea's Demographic Divided: Echoes of the Past or Prologue to the Future?* Washington, D.C.: Rowman & Littlefield / Center for Strategic & International Studies, 2019.

Tharoor, Ishaan. "South Korea Just Showed How the World How to Do Democracy." *Washington Post*, May 10, 2017. https://www.washingtonpost.com/news/worldviews/wp/2017/05/10/south-korea-just-showed-the-world-how-to-do-democracy/.

"What Moon Jae-in Pledged to Do as President." *Korea Herald*, May 10, 2017. http://www.koreaherald.com/view.php?ud=20170509000521.

Winters, Matthew S., and Rebecca Weitz-Shapiro. "Lacking Information or Condoning Corruption: When Do Voters Support Corrupt Politicians?" *Comparative Politics* 45, no. 4 (2013): 418–36.

World Inequality Database. "Korea." Accessed November 28, 2021. https://wid.world/country/korea/.

Yeo, Andrew. "Has South Korean Democracy Hit a Glass Ceiling? Institutional-Cultural Factors and Limits to Democratic Progress." *Asian Politics & Policy* 12, no. 4 (2020): 539–58.

You, Jong-Sung. "The 'Cheonan' Incident and the Declining Freedom of Expression in South Korea." *Asian Perspective* 38, no. 2 (2015): 195–219.

CHAPTER THREE

The Weakness of Party Politics and Rise of Populism in Korea

Kwanhu Lee

It was once widely believed among scholars that Korea's democracy was undergoing a stage of stable democratic consolidation after transitioning from authoritarianism in the late 1980s.[1] For example, at the 1997 conference of the International Political Science Association, numerous Korean and foreign scholars would have agreed that "Korea has entered the stage of democratic consolidation, and although there are many obstacles to overcome, there is a widespread consensus that there is no longer a danger of reverting to authoritarian rule."[2] In particular, the development of political parties and electoral institutions fostered structural conditions regarded as integral to democratic consolidation, along with a stable rule of law and the vitalization of civil society.

However, after 2007, Korean scholars began to argue that using only (1) interparty competition and (2) two or more transfers of power as the standards by which to determine consolidation reflected an extremely narrow understanding of the term.[3] Even if there was such a thing as democratic consolidation, it was now apparent that there was an expansive "gray zone" between firmly established democracies and

1 The views expressed in this chapter are those of the author alone.
2 Choi Sang-Ryong, "Democratization in Korea Is at the Stage of Consolidation" [in Korean], *Daehak Sinmun*, September 1, 1997.
3 Jang Hoon, "Reflections and Prospects of Korean Democracy" [in Korean], in *Crisis and Prospects of Korean Democracy: Democratization, Globalization, and De-security* (Seoul, Korea: Ingansarang, 2013); Shin Myung-Soon, "Theoretical Review of Democratization and Democratization Movement" [in Korean], in *Democratization and Democratization Movement in Korea: Success and Frustration* (Seoul, Korea: Hanul, 2016).

nascent democracies that had just transitioned from authoritarianism. In Korea, this manifested itself as an extended period of tedious and excruciating trench warfare between the old authoritarian political forces that had overseen industrialization and new political actors who spearheaded the democratization movement.[4] Korea finally seemed to exit this gray zone with the impeachment of President Park Geun-Hye, the daughter of military dictator Park Chung-Hee, in 2017. This moment marked the end of a generation following the democratic transition of 1987, and the end of two eras since the beginning of authoritarianism. After the inauguration of the Moon Jae-In administration in 2017, many expected the stabilization of party politics and (re)consolidation of democracy. However, it seems that these expectations have not been met. Political parties, their supporters, and citizens regard one another with a strong sense of hostility.[5] Political polarization is getting stronger not only among politicians, but also among the general public.[6] It appears that Korea is still in the gray zone on the road to democracy.

The events of 2016 and 2017—the candlelight protests and the impeachment of President Park Geun-Hye—erupted from the accumulation of several problems during the democratization phase. This chapter will mainly focus on this period of democratization, which can be described as an unstable deepening of liberalization.

Democracy after the Democratic Transition (1987–2017)

The obstacles and constraints that emerged during the time of democratization were structural legacies of modernization and industrialization under authoritarian rule. This section will thus begin with a brief overview of the authoritarian era, as a prologue to the democratization

4 Kim Jong-Yeop, "The 87-Year Regime in Education: Between Democratization and Neoliberalism" [in Korean], *Economy and Society* 84 (2009): 40–69; Kwanhu Lee, "Formation of Korean Democratic Ideology: Constitutionalism, Democratic Republic, National Sovereignty" [in Korean], in *Korean Democracy, 100 Years of Revolution: 1919–2019* (Seoul, Korea: Hanul, 2019).

5 Choi Jang-Jip, "The Crisis and Consolidation of Korea's Democracy, and Alternatives for a New Political Order" [in Korean] (Paper presented at "Kim Dae-Jung and Democracy: Thought and Practice" at Kim Dae-Jung Library at Yonsei University, December 9, 2019).

6 For a closer analysis of the present state of Korean politics, see chapters 1 and 10.

phase, and then examine this phase further by dividing it into three parts: the 1987, 1997, and 2007 regimes.

Authoritarian rule: 1948–87

For nearly forty years from the founding of the Republic of Korea in 1948 until 1987, the country was essentially ruled by three presidents: Syngman Rhee (1948–60), Park Chung-Hee (1961–79), and Chun Doo-Hwan (1980–88). The usual institutions of democracy—including the legislature, the judiciary, and the press—existed only as a formality. During this period, party politics were also inexorably tied to the division of the peninsula, as it was difficult for any political party to espouse progressive policies or advocate peaceful exchanges with North Korea. In particular, the execution of Cho Bong-Am in 1956 on espionage charges[7] had a traumatic effect on politicians who later struggled against authoritarian rule through party politics. Cho was the leader of the Progressive Party, which advocated social democratic policies, and a leading rival to Syngman Rhee. Kim Dae-Jung, who was a formidable rival to Park Chung-Hee, faced numerous death threats. Immediately after taking over power in a coup in December 1979, Chun Doo-Hwan also sentenced Kim to death on sedition charges in 1980. Whenever they faced a challenge to their political legitimacy, authoritarian governments turned to anti-communism and focused attention on the North Korean threat. They also did not hesitate to wield coercive state power through declarations of martial law, constitutional reforms giving the president absolute authority, and various "presidential emergency measures."

It was difficult for civil society to develop under authoritarian rule, which in turn gave rise to an increasingly repressive state.[8] The constitution's amendment in 1972 to give the president a lifetime term was made possible by not only the physical coercion of the state but also its hegemonic rule over all civil society organizations. Because the oppressive legal and state apparatus did not permit a public sphere for political dialogue, the struggle against dictatorial rule was led by a handful of intellectuals and students instead of political parties or civil

7 This case is referred to as a "judicial murder" both at home and abroad.

8 This vicious circle was gradually broken by the quantitative and qualitative growth of university students in the 1980s, the victory of the opposition party in the 1985 election, and the consolidation of anti-government forces.

society actors. There were sporadic protests by workers, farmers, and the urban poor, but these efforts did not coalesce into a meaningful political force. With few exceptions, those who resisted authoritarian rule typically adopted a moderate stance in favor of liberal democracy.[9]

Nonetheless, some politicians in the opposition party and intellectuals continued to fight for democracy. Paradoxically, the reason why South Korea's democracy could not be completely suffocated was the presence of North Korea. South Korea's regimes were always compelled to advocate for liberal democracy, as opposed to the communist North, and educate the people regarding its importance. Thus, the people came to have a strong belief in liberal democracy. But without following basic democratic procedures, such as periodic elections, the South Korean government could hardly claim superiority over the North. Opposition parties and students argued that there was no reason to defend a non-democratic government. South Korea's dictators were trapped by this dilemma. In effect, in South Korea, liberal democracy undergirded the legitimacy of the state. Thus, calls to uphold liberal democracy always had a strong justification.

Three phases of democratization

The democratic transition of 1987 occurred through a political compromise, culminating in the creation of a "liberal" democracy. This consisted, in essence, of political and economic liberation from coercive state power. However, liberalization in this context primarily referred to a very basic level of everyday and political freedoms and a market economy free from government pressure—far from the liberalism that includes citizenship and social culture, and guarantees a wide range of collective and individual freedoms for civil society, artists, journalists, politicians, and businesses.[10]

1987–1996: POLITICAL LIBERALIZATION AND THE END OF MILITARY DICTATORSHIP

The thirty-year period of democratization (1987–2017) started with securing the minimal political and social freedoms necessary for

9 Kim Young-Rae, "The Democratic Movement of the Third Republic" [in Korean], in *The Democratic and Democratization Movement in Korea*, ed. Shin Myung-Soon (Seoul, Korea: Hanul, 2016).
10 See chapter 1 for a discussion of related issues.

democracy. In political terms, many Koreans believed that democratization meant removing military-authoritarian rule, reclaiming the people's right to vote for the president, limiting presidents to one term in office, and ensuring free and fair elections. For the vast majority of citizens, the most tangible change was the enjoyment of political freedoms in everyday life and participation in free and fair elections. For society as a whole, the greatest transformation was the protection of the freedoms of association and assembly, as well as that of the press.

With the restoration of party politics, key political actors shifted during this first stage of liberalization. Intellectuals and student activists who had spearheaded the resistance against the authoritarian regime were absorbed into the formal political sphere. Kim Young-Sam and Kim Dae-Jung, who respectively represented the Gyeongsang and Jeolla regions as major opposition leaders, actively recruited these individuals into politics. This group of individuals continued to grow throughout the democratization phase and came to form the mainstream of party politics in Korea. On one side, the precursor to the Conservative Party was formed when Kim Young-Sam and his group joined forces with Roh Tae-Woo—Chun Doo-Hwan's successor—and won the presidential election in 1992. This coalition consisted of former pro-democracy activists and moderate forces from the military. On the other side of the political spectrum, intellectuals and student leaders from the pro-democracy movement supported Kim Dae-Jung and formed the Democratic Party. They won the presidential election in 1997 and in 2002.

Through this process, a two-party system began to take shape in Korea: the Democratic Party and the Conservative Party.[11] There were, on occasion, minor progressive or centrist parties that won 5–10 percent of seats in the National Assembly and held the casting vote. Nevertheless, the two major parties won an overwhelming majority of seats in almost every legislative election. In most cases, presidential elections were a two-way race with a less than 5 percent margin of victory

11 In the three decades following the transition to democracy, Korea's political parties frequently changed their names and underwent mergers and dissolutions. A plethora of new parties also appeared on the scene during this period. However, the political landscape was dominated by the precursors to the two major parties that exist today: the Democratic Party of Korea (relatively progressive) and the People Power Party (conservative). Unless specified otherwise, the forerunners to these two parties are hereafter referred to as the "Democratic Party" and the "Conservative Party."

between the two major candidates, regardless of the presence of a third candidate. Those third candidates or third parties that emerge on occasion have as yet been unable to overcome the institutional constraints of presidential and parliamentary elections held under a majoritarian electoral system.

Meanwhile, the two main political parties had no major differences on key policy issues. They shared a common antipathy toward the excessive political control over society and the economy seen during the authoritarian era. There were some notable differences in attitude toward former officials of the authoritarian regime or regarding the pace of democratization (e.g., the introduction of local elections). Nevertheless, there was a broad consensus on the overall direction of political and economic liberalization. In this atmosphere, large conglomerates (*chaebol*) strengthened their market dominance, and the relationship between the state and the *chaebol* changed from subordination to cooperation.

In addition, civil society grew rapidly. Now that the freedom of association had been secured, a wide array of labor unions formed after 1989.[12] Male workers at large conglomerates were able to legally form labor unions as part of the overall shift toward political liberalization. By exercising their right to strike, they obtained the wage increases that had been delayed throughout the industrialization phase of the 1960s and 1970s. This gave rise to the emergence of a middle class built around full-time workers at large conglomerates, but it also contributed to the formation of a dual labor market—with vast wage differences between large conglomerates and small and medium enterprises—and resulting social inequality.

1997–2006: ECONOMIC LIBERALIZATION AND THE ASIAN FINANCIAL CRISIS

The second phase of the democratization period centered on a top policy priority of Kim Young-Sam's government (1993–98): globalization. The Kim government swiftly dismantled the protectionist safeguards that had been the mainstay of Korea's industrial policy for decades and opened the door to free trade. Among these measures, the wholesale

12 Shin Gi-Wook et al., "The Korean Democracy Movement: An Empirical Overview," in *South Korean Social Movements: From Democracy to Civil Society*, Gi-Wook Shin and Paul Y. Chang, eds. (Milton Park: Routledge, 2011), 21–40.

liberalization of the foreign exchange market put Korea's economy at significant risk. It was difficult for the government to properly identify short-term speculative capital flows, and there was a lack of policy levers to adequately prepare for shocks from foreign financial markets. The Kim government failed to promptly respond to developments in the foreign exchange market and unexpectedly found itself on the brink of a sovereign default. Numerous banks and companies went bankrupt, and the number of unemployed individuals tripled following the onset of the Asian financial crisis in 1997. In 1998, nearly 1.5 million Koreans found themselves out of work.[13]

This unprecedented economic crisis set the stage for the first peaceful transfer of power in Korea's history, with an opposition candidate achieving victory in a presidential election almost fifty years after the founding of the country. Even before entering office, President-elect Kim Dae-Jung promised to accept a bailout from the International Monetary Fund (IMF) to stave off a sovereign default. As part of the bailout, the government had no choice but to liberalize the economy—and to an extent that even the IMF later admitted was excessive. Neoliberalism was adopted wholesale. Restrictions on foreign direct investment were almost entirely removed, and many public enterprises were privatized at once. Credit cards were issued without regard for income or credit scores in an effort to boost domestic demand. Companies were permitted to carry out massive layoffs for business reasons. Korea managed to avoid a sovereign default, but the side effects were devastating. Speculative investors made large profits by acquiring companies that faced a liquidity crisis and reselling them after restructuring.[14] The provision of public services was weakened, and the widespread misuse of credit cards led to an enormous increase in credit delinquencies.

Korea was still a developing country at the time of the financial crisis. It did not have a robust welfare system relative to West European

13 The number of unemployed individuals almost tripled from 435,000 (unemployment rate 2.0 percent) in 1996 and 560,000 (2.6 percent) in 1997 to 1.49 million (7.0 percent) in 1998. This remained at 1.37 million (6.3 percent) in 1999. See Statistics Korea, https://kosis.kr/index/index.do.

14 Lone Star, a Texas-based private equity firm, acquired the Korea Exchange Bank and gained a profit of over $3.5 billion after reselling it. Subsequently, Lone Star claimed, through the World Bank's International Centre for Settlement of Investment Disputes, an additional $4.5 billion in damages from the Korean government for its "belated approval" of the sale. This trial was still ongoing as of early 2022.

countries, and it was lacking in private charities compared to the United States. With insufficient social aid from both the public and private sectors, individuals and their families were left to shoulder the pain and suffering that came from unemployment and bankruptcy. Those who lost their jobs from large-scale layoffs could not return to their original workplace or find employment elsewhere. As a result, Korea came to have one of the highest self-employment levels of any OECD country after 1997.[15] There was intense competition in the restaurant industry, which constituted the vast majority of the self-employment sector.[16] Some *chaebol* companies were dismantled and sold off, but others recovered after receiving financial assistance and increased their dominance over the domestic market.[17]

These trends were greatly affected by the pervasive influence of neoliberal ideology across the international economy. However, the Korean government did not have the capacity to properly coordinate or manage the reforms undertaken to comply with the requirements of structural adjustment. Korea's economy was left exposed to volatile foreign markets due to hasty liberalization. As a result, the events of 1997 gave rise to some of the highest levels of income inequality in the world.[18]

---

15 In 2019, the proportion of self-employed individuals in Korea was 24.6 percent, ranking eighth among OECD countries. This figure is about four times that of the United States and is also higher than that of Italy and Spain. See OECD, "Self-Employment Rate," accessed December 1, 2021, https://data.oecd.org/emp/self-employment-rate.htm.

16 Korea's fried chicken is renowned among food lovers. Interestingly, this is because many unemployed individuals entered this market following the 1997 crisis. The recipe for fried chicken is relatively simple, which made it easy for newcomers to open a restaurant, and there were numerous franchises looking to open new locations. Fried chicken is commonly enjoyed with beer in Korea, which meant that there was high popular demand. However, given the large number of individuals who entered the market, not everyone succeeded.

17 Aggregate concentration (the share of large business groups in the overall national economy, accounting for market capitalization, sales, shipments, net income, added value, assets, employment, etc.) of the ten largest conglomerates rose from 77.78 percent in 1995 to 90.74 percent in 2007. See Choi Jeong-Pyo, "Succession of Chaebols and the Change in Economic Concentration" [in Korean], *Journal of Business History* 26, no. 2 (2011): 181–99.

18 In terms of the Gini coefficient and Palma ratio, which are indicators of inequality, Korea records some of the highest figures, along with the United States and the United Kingdom. See OECD, "Income Inequality," accessed December 1, 2021, https://data.oecd.org/inequality/income-inequality.htm.

During this period of economic liberalization, the Democratic Party retained power with the victory of Roh Moo-Hyun in the 2002 presidential election. The five years of the Kim Dae-Jung government were not long enough to erase from people's minds the incompetence of the Kim Young-Sam government, whose missteps had precipitated a disastrous financial crisis. Many were still reeling from the trauma of unemployment, and voters were not prepared to put their trust in the Conservative Party. For the conservative candidate, Lee Hoi-Chang, a former judge who had entered politics at the urging of Kim Young-Sam, it was the second consecutive defeat in a presidential race.

The Democratic Party also got a majority in the National Assembly for the first time following the 2004 legislative election. Taking advantage of its dominant position, the party pursued a variety of political reforms. This effort was led by the so-called 386 generation of politicians, who solidified their position as the party's mainstream. Pushing aside the group of Kim Dae-Jung loyalists who had struggled against the dictatorship of Park Chung-Hee,[19] leading individuals from the campus pro-democracy movement of the 1980s took center stage. The label "386" reflects the fact that they were in their thirties when the term was coined in the 1990s, attended college in the 1980s, and were born in the 1960s. The 386 generation of politicians forms the core of the Democratic Party to this day. Their primary political objective was the complete eradication of authoritarian legacies, including the National Security Law. This brought them into conflict with party elders, who supported gradual reform. They openly challenged the establishment, revising the Private School Act and clashing with the conservative press. Conservative political forces stubbornly resisted these changes.

In this second phase of democratization, one of the most notable political and social changes was the emergence of a broad coalition of conservatives in civil society. Since conservatives have always had almost complete control of the state and the political arena, they did not need a visible presence in civil society. After dominating the political scene for nearly fifty years, however, they had been defeated in two consecutive presidential elections in 1997 and 2002. In response to these setbacks in the political arena, conservative forces attempted to attain hegemony in civil society and launched a new conservative

19 This group is called the "Donggyo-dong faction," in reference to the address of President Kim Dae-Jung's private residence in Seoul.

movement based on an ideology called the "New Right." This prompted a conservative alliance that extended beyond the political party and included the press, civil associations, and religious actors (Protestant evangelicals).[20]

However, it was unclear precisely what values the conservatives could defend. Focusing on issues of national security and anti-communism was no longer effective. Moreover, liberal political forces had adopted political and economic reform and neoliberalism as their core values, both in the first and second phases of democratization. Instead of formulating a new set of values, the conservatives decided to center their efforts on a symbolic character, Park Chung-Hee, who had led Korea's modernization. No living politician could unite and mobilize the conservatives in the same way that he could. In addition, there was an obvious way to appeal to his legacy. Park Geun-Hye—Park's daughter—appeared on the political scene, assumed leadership of the party, and rallied support.

While her political ability was largely unknown, Park Geun-Hye personified the political legacy of her father. Centrist and right-leaning voters older than forty, who had grown up under the Park Chung-Hee regime, had a sense of nostalgia for the former president.[21] There was also hostility toward the rapid political and social reforms that had been set in motion by the Roh Moo-Hyun government and the 386 genera-

---

20 The political role of the Korean church emerged in this period and continues to be very prominent today. There are two key reasons for this phenomenon. First, several large churches and Christians moved from North Korea to South Korea during the Korean War, internalizing intense anti-communism in the process. The other is that some church leaders and politicians who were supported by these conservative churches were directly affected by the 2016 Private School Act, because they owned many private school foundations. Some of these foundations were accused of serious corruption.

21 According to the 2010 Korea Democracy Barometer survey, there is a huge generational and ideological gap in perceptions of Park Chung-Hee. Among those who chose Park Chung-Hee as the best president in modern Korean politics, the age composition was as follows: sixties or older (30 percent), fifties (25 percent), and forties (23 percent). The proportion in their thirties and twenties was only 8 percent and 11 percent, respectively. Fifty-four percent of conservative respondents considered Park Chung-Hee the best president, while only 17 percent of progressive respondents gave the same response. See Kang Woo-Jin, "Park Chung Hee Syndrome and Korean Democracy: Centering on Four Important Issues" [in Korean], *Korea and World Politics* 29, no. 2 (2013): 73–105.

tion of politicians. The conservatives successfully realigned themselves behind Park Geun-Hye in this context and began to achieve one electoral victory after another following the 2004 legislative election.

2007–17: THE RETURN OF THE CONSERVATIVES AND PARK CHUNG-HEE SYNDROME

In large part, the 2007 presidential election was a referendum on the ten-year rule of the progressive administrations. Radical reforms had drawn the opposition of centrist and conservative voters, while progressive voters withdrew their support because of the income inequality that had resulted from economic liberalization. It is interesting to note, however, that the beneficiary of these political trends was Lee Myung-Bak, not Park Geun-Hye.

Lee, a former Hyundai executive who became the mayor of Seoul, narrowly defeated Park in the party primary. If Park personified the Park Chung-Hee of the past, Lee represented a Park Chung-Hee of the present. He pledged to alleviate economic inequality by achieving a 7 percent annual economic growth rate—a twenty-first-century reincarnation of Park Chung-Hee's policies of modernization.

The trends of this time were sustained by the pillars set up in the first pause of democratization since 1987 (political liberalization) and the second pause since 1997 (neoliberal economic policy). But the Conservative Party, secure in its dominant political position, became absorbed in internal struggles. While in power, each faction prioritized rent-seeking over the proper management of state affairs. The *Sewol* ferry disaster is illustrative. The ferry was operated under safety regulations that had been relaxed under the Lee Myung-Bak government. When the *Sewol* encountered fatal issues on the morning of the disaster, President Park did not receive proper reports or issue timely directions to the appropriate authorities. More than three hundred individuals, many of them high school students on a field trip, lost their lives. This tragedy had a critical effect on President Park's impeachment and the Conservative Party's defeat in the subsequent presidential election in 2017.

Korean civil society was characterized by the rise of progressive civic groups during the 1987 regime and the emergence of a conservative civil society during the 1997 regime. Under the 2007 regime, there was a severe confrontation between the left and the right in civil society, and the government responded by taking direct action against civil society. The Lee Myung-Bak administration faced candlelight demonstrations opposing the import of U.S. beef and the Four Major Rivers Project in its early days.[22] In response, the Lee government implemented a "blacklist" policy to block or reduce financial support for opposing civil society organizations and a "whitelist" to increase support for pro-government organizations, such as the Saemaul movement Central Association, the Freedom Federation, and the Live Right Central Association. The Park Geun-Hye administration continued this practice, and many civic groups under government surveillance and sanctions became critical of the government.[23] The blacklisting of artists, including famous actors and directors such as Bong Joon-Ho, the Oscar-winning director of the film *Parasite*, became one of the main reasons for the impeachment of President Park Geun-Hye.

The impeachment of President Park Geun-Hye

The latter half of 2016 was a turning point in the political transformation that swept the country. There was a scandal surrounding Choi Soon-Sil's illegal involvement in state affairs, and this prompted candlelight demonstrations across the country.[24] However, the decisive inflection point was the 19th National Assembly election of April 2016.

---

22 When the Four Major Rivers Project was announced in early 2009, critics suspected that it was a mere name change for the Grand Korean Waterway. The overall project was broken into three project sets: revitalizing the four rivers, projects on their fourteen tributaries, and refurbishing other smaller-sized streams. This project attracted significant criticism from environmental groups in South Korea and foreign groups such as Friends of the Earth. Also, Lee's push for the project's swift approval in the National Assembly reminded some of his persona as the former CEO of the Hyundai Engineering & Construction Co. Ltd., where he was nicknamed the "Bulldozer." For further details, see "The Environmental Fallout of the Four Major Rivers Project," *Hankyoreh*, August 3, 2013, http://english.hani.co.kr/arti/english_edition/e_national/598190.html.

23 Joo Sung-Soo, "Financial Relations between Government and Civil Society: A Paradigm Shift from Supporting to Cooperation" [in Korean], *Civil Society and NGO* 15, no. 2 (2017): 3–33.

24 Choi Soon-Sil was the protagonist in a 2016 political scandal regarding her influence over President Park Geun-Hye. Choi had inappropriate access to, and possible influence over, President Park. Choi, who had absolutely no official position in government, had allegedly been given regular reports on Park's schedule, speeches, and political and personnel arrangements. She had even seen classified information on secret meetings with North Korea. Choi was indicted for extorting bribes, abusing power, and leaking classified documents. Choi was also accused of

For the first time, President Park Geun-Hye, who had been hailed the "Queen of Elections," suffered defeat in an election campaign that she had overseen. The Democratic Party fared poorly in its traditional stronghold of Honam (Gwangju and Jeolla provinces), winning only three of the twenty-eight constituencies in that region. Nevertheless, it won 123 seats overall out of three hundred seats, one more than the ruling party. The ruling party's defeat was commonly attributed to the *Sewol* ferry disaster, presidential overreach in party affairs, intraparty conflict, and the rise of the People's Party—a centrist third party led by Ahn Cheol-Soo—which won thirty-eight seats.

The *Sewol* ferry disaster raised doubts about the competence of the Park administration, especially among younger voters. The election recorded the greatest turnout of voters in their twenties (52.7 percent) in two decades. This was greater than the turnout for the same age group in the 17th National Assembly election of 2004, when the Democratic Party achieved an overwhelming victory during the impeachment trial against President Roh Moo-Hyun, and 11.2 percentage points greater than the previous election in 2012. There was also greater turnout among younger age groups compared to the previous legislative election (45.5 percent to 50.5 percent among ages 30 to 39, and 52.6 percent to 54.3 percent among ages 40 to 49).

The Choi Soon-Sil scandal then began to surface in the press during the summer of 2016. This must be understood in the context of President Park's lame-duck period, which essentially began with the conservatives' unexpected defeat in the April elections. Some reporters had already begun to investigate the corruption surrounding Choi Soon-Sil and her interference in state affairs, but there had been no meaningful progress before the election. Following the election, the benign negligence and active cooperation of sources within the government added fuel to the fire. The flood of revelations in the press sparked the candlelight protests, which ultimately led to Park's impeachment in 2017.

A critical step in this chain of events was the passage of an impeachment resolution in the National Assembly in December 2016 that initiated the impeachment trial before the Constitutional Court. The resolution required a two-thirds majority in the National Assembly. It could not have passed if the ruling party, with its 122 seats, had unanimously opposed the resolution. However, the center-right politicians

having pressured Ewha Womans University to change their admission criteria to admit her daughter, Jung Yoo-Ra.

TABLE 3.1 The three phases of Korea's democratization (1987–2017)

	1987–1996	1997–2006	2007–17
Presidents	Roh Tae-Woo Kim Young-Sam	Kim Dae-Jung Roh Moo-Hyun	Lee Myung-Bak Park Geun-Hye
Objective	"Soft landing" from authoritarianism to democracy	Dual development of democracy and market economy	Recreating the Park Chung-Hee era vision of high economic growth
Means	Liberalizing reforms	Replacing the ruling political class	Restoring close ties between the state (bureaucracy) and the private sector (*chaebol*)
Problems	Insufficient governing ability	Incongruity between means and objectives	Factional politics and rent-seeking
Result	Economic crisis → transfer of power	Reform fatigue → transfer of power	Corruption, impeachment → transfer of power

SOURCE: Author.

whom President Park had sought to oust from the party voted in favor. These individuals subsequently left the ruling party and formed a splinter party. Overall, the antipathy of center-right voters toward the sharp ideological right turn under President Park contributed to the impeachment decision.

The 2007 regime marked the beginning and the end of the Park Chung-Hee syndrome. It was a brief return to power for the authoritarian right, which drew on anti-communist ideology and the legacy of modernization and industrialization. Ironically, Park ended her father's legacy with the political catastrophe of impeachment. President Park's failures left conservatives with the fundamental task of how to shed a reputation of incompetence, corruption, and obsolescence. Questions of policy and ideology were secondary to this challenge.

The three stages of the democratization phase are summarized in table 3.1.

Korean Democracy in Peril: Simultaneous and Contradictory Demands of Three Objectives

The impeachment of President Park Geun-Hye meant the end of the 2007 phase of democratization, but it also revealed the fundamental flaws of the 1987 phase. Korean politics has succeeded in escaping from authoritarianism after 1987, but it had also shown serious flaws in the quality of its democracy, particularly in the stable development of party politics. In fact, this weakness was caused not only by democratization since 1987, but also by structural problems inherent in the Korean government, which had been pursuing modernization since the founding of the country.

Ever since the founding of the Republic in 1948, the Korean government has pursued three objectives: industrialization, democratization, and social justice. There was a strong emphasis on the economic task of industrialization during the 1960s and 1970s. After this goal was achieved to a certain degree, the 1980s were marked by a focus on the political task of democratization. During the 1990s, the financial crisis and the adoption of neoliberal economic policies gave rise to demands for social justice and the alleviation of structural inequalities.

It is especially important to note that the overriding task of each era was not fully resolved before the onset of the next. These old, unresolved tasks gave rise to new and increasingly complex demands in subsequent years. The imperatives of industrialization and economic growth continued to be emphasized after the 1980s and until the Lee Myung-Bak and Park Geun-Hye governments. Democratization and liberalization had to be pursued alongside a policy of state-driven economic growth and efforts to overcome economic crises. The pursuit of these goals had the side effect of exacerbating socioeconomic inequalities. As a result, during and after the 1990s, the government was confronted with the additional task of addressing these inequalities. The interrelated and contradictory demands of democratization and authoritarianism, liberalization and the alleviation of socioeconomic inequalities, and economic growth and redistribution all surfaced simultaneously.

The widespread popularity of phrases such as "*Hell-Joseon*" and "*Gap-jil*" in recent years clearly illustrates this contradiction.[25] The first is a neologism that combines "hell," which reflects an extreme degree of socioeconomic inequality, and the Joseon dynasty, which refers to the steep decline in intergenerational social mobility. In the second, "*gap*" refers to powerful actors who rank higher in the socioeconomic

25 According to a recent OECD report, Korea ranked seventh in terms of the Gini measure of inequality. It has the third-highest overall relative poverty rate among OECD countries. See *OECD Economic Surveys Korea: 2020* (Paris, France: OECD Publishing, 2020).

hierarchy, and "*jil*" indicates unethical and wrongful behavior that occurs in an informal way.

It is startling that the development of a capitalist economy through industrialization has resulted in a return to premodern social characteristics. This is the reality of Korea's society today: the absence of social justice from the lives of individual citizens far outweighs the economic and legal justice achieved through modernization. Put differently, the individual rights and human dignity attained through democratization have not been adequately respected or protected under a state that was molded by industrialization and modernization. This is a major source of social conflict and contradiction in contemporary Korea. There are no obvious solutions in sight, however. In political terms, there are simultaneous demands for the greater institutionalization of representative democracy and the expansion of direct (participatory) democracy. As a solution to the underdevelopment of democracy, one side argues that a higher level of institutionalization is necessary, while the other side argues that more political participation of individuals is a priority. In social terms, there are concurrent arguments in favor of a more equitable *Gemeinschaft* and a mutually beneficial *Gesellschaft*. As a solution to socioeconomic polarization and cleavages, one side insists on strengthening the sense of community, while the other side argues that it is better to establish a healthy competitive society.

Korea's party system, even in today's post-2017 democratization era, still lacks the capacity to resolve the simultaneous eruption of conflicting issues that accumulated throughout the authoritarian and democratization eras. The current political landscape in Korea is characterized by severe conflict between the two leading political parties and their respective supporters. However, these two parties do not meaningfully differ in ideological terms. The main problem is not ideological polarization, but rather political polarization and the radicalization of political behavior amplified by social media. In the past, the key axis of party conflict was regionalism. But now, intergenerational divides have further complicated the battle lines, with greater polarization among intellectuals and the media. There is aggressive and hostile discourse around online political fandoms, and there is a stronger tendency to apply a binary, tribal logic when discussing political issues.[26]

---

26 Shin Gi-Wook, "South Korea's Democratic Decay," *Journal of Democracy* 31, no. 3 (July 2020): 100–14.

These trends have been labeled as "populism," in reference to similar developments in other democracies around the world. Among many causes, perhaps the most fundamental is the weakness of party politics. Korea's populism is unique in that the major political cleavages are not defined by ethnicity, race, or inequality, but rather by decades-old and "false" ideological conflicts that originate from the division of the peninsula.

Populism in the Post-Democratization Era

This section begins by examining the discourse surrounding "pro–North Korean leftists" (*jong-book jwa-pa*), a crucial element in the prehistory of populism in Korea. It then analyzes the conceptual ambiguity of contemporary Korean populism and discusses potential solutions to these political issues.

The rise and fall of the "pro–North Korea leftist" discourse

During Korea's democratization, conservative parties adopted a strategy of uniting their supporters by inciting fear. The most commonly deployed political frame was that of "pro–North Korean leftists." This condenses abstract anti-communist ideology into concrete, but exaggerated and distorted terms. It was frequently used during election campaigns to instill fear among citizens and rally them around the conservative cause. The Conservative Party often relied on this frame when criticizing the Democratic Party's foreign, welfare, and economic policies. Instead of engaging in a complex debate about the contents, anticipated effects, or beneficiaries of particular policies, it sought to achieve political victory by framing the Democratic Party as pro–North Korean leftists.[27] This frame was possible because the Cold War had not yet ended on the Korean Peninsula. There are two intriguing aspects to this political frame. The first is that it attaches the "pro–North Korean" label to leftists, and the second is its strong but limited efficacy in terms of its target audience.

The "pro–North Korean" label did not enter political parlance until the 1990s. In the past, the term "leftist" was readily associated with pro-communist attitudes and widely regarded as referring to a public

27 This can be readily understood as a direct application of George P. Lakoff's theory of political framing.

enemy. Within ten years of the end of the Cold War, however, Koreans were no longer fearful of communism or socialism as ideologies. There was a sense of ideological superiority; in the words of Francis Fukuyama, "history had ended with the triumph of liberal democracy." Moreover, the Roh Tae-Woo government's (1988–93) *Nordpolitik* and the subsequent pursuit of globalization under Kim Young-Sam gave Koreans greater confidence on the international stage.[28]

It was in this context that the Kim Dae-Jung government pursued its "Sunshine Policy" toward North Korea. Instead of simply attacking the government as leftists, conservatives introduced the prefix of "pro–North Korean" and "North Korean sympathizer" to draw attention to the tangible security threat posed by Pyongyang. North Korea experienced a domestic crisis due to a devastating famine during the 1990s, and it attempted to draw the attention of the international community. Accordingly, there was a series of small-scale military provocations near the inter-Korean border, and the nuclear crisis continued to escalate.[29] The conservatives' political framing was relatively successful. This frame later manifested itself in the Lee Myung-Bak government's hardline North Korea policy of "Vision 3000: Denuclearization and Opening,"[30] as well as the Park Geun-Hye government's pursuit of "unification by absorption."[31] These aggressive political frames prompted a military reaction from North Korea. During the

---

28 *Nordpolitik* refers to the normalization of diplomatic relations with Russia and China. This was a marked departure from Korea's previous policy of not establishing diplomatic ties with countries in the communist bloc.

29 South Korean casualties were as follows: Gangneung submarine infiltration incident (1996): twelve killed and twenty-seven wounded; First Battle of Yeonpyeong (1999): nine wounded; Second Battle of Yeonpyeong (2002): one patrol boat sunk, six men killed, and eighteen wounded.

30 Under this policy, Seoul would reject any dialogue with Pyongyang in which it could use its nuclear program as leverage. Instead, Seoul would strengthen sanctions to increase pressure on the North Korean economy and push Pyongyang toward economic reform. This would increase North Korea's per capita GDP from $500 to $3,000, thereby providing the foundation for unification. However, this policy vision was not realized.

31 This vision was outlined in detail in President Park's "Dresden Declaration" on March 28, 2014. The speech was given in Dresden, a city that had fallen into disrepair under East German rule. There were also protests in Dresden immediately before the collapse of the Berlin Wall. Because the implication was that the city had prospered after unification, North Korea reacted strongly to this speech. It was later revealed that Choi Soon-Sil had personally edited the text of the speech, which contributed to the political momentum that led to Park's impeachment.

Lee Myung-Bak administration, North Korea attacked the naval vessel *Cheonan* and bombarded Yeonpyeong Island. It conducted nuclear tests and missile launches during the Park Geun-Hye administration.[32]

At the same time, there are limits to the efficacy of this political frame. Tying "leftists" to a "pro–North Korean" stance highlights a clearly visible enemy. However, this framing immediately loses its power when the situation on the Korean Peninsula shifts toward peaceful dialogue and détente, as when the Moon Jae-In government has sought to improve inter-Korean relations. Moreover, after repeated nuclear crises over the past two decades, many Korean citizens now regard Pyongyang's threats as nothing more than diplomatic rhetoric. Also, the "pro–North Korea leftist" frame has a narrow audience, split along generational and regional lines.[33] The results of the four nationwide elections since 2016 show this clearly. Deploying this frame reinforces political isolation: the conservative mainly appeals to elderly voters, and therefore the political efficacy of this frame is likely to decline over time.

Starting in the mid-2000s, a small but vocal minority of conservative politicians called for the party to abandon the "pro–North Korea leftist" framing. These politicians, who belonged to the center-right, were commonly associated with Yoo Seong-Min.[34] Although the impeachment

---

32 South Korean casualties were as follows: sinking of the *ROKS Cheonan* (2010): forty-six killed and fifty-eight wounded; bombardment of Yeonpyeong Island (2010): two soldiers and two civilians killed, nineteen soldiers and three civilians wounded.

33 Kim Young-Tae, "The 2007 Presidential Election and Effects of 'North Korean Variables'" [in Korean], *Journal of Political Science and Communication* 10, no. 2 (2007): 65–77; Jeong Han-Wool, "Trends and Prospects for Generation Voting Research and the 21st General Election" [in Korean], *Journal of Korean Social Trend and Perspective* 109 (2020): 74–96; Lee Sung-Woo, "A Study of Perceptions of North Korean Issues according to Security Situation around the Korean Peninsula: Comparing on 2018 and 2019" [in Korean], *Korea and World Politics* 36, no. 4 (2020): 109–35.

34 Yoo Seong-Min is a prominent conservative politician who is an economist by training (he received a BA in economics from Seoul National University in 1982, and a PhD in economics from the University of Wisconsin–Madison in 1987). He was first elected as a Conservative Party member of the National Assembly in 2004. He was elected to the National Assembly another three times (over a period of sixteen years) and ran for the 2017 South Korean presidential election. When he served as the floor leader of the ruling party in the Park Geun-Hye administration, he was the leader of moderate, center-right politicians within the party. In a speech before the National Assembly, he criticized President Park Geun-Hye's

crisis was the immediate cause of the splintering of the Conservative Party in 2017, the underlying cause was a fundamental disagreement about the ideological identity of the party—including debates over the use of the "pro–North Korea leftists" framing. The phrase began to lose political traction after the impeachment crisis.

Now that the ideological substance of the political conflict had disappeared, the two major parties needed a way to effectively mobilize and unite their supporters. They leveraged the fact that many Koreans had a strong antipathy toward one-party rule, and charismatic rule, to create solidarity among their supporters.[35] The two major parties thus charged their opponents with these attributes, and the political discourse of populism emerged as a result.

The discourse of populism

CHOI JANG-JIP'S CRITICISM OF THE MOON ADMINISTRATION

Since the candlelight protests of 2016, both the Conservative and Democratic parties have criticized each other as populist. The former labeled the candlelight protests as "left-wing populism," while the latter criticized the conservatives' *Taegukgi* protests, which emerged in reaction to the candlelight protests, as "far-right populism." The intensification of political conflicts and the binary, tribal logic that dominates Korean politics today are influenced by this populist discourse.[36]

In Korea, many scholars agree that populism is a powerful and indisputable phenomenon. One of the leading proponents of this view is Choi Jang-Jip, one of the most frequently cited authors on Korean politics among both Korean and foreign scholars.[37] At an academic

---

return to hardline conservatism, causing a stir. President Park ordered the party not to nominate Yoo in the next general election. As this intraparty conflict grew, party supporters became divided, and the ruling party was defeated in the election. This defeat precipitated President Park's impeachment.

35 See chapter 10 in this book.

36 Byongjin Ahn, in chapter 1, argues that Korean progressives are not populist but illiberal. While the relationship between populism and liberalism can be defined in various ways, it seems relatively clear that populism is one of the symptoms of anti-liberal democracy. See also Yascha Mounk, *The People vs. Democracy: Why Our Freedom Is in Danger and How to Save It* (Cambridge: Harvard University Press, 2018).

37 For example, see Choi Jang-Jip, *Democracy after Democratization: The Korean Experience* (Stanford: Shorenstein Asia-Pacific Research Center, 2012).

symposium in late 2019 to commemorate the tenth anniversary of the passing of President Kim Dae-Jung, Choi gave a blistering criticism of populist tendencies in contemporary Korean politics.[38] In assessing the late president's legacy, Choi praised the Kim Dae-Jung government for emphasizing a politics of cooperation over conflict and confrontation, declining to settle old political scores over the legacies of the authoritarian era, and pursuing minimalist and gradual reforms instead of maximalist goals. These achievements contributed to the consolidation of Korea's democracy, according to Choi.

In his remarks, Choi noted with concern that Korea's democracy is facing a crisis as the achievements of the Kim Dae-Jung government fade away. He attributed this to several causes. The mainstream of the Democratic Party is engaged in a pitched battle over historical issues and pursuing radical reforms under the banner of "eradicating deep-rooted evils" (*jeok-pye cheong-san*) while taking a maximalist position. Moreover, the power of the Blue House has been strengthened, and the government has been filled with staff from Moon's election campaign instead of being centered around the party. There is a prevailing emphasis on winner-takes-all politics, and Carl Schmitt's vision of confrontational politics has been widely adopted. The tight-knit circle of familial loyalty among the 386 generation of politicians is also a contributing factor.[39]

Choi cited the immaturity of Korea's civil society as the fundamental reason for these problems. In his view, the fusion of a weak civil society and a strong state manifested itself as populism. The ruling elite mobilized civil society organizations in a top-down fashion, leading to the formation of a clientelist relationship with political supporters and donors. This, in turn, led to the creation of political groups that drove political polarization. To address these problems, Choi proposed reducing the state's power, dispersing power away from the president, fostering a mature civil society, and disseminating a pluralist vision of politics.[40]

Before assessing his proposals, let us first closely examine Choi's diagnosis of why populism emerged in Korean politics. He argues that the two progressive administrations after Kim Dae-Jung—those of Roh Moo-Hyun and Moon Jae-In—veered away from political pluralism,

38 Choi, "The Crisis and Consolidation of Korea's Democracy."
39 Choi, "The Crisis and Consolidation of Korea's Democracy."
40 Choi, "The Crisis and Consolidation of Korea's Democracy."

throwing Korea's democracy off the path of consolidation and into crisis. The various causes he cites for this development can be summarized as the Democratic Party mainstream's headlong pursuit of radical social reform. Choi attributes this to an underlying anti-democratic, anti-political intent among progressives, which explains why Korea's political structure has turned toward a populist democracy lacking in liberal constitutionalism. The political forces that controlled the Blue House and held a majority in the National Assembly ignored the opposition and mobilized its supporters to drive political confrontation and conflict. This led to the emergence of populism.

386's apologia

Why did the 386 generation of politicians—the current mainstream of the Democratic Party—come to engage in this confrontational style of politics? The answer to this question can be summarized in two parts: Roh Moo-Hyun and civil society. In particular, two defining experiences in Roh Moo-Hyun's political career had a critical impact.[41]

The first is the impeachment of President Roh in 2003. After the first-ever peaceful transfer of power in 1997 with the election of Kim Dae-Jung, the conservatives' resistance was not as intense as expected. The Kim Young-Sam government had gone to the precipice of a sovereign default during the financial crisis, and Kim Dae-Jung was also a political heavyweight. However, the conservatives' reaction was notably different after the 2002 presidential election, when Roh Moo-Hyun defeated Lee Hoi-Chang. They did not want to recognize a president who had not attended college, a president who had been an outsider even within his own party. Furthermore, Roh's nonhierarchical, horizontal style of leadership—as displayed in his words and actions—clashed with conservative values not just in the political arena, but also in civil society.[42] The conservatives, who held a majority in the National Assembly, eventually impeached President Roh. He was reinstated after the Constitutional Court dismissed the impeachment case, but the pro-Roh 386 politicians believed that the Conservative Party still refused to acknowledge its defeat in a free and fair democratic election.

---

41 Here, I focus on decisive events in the context of Korea's recent political history. See chapter 1 for a discussion of the characteristics of the 386 politicians.

42 Park Dong-Cheon, "An Evaluation of President Roh Moo-Hyun: Focusing on His Manner of Speech" [in Korean], *Social Science Research* 16, no. 1 (2008): 114–45.

The second is President Roh's death. During the first year of the Lee Myung-Bak government, Roh, his family members, and close aides were investigated on corruption charges. Roh committed suicide, leaving behind a final note which implied that political retaliation would not cease as long as he was alive. Once again, the pro-Roh 386 politicians believed that the Conservative Party, which had never truly accepted Roh as president, had politically pressured him to the point of death with an excessive prosecutorial investigation after he had left office. In their eyes, there could no longer be any meaningful dialogue or compromise with the Conservative Party. Since President Roh's death, Korea's politics has become an all-out war between two irreconcilable opponents.

The 386 generation of politicians is also likely to diverge from Choi Jang-Jip in their understanding of civil society. While the Democratic Party seized both the presidency and the legislature for the first time after the 2002 presidential election and the 2004 National Assembly elections, it failed to make meaningful progress in implementing reforms. A broad coalition consisting of the Conservative Party, the conservative press, and like-minded civil society actors—including Protestant churches and related organizations—played a central role in resisting these reforms. At the time, the Conservative Party and conservative media outlets criticized the ruling party for displaying an aggressive attitude, acting as if it had the weaker hand when it had already come to power through electoral victories. The 386 politicians had a different story to tell, however. While they had seized political power through elections, civil society was still dominated by conservative forces due to decades of authoritarian rule and the influence of anti-communist ideology. To borrow Antonio Gramsci's terminology, they had won the "war of maneuver" in the formal political sphere, but they had not yet won the "war of position" over civil society that was necessary for achieving hegemony.[43]

Consequently, the 386 politicians do not attribute their failed attempts at radical reform to an anti-democratic or anti-political intent. Instead, they believe that the dominance of conservative civil society came into full view after the 1997 presidential election, which marked the first transfer of power and heralded the beginning of a meaningful competition in the formal political sphere. This dominant position had

43 Antonio Gramsci, *Selections from the Prison Notebooks* (New York: International Publishers, 1971), 233–39.

previously been hidden behind the political arena, and conservative civil society actors had no reason to make themselves visible. To this day, the 386 politicians largely maintain this view. It explains why the Democratic Party, after having won all four nationwide elections since 2016, still adopts a highly confrontational stance.

Because of these fundamental differences in their interpretation of events, the 386 politicians—the current mainstream of the Democratic Party—are unlikely to agree with Choi Jang-Jip's proposals to "reduce the state's power, disperse power away from the president, foster a mature civil society, and disseminate a pluralist vision of politics."[44] Instead, they believe that they still lack the political power to attack the formidable ramparts of conservative civil society, as well as the Prosecution Service and the conservative press. Furthermore, they also believe that the president has insufficient authority to change the political landscape in their favor. In their view, it is vital to incapacitate the enemy through direct confrontation rather than through dialogue or compromise. The territory of civil society is occupied by conservative forces who can engage in political retribution at any time. Reaching out to the other side in good faith, as President Roh did toward the end of his term by proposing a coalition government, would be unwise. Only by inflicting significant damage on the opponent is it possible to convince them that a mutual cycle of political retribution is not in anyone's interest.

This state of affairs in Korean politics resembles the Cold War–era arms race between the United States and the Soviet Union. The world experienced perilous crises during that time, including the Cuban Missile Crisis. Similarly, Korean politics is also highly likely to undergo crises of various forms. Like the U.S. and Soviet governments during the Cold War, Korea's political parties exaggerate each other's threats and attempt to rally domestic supporters around these threats. A high level of mutual hostility has enabled each party to rally a great deal of public support. The Conservative Party tends to rely on only its traditional base of supporters, while the Democratic Party narrowly focuses on supporters of the 386 generation. The impeachment of President Park Geun-Hye, the candlelight protests, and the recent emergence of populism are all symptoms of this tendency. This is not a strengthening of party identification. Instead, it is a regression in democratic party politics, which has been reorganized around a small band of zealous

44 Choi, "The Crisis and Consolidation of Korea's Democracy."

supporters. Korean politics today is not a debate or negotiation about the welfare of the entire nation, or about the value of democracy, freedom, justice, peace, reconciliation, or fair distribution. Instead, it resembles a fight between gladiators in the Colosseum, where the oppression and condemnation of opponents by any means is the primary objective.

It is also possible to extend the Cold War analogy to assess possible ways that the stand-off in Korean politics may end. One is the defeat and dissolution of one side (both major parties may hope for this outcome). In this scenario, a centrist or a progressive third party would likely emerge to fill the void. Another possible outcome is a political compromise between the two parties, just as the United States and the Soviet Union engaged in arms control negotiations. There could be an institutional compromise on creating a parliamentary system, which would allow for a coalition government, or a semi-presidential system. Beyond institutional solutions, one could imagine a generational change within the two major parties. For example, in the next presidential and legislative elections, the 386 generation could step out of the limelight in the Democratic Party. Similarly, the generation of anticommunist politicians could exit the scene in the Conservative Party. Such a change is unlikely to be voluntary, however. It will happen only when the next generation boldly enters the political arena.

The Future of Korean Democracy: Not the President, but Party Politics

Although this chapter critically reviews many problems associated with Korean democracy, especially the immaturity of party politics, it is also clear that Korean politics has steadily developed over the past seventy years. In the thirty years since democratization, Conservative and Democratic parties have taken turns holding office, each for about ten years. This shows the effectiveness of free and fair elections. While support for democracy is weakening around the world,[45] many Koreans still strongly support it.[46] Party politics has not stabilized, and immature politicians have occasionally emerged, but citizens have quickly recti-

45 Roberto Foa and Yascha Mounk, "The Danger of Deconsolidation: The Democratic Disconnect," *Journal of Democracy* 27, no. 3 (July 2016): 5–17.

46 Seo Bok-Kyung, *Inside and Outside the Impeachment Square* [in Korean] (Seoul, Korea: Chaekdam, 2017); see also chapter 10 in this book.

fied such problems through elections or direct protests. Compared to many countries where people's belief in democracy has clearly declined, Korea seems to be on the path to liberal democracy, even though there are cycles of progress and setback. The people have acted as a check and balance to keep Korea's democracy on course. It is hoped that the populist symptoms that are currently appearing will be pushed aside faster than in Europe or the United States.

If democracy depends on fair elections and strong public support for democratic institutions, then South Korea's democracy is certainly working. What is not working is party politics, which is a core mechanism of representative democracy. As we have seen, prior to democratization, Korean politics had pursued modernization—industrialization, democratization, and the realization of social justice—while being trapped in a very narrow ideological landscape. Even after democratization, the extreme focus on ideological issues was not completely resolved, and even after the Cold War, it did not easily disappear due to the presence of North Korea—a hostile adversary armed with nuclear weapons. In the process, Kim Dae-Jung's achievements in overcoming the financial crisis were undermined, and Roh Moo-Hyun, who had sought political compromise, suffered political retaliation and committed suicide. Currently, the two main political parties in South Korea are mobilizing their supporters against each other, as either descendants of the left or of the dictatorship.

In this polarization of party politics, the policy debates that have critical implications for the people have all but disappeared. In particular, Korea's party politics have been incompetent in resolving economic polarization, which has rapidly intensified in the period of democratization. The emergence of populism indicates a serious problem in the proper functioning of party politics. It has been argued that populism is rooted in anti-elite sentiment among the people,[47] and also in dissatisfaction with a party system that fails to adequately represent a hidden majority.[48]

The precise causal relationship between socioeconomic inequality and populism is unclear. Nevertheless, the two phenomena are undoubtedly related. Populism rejects political solutions to social problems (and

47 John Judis, *The Populist Explosion* (New York: Columbia Global Reports, 2016); Paul Taggart, *Populism* (Buckingham: Open University Press, 2000).
48 Jan-Werner Müller, *What Is Populism?* (Philadelphia: University of Pennsylvania Press, 2016).

is characterized by an anti-political stance, political cynicism, and free-market fundamentalism) and is hostile toward the weak and the vulnerable (expressed through hatred toward minorities, anti-immigrant attitudes, and opposition to welfare policy and anti-discrimination measures). Party politics' failure to resolve socioeconomic polarization has had widespread effects on youth unemployment, fairness in employment, the legitimacy of inheritances through real estate, and inequality due to social capital. The scandal surrounding Cho Kuk, former minister of justice and a professor at Seoul National University, and his family exemplified all of these problems.[49] In the case of South Korea, we can say that socioeconomic inequalities may not be a direct cause or effect of populism, but alleviating inequality will help counter populist ideologies and weaken populist phenomena.

In Korea, party politics has failed to solve socioeconomic problems. Instead, it relied on one individual—the president—yet again. However, such an approach is not the right answer, as we have seen during the last democratization period, and even after the impeachment of Park Geun-Hye. What is needed in Korean politics is the development of a robust party politics that can promptly identify and address social problems through carefully devised and effective policies. Two changes are necessary for the development of party politics in Korea: the transformation of the presidential system and diversity in political representation.

It is difficult to suddenly change the presidential system, which has been in operation for more than seventy years, into a parliamentary system. The alternative is to change the character of the Korean presidential system, which is often criticized for being "imperial." The excessive concentration of power in the Blue House makes the system prone to abuses of power and corruption, including through personnel appointments. However, in terms of achieving political outcomes, especially when considering the relationship with the legislative branch, it is difficult to see the executive branch as imperial. There is a dual legitimacy in Korea's presidential system: both the president and members of the National Assembly are directly elected by the people. This dual legitimacy often creates a deadlock between the president and the National Assembly, making it difficult for them to reach any agreement

49 "'Gold-Spoon' Children Shakes South Korea's Political Elite," *New York Times*, October 21, 2019, https://www.nytimes.com/2019/10/21/world/asia/south-korea-cho-kuk-gold-spoon-elite.html.

and giving rise to political polarization. Therefore, it is vital to construct a functioning presidential system that is not imperial and also avoids political polarization. A decentralized presidential system that separates the powers of the president and prime minister is one possibility. Currently, many politicians and political scientists in Korea are interested in this option. If the next president pursues constitutional reform, this change may be possible.

Promoting diversity in political representation is a more fundamental issue. As Korean society becomes increasingly unequal, more and more individuals will fall by the wayside amid the fierce competition. These individuals will eventually form an "invisible majority." Their discontent will continue to build as long as politics fails to speak to their own life experiences. It was once accepted without question that democracy is a rule by the majority. However, it is now becoming clear that politics was always dominated by the few, who were vastly overrepresented. There are many reasons—including substantial differences in the level of education, personal wealth, and social status—why Korea's political representatives today may be regarded as the elite.[50] Moreover, in their personal and public interactions, these representatives mostly come into contact only with elites who belong to the middle or upper classes.

Both the Democratic and Conservative parties must therefore take proactive steps to expand political representation beyond the elite. This change can be made by reforming the electoral system, which could increase the diversity of political representatives. The current election law encourages zero-sum competition between the two major parties; the rules and formulas for allocating seats favor only these two parties. It is also necessary to introduce a candidate nomination system that can increase representation across generations, age, region, and class in parties. There must be a meaningful effort to incorporate the "invisible" voices of the majority into the political arena. This requires greater diversity within political parties. There need to be many more politicians who represent women, youth, the elderly, the poor, casual workers, and many other minorities. Improving representation in this way will bring much-needed energy and vitality to political parties. For

---

50 Kwanhu Lee, "Consideration of Political Representatives after Democratization in Korea—Members of the National Assembly" [in Korean], *Citizen and World* 29 (2016): 27–56; Kim Yong-Cheol, "Socioeconomic Inequalities and Korean Democracy: Is It a 'Good' Democracy?" [in Korean], *Memory & Vision* 42 (2020): 58–97.

the vast majority of ordinary citizens, the most common way to make their voices heard is through mass public opinion. We must now create avenues and mechanisms that empower citizens to directly influence the political agenda through their representatives.

Bibliography

Choi, Jang-Jip. *Democracy after Democratization: The Korean Experience*. Stanford: Shorenstein Asia-Pacific Research Center, 2012.

———. "The Crisis and Consolidation of Korea's Democracy, and Alternatives for a New Political Order." [In Korean.] Paper presented at "Kim Dae-Jung and Democracy: Thought and Practice" at Kim Dae-Jung Library at Yonsei University, December 9, 2019.

Choi, Jeong-Pyo. "Succession of Chaebols and the Change in Economic Concentration." [In Korean.] *Journal of Business History* 26, no. 2 (2011): 181–99.

Choi, Sang-Ryong. "Democratization in Korea Is at the Stage of Consolidation" [in Korean], *Daehak Sinmun*, September 1, 1997.

Hankyoreh. "The Environmental Fallout of the Four Major Rivers Project." August 3, 2013. http://english.hani.co.kr/arti/english_edition/e_national/598190.html.

Foa, Roberto, and Yascha Mounk. "The Danger of Deconsolidation: The Democratic Disconnect." *Journal of Democracy* 27, no. 3 (July 2016): 5–17.

"Coddling of 'Gold-Spoon' Children Shakes South Korea's Political Elite." *New York Times*, October 21, 2019. https://www.nytimes.com/2019/10/21/world/asia/south-korea-cho-kuk-gold-spoon-elite.html.

Gramsci, Antonio. *Selections from the Prison Notebooks*. New York: International Publishers, 1971.

Jang, Hoon. "Reflections and Prospects of Korean Democracy." [In Korean.] In *Crisis and Prospects of Korean Democracy: Democratization, Globalization, and De-security*. Seoul, Korea: Ingansarang, 2013.

Jeong, Han-Wool. "Trends and Prospects for Generation Voting Research and the 21st General Election." [In Korean.] *Journal of Korean Social Trend and Perspective* 109 (2020): 74–96.

Joo, Sung-Soo. "Financial Relations between Government and Civil Society: A Paradigm Shift from Supporting to Cooperation." [In Korean.] *Civil Society and NGO* 15, no. 2 (2017): 3–33.

Judis, John. *The Populist Explosion*. New York: Columbia Global Reports, 2016.

Kang, Woo-Jin. "Park Chung Hee Syndrome and Korean Democracy: Centering on Four Important Issues." [In Korean.] *Korea and World Politics* 29, no. 2 (2013): 73–105.

Kim, Jong-Yeop. "The 87-Year Regime in Education: Between Democratization and Neoliberalism." [In Korean.] *Economy and Society* 84 (2009): 40–69.

Kim, Yong-Cheol. "Socioeconomic Inequalities and Korean Democracy: Is It a 'Good' Democracy?" [In Korean.] *Memory & Vision* 42 (2020): 58–97.

Kim, Young-Rae. "The Democratic Movement of the Third Republic" [in Korean]. In *The Democratic and Democratization Movement in Korea*, edited by Shin Myung-Soon. Seoul, Korea: Hanul, 2016.

Kim, Young-Tae. "The 2007 Presidential Election and Effects of 'North Korean Variables'." [In Korean.] *Journal of Political Science and Communication* 10, no. 2 (2007): 65–77.

Lee, Kwanhu. "Consideration of Political Representatives after Democratization in Korea—Members of the National Assembly." [In Korean.] *Citizen and World* 29 (2016): 27–56.

———. "Formation of Korean Democratic Ideology: Constitutionalism, Democratic Republic, National Sovereignty." [In Korean.] In *Korean Democracy, 100 Years of Revolution: 1919–2019*. Seoul, Korea: Hanul, 2019.

Lee, Sung-Woo. "A Study of Perceptions of North Korean Issues according to Security Situation around the Korean Peninsula: Comparing on 2018 and 2019." [In Korean.] *Korea and World Politics* 36, no. 4 (2020): 109–35.

Mounk, Yascha. *The People vs. Democracy: Why Our Freedom Is in Danger and How to Save It*. Cambridge: Harvard University Press, 2018.

Müller, Jan-Werner. *What Is Populism?* Philadelphia: University of Pennsylvania Press, 2016.

OECD (Organisation for Economic Co-operation and Development). *OECD Economic Surveys Korea: 2020*. Paris, France: OECD Publishing, 2020.

———. "Income Inequality." OECD Data. Accessed December 1, 2021. https://data.oecd.org/inequality/income-inequality.htm.

———. "Self-Employment Rate." OECD Data. Accessed December 1, 2021. https://data.oecd.org/emp/self-employment-rate.htm.

Park, Dong-Cheon. "An Evaluation of President Roh Moo-Hyun: Focusing on His Manner of Speech." [In Korean.] *Social Science Research* 16, no. 1 (2008): 114–45.

Seo, Bok-Kyung. *Inside and Outside the Impeachment Square.* [In Korean.] Seoul, Korea: Chaekdam, 2017.

Shin, Gi-Wook. "South Korea's Democratic Decay." *Journal of Democracy* 31, no. 3 (July 2020): 100–14.

Shin, Gi-Wook et al. "The Korean Democracy Movement: An Empirical Overview." In *South Korean Social Movements: From Democracy to Civil Society*, edited by Gi-Wook Shin and Paul Y. Chang, 21–40. Milton Park: Routledge, 2011.

Shin, Myung-Soon. "Theoretical Review of Democratization and Democratization Movement." [In Korean.] In *Democratization and Democratization Movement in Korea: Success and Frustration.* Seoul, Korea: Hanul, 2016.

Statistics Korea. https://kosis.kr/index/index.do.

Taggart, Paul. *Populism*. Buckingham: Open University Press, 2000.

CHAPTER FOUR

The Politicization of Civil Society

No Longer Watchdogs of Power, Former Democratic Activists Are Becoming New Authoritarian Leaders

Myoung-Ho Park

"Can our democracy really overcome this crisis?" During the interpellation session of the 21st National Assembly's first regular session in the fall of 2020, Representative Jang Hye-Young of the progressive Justice Party posed this question to the floor. In her words, "the very individuals who were once the most powerful agents of change have now become the establishment. They now only speak of change as they stand in its way. This is the unfortunate reality that is in front of us today."[1]

Jang continued with another question: "How is it that the burning hearts that vowed to fight for a fair and equal world where everyone could live in dignity—to fight without care for love, honor, or fame—have grown so cold?" Once again, in her words, "we had hoped that when the protagonists of the democratization movement came to power by democratic means, they would not only sweep away the age-old issues that beset our society, but also bravely confront the challenges we face in this new era." Jang also underlines a commonly felt disappointment with Moon's administration: "In 2017, when the Moon Jae-In administration entered office amidst cries of bewilderment and anger about the state of our country, many citizens were filled with hope. I was one of those citizens."[2]

1 Jang Hye-Young, "A Message from a Politician Born in 1987 to the Youth of 1987" [in Korean], September 16, 2020, http://janghyeyeong.com/28/?q=YToyOntzOjEyOiJrZXl3b3JkX3R5cGUiO3M6MzoiYWxsIjtzOjQ6InBhZ2UiO2k6Mjt9&bmode=view&idx=4962881&t=board.

2 Jang Hye-Young, "A Message from a Politician Born in 1987."

Her criticism can also be applied to Korea's civil society. How can we characterize the relationship between civil society and state power under the Moon administration? Specifically, are the actions of civil society and civic movements simply another form of political behavior, like that of political parties, or has civil society become a stepping-stone on the path to political power?

Korea's civil society has previously been noted for its contributions to Korean democratization.[3] However, many in Korea—progressives and conservatives alike—are beginning to question whether civil society is now playing a role in Korea's democratic recession. There is a profound self-recognition that "we are faced with a new problem of how to halt the erosion of democracy and move toward its restoration and development."[4] Representative Jang's critique can be understood in the same vein. Paradoxically, the former protagonists of democratization are now posing a threat to liberal democracy.[5]

Concerns about a crisis of democracy have been widely raised among political circles in Korea. Critics contend that an increasingly powerful "imperial presidency" has undermined Korea's democratic system of government. The prospect of implementing meaningful checks and balances, with a greater decentralization of power, continues to recede. Kim Chong-In, the former leader of the conservative People Power Party, noted that "this is an era where those who are elected to power are now dismantling democracy."[6]

Has Korea's civil society truly become a disruptive force in the country's democracy, instead of driving its progress? If so, why and through what steps did civil society arrive at this state? Furthermore, how has Korea's civil society been politicized, and what are the consequences of this development?

---

3 Shin Gi-Wook and Paul Y. Chang, *South Korean Social Movements: From Democracy to Civil Society* (Milton Park: Routledge, 2011).

4 Ko Jeong-Ae, "Erosion of Democracy after the Candlelight Protests: The Elite of the Pro-Democracy Student Movement are the Problem," *JoongAng Ilbo*, August 7, 2020, https://www.joongang.co.kr/article/23843114.

5 Shin Gi-Wook, "Korean Democracy Is Sinking under the Guise of the Rule of Law," Walter H. Shorenstein Asia-Pacific Research Center, April 2020, https://fsi.stanford.edu/news/korean-democracy-sinking-under-guise-rule-law.

6 "Kim Chong-In of the People Power Party Holds Emergency Press Conference in Response to Suspension of Prosecutor General Yoon Seok-Youl," *YTN News*, November 25, 2020, https://www.ytn.co.kr/replay/view.php?idx=21&key=202011251430375620.

This chapter attempts to answer these questions. In doing so, it first briefly examines the existing literature to outline the basic and defining characteristics of civil society. It then assesses the achievements of Korea's democracy and the evolution of its civil society, as well as trends in public trust in civil society over time. Lastly, it analyzes the politicization of Korea's civil society and concludes by discussing its implications for Korean democracy.

Democracy and Civil Society

The definition of civil society has long been a subject of debate. Aristotle's use of civil society as a synonym for the state or a political community reflects the commonly held understanding of the concept in ancient Greece. The city-states of ancient Greece were communities of public citizens who participated in the formulation and realization of the public good—in other words, a civil society. This understanding of civil society persisted until the Roman Republic.[7]

A different conception of civil society emerged in the modern era. To John Locke and Jean-Jacques Rousseau, civil society represented a state or a government that ruled through laws, in contrast to the state of nature. Civil society represented a social order of enlightened or civilized citizens who actively participated in public life and whose mutual relations were regulated by laws. By this understanding, civil society is a community of citizens who possess a public spirit and public virtues.[8]

It is only in the nineteenth century that a conception of civil society independent of the state or a political community began to take shape. In this view, civil society did not directly belong to or rely upon the state. Instead, it referred to the private market economy, social classes, companies, and welfare institutions, which were all regulated by civil laws. At its core, civil society was a "bourgeois society" centered on private property, but it also included self-interested citizens who engaged in commercial activities and citizens with public virtues. Adam Smith considers such individuals as ethical citizens with "moral sentiments."[9]

7 Victor Davis Hanson, *A War Like No Other: How the Athenians and Spartans Fought the Peloponnesian War* (New York: Random House, 2009).
8 Im Hyug-Baeg, "Revival and Development of Korean Civil Society After Democratization" [in Korean], *Oughtopia* 24, no. 1 (2009): 137–69.
9 Im, Hyug-Baeg, *Democracy in the Era of Globalization* [in Korean] (Seoul, Korea: Nanam, 2000).

In contemporary usage, civil society includes private associations and entities that exercise a certain degree of autonomy from the state. Alexis de Tocqueville's conception of civil society continues to be most influential today, and it also aligns with Montesquieu's notion of mediating associations. Civil society, in this account, is a "nonstate" domain in which citizens and associations engage in autonomous activities. It is also a space of mediation that is not individual, familial (private), or market-based in character. At the same time, as a voluntary and self-governing association of citizens, it ultimately prioritizes public objectives even as it draws attention to public issues and articulates its own interests. Moreover, unlike political parties, it does not seek to resolve issues by exerting control over the state.

Civil society is a social domain that consists of voluntary associations that exist between the individual and the state, and it is also a public domain that is created by proactive citizens.[10] It is now widely understood as "a general concept that encompasses civil society organizations (CSOs), nongovernmental organizations (NGOs), and nonprofit organizations (NPOs)."[11] The growth and maturation of civil society can be empirically measured by the increase in the number of CSOs and greater public participation in these organizations. Given this definition, civil society has the following defining characteristics.

First, autonomy from the state is the cornerstone of civil society. It does not seek political power and is the product of liberalism. The distinction between the state and civil society is foundational to liberalism, and a separation between the two is a tangible expression of liberal ideals.[12]

Second, the identity of civil society is built on pursuing the public good. It can gain the trust of citizens and affirm its identity only when it pursues the public interest as a public organization. In keeping a watchful eye over the state and the market, it maintains a tense relationship with political power. Civil society can help resolve social conflicts, restore a sense of community, and effectively function as a

10 Kim Young-Rae, "Restoring the Values of Democracy and Civil Society" [in Korean], *NGO Research* 5, no. 1 (2007): 1–25; Choi Jang-Jip, *Democracy after Democratization* [in Korean] (Seoul, Korea: Humanitas, 2005).

11 Kim, "Restoring the Values of Democracy and Civil Society," 3.

12 Nancy L. Rosenblum, "Civil Societies: Liberalism and the Moral Uses of Pluralism," *Social Research* 61, no. 3 (Fall 1994): 539–62.

forum for social dialogue only when it stays true to this foundational identity.[13]

Third, transparency is essential to civil society. Trust in CSOs hinges on the transparency of their operations and decision-making procedures. If certain board members monopolize control over an organization's activities and decision-making processes, or if its finances are not clearly accounted for, then its transparency is threatened. Receiving substantial assistance from the government or from private companies, whether directly or indirectly, can also have the same effect.

Fourth, civil society as a whole must be democratic in nature and possess professional knowledge and expertise in the issue areas that it addresses. Its operations and decision-making procedures must be democratic, and it must be capable of presenting viable policy options to address the failures of the state or the market.

Fifth, civil society would lose its vitality without the voluntary participation of citizens. At their core, civil society movements draw on the dedication of individual citizens who form the basis for grassroots movements. It is impossible to envision a civic movement without citizens.

Ultimately, the CSOs that make up civil society pursue public interests and are nonpartisan, neutral, autonomous, nonprofit, and voluntary in character.[14] To the extent that Korea's civil society is facing a crisis, the key to restoring the public's trust lies in defending its identity by demonstrating responsibility, transparency, democracy, and professionalism.

These characteristics of civil society are critical for defending and improving democracy. As a political system, democracy was founded on the assumption that those in positions of power could abuse their authority for corrupt purposes. Democracy always maintains a suspicious attitude toward those in power, relying on checks and balances to keep a watchful eye. Civil society is the soil in which this democratic "system of monitoring" takes root. Does Korea's civil society play such a role?

---

13 Aisha Ghaus-Pasha, "Role of Civil Society Organizations in Governance" (paper presented at *6th Global Forum on Reinventing Government Towards Participatory and Transparent Governance*, Seoul, Korea, May 2005).

14 Lester M. Salamon, *America's Nonprofit Sector: A Primer* (Washington, DC: The Foundation Center, 1999).

The Evolution of Korea's Civil Society

To understand the current characteristics of Korea's civil society, it is necessary to first examine its origins. In particular, the history of Korea's civil society must be understood in the context of the country's democratization in 1987 and the ascendance of progressive politics in the late 1990s and early 2000s.

Civil society and Korea's democratization

According to Mainwaring and Bizarro, Korea is one of the eight most successful democracies among the ninety-one countries that democratized during the so-called "Third Wave" between 1974 and 2012. Of these countries, only twenty-three (25 percent) are classified as having achieved "major democratic advances." Among these cases, only eight have successfully become strong liberal democracies. Korea is second only to Portugal in this respect.[15]

This democratic advance cannot be understood separately from Korea's civil society, which played a critical role in both the transition to democracy and its subsequent consolidation. In particular, 1987 was a watershed moment in the emergence of Korea's civil society.[16] Organizations such as the Citizens' Coalition for Economic Justice (CCEJ), People's Solidarity for Participatory Democracy (PSPD), and the Korea Federation for Environmental Movements (KFEM) came to form the backbone of Korea's civil society. They played a leading role in catalyzing various reforms. The CSOs that led the fight for democracy, along with those that appeared shortly after democratization, solidified their role as key players who proposed policy measures in response to the failures of the government or the market. Drawing on the public's unwavering trust, these organizations steadily grew into important actors in Korea's political process.

Such a rapid growth of civil society was not confined to Korea. In the twentieth century, four crises set the stage for the development of civil society worldwide: the crisis of the welfare state, the crisis of development, the environmental crisis, and the crisis of socialism. Economic

---

15 Scott Mainwaring and Fernando Bizarro, "The Fates of Third-Wave Democracies," *Journal of Democracy* 30, no. 1 (January 2019): 99–113.
16 Kim, "Restoring the Values of Democracy and Civil Society."

growth also contributed to the evolution of civil society.[17] Moreover, global trends such as the Third Wave of democratization and the "associational revolution"[18] were important contributing factors. In sum, the twenty-first century can be called the century of civil society. The era of "associative democracy" led by civil society has come to fruition in many countries, including Korea.[19]

The key juncture in the growth of Korea's civil society was democratization in 1987. Previously, state-society relations in Korea could be characterized as those of a "strong state" versus a "contentious society."[20] During the authoritarian era, Korea's market-authoritarian state sought to demobilize and dissolve civil society. CSOs remained under the firm control of the state's legal, financial, and bureaucratic sanctions and incentives.[21] Democratization led to an eruption of diverse demands that had been repressed under the authoritarian regime. Korea's civil society thereby came to form a wide array of interest groups that took on a public character, structuring themselves into organizations as they grew.[22]

Civil society was a driving force for reforms in many areas: purging the legacies of the military dictatorships, enacting political reforms, expanding social welfare institutions, securing and expanding labor rights, safeguarding and improving human rights, and protecting the environment. In particular, CSOs gained the public's trust by making decisive contributions in purging the legacies of authoritarian rule.

17 Lester M. Salamon, "The Rise of the Nonprofit Sector," *Foreign Affairs* 73, no. 4 (1994): 109–22.

18 Ooi defines associational revolution as "a massive array of self-governing private organizations, not dedicated to distributing profits to shareholders or directors, but pursuing public purposes outside the formal apparatus of the state." Giok Ling Ooi, "Civil Society and the Urban Environment," in *Cities and the Environment : New Approaches for Eco-Societies*, eds. Takashi Inoguchi, Edward Newman, and Glen Paoletto (United Nations University Press, 1999), 107.

19 Samuel P. Huntington, *Third Wave: Democratization in the Late Twentieth Century* (Norman, OK: University of Oklahoma Press, 1991).

20 Hagen Koo, "Strong State and Contentious Society," in *State and Society in Contemporary Korea*, ed. Hagen Koo (Ithaca: Cornell University Press, 1993), 231–50.

21 Song Ho-Keun, "Democratization of Korea's Society: State-Civil Society Relations" [in Korean], in *The Dynamic Relationship Between Political and Social Democratization: International Comparative Research* (Chuncheon, Korea: Hallym University Center for Social Research, 1996).

22 Kim Young-Rae, *Interest-Group Politics and Interest-Based Conflicts* [in Korean] (Seoul, Korea: Hanul, 1997).

They also pursued the public interest across a variety of other issues, such as addressing real estate speculation, reforming financial institutions, and combating political corruption.

Prior to democratization, civil society typically takes on a "defensive" character shaped by "limited pluralism" under authoritarian rule. With democratization, it develops into an "emergent" civil society and then into a "mobilizational" civil society. Following democratization, it becomes an "institutional" civil society that helps institutionalize and consolidate the nascent democracy.[23] In Korea, mobilizational civil society played a central role in the democratization process.[24]

Civil society after 1987

Institutional civil society developed in two directions following democratization.[25] The first category of organizations sought to raise awareness and mobilize citizens' interest to create pressure for tangible change in specific issue areas. Examples include the Korean Teachers and Education Workers Union (*Jeon-gyo-jo*), Lawyers for a Democratic Society (*Minbyun*), Professors for Democracy (*Mingyohyup*), and organizations that focused on environmental protection, gender equality, and consumer protection.[26] The second category of organizations includes those that address a wide range of related issues, such as the Citizens' Coalition for Economic Justice and People's Solidarity for Participatory Democracy.[27]

Figure 4.1 shows changes in the structure of Korea's civil society before and after democratization. Before 1987, most CSOs focused on anti-regime activities with the goal of democratization. This dates back to the presidency of Syngman Rhee and also includes the Park Chung-Hee and Chun Doo-Hwan regimes. Civil society diversified

23 Marcia A. Weigle and Jim Butterfield, "Civil Society in Reforming Communist Regimes: The Logic of Emergence," *Comparative Politics* 25, no. 1 (October 1992): 1–23.

24 Shin and Chang, eds., *South Korean Social Movements.*

25 Im, "Revival and Development of Korean Civil Society."

26 Park Sang-Hoon, "General Election Civic Movement: Korea's Democracy and the Emergence of a New Social Movement" [in Korean], *Graduate Journal of the Hankuk University of Foreign Studies* (2000).

27 Choi Jang-Jip, "Korea's Democratization, Civil Society, and Civic Movement: The Significance of the 2000 General Election Coalition" [in Korean] (paper presented at *Conference of the Korean Political Science Association,* February 10, 2000).

FIGURE 4.1 Changes in the nature and diversity of Korea's civil society organizations (CSOs), 1950–2020

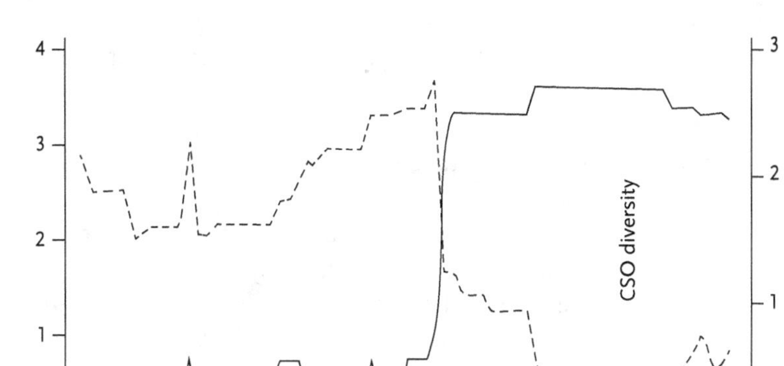

SOURCE: Jung Jai-Kwan, "The Role of Civil Society in South Korean Democracy: Liberal Legacy and Its Pitfalls," East Asia Institute Issue Briefing (2020).

with democratization, and CSOs expanded across many issue areas. There was a fundamental change in Korea's civil society after 1987, with a diverse array of organizations taking shape.

There was a particularly rapid growth of civil society during the Kim Young-Sam and Kim Dae-Jung administrations, in both quantitative and qualitative terms. The number of CSOs increased from approximately 3,500 in 1997 to 6,000 in 2000, and the number of CSO offices doubled from 10,000 to 20,000 over the same period.[28] At the same time, Korea's civil society began to divide into two broad categories: people's (*minjung*) movements and citizens' (*simin*) movements.[29] While the former prioritizes field activities, centered on the existing popular democratic movement, over entering the government system, the latter aims to participate in the system, such as by taking part in political parties and civic group activities. CSOs are a representative

28 Im, "Revival and Development of Korean Civil Society."

29 Kim Ho-Ki, "The Structure and Change of Civil Society, 1987–2000" [in Korean], *Korean Society* 3 (2000): 63–87.

example of citizens' (*simin*) movements. CSOs were formed around an ever-widening set of issues, including economic justice, citizen participation, environmental protection, women's rights, social welfare, transportation, media accountability, consumer protection, election monitoring, and the protection of foreign migrant workers.[30] Major achievements during this period included the "real name" financial transparency reforms, the Assistance for Non-Profit Organizations Act, and the Anti-Corruption Act.

Korea's civil society was characterized by two key trends in the post-democratization period. The first was the integration of civil society, CSOs, and civic movements. The origins and developmental process of Korea's civil society differ from those of many Western countries. Among these other countries, civil society began as a strata of interest groups situated between the state and individual that organized and represented particular socioeconomic interests. By contrast, Korea's civil society was centered primarily on the urban, educated middle class and around the pursuit of values. Korean movements around consumer rights, environmental protection, and women's rights are key examples. These movements encompass a truly wide array of issues, ranging from human rights and the legacies of Japanese colonial rule to current issues in Korea-Japan relations.

The second is the prioritization of the public interest. If the growth and maturation of Korea's civil society are measured in terms of the number of organizations or the scope of their activities, then Korea's civil society—in line with the first characteristic described above—can be understood as a civic movement of CSOs. As such, Korea's CSOs are fundamentally different from interest groups, which are built around specific vocations or producer organizations, which advance their own socioeconomic interests. Instead of pursuing particularistic interests, Korea's civic movements emphasized the pursuit of public values above all else.

Civil society takes center stage (early 2000s)

The 2000 general election was another turning point for Korea's civil society. The campaign to defeat particular candidates or prevent

30 Seong Kyoung-Ryung, "Civil Society and Democratic Consolidation in Korea, 1987–1996: Great Achievement and Remaining Problems" [in Korean] (paper presented at the Conference on "Consolidating Democracy in South Korea," Korea University Ilmin International Research Institute, 1996).

individuals from earning a political party's nomination was particularly notable.[31] Major CSOs—including PSPD and KFEM—formed a nationwide coalition and exerted a powerful impact on the elections by singling out particular politicians.[32] Fifty-nine of the eighty-six candidates who were called out by the coalition lost their seats. These CSOs exerted a powerful influence over public opinion, even though their initiative violated electoral laws that prohibited nonpolitical parties from interfering in the election by engaging in such activities.

This coalition of CSOs, drawing on a fervent desire among citizens for political reform, wrote a new chapter in the history of Korea's civic movements. They coordinated to overcome a fundamental limitation of Korea's democracy; despite a transfer of power to the opposition in 1997, the same group of individuals had remained in politics.[33] This campaign continued with a citizens' ombudsman movement that monitored the party primaries ahead of the 2002 presidential election and joined another coalition of CSOs to address the 2004 general election. Korea's civil society became a key driver of political reform through these initiatives, which were successful in promoting the transparency and openness of general election campaigns.

After these developments, it became impossible to discuss policymaking and policy implementation in Korean politics without considering the direct participation of CSOs in the decision-making process.[34] In a public opinion survey published by *Sisa Journal* on October 28, 2004, about the most powerful and influential actors in Korean society, CSOs ranked in first place. This clearly shows the dominant political influence of civil society at the time.

Under the Roh Moo-Hyun administration, which began its term in 2003, a new office to engage civil society was created within the Blue House. Individuals who were directly or indirectly tied to CSOs also began to enter government *en masse*. For example, the presidential transition team of president-elect Roh recruited ten of its fifty-five high-level personnel committee members from civic groups.[35] Com-

31 Kim, "Restoring the Values of Democracy and Civil Society."

32 General Election Citizens' Coalition, *General Election Coalition White Paper* [in Korean], vols. I–II (Seoul, Korea: 2001).

33 Im, "Revival and Development of Korean Civil Society."

34 Kim, "Restoring the Values of Democracy and Civil Society."

35 "Reflections on Ten Years of the Kim Dae-Jung & Roh Moo-Hyun Administrations: CSOs Stained by Political Power" [in Korean], *Donga Ilbo*, January 4, 2008, https://www.donga.com/news/Politics/article/all/20080104/8529887/1.

pared to previous administrations, the Roh administration had the most individuals with a civil society background in the Blue House, in government, and in various official committees.[36]

The Roh administration marked a golden age for Korea's civil society. There were even discussions about a "coalition" between the Roh administration and civil society.[37] It was in this context that a large number of individuals with a CSO background entered politics through the 2004 general election and the 2002 and 2006 local elections. To this day, the political participation of CSOs, including through members' entry into political office, is accepted as the norm.

Korea's civil society thus became a key axis of political power. Following the 2004 general election, its growing political influence prompted both internal and external criticism. Some of this focused on the emergence of an "elite" within the civic movements.[38] In other words, while civil society had expanded its political influence by building a civic movement, it was criticized for neglecting issues that directly affected the daily lives of its members. It was also lacking in its efforts to devise and advocate for policies to address these issues. Civil society was no longer seen as the defender of democracy that it had once been.[39]

Civil society loses the public's trust

Korean public opinion began to turn against civil society as a result of these developments. Figures 4.2 and 4.3 and table 4.1 illustrate the changes over time in the public's view of the trustworthiness and integrity of civil society.

For instance, trust in civil society began to fall sharply during the second half of the Roh administration. Though civil society ranked first in surveys of the most influential actors in Korean society in 2003 and 2004, it dropped to fifth in 2005 and sixth in 2006.[40] Similarly, there was a decline in press coverage of major CSOs, including CCEJ, PSPD,

---

36 Kim, "Restoring the Values of Democracy and Civil Society."
37 Kim, "Restoring the Values of Democracy and Civil Society."
38 Cha Myeong-Je, "Decentralizing Civic Movements: Shift to Region-Centered Focus" [in Korean], *Civil Society* 18 (2005).
39 Choi Jang-Jip, *Democracy after Democratization* [in Korean] (Seoul, Korea: Humanitas, 2005).
40 "The Current State of Korea's Middle Class" [in Korean], *Seoul Shinmun*, May 25, 2007, https://www.seoul.co.kr/news/newsView.php?id=20070525002008.

FIGURE 4.2 Proportion of the public that trusts civil society, across three years

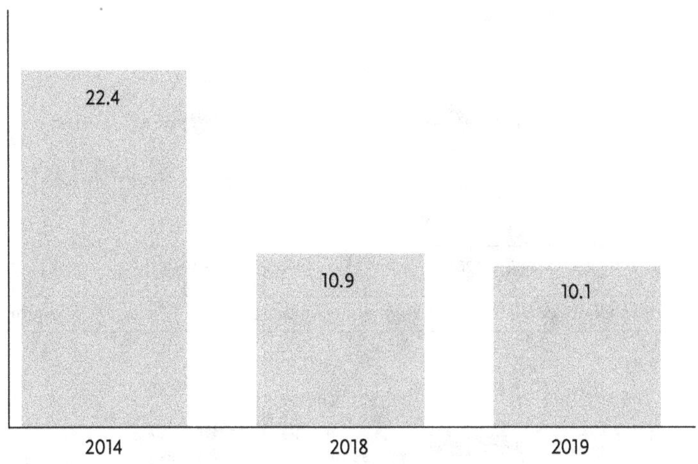

SOURCE: Korea Institute of Public Administration, Korea Social Integration Survey 2014; Korea Social Integration Survey 2018; Korea Social Integration Survey 2019, https://www.kipa.re.kr/site/kipa/research/selectReList.do?seSubCode=BIZ017A001.

and KFEM over the same time period.[41] A decline in the membership of CCEJ and PSPD also confirmed a crisis in civil society.[42] Activists themselves acknowledged its diminishing stature. In a survey of full-time CSO employees in 2007, 49 percent of respondents stated that Korea's civil society was in a state of crisis.[43]

This crisis was a long time coming. As shown in figure 4.2, the Korean public's trust in civil society plunged from 2014 to 2019. Over 20 percent of respondents in 2014 stated that they trusted civil society, but this was cut in half by 2018 and fell to only 10 percent in 2019.

Figure 4.3 outlines the public's assessment of the PSPD's trustworthiness and its influence in Korean society. The PSPD, established in 1994 with around 200 founding members, is an NGO that advocates for progressive policies. In the past twenty years, it has been involved in

41 Joo Sung-Soo, *Korea NGO Report* (Seoul, Korea: Hanyang University Press, 2004).

42 Ha Seung-Chang, "The Limitations of Civic Movements in the 1990s" [in Korean], *Korea NGO Report* (2006).

43 "Why Is There a Crisis in Civic Movements? 46 percent Point to Rightward Shift of Society" [in Korean], *Hankyoreh*, March 22, 2007, https://www.hani.co.kr/arti/society/society_general/198139.html.

FIGURE 4.3 Changes in the perceived influence and trustworthiness of the People's Solidarity for Participatory Democracy, 2005–13

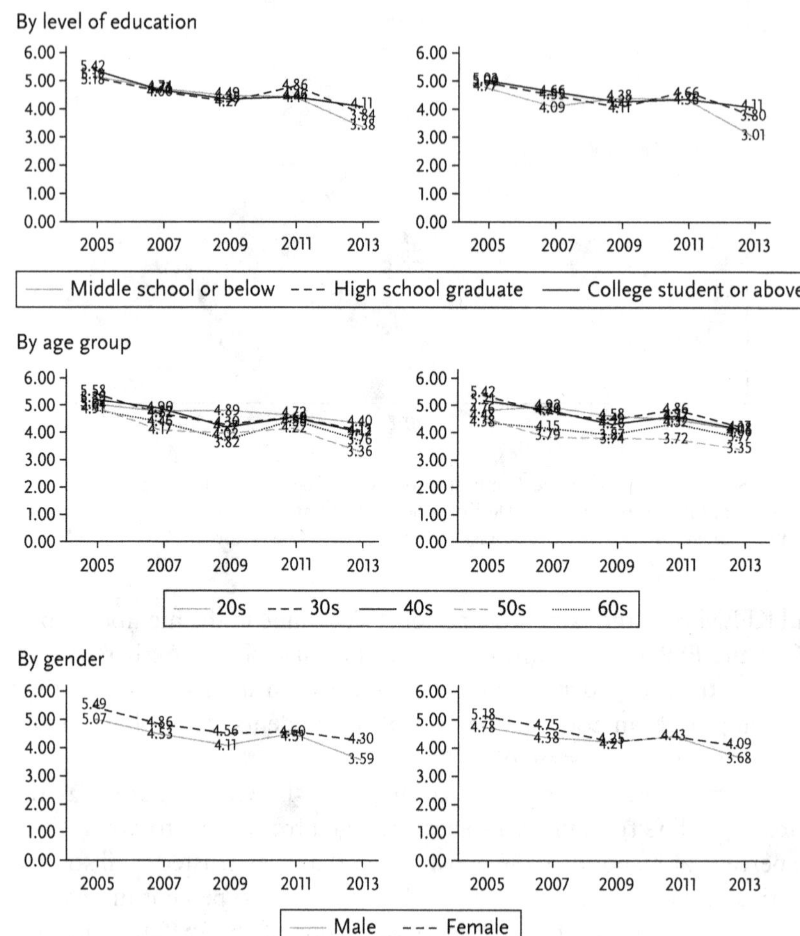

SOURCE: Jeong Han-Wool, "Assessing the Crisis of Public Trust in Korean NGOs and Seeking Alternatives: Changes in the Perception of Government-NGO Relations and the Weakening of Political NGOs" [in Korean], *Citizen and the World* 29 (2016): 113–14.

various civic movements and socioeconomic reforms and is widely regarded as the most powerful CSO in Korea. However, figure 4.3 shows an overall decline in the public's assessment of PSPD from 2005 to 2013, regardless of age group, sex, or level of education.

The same trend can be found with regards to the ideologically more neutral CCEJ or the conservative "New Right" movement. Founded

TABLE 4.1 The ten most powerful actors and organizations in Korea, as rated by respondents over several years

	1989	1990	1992	1999	2004	2007	2009	2011	2013
1	Blue House	DLP	DLP	Politicians	**NGOs**	GNP	GNP	GNP	Saenuri Party
2	*Chaebol*	PDP	Press	Business sector	Uri Party	Press	Democratic Party	Samsung	Samsung
3	Military	FKI	NSPA	**NGOs**	Press	Business sector	Press	Press	Nat'l Assembly
4	Press	NCSR	Blue House	Press	GNP	Politicians	Nat'l Assembly	Nat'l Assembly	Democratic Party
5	Exec. branch	CNDM	*Chaebol*	Democratic Party	Politicians	Samsung	Samsung	Large companies	Press
6	NSPA	NCTU	TK faction	Religious entities	Nat'l Assembly	Nat'l Assembly	**NGOs**	Politicians	Prosecution service
7	Students	Military	Opposition parties	Exec. branch	Business sector	**NGOs**	Prosecution service	Political parties	NIS
8	Nat'l Assembly	Religious entities	Exec. branch	Labor unions	Religious entities	UNDP	KCTU	Democratic Party	Political parties
9	Ruling party	Press	Military	FKI	Business-people	FKI	FKI	**NGOs**	Large companies
10	United States	Exec. Branch	**NGOs**	GNP	Samsung	Exec. branch	Business sector	Prosecution service	Politicians

NOTE: GNP = Grand National Party; DLP = Democratic Liberal Party; PDP = Peace Democratic Party; UNDP = United New Democratic Party; NSPA = National Security Planning Agency; NIS = National Intelligence Service; FKI = Federation of Korean Industries' NCSR = National Council of Student Representatives; CNDM = Coalition for a National Democratic Movement; KCTU = Korean Confederation of Trade Unions; NCTU = National Council of Trade Unions.

SOURCE: *Sisa Journal* surveys, 1989–2013.

FIGURE 4.4 Trends in the perceived influence and trustworthiness of civil society, by organization, 2005–13

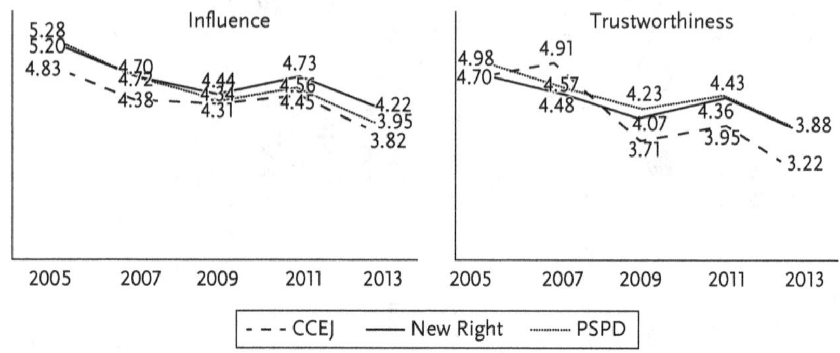

SOURCE: Jeong Han-Wool, "Assessing the Crisis of Public Trust in Korean NGOs and Seeking Alternatives: Changes in the Perception of Government-NGO Relations and the Weakening of Political NGOs" [in Korean], *Citizen and the World* 29 (2016): 100.

in 1989, the CCEJ has been a key advocate for economic justice, democratic and social development, and environmental protection. The New Right movement was founded in 2005 by individuals holding neoconservative values. Despite differences in ideological orientation, all three CSOs show an overall decline in both influence and trustworthiness.

The crisis of Korea's civil society after 2004 can also be seen in the results of annual surveys conducted by the *Sisa Journal*, in which respondents are asked to list the ten most powerful actors or institutions in Korea.[44] NGOs ranked in first place in 2004 but fell in subsequent years. They were no longer in the top ten in 2013, indicating that they had lost the public's favor.

The Politicization of Korea's Civil Society and Its Consequences

Declining trust in civil society in Korea can be attributed to its politicization. The concept of politicization can be defined and applied in many ways. For example, in the context of public administration,

44 Because the question is open-ended, some of the responses are not mutually exclusive.

it is defined as "the substitution of political criteria for merit-based criteria in the selection, retention, promotion, rewards, and disciplining of members of the public service."[45] In the context of civil society, politicization begins from the participation of personnel in institutional politics—that is, entering elected office, being appointed to public office, or participating in semi-public institutions. In Korea, a large number of individuals with extensive experience in civil society have entered the government. As of June 2020, nine out of fifty-four secretaries (17 percent) at the Blue House were from civic organizations such as the PSPD and *Minbyun*. In addition, three out of eighteen ministers in the Moon administration had an extensive career in civil society, and 11 percent of the representatives in the ruling Democratic Party were previously involved in various civic organizations.[46]

In the 21st National Assembly elections in April 2020, individuals who belonged to a particular civic movement created a makeshift political party to run for office, and many were elected. Never before had so many individuals with a civil society background entered the National Assembly. Civic movements have now become political parties, and political parties have become civic movements. Civil society and civic movements have been entirely absorbed into the formal political sphere, which includes the state.[47] In Korea, the acronym NGO may be more accurately defined as "next" governmental organization (next in line to public office) or "near" governmental organization.

This outcome could have been readily anticipated in the early 2000s. Following the 2004 general election, Korea's civil society and civic movements solidified their role as influential political actors. The results of the 21st National Assembly elections in 2020 represent a culmination of this trend. As Kim Dong-No warns, "civil society loses its autonomy when it becomes excessively politicized and the boundary between the state and civil society is demolished."[48]

---

45 B. Guy Peters and Jon Pierre, eds., *Politicization of the Civil Service in Comparative Perspective: The Quest for Control* (London: Routledge, 2004), 2.

46 "Nine Blue House Aides, Three Ministers, Nineteen Ruling Party Members: Civil Society in Power," *Chosun Ilbo*, June 2, 2020, https://www.chosun.com/site/data/html_dir/2020/06/02/2020060200103.html.

47 Choi Jang-Jip, "Reconsidering Korean Democracy: Crisis and Alternative" [in Korean], *Journal of Korean Politics* 29, no. 2 (2020): 1–26.

48 Kim Dong-No, "Overpoliticization of Civil Society and Its Declining Social Significance" [in Korean], *Korean Journal of Humanities and the Social Sciences* 37, no. 3 (2013): 82.

To a certain extent, the politicization of Korea's civil society through the entry of CSO members into politics was expected. The urban, educated middle class formed the core of the pro-democracy movement in the 1980s, and this movement developed into the civic movements of the 1990s. Participants in these movements supplemented and supported the progressives' political and social base. The rapid expansion of civil society's political influence under the Roh and Moon administrations was an entirely natural consequence of these trends.[49]

This phenomenon has had adverse side effects, however. For instance, there has been an increase in civic associations that display "rent-seeking" behavior. There is thus a tendency to prioritize the limited interests of specific groups or regions of the country at the expense of the public interest. A political union between the state and civil society eventually degenerates into a mutually dependent, clientelistic relationship. Political support is provided in return for favors and benefits, and this relationship has now extended into local government.[50]

The *politicization of personnel* from civil society also leads to the *politicization of policy*. CSOs, individuals from CSOs, and their preferences become increasingly influential in the Blue House, in government, and in political parties throughout the policymaking and policy implementation process. One prominent example of such an official in the Moon administration is Kim Sang-Jo. An economist by training, Kim served as the chief of the Economic Reform Center at the PSPD, and he strongly supports the notion of a "fair" economy. He was appointed as the senior presidential secretary for policy planning in 2019, and his two predecessors were also deeply involved in CSOs before entering the Blue House.

The politicization of civil society, CSOs, and civic movements in Korea drives the government into a polarized state of confrontation. Civil society becomes a means of mobilizing ordinary citizens in a divisive, partisan politics of confrontation and stalemate. The polarized mobilization of civil society poses a threat to institutional politics, which is centered on political parties and the National Assembly.

This can be seen in the clash between *Moon-ppa* (fervent supporters of President Moon Jae-In) and the conservative *Taegukgi* brigade, and their respective protests held at Seocho-dong (the location of the Supreme Prosecutor's Office) and Gwanghwamun Plaza. Politicization

49 Choi, "Reconsidering Korean Democracy."
50 Choi, "Reconsidering Korean Democracy."

itself has become polarized. There is strong distrust between groups and between individuals. A black-and-white logic of good and evil dominates political discourse, precipitating a crisis of democracy. Politicization, political polarization, and confrontation have become Korea's "new normal."[51] Korea's civil society no longer functions as an independent, autonomous domain for public dialogue. Instead, civil society has been subordinated to partisan political interests. It does not enable a public discussion that crosses political and partisan divides.

After civil society achieves hegemony through various forms of politicization, it can display authoritarian tendencies. In extreme cases, CSOs may act like "religious fundamentalist [or] ethnic chauvinist" organizations by "[seeking] to monopolize a functional or political space in society," thereby threatening the pluralism of civil society.[52] Such tendencies are now evident throughout Korea's civil society, CSOs, and civic movements. In fact, from its origins, Korea's civil society had a fundamentally dual character. As it experienced an internal conflict with Western individualism and liberalism, Korea's civil society came to have a complex, overlapping nature. It is a "dual" civil society in which traditionalism and modernism, competition and solidarity, and familism and individualism coexist.[53] This can be understood as a cultural lag arising from a tension between Korean culture and Western institutions.

Democracy cannot be sustained with only institutions and procedures. There must also be a civic culture that is characterized by pluralistic values and norms that emphasize equality, a public interest that surpasses individual self-interest, respect for the rule of law, proactive participation through voluntary associations, and consensus-building through dialogue and persuasion.[54] The failure to internalize and practice democratic norms leads to authoritarian tendencies in civil society, CSOs, and civic movements. As Ahn points out in chapter 1, Korea's progressives failed to internalize liberal values while fighting against authoritarian regimes. In turn, these tendencies create obstacles to a

51 Shin, "Korean Democracy Is Sinking."

52 Larry Diamond, "Rethinking Civil Society: Toward Democratic Consolidation," *Journal of Democracy* 5, no. 3 (July 1994): 7.

53 Kim Ho-Ki, "Reflections on Korea's Civil Society and Its Prospects" [in Korean], *Economy and Society* 48 (2000): 8–34.

54 Gabriel Almond and Sidney Verba, *The Civic Culture: Political Attitudes and Democracy in Five Nations* (Newbury Park: Sage Publications, 1989); Kim, "Reflections on Korea's Civil Society."

politics of mutual recognition, toleration, and forbearance. This can explain why familism and quasi-familism, not liberalism, affect the decision-making and personnel practices of Korea's CSOs and civic movements, manifesting as "group egoism."

Conclusion

The politicization of civil society, which began during the Roh administration, reached its climax during the Moon administration. As noted above, the Roh administration marked a "golden age" for civil society in Korea. Many individuals from civil society entered the political realm through the 2004 general election and the 2002 and 2006 local elections. CSOs had become a stepping-stone for those seeking to enter public office, and the politicization of CSOs is accepted as a norm.

It is no exaggeration to say that civil society is at the core of the Moon administration, and the politicization of civil society is reaching its peak. Civil society has entered the Blue House and the National Assembly in large numbers and exerted enormous influence on important policies. Perhaps the most representative examples of the politicization of civil society are the nuclear phase-out policy and the exercise of shareholder rights by the National Pension Service; these policy directions, sudden departures from the past, have been continuously advocated by civil society and were realized by the Moon administration.

The large-scale entry of civil society forces into political affairs has harmed Korea's democracy. Civil society has lost its political independence, and it has thus lost the public's trust. Korea's civil society is undergoing an identity crisis. It has strayed too far from its original mission of acting as a check on government power and advancing policy alternatives affecting important social and economic issues. Instead, it has become closely intertwined with the government and with political parties. CSOs have become political insiders, displaying organizational selfishness, and acting like any other interest groups.

No one can deny the crucial role that civil society has played in Korea's path to democracy. However, as its political influence has grown, Korea's civil society has become highly politicized. It is no longer the defender of democracy that it once was. Still, I expect civil society to eventually return to its former role in due time. For this to happen, it must distance itself from activist political forces with which it has allied in its pursuit of political power. Without meaningful depoliticization, civil society cannot reasonably justify its existence. It is now time for the generation of former pro-democracy activists, who have lost sight of their original goals, to step aside and yield power to the next generation.

Bibliography

Almond, Gabriel, and Sidney Verba. *The Civic Culture: Political Attitudes and Democracy in Five Nations*. Newbury Park: Sage Publications, 1989.

Cha, Myeong-Je. "Decentralizing Civic Movements: Shift to Region-Centered Focus." [In Korean.] *Civil Society* 18 (2005).

Choi, Jang-Jip. "Korea's Democratization, Civil Society, and Civic Movement: The Significance of the 2000 General Election Coalition." [In Korean.] Paper presented at the Conference of the Korean Political Science Association, February 10, 2000.

———. *Democracy after Democratization*. [In Korean.] Seoul, Korea: Humanitas, 2005.

———. "Reconsidering Korean Democracy: Crisis and Alternative." [In Korean.] *Journal of Korean Politics* 29, no. 2 (2020): 1–26.

"The Current State of Korea's Middle Class." [In Korean.] *Seoul Shinmun*, May 25, 2007. https://www.seoul.co.kr/news/newsView.php?id=20070525002008.

Diamond, Larry. "Rethinking Civil Society: Toward Democratic Consolidation." *Journal of Democracy* 5, no. 3 (July 1994): 4–17.

Gebremedhin, Naigzy. "Cities and the Environment: New Approaches for Eco-Societies." *Environment* 42, no. 9 (2000): 42.

General Election Citizens' Coalition. *General Election Coalition White Paper*, vols. I-II. [In Korean.] Seoul, Korea: General Election Citizens' Coalition, 2001.

Ghaus-Pasha, Aisha. "Role of Civil Society Organizations in Governance." Paper presented at the 6th Global Forum on Reinventing Government Towards Participatory and Transparent Governance, Seoul, Korea, May 2005.

Ha, Seung-Chang. "The Limitations of Civic Movements in the 1990s." [In Korean.] *Korea NGO Report*, 2006.

Hanson, Victor Davis. *A War Like No Other: How the Athenians and Spartans Fought the Peloponnesian War*. New York: Random House, 2009.

Huntington, Samuel P. *Third Wave: Democratization in the Late Twentieth Century*. Norman: University of Oklahoma Press, 1991.

Im, Hyug-Baeg. "Revival and Development of Korean Civil Society after Democratization." [In Korean.] *Oughtopia* 24, no. 1 (2009): 137–69.

———. *Democracy in the Era of Globalization*. [In Korean.] Seoul, Korea: Nanam, 2000.

Jang, Hye-Young. "A Message from a Politician Born in 1987 to the Youth of 1987." [In Korean.] September 16, 2020. http://janghyeyeong.com/28/?q=YToyOntzOjEyOiJrZXl3b3JkX3R5cGUiO3M6MzoiYWxsIjtzOjQ6InBhZ2UiO2k6Mjt9&bmode=view&idx=4962881&t=board.

Jeong, Han-Wool. "Assessing the Crisis of Public Trust in Korean NGOs and Seeking Alternatives: Changes in the Perception of Government-NGO Relations and the Weakening of Political NGOs." [In Korean.] *Citizen and the World* 29 (2016): 85–123.

Jung, Jai-Kwan. "The Role of Civil Society in South Korean Democracy: Liberal Legacy and Its Pitfalls." East Asia Institute Issue Briefing, 2020.

Joo, Sung-Soo. *Korea NGO Report*. Seoul, Korea: Hanyang University Press, 2004.

Kim, Dong-No. "Overpoliticization of Civil Society and Its Declining Social Significance." [In Korean.] *Korean Journal of Humanities and the Social Sciences* 37, no. 3 (2013): 59–85.

Kim, Ho-Ki. "Reflections on Korea's Civil Society and Its Prospects." [In Korean.] *Economy and Society* 48 (2000): 8–34.

———. "The Structure and Change of Civil Society, 1987–2000." [In Korean.] *Korean Society* 3 (2000): 63–87.

Kim, Young-Rae. *Interest-Group Politics and Interest-Based Conflicts*. [In Korean.] Seoul, Korea: Hanul, 1997.

———. "Restoring the Values of Democracy and Civil Society." [In Korean.] *NGO Research* 5, no. 1 (2007): 1–25.

Ko, Jeong-Ae. "Erosion of Democracy after the Candlelight Protests: The Elite of the Pro-Democracy Student Movement Are the Problem." *JoongAng Ilbo*, August 7, 2020. https://www.joongang.co.kr/article/23843114.

Koo, Hagen. "Strong State and Contentious Society." In *State and Society in Contemporary Korea*, edited by Hagen Koo, 231–50. Ithaca: Cornell University Press, 1993.

Korea Institute of Public Administration. *Korea Social Integration Survey 2014*. [In Korean.] https://www.kipa.re.kr/site/kipa/research/selectReList.do?seSubCode=BIZ017A001.

———. *Korea Social Integration Survey 2018*. [In Korean.] https://www.kipa.re.kr/site/kipa/research/selectReList.do?seSubCode=BIZ017A001.

———. *Korea Social Integration Survey 2019*. [In Korean.] https://www.kipa.re.kr/site/kipa/research/selectReList.do?seSubCode=BIZ017A001.

Ooi, Giok Ling. "Civil Society and the Urban Environment." In *Cities and the Environment: New Approaches for Eco-Societies*, edited by Takashi Inoguchi, Edward Newman, and Glen Paoletto. (New York: United Nations University Press, 1999).

Mainwaring, Scott, and Fernando Bizarro. "The Fates of Third-Wave Democracies." *Journal of Democracy* 30, no. 1 (January 2019): 99–113.

"Nine Blue House Aides, Three Ministers, Nineteen Ruling Party Members: Civil Society in Power." *Chosun Ilbo*, June 2, 2020. https://www.chosun.com/site/data/html_dir/2020/06/02/2020060200103.html.

Park, Sang-Hoon. "General Election Civic Movement: Korea's Democracy and the Emergence of a New Social Movement." [In Korean.] *Graduate Journal of the Hankuk University of Foreign Studies* (2000).

Peters, B. Guy, and Jon Pierre, eds. *Politicization of the Civil Service in Comparative Perspective: The Quest for Control*. London: Routledge, 2004.

"Reflections on Ten Years of the Kim Dae-Jung & Roh Moo-Hyun Administrations: CSOs Stained by Political Power." [In Korean.] *Donga Ilbo*, January 4, 2008. https://www.donga.com/news/Politics/article/all/20080104/8529887/1.

Rosenblum, Nancy L. "Civil Societies: Liberalism and the Moral Uses of Pluralism." *Social Research* 61, no. 3 (Fall 1994): 539–62.

Salamon, Lester M. "The Rise of the Nonprofit Sector." *Foreign Affairs* 73, no. 4 (1994): 109–22.

———. *America's Nonprofit Sector: A Primer*. Washington, DC: The Foundation Center, 1999.

Seong, Kyoung-Ryung. "Civil Society and Democratic Consolidation in Korea, 1987–1996: Great Achievement and Remaining Problems." [In Korean.] Paper presented at the Conference on

"Consolidating Democracy in South Korea," Korea University Ilmin International Research Institute, 1996.

Shin, Gi-Wook. "Korean Democracy Is Sinking under the Guise of the Rule of Law." Walter H. Shorenstein Asia-Pacific Research Center, April 2020. https://fsi.stanford.edu/news/korean-democracy-sinking-under-guise-rule-law.

Shin, Gi-Wook, and Paul Y. Chang, eds. *South Korean Social Movements: From Democracy to Civil Society*. Milton Park: Routledge, 2011.

Song, Ho-Keun. "Democratization of Korea's Society: State-Civil Society Relations." [In Korean.] In *The Dynamic Relationship between Political and Social Democratization: International Comparative Research*. Chuncheon, Korea: Hallym University Center for Social Research, 1996.

Weigle, Marcia A., and Jim Butterfield. "Civil Society in Reforming Communist Regimes: The Logic of Emergence." *Comparative Politics* 25, no. 1 (October 1992): 1–23.

"Why Is There a Crisis in Civic Movements? 46 percent Point to Rightward Shift of Society." [In Korean.] *Hankyoreh*, March 22, 2007. https://www.hani.co.kr/arti/society/society_general/198139.html.

CHAPTER FIVE

The Politicization of the Judiciary in Korea

Challenges in Maintaining the Balance of Power

Seongwook Heo

Four years have passed since the inauguration of President Moon Jae-In on May 10, 2017. As other chapters of this volume discuss, there are many signs of "democratic decay" in Korean society and politics. Important developments in the judiciary are indicative of two unsettling trends under the current administration: the politicization of the judiciary and the judicialization of politics. The former refers to judges deciding cases in courts along partisan lines, and the latter refers to courts increasingly addressing public policy questions and political controversies (e.g., election processes or scrutiny of executive branch behavior).

These trends are not unique to Korea. Most advanced countries have undergone similar experiences during the process of democratic development. They are not entirely new to Korea either. Nonetheless, these trends have become more salient in Korea following the impeachment of former president Park Geun-Hye in 2017 and the unprecedented arrest of former chief justice Yang Seung-Tae, whose trial is ongoing as of this writing in September 2021.

It is therefore critical to reconsider the events of the past four years and their impact on major Supreme Court cases from the perspective of democracy, rule of law, and the separation of powers. This chapter examines key events and cases that reflect the politicization of the judiciary and the judicialization of politics between 2017 and 2021 and discusses their implications for Korean democracy.

Background and Recent Political Context

Before examining specific court rulings issued during the Moon administration, this section provides an overview of judicial institutions in Korea and recent political events during the Moon administration as they relate to the judiciary. In particular, the administration's campaign to "eradicate deep-rooted evils" has given rise to worrying developments in the courts.

Constitutional provisions

Like that of many other developed democracies, the Constitution of the Republic of Korea strictly prescribes the independence of judicial power:

Article 101
1. Judicial power shall be vested in courts composed of judges.

Article 103
Judges shall rule independently according to their conscience and in conformity with the Constitution and the law.

Article 105
1. The term of office of the chief justice shall be six years and he or she shall not be reappointed.
2. The term of office of the justices of the Supreme Court shall be six years and they may be reappointed as prescribed by law.

It is important to note that the term of a Supreme Court justice is six years, while the president has a single five-year term. The one-year difference is intentional. By design, the Constitution ensures that judicial power is not fully subordinated to prevailing political trends during a certain period.

Another unique feature of Korea's Constitution is that it creates a dual system featuring both a Supreme Court and a Constitutional Court. This is starkly different from the U.S. judicial system, in which the Supreme Court deals with the judicial review of constitutionality. It is also different from the German judicial system, in which the Constitutional Court is the highest court in the land, given that the judicial decisions of the general court are reviewable by the Constitutional Court.

In Korea, the Constitutional Court is the highest court charged with reviewing the constitutionality of legislation and actions taken by government agencies. However, general court decisions cannot be reviewed by the Constitutional Court. The Supreme Court is the highest court in general civil, criminal, and administrative matters. Suffice to say, this dual structure was the result of a concerted effort to strike a balance of power between the judiciary and the political sphere.[1]

The impeachment of former president Park and its impact on the composition of the Supreme Court

The term of former president Park Geun-Hye was supposed to last until February 2018. During that term, she was due to nominate a new chief justice and four additional justices of the Supreme Court. Because she was impeached on March 10, 2017, however, those appointments were transferred to President Moon, enabling him to nominate thirteen out of fourteen Supreme Court justices during his term. The situation of the Constitutional Court was no different. Due to Park's impeachment, Moon had the opportunity to compose the Constitutional Court almost in its totality, including the chief justice. Even though the independence of the judiciary is strictly prescribed in the Constitution, the executive branch tends to appoint judges who share its political and ideological preferences to the highest court. The Blue House typically resorts to so-called court packing to alter the composition of the courts in its favor. However, no administration has had the opportunity to alter the courts' composition as much as Moon's.

Many advanced countries, including the United States, have sought to prevent this outcome by establishing institutional and conventional safeguards to protect judicial independence.

In the United States, after the death of Justice Antonin Scalia in February 2016, President Barack Obama sought to nominate a successor before stepping down from power in January 2017. However, he was unable to do so because of institutional constraints and prevailing norms. Obama did not have the time or the political clout to push through the Senate nomination process for Merrick Garland, who was

1 There is an important institutional history behind this judicial structure, which is beyond the scope of this chapter. For an extensive discussion of this topic, see Sung Nak-In, *Constitutional Law* [in Korean], 17th ed. (Seoul, Korea: Bobmunsa, 2017), 757–62.

later appointed as the Biden administration's attorney general. The vacant Supreme Court position was later filled by Justice Neil Gorsuch, who was nominated by President Donald Trump. This is one example of how constitutional and normative constraints on the executive branch limit its ability to shape the composition of the Supreme Court in U.S. politics.[2]

From the very beginning, President Moon sought to mold the Supreme Court and the Constitutional Court in line with the political and ideological preferences of his administration. In particular, he heavily recruited justices from liberal lawyers' groups, including the *Wooribeop* Study Group (WSG), the International Human Rights Law Study Group (IHRLSG), and Lawyers for a Democratic Society (LDS; commonly called *Minbyeon*), all of which are well known for their liberal views.[3] In fact, Moon himself was a former member of the LDS.

As of March 2021, among the eleven Supreme Court justices nominated by President Moon, including Chief Justice Kim Myeong-Soo, more than half were from these three groups. Moreover, among the eight Constitutional Court justices nominated by President Moon, including Chief Justice Yoo Nam-Seok, five justices were from these three groups. This ideological leaning in the composition of the Supreme Court and the Constitutional Court is unprecedented, and it could easily lead to the politicization of the judiciary and even an erosion of the separation of powers. It has already resulted in new rulings on politically sensitive cases, with significant repercussions for Korean society and politics.[4]

Moon's campaign to eradicate "deep-rooted evil" in the judiciary

The Moon administration went even further by appointing Kim Hyeong-Yeon, a sitting judge, to a senior position in the Blue House. Public prosecutors have been appointed to such positions in the past,

2 It should be noted that Trump upended these constraints when he nominated Amy Coney Barrett to the Supreme Court immediately before the 2020 presidential election.

3 WSG and IHRLSG are study groups composed of sitting judges who share politically liberal ideas. LDS is an association of liberal lawyers outside the court.

4 For a detailed analysis, see Lee Yoo-Jeong and Lee Soo-Jeong, "Constitutional Court Rulings Decided by the Same 4 Progressive Justices + 1 in 32 of 33 Cases" [in Korean], *JoongAng Ilbo*, March 23, 2021, https://news.joins.com/article/24017996.

and this practice has been widely criticized. Kim's appointment was the first time that a sitting judge was appointed to such a position since the end of the military regime in Korea in 1987.

Kim was a key member of the IHRLSG and joined the Blue House as a secretary to the president for legal affairs. He was presumed to be closely involved in the Moon administration's campaign to "eradicate deep-rooted evil" in the judiciary. He was succeeded by Kim Young-Shik, a judge who had just retired from the bench. These two appointments severely undermined the principle of separation of powers and judicial independence.

The early days of the Moon administration were characterized by harsh investigations aimed at former government officials, including former presidents Park and Lee Myung-Bak. Major figures of the judiciary, including the former chief justice and justices of the Supreme Court and many other senior judges, could not escape investigation and conviction.[5] Former chief justice Yang was arrested on forty-seven charges relating to actions taken during his term in office and is currently facing trial as of September 2021.

Many other judges who had served as staff members for the chief justice at the Judicial Administration Office were also investigated and convicted.[6] In addition, more than one hundred judges were summoned by prosecutors as persons of interest or witnesses.[7] This is unprecedented in Korea's judicial history. Even under military dictatorships, investigations and convictions of this magnitude against incumbent judges did not take place.

Of course, judges are not exempt from the rule of law. They should be tried and punished if they are found guilty. However, considering the constitutional importance of judicial independence, the criminal

---

5 Lim Jae-Woo, "Former Chief Justice Yang Seung-Tae Arrested and Indicted, Former Supreme Court Justices Park Byeong-Dae and Go Yeong-Han Also Indicted" [in Korean], *Hankyoreh*, February 11, 2019, http://www.hani.co.kr/arti/society/society_general/881622.html.

6 The Judicial Administration Office is an office in the Supreme Court that oversees the administration of the judicial system. Unlike the U.S. judicial system, administrative matters are handled by judges in that office under the concentrated authority of the chief justice. Generally, elite judges are recruited to this office, and these judges do not open their courtroom while serving in this office.

7 "Remaining Investigations Regarding the Alleged Abuse of Judicial Authority: Taking Aim at 100 Judges before Looking Elsewhere" [in Korean], *Newsis*, February 11, 2019, https://newsis.com/view/?id=NISX20190211_0000554680&cid=10201.

prosecution of judges following a shift in political power, especially in the "revolutionary" atmosphere after the candlelight protests and impeachment, should have been handled with the utmost caution.

If criminal investigations against judges are tied to internal power struggles in the courts between the traditional elite group of judges and a progressive, ideological faction of judges, these investigations are a reason for serious concern.[8] Moreover, three judges who took leading roles in attacking the former chief justice cast aside their robes and became candidates for the ruling Democratic Party of Korea in the April 2020 National Assembly elections.[9] As discussed below, one of these former judges has spearheaded the impeachment of a sitting senior judge. These developments pose a grave threat to the principle of judicial independence in Korea.

The Judicialization of Politics and the Politicization of the Judiciary in Korea

Under Korea's authoritarian regimes, few politically important cases were sent to the court for judicial review.[10] Instead, they were mostly dealt with by political leaders through informal means. After democratization in 1987 and especially with the start of the new millennium in 2000, Korean politics became more open and participatory. Many new

---

8 Toward the end of former chief justice Yang's term in office, there was tension between the traditional elite group of judges at the Judicial Administration Office and the group of liberal judges. The members of IHRLSG voiced dissent against Chief Justice Yang's policies, which included an effort to reform the appeals system to the Supreme Court. This tension ruptured after one judge in the IHRLSG claimed that the Judicial Administration Office had compiled a "blacklist" of liberal judges. After Moon was elected as president, this issue led to the prosecution of former chief justice Yang and many other judges at the Judicial Administration Office. The judge in the IHRLSG who first raised this issue was later elected as a legislator for the ruling party. For further details, see Jeong Joon-Yeong, "A Heavier Burden for the Chief Justice: The 'Blacklist' Investigation Deepens Conflict and Mistrust" [in Korean], *Chosun Ilbo*, May 26, 2018, https://www.chosun.com/site/data/html_dir/2018/05/26/2018052601309.html.

9 Gi-Wook Shin, "South Korea's Democratic Decay," *Journal of Democracy* 31, no. 3 (July 2020): 100–14.

10 For more on the judicialization of politics and the politicization of the judiciary in Korea, see Seongwook Heo, "Politics and the Law—A Positive Analysis of Statutory Interpretation" [in Korean], *Seoul National University Law Review* 46, no. 2 (June 2005): 344–76.

groups and individuals made themselves heard in the formal political sphere. This provided more transparency to politics, which was a positive development for Korean democracy.

At the same time, those who had failed to attain a majority in elections began to bring political cases to court. This marked the beginning of the "judicialization of politics"—the pursuit of political objectives by judicial means. Two cases brought before the Constitutional Court—the impeachment of former president Roh Moo-Hyun (2003–08) and a 2004 suit opposing the constitutionality of moving the capital city from Seoul to Sejong—were the most prominent examples of this trend.

While the Constitutional Court's decisions in these two cases invited a great deal of debate and even some controversy, both from academic and political circles, they were largely seen as positive. With these cases, many political issues and decisions came under the purview of democratic politics, given the possibility of judicial review by the courts.[11]

After seeing that major political issues could be sent to the judiciary and be decided upon by judges, politicians and civic groups alike became more interested in the nomination process for the judiciary. Ideological groupings of judges began to form inside the courts and voice positions on political issues. With the end of the military dictatorship in 1987, many liberal activists returned to university campuses, took the bar examination, and became judges. Many maintained their political and ideological preferences, and they created or joined liberal judges' groups like the WSG or the IHRLSG. Of course, judges dealing with political cases cannot be completely neutral. However, it is a different matter when judges create factions within the court and take collective action based on common political views.

All of the above developments point to the "politicization of the judiciary." Given these trends, one of the main responsibilities of the chief justice of the Supreme Court was to protect the court's political independence. Several chief justices, from the early 2000s onward, tried to do so by establishing and building up the Supreme Court's main administrative office, which was filled with elite judges. In Korea, as elsewhere, the judiciary attracts an extraordinarily talented and brilliant group of individuals. The elite judges who staffed the Judicial Administration Office were extremely devoted and efficient. Until the mid-2010s, the Korean judicial system selected judges from among elite lawyers who had graduated from the Judicial Research and Education

11 Heo, "Politics and the Law, 344–47.

Institution with the highest scores. In Korea, everyone who passed the judicial exam had to attend this institution for two years.[12] Under this system, relatively young lawyers in their twenties could become judges without any prior experience as attorneys. They learned practical skills and built their knowledge of judicial trials from their seniors through an apprenticeship system. Combined with a very selective and merit-based promotion scheme, this system provided a solid foundation for the bureaucracy within the judiciary.

Combined with the bureaucratic system of the court, the Judicial Administration Office gave "emperor-like" superpowers, in the words of some observers, to the chief justice. Authority over the court's budget and the promotion of judges was concentrated in the hands of the chief justice through this office. This raised concerns about the fairness of trials, not only from outside the court, but also from within. As noted above, this office became a major target of the campaign to "eradicate deep-rooted evils" in the judiciary.

Major Cases in the Supreme Court and Lower Courts

The new composition of the Supreme Court and the Constitutional Court under the Moon administration predictably led to new rulings in politically sensitive cases. Although it is still premature to conduct a thorough analysis of these cases, this section offers an outline of major trends at the Supreme Court and the lower courts. The Moon administration's practices of "court packing" have been mainly focused on the Supreme Court. In the lower courts, sitting judges are essentially maintaining their portfolios. Thus, with few exceptions, the lower court decisions discussed below are better understood as examples of the judicialization of politics rather than the politicization of the judiciary.

Supreme Court cases

The following cases are examples of major decisions by the newly composed Supreme Court that dealt with politically sensitive issues. These decisions are controversial because they employed different legal

12 This system was abolished in 2007 with the introduction of a U.S.-style law school system, along with a new bar exam system.

rationales compared to past Supreme Court decisions. They also sometimes relied on unusual legal rationales to justify their conclusions.

THE CASE OF FORCED WORKERS DURING JAPANESE COLONIAL RULE (SUPREME COURT DECISION 2013DA61381, DELIVERED OCTOBER 30, 2018)

This case addressed whether Japanese corporations with origins in companies that had been complicit in war crimes during World War II were liable for damages to the plaintiffs, Koreans who had worked as laborers during the war. During the colonial period, especially toward the end of World War II, many Koreans moved to Japan and were hired by Japanese companies that produced war materials. After Japan's surrender in 1945, these workers returned to Korea with unpaid wages.

This case involved several difficult legal issues that had to be resolved for the plaintiffs to win damages against the defendant company. The first was whether the identity of the defendant company could be understood as being the same as that of the old company that had produced war materials in the 1940s. Considering that the original companies were dissolved during the Allied occupation of Japan under General MacArthur after the war and the current defendant company was newly formed, there were complicated legal considerations on this point. The second was whether monetary obligations between the parties had already been resolved by the San Francisco Peace Treaty of 1951 and the Korea-Japan Claims Agreement of 1965. The third was whether the plaintiffs could prove the existence and amount of credit against the defendant company that had not yet been paid, and if not, whether they could claim compensation for psychological damages. The Supreme Court accepted the first and third issues in favor of the plaintiffs, and its main arguments and considerations were focused on the second question. The Supreme Court *en banc* decided that the defendant company was liable, with the majority opinion stating that the plaintiffs' claim had neither been included in nor resolved by the San Francisco Peace Treaty of 1951 or the Korea-Japan Claims Agreement of 1965.[13]

---

13 One noteworthy but unfortunate story about this case is that of former chief justice Yang who is, as of September 2021, facing trial on the charge that he deliberately delayed the trial and decision of this case in collusion with the Ministry of Foreign Affairs to gain political support for reforming the appeals system to the

The underlying rationale of the majority opinion was as follows. First, the claims of the plaintiffs are against the inhumane activities of a Japanese company, which was based on the Japanese government's illegal colonization of the Korean Peninsula and war of aggression.

Second, the aim of the Korea-Japan Claims Agreement of 1965 was to politically resolve the financial and civil credit/debt issues between the two countries following the San Francisco Peace Treaty of 1951, not to resolve individual and nationwide damages related to Japan's illegal colonization. Third, it is unclear whether the money paid by the Japanese government to the Korean government under Article 1 of the 1965 agreement, for purposes of economic cooperation, can be legally understood as having compensational relations with the claims referenced in Article 2. Lastly, considering that the Japanese government was still denying the illegality of colonization during the negotiations for the 1965 agreement, it is difficult to argue that the plaintiffs' claims are covered under the agreement.[14]

The Japanese government disagreed with this decision on the grounds that all the claims of the plaintiffs had been included in and resolved by the 1965 agreement. Moreover, the Japanese government also argued that this decision differed from the position of the Korean government under President Roh Moo-Hyun, who compensated the plaintiffs with a budget prepared under a special legislation.

Following this decision, district court judges allowed the plaintiffs to seize the assets of the defendant company that were in Korea. This brought the Korea-Japan bilateral relationship to its worst point in

---

Supreme Court. At that time, Yang was devoted to reforming the appeals system for the Supreme Court. The Korean Supreme Court, composed of fourteen justices including the chief justice, then dealt with more than forty thousand cases per year. In comparison, the U.S. Supreme Court, composed of nine justices, delivers about eighty decisions a year. Yang hoped to create a new appellate court to lighten the caseload, allowing the Supreme Court to concentrate on a smaller number of significant cases. To implement these reforms, the Supreme Court needed support from both the Blue House and the National Assembly.

14 There was also a separate opinion from three justices. They argued that the plaintiffs' claims were covered by the 1965 agreement, but there had not been clear agreement between the two governments regarding the extinction of individual claims. These justices stated that the agreement only waives the right to diplomatic protection. Thus, the plaintiffs could sue the defendant company for damages. Against the majority and separate opinions, there was another dissenting opinion from two justices. It stated that individual claims and rights were also included in the agreement. Therefore, the plaintiffs could not sue the Japanese company.

the postwar period.[15] Both countries took retaliatory measures, ranging from economic sanctions to immigration measures. The Japanese government restricted the export of materials that were critical to the production of semiconductors in Korea. In return, the Korean government took actions to effectively terminate its General Security of Military Information Agreement with Japan, an agreement that was essential for the sharing of military information between the two countries.

On June 7, 2021, the Seoul Central District Court dismissed another plaintiffs' suit against sixteen Japanese companies. This suit, in terms of key facts and legal issues, was very similar to the case that led to the Supreme Court decision discussed above. However, the presiding judge in this case explicitly stated that this decision followed the minority opinion of the Supreme Court's decision. Lower courts are not obligated to follow every Supreme Court decision. Nevertheless, considering that the Supreme Court's *en banc* decision was delivered after lengthy societal and judicial debates, the Seoul Central District Court's 2021 decision came as a surprise. It is yet too early to accurately evaluate these decisions from an academic perspective, but these cases can surely be counted as salient examples of the politicization of the judiciary in Korea.

THE CASE OF GYEONGGI PROVINCE GOVERNOR LEE JAE-MYUNG (SUPREME COURT DECISION 2019DO13328, DELIVERED JULY 16, 2020)

This is a criminal case concerning former governor Lee Jae-Myung, who, at the time of this writing, is a leading presidential contender for the ruling party. He was charged with violating Article 250 of the Public Official Election Act, which prohibits false statements during campaigns for public office. During a televised debate in his campaign for governor, Lee was asked by the opposing candidate whether he had used his authority as the mayor of Seongnam city to force his brother to be hospitalized at a psychiatric hospital. Lee was charged with falsely stating no in response to that question during a televised debate.

At the appellate court, he was sentenced to a monetary penalty of ₩3,000,000 on the grounds that his statement was false. The Public

15 Jo Ki-Won and Park Min-Hee, "Japan Voices Opposition to Ruling in Forced Labor Case, Pressuring the Korean Government on All Fronts" [in Korean], *Hankyoreh*, November 6, 2018, http://www.hani.co.kr/arti/politics/diplomacy/869133.html.

Official Election Act prescribes that a candidate forfeits the election when sentenced to a monetary penalty of more than ₩1,000,000. Therefore, if the appellate court's decision had been upheld by the Supreme Court, he would have been deprived of his governorship and barred from running for public office for five years.

According to Korea's Criminal Procedure Act, each party can only argue about the legal issues of the appellate court decision, not about fact-finding or the weighing of penalties. Therefore, the odds that the verdict would be overturned by the Supreme Court were not high. According to well-established precedents, his debate statement met the bar to violate the Article 250 requirement of the Public Official Election Act.

Led by Chief Justice Kim, the Supreme Court *en banc* remanded the case to the appellate court with the intent of not guilty. The opinions of the justices were split. The majority of seven justices voted not guilty, and the minority of five justices voted guilty. Five justices of the eight nominated by President Moon, and including the chief justice, voted not guilty on the grounds that Governor Lee's statement was not an "actively" false statement; rather, he was passively saying no to his opponent's question. However, the minority view pointed out that his denial was still a false statement according to the verified facts. At the remanded appellate court, Governor Lee was found not guilty, and this decision was confirmed. According to Korea's Criminal Procedure Act, the remanded court is obligated to follow the Supreme Court's remanding opinion.

It is not yet clear how much political reasoning was involved in this case, but the resulting decision has already had a great impact on Korean politics, considering that former governor Lee is a leading contender for president.[16] Moreover, the general attitude of the Supreme Court toward political issues appears to have changed subtly but significantly after President Moon's reconstitution of the courts, and it is more actively involved in political decisions.

One way of justifying the new majority opinion in Governor Lee's case would be to place greater emphasis on the democratic legitimacy of elections. Korea's election laws are extremely strict in their regulation of campaign finances and false statements. Given the complex political realities of election campaigns, which cannot rigorously adhere

16 *Editor's note:* On October 10, 2021, Lee Jae-Myung was confirmed as the ruling party's presidential candidate for the March 2022 election.

to all these regulations, such laws can enable prosecutorial agencies to challenge election results. This undermines one of the fundamental pillars of democracy. Even with this justification, however, the legal rationale of the majority opinion is far from robust. During the gubernatorial campaign, the controversy surrounding the hospitalization of Lee's brother was hotly debated before the television debate. It is difficult to argue that Lee passively said no in response to an unexpected question from the other candidates.

THE CASE OF THE TEACHERS AND EDUCATION WORKERS UNION (SUPREME COURT DECISION 2016DU32992, DELIVERED SEPTEMBER 3, 2020)

The Labor Union Act of Korea states that when a union accepts a person who does not work in the company as its member, it cannot be legally protected by the act. Until 2013, the Korean Teachers and Education Workers Union (KTU) included as members those who had been fired from their jobs due to illegal activities. The Ministry of Education ordered a correction of this status twice, in 2010 and in 2012, but the union did not comply. Then, on October 24, 2013, the Ministry of Education delivered a notice that the KTU was no longer a legally protected union under the Labor Union Act.[17]

The KTU requested the cancellation of this notice. After being rejected by the ministry, it brought the case to court. The district court and the appellate court rejected the claim on the basis that the notice was a legal action under the statute. The union then brought the issue to the Constitutional Court, claiming that this article of the Labor Union Act was unconstitutional. However, the Constitutional Court likewise rejected the union's claim, confirming the article's constitutionality. The plaintiff brought the case to the Supreme Court, claiming that the Ministry of Education's decision was illegal.

Within this context, the general expectation regarding this case at the Supreme Court was that the claim would be rejected again. Unexpectedly, however, the Supreme Court *en banc* accepted the KTU's claim, cancelled the ministry's notice, and remanded the case to the

---

17 This "notice" was different from an "order" in regular administrative decisions. While an "order" has an administrative effect by itself, a "notice" is not understood as having its own administrative effect other than a procedural effect. In this case, the effect on the legal status of the KTU had already been decided by the statutory requirement. In this context, the legal identity of a "notice" became a critical issue in this case.

appellate court. Another surprise was the legal reasoning the Supreme Court employed in accepting the union's claim. The majority opinion reasoned that under the "non-delegation doctrine," there should have been delegation from the statute not only about the qualifications necessary to be considered a legal union, but also about the notification process for the delivery of the notice to be legally valid. Against this majority opinion, there were dissenting views from the other four justices. In general, it is common for a statute to stipulate the requirements for a certain legal status, and thereafter, for administrative legislation to prescribe the details of the process. This Supreme Court decision conflicts with precedents. The minority opinion took the conventional position and argued that the Labor Union Act does not violate the "non-delegation doctrine."

After the decision, there was also debate in legal circles regarding the status of Chief Justice Kim. Korea's Civil Procedure Act prohibits a judge from considering a case that he or she has been previously involved in. Of the thirteen justices, Justice Kim Seon-Soo had recused himself from the case because he had been involved in the litigation of this case as a lawyer representing the union before being appointed to the Supreme Court.[18] However, Chief Justice Kim remained as the presiding judge even though he was involved in a related case five years earlier, ruling in favor of the KTU.[19] The KTU is a powerful actor in Korea's progressive politics, and the judges appointed by President Moon went against precedent to open the way for the KTU to regain its legally protected status as a labor union.

Lower court cases

The following are examples of major decisions by the lower courts (district and appellate courts) that address political issues. Considering that "court packing" has not yet had a substantial impact on these lower courts, these cases are examples of the judicialization of politics in the sense that political issues are brought to the court for judicial review.

---

18 He had been a leading figure at the LDS and had no career as a judge before being nominated as a justice.

19 For further details, see Yang Eun-Gyeong, "The Controversial Role of Chief Justice Kim, Who Had Ruled in Favor of the KTU" [in Korean], *Chosun Ilbo*, September 7, 2020, https://www.chosun.com/national/court_law/2020/09/07/JMJFTPPQQBATVDHEFZJEWMNVQE/.

THE VALIDITY OF DISCIPLINARY MEASURES TAKEN AGAINST PROSECUTOR GENERAL YOON SEOK-YOUL BY JUSTICE MINSTER CHOO MI-AE

Korean conservatives satirically note that the term of Justice Minister Choo Mi-Ae was devoted to attacking and ousting former prosecutor general Yoon Seok-Youl. Choo suspended Yoon and subjected him to disciplinary measures on the grounds that he had been delinquent in carrying out his duties as a prosecutor, had involved himself in politics by not actively requesting to have his name removed from polling for the next presidential election, and had illegally gathered private information on judges. It is widely suspected that her attempt to remove him from office was politically motivated because he was investigating key figures in the Moon administration.

The administrative court dismissed all of Choo's claims against Yoon and accepted Yoon's request to suspend the disciplinary measures ordered by Choo in December 2020. The court ruled that there was not enough evidence to suspend Yoon, and that Yoon could possibly face irreversible damages from his suspension.

Choo's actions are a clear example of the judicialization of politics in Korea. It should be noted, however, that the administrative court's decision went against the wishes of the ruling party and severely weakened Choo's leadership. She left office before Yoon, who quit his job in March 2021 to protest the sweeping prosecutorial reforms proposed by the ruling party. He has since declared his candidacy for the next presidential election as a member of the opposition People Power Party.[20]

CLAIMS OF MONETARY DAMAGES BY SO-CALLED COMFORT WOMEN AGAINST THE JAPANESE GOVERNMENT

In January 2021, a panel of judges at the Seoul Central District Court accepted the request of so-called comfort women against the Japanese government for monetary damages. The plaintiffs claimed that the Japanese government forcibly recruited them as "comfort women" for the Japanese military. The court accepted the plaintiffs' claims and ordered compensation for psychological damages.

The legal reasoning of this decision essentially follows that of the forced laborer case discussed above, but this case differs significantly

---

20 *Editor's note*: Yoon Seok-Youl won the Korean presidential election in March 2022.

in that it directly concerns a foreign government. In this setting, the rule of sovereign immunity applies as a basic principle of international law. Nonetheless, it can be charged that the court made this decision for political reasons, cognizant of the state of bilateral relations between Seoul and Tokyo. The enforceability of the ruling is already being questioned and debated among lawyers. In this sense, this case can be counted as another example of the politicization of the judiciary.

Another ongoing development is that of another panel of judges at the Seoul Central District Court, which delivered the opposite verdict in response to the same request from different plaintiffs in April 2021. This new panel of judges accepted sovereign immunity as a basic principle of international law. This issue will be finalized at the Supreme Court.

THE CRIMINAL CASE AGAINST SAMSUNG CHAIRMAN LEE JAE-YONG

Lee Jae-Yong was found guilty and imprisoned in January 2021 on the charge that he had illegally provided money and horses to former president Park and her friend Choi Soon-Sil, who was deemed to share "common economic interests" with Park. Even though former president Park did not directly receive any money from Samsung, the prosecutors devised the concept of "common economic interests" in this case, which the court accepted as valid. During the last trial at the High Court, the presiding judge ordered the defendant to create a "Samsung compliance committee," with the understanding that it could be considered a mitigating factor in the court's sentencing.

Some commentators have criticized the decision on the grounds that the court was unduly influenced by political considerations in its sentencing, given Samsung's international and domestic standing. Since the beginning of the Biden administration, the United States has been strongly urging the Korean government, Samsung, and other Korean conglomerates to join forces with other allies against China in the intensifying conflict over semiconductors. In this context, the potential pardoning of Lee was considered politically significant. Additionally, Samsung plays a substantial role in Korea's economy and its politics. The numerous lawsuits and criminal trials surrounding the Lee family, including issues related to the inheritance that former chairman Lee Geon-Hee left to Lee Jae-Yong and his sisters, take on a political character. Lee Jae-Yong was released on parole in August 2021.

THE IMPEACHMENT OF INCUMBENT JUDGE LIM SEONG-GEUN BY THE RULING PARTY IN 2021

At the end of January 2021, the ruling Democratic Party initiated the impeachment of incumbent judge Lim Seong-Geun, who was charged with being involved in alleged misconduct that had occurred under former chief justice Yang. Lim was indicted on the criminal charge that he had tried to influence the defamation case concerning former president Park while working as a supervising judge for criminal cases at the Seoul High Court. The National Assembly, in which the ruling bloc held over 60 percent of the 300 seats, passed a motion to impeach Lim. The case has been moved to the Constitutional Court, which will make a final decision on the impeachment.

Lim's impeachment trial has raised complex legal and political concerns about the independence of the judiciary in Korea and the proper role of the chief justice in defending it. First, even though Lim was found not guilty at the district court trial in February 2020, the ruling party forced through the impeachment motion at the National Assembly in February 2021. One could raise legal questions about whether the impeachment process fully adhered to due process and what the constitutional merits of the impeachment trial would be. Lim was also found not guilty by the appellate court in August 2021. Second, since Lim's term as a judge already expired at the end of February 2021, the impeachment could be considered moot. Third, shortly after the passage of the impeachment motion, a recording of Chief Justice Kim speaking to Lim about his resignation was publicly released. Refusing to accept Lim's resignation, Kim said that due to political maneuvers at the National Assembly to impeach judges who had been involved in the alleged misconduct under former chief justice Yang, he would face heavy criticism if he accepted Lim's resignation. If the recording fully and accurately represents Chief Justice Kim's views, it is direct evidence that the judiciary has been politicized in a profound way. This recording contradicted Chief Justice Kim's statement to the National Assembly and to the public. On October 28, 2021, the Constitutional Court acquitted the case on the grounds that Lim was already retired and thus not subject to impeachment.

Conclusion

It is a legal maxim that a trial must be fair in appearance as well as in substance. It also takes a long time for the judiciary to acquire citizens' trust in its impartiality, and a reputation for reliability. As the judiciary is a branch of government with no sword and no wallet, all it can do to garner trust is to give everyone a fair trial and reach fair decisions. Just one failure in this regard might undermine trust in the judicial system.

In terms of fairness, what has occurred in Korea's judiciary over the past four years is a tragedy—for those directly involved in the cases and for the nation as a whole. Citizens have learned that the judiciary can become a political battlefield, especially following a shift in political power. After seeing that the highest court can be filled with judges who share views with the politicians in power, and witnessing the subsequent impact on judicial decisions, the Korean public considers the judiciary as just another field for fighting dirty political battles. Those who hold political power in the future will make it a priority to reconstitute the court by any means, which may again entail investigation and prosecution for their own ends rather than for the pursuit of justice.

Unfortunately, it could take a long time for the Korean judiciary to regain its authority as the last safeguard for justice and fairness. Nevertheless, I still hope that this chain of events will eventually lead to a brighter future. Korea's remarkable achievements in economic development and democratization cannot solely be attributed to good fortune. The country will surely emerge from the current crisis with a more robust liberal democracy and a strongly independent judiciary.

Bibliography

Heo, Seongwook. "Politics and the Law—A Positive Analysis of Statutory Interpretation." [In Korean.] *Seoul National University Law Review* 46, no. 2 (June 2005): 344–76.

Jeong, Joon-Yeong. "A Heavier Burden for the Chief Justice: The 'Blacklist' Investigation Deepens Conflict and Mistrust." [In Korean.] *Chosun Ilbo*, May 26, 2018. https://www.chosun.com/site/data/html_dir/2018/05/26/2018052601309.html.

Jo, Ki-Won, and Park Min-Hee. "Japan Voices Opposition to Ruling in Forced Labor Case, Pressuring the Korean Government on All

Fronts." [In Korean.] *Hankyoreh*, November 6, 2018. http://www.hani.co.kr/arti/politics/diplomacy/869133.html.

Lee, Yoo-Jeong, and Lee Soo-Jeong. "Constitutional Court Rulings Decided by the Same 4 Progressive Justices + 1 in 32 of 33 Cases." [In Korean.] *JoongAng Ilbo*, March 23, 2021. https://news.joins.com/article/24017996.

Lim, Jae-Woo. "Former Chief Justice Yang Seung-Tae Arrested and Indicted, Former Supreme Court Justices Park Byeong-Dae and Go Yeong-Han Also Indicted." [In Korean.] *Hankyoreh*, February 11, 2019. http://www.hani.co.kr/arti/society/society_general/881622.html.

"Remaining Investigations Regarding the Alleged Abuse of Judicial Authority: Taking Aim at 100 Judges before Looking Elsewhere." [In Korean.] *Newsis*, February 11, 2019. https://newsis.com/view/?id=NISX20190211_0000554680&cid=10201.

Shin, Gi-Wook. "South Korea's Democratic Decay." *Journal of Democracy* 31, no. 3 (July 2020): 100–14.

Sung, Nak-In. *Constitutional Law.* [in Korean], 17th ed. Seoul, Korea: Bobmunsa, 2017.

Yang, Eun-Gyeong. "The Controversial Role of Chief Justice Kim, Who Had Ruled in Favor of the KTU." [In Korean.] *Chosun Ilbo*, September 7, 2020. https://www.chosun.com/national/court_law/2020/09/07/JMJFTPPQQBATVDHEFZJEWMNVQE/.

CHAPTER SIX

Two Divergences in Korea's Economy and Democracy

Regional and Generational Disparities

Jun Ho Jeong and Il-Young Lee

Democratization in 1987 was an important turning point in Korea's political history, and it also had a profound impact on subsequent socioeconomic developments. There has been a widespread recognition that the "1987 system" has hitherto continued to function in Korea. However, there are various interpretations of the 1987 system. A book entitled *The Discourses of the 1987 Political Order*, a compilation of views from various sources, describes several discursive terrains.[1] One contributor points to the dual structure of institutional and noninstitutional politics established since democratization and identifies a periodic cycle of change and stagnation, and of aspirations and disappointments as structural characteristics of the 1987 system. Another claims that before and after democratization, the economic system has transformed from a catch-up economy at the national level into a system that adapts to globalization and East Asian production networks. Yet another view focuses on the political and economic momentum after the 1997 Asian financial crisis, stressing the importance of neoliberalism's introduction to Korea's social changes.

Noting that democracy is closely linked to the economic system, we examine how regional and generational disparities have developed over time and how they have affected and will affect democracy in Korea. Although political scientists such as Choi Jang-Jip point to the absorption of civil society and civic movements into the state as a key

1 Kim Jong-Yeop, *The Discourses of the 1987 Political Order* [in Korean] (Paju, Korea: Changbi Publishers, 2009).

force that weakened the 1987 system,[2] we instead consider the regional and generational disparities that have appeared and worsened since the global financial crisis of 2008. In our view, these disparities are fundamental forces behind the erosion of the 1987 system.

Regional Divergences

The issue of regional disparities has been a key factor in shaping Korea's political landscape. It has been usually discussed in four ways: urban vs. rural, major cities vs. small- and medium-sized cities, the capital region vs. other regions, and the Yeongnam region vs. the Honam region (i.e., the Seoul-Busan corridor vs. other regions). In this chapter we focus on disparities between the capital and other regions, with particular attention to trends that have emerged since the 2010s. Such disparities can be understood in terms of the income gap and power imbalance between Seoul—including the wider capital region—and the rest of the country.

Korea's capital region was formed through the outward expansion of Seoul. Ever since the early stages of economic development in the 1960s, the capital region has been at the forefront of the daily lives of the Korean people due to matters of national security, overpopulation, and the housing problem. While inequality between the Yeongnam and Honam regions still remains a potent force for political mobilization, it is becoming less salient. Rather, the disparity between the capital region and the rest of the country is beginning to manifest itself in the form of a center-periphery power imbalance. This divide gives rise to a difference in both socioeconomic opportunities and identities. This gap, which is the key regional divide in Korea today, has recently shown signs of developing into a problem as serious as the North-South divide in England.

Income and industrial structure

Let us examine this regional disparity using the three measures of aggregate economic income: production, distribution, and expenditure (consumption). A measure of real gross regional domestic product (GRDP) per capita in terms of production income reveals the geographic

2 Choi Jang-Jip, "Reconsidering the Korean Democracy: Crisis and Alternative" [in Korean], *Journal of Korean Politics* 29, no. 2 (2020): 1–26.

distribution of industries in Korea. As indicated in figure 6.1, panel A, regional disparities in real GRDP per capita began to emerge in 1996, just before the Asian financial crisis, and steadily grew until 2011, the last year of the Lee Myung-Bak administration.[3] This can be traced to the difference in productive capacity between industrial clusters. These clusters include both primary material industries and processing and assembly industries—such as electronics, automobiles, semiconductors, petrochemicals, and shipbuilding—that are the flagship industries of Korea's economy.

The prevailing model of export-driven growth, centered on large conglomerates, gave rise to regional production disparities after the 1997 Asian financial crisis. Some conglomerates that survived the restructuring resulting from the crisis have since become competitive on the global stage, and this has been reflected differentially in the productivity of their plants located in the noncapital region. Major manufacturing clusters are located in the capital region, the North and South Chungcheong provinces, South Jeolla Province, Ulsan, and the North and South Gyeongsang provinces. Figure 6.1, panel B, shows that real GRDP per capita is higher than the national average in these manufacturing regions. However, this gap has declined since 2012 as key industries, including the automotive and shipbuilding industries, underwent restructuring.[4]

If a company locates its headquarters in the capital region and its branch plants in other parts of the country, the production income generated through the industrial clusters does not remain in that region. It partly flows to the capital region in the form of employee compensation, operating surplus, and property income. Real gross regional income (GRI) per capita as a measure of distribution income, which accounts for this cross-regional movement of production income, displays a similar trend to that of real GRDP per capita. However, regional disparities in real GRI per capita have been growing since 2015.[5]

3 Some large companies, such as Hanbo Steel, went bankrupt in the mid-1990s following their involvement in political corruption scandals.

4 In 2012, growth in global trade stagnated due to the 2008 global financial crisis and China's shift toward greater domestic insourcing of parts and materials.

5 The Korean economy faced a recession in the early and mid-2010s due to a decline in global trade growth and the restructuring of its shipbuilding and automobile industries. In order to boost the economy, the Park Geun-Hye administration attempted to ease regulations around the real estate market in 2014–15.

FIGURE 6.1 Trends in regional income disparities over time

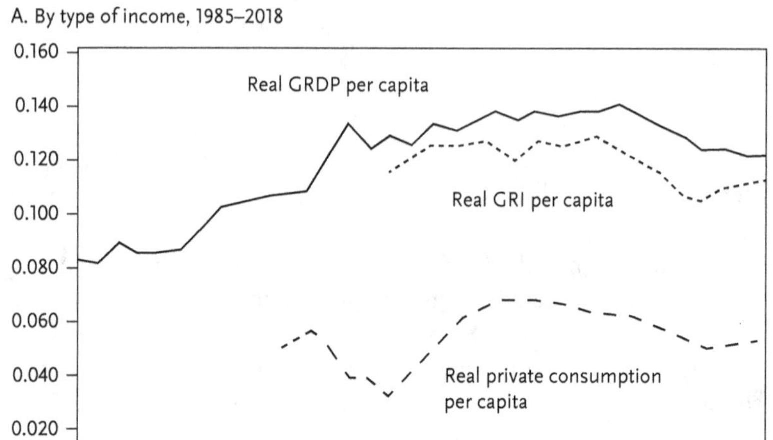

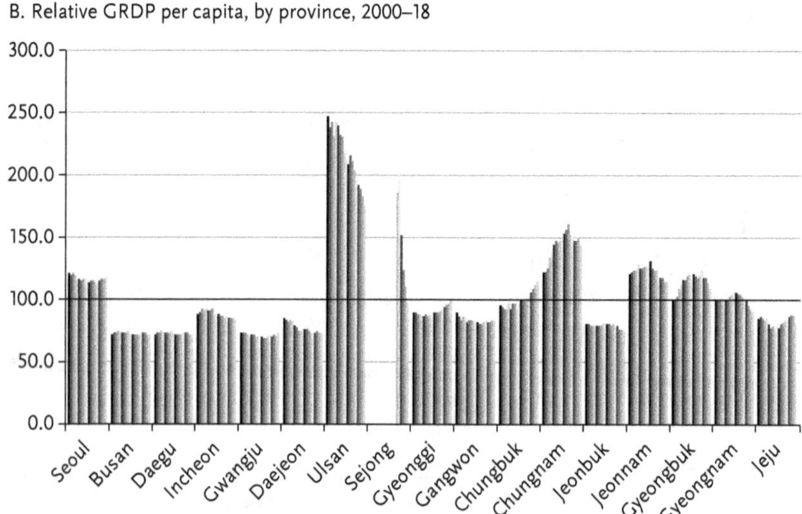

C. Relative GRI per capita, by province, 2000–18

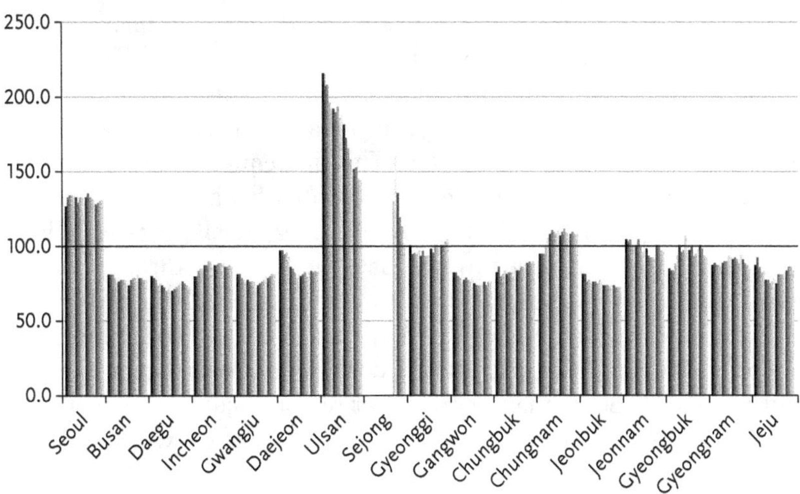

D. Relative private consumption per capita, by province, 2000–18

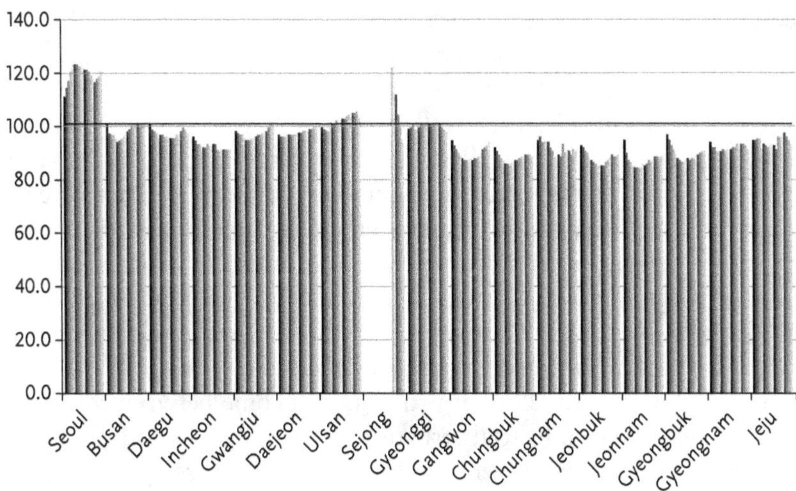

NOTE: Based on real prices in 2015. The province (primary administrative division) is used as the unit of analysis. A cross-regional measure of inequality is calculated using a population-weighted Gini coefficient. The relative level for each province/region is represented using 100 as the national average. GRDP = gross regional domestic product; GRI = gross regional income.
SOURCE: Statistics Korea, http://kosis.kr.

This can be attributed to the relative increase in real GRI per capita for the capital region compared to the rest of the country.

Real private consumption per capita as a measure of expenditure income accounts for taxes and transfers and the effect of financial markets as applied to real GRI per capita. As a result, the difference between regions is substantially smaller. Regional disparities in private consumption decreased following the global financial crisis but appear to be increasing again since 2015. The tightening of regulations on household lending following the 2008 global financial crisis contributed to the temporary decline.[6] However, these regulations were loosened after 2014 in an effort to stimulate the economy through the real estate market. By increasing access to credit, especially in and around Seoul, this policy has once again increased regional disparities in consumption. In particular, real private consumption per capita is significantly higher in Seoul than in any other region (figure 6.1, panel D).

Thus, economic inequality between regions has shown a markedly different trend since the mid-2010s. There has been little change since 2015 in terms of real GRDP per capita, but there has been a shift in terms of both real GRI and private consumption per capita. During the mid-2010s, the Park Geun-Hye administration sought to stimulate the economy through the real estate market. This economic stimulus appears to have exacerbated regional economic disparities in terms of real GRI and private consumption.

Regional income disparities reflect the spatial divisions of labor that arise from the organizational structure of large firms.[7] As shown in figure 6.2, the capital region accounts for 55 to 70 percent of each component of distribution income—employee compensation, operating surplus, and property income. This is substantially larger than the share of the population that resides in the capital region, which is approximately 50 percent. The concentration of distribution income in the capital region has been on the rise since 2015.

As noted above, the flow of production income between regions is strongly related to industrial structure. Between 2000 and 2018, the proportion of primary material industries and processing and assembly industries in a given region explains 77.8 percent of the variation

6 Jeong Jun Ho, "Regional Income Disparities and Risk Sharing in Korea" [in Korean], *Space and Environment* 28, no. 2 (2018): 12–44.

7 Doreen Massey, *Spatial Divisions of Labour: Social Structures and the Geography of Production* (London: Macmillan, 1984).

in income outflow. Large conglomerates operate plants outside of the capital region in these industries, and these plants have essentially no autonomy in their operations.

Because of a downturn in the volume of international trade, foreign value added as a proportion of Korea's exports has fallen since 2011. The capital region's GRI as a share of total GRDP has begun to fall as a result (figure 6.2, panel B). This implies that Korea's system of branch plants is closely tied to international trade and global value chains. The recent decline in the volume of international trade is due to structural factors including the U.S.-China trade war, a dramatic increase in China's self-sufficiency with regard to parts and components, and the residual effects of the global financial crisis. The COVID-19 pandemic is adding fuel to the fire in this regard. Thus, it is unlikely that the institutional and material conditions for expanding exports at the international level will improve in the short term. This implies that the export-driven system of branch plants operated by large conglomerates has, in some ways, reached its limit. Currently, regional disparities in production income are narrowing due to restructuring in existing industrial hubs. However, this trend is likely to reverse as newly emerging industries, including the information technology and biotechnology sectors, become increasingly concentrated in the capital region.

Under the system of branch plants, a portion of production income flows out from noncapital region industrial areas (responsible for "execution") and into the capital region and other major metropolitan areas (responsible for "conception"). This is due to two factors: work-home separation for executives and workers who commute to their working places, and the transfer of operating surpluses from branch plants to headquarters, which are spatially distinct. It is also important to note that real estate and other assets in the capital region and other major metropolitan areas are used as a means to hedge against income shocks. From 2000 to 2018, the total income that flowed into the capital region was ₩1,160.2 trillion (nominal value), of which ₩758.0 trillion came to Seoul. The total income that flowed into the four other metropolitan areas of Busan, Daegu, Gwangju, and Daejeon was ₩305.7 trillion. In the case of Ulsan—a major hub for the automobile, shipbuilding, and chemical industries—₩190 trillion flowed out to other regions. This clearly shows the outflow of income from noncapital regions to the capital region and other major metropolitan areas (figure 6.2, panel D).

This concentration of distribution income in the capital region has effects that extend beyond economic indices. It narrows the gap

FIGURE 6.2 Regional income disparities and income flow trends in regional share, 2000–18

A. By GRI components in capital region

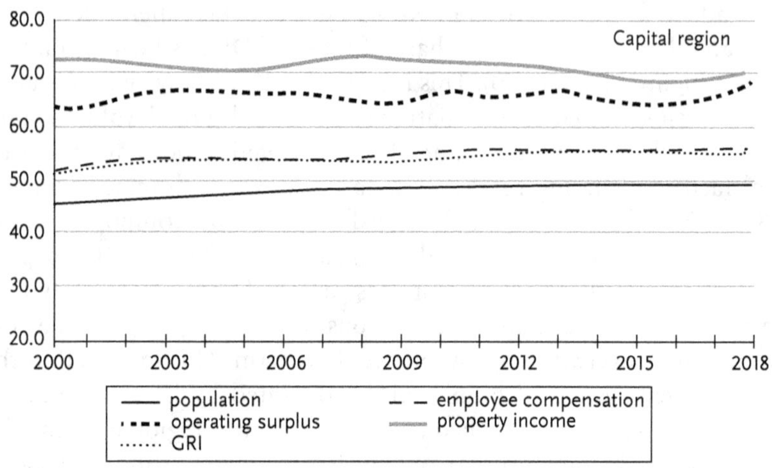

B. Branch plants and changes in the global value chain, and capital region income

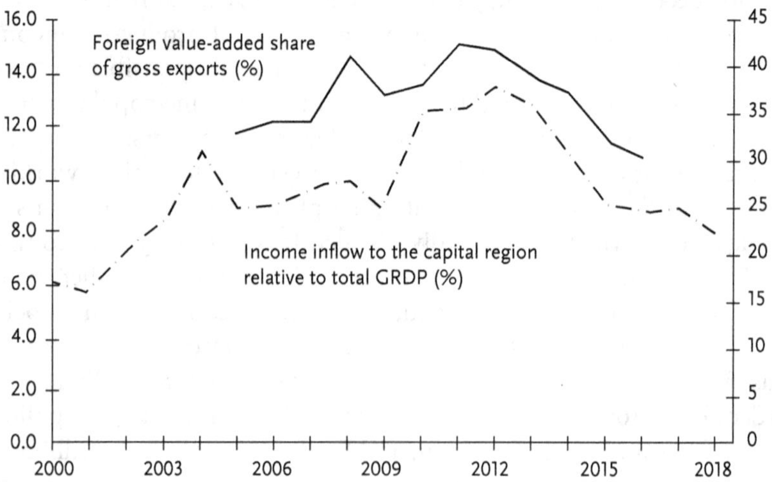

C. Income flow between regions and industrial structure

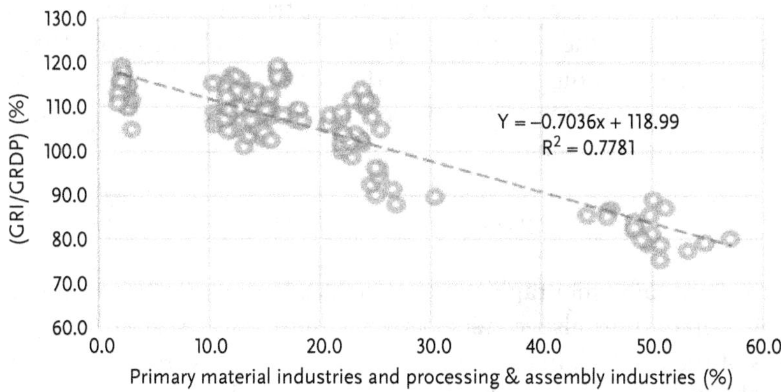

D. Movement of income across regions: amount (nominal) and spatial flow

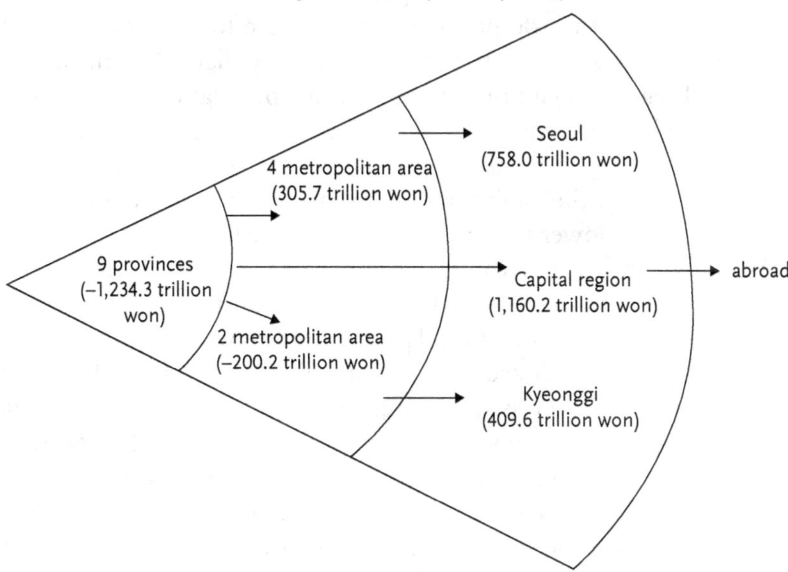

NOTE: "Primary material industries and processing & assembly industries" refers to the sum (regional accounts) of the following industries: coal & oil, chemical products, nonmetal minerals & metal products, electronics & precision instruments, transport equipment, and other manufacturing. The graphs consider four major metropolitan areas (305.7 trillion KRW): Busan, Daegu, Gwangju, Daejeon; two major metropolitan areas (200.2 trillion KRW): Incheon, Ulsan; and nine provinces (1,234.3 trillion KRW): Sejong, Gangwon, N. Chungcheong, S. Chungcheong, N. Jeolla, S. Jeolla, N. Gyeongsang, S. Gyeongsang, Jeju. GRDP = gross regional domestic product; GRI = gross regional income.
SOURCE: Statistics Korea, http://kosis.kr; OECD Statistics, https://stats.oecd.org/.

between GRDP and GRI within the capital region, thereby reducing the imbalance between production and distribution income. Furthermore, it solidifies the geographic hierarchy in which the capital region is at the "commanding heights" of the economy, with spatial separation between companies' headquarters in the capital region and branch plants outside the capital region.[8]

Demographic issues

The severity of demographic issues, such as Korea's low birth rate and aging population, also differs between the capital region and other parts of the country. In an aggressive effort to address regional disparities, the Roh Moo-Hyun administration created the new administrative capital of Sejong and relocated government ministries and public enterprises to that city. It also created "innovation cities" outside the capital region. Still, the concentration of population in the capital region has continued to increase despite these proactive efforts, with over half the population residing in the capital region. As figure 6.3 illustrates, the capital region's share of the working-age population (aged 15–64) has exceeded 50 percent since 2007. The capital region's share of the country's youth (aged 15–24) is also projected to surpass 50 percent in 2022. Conversely, the capital region's share of the elderly population (aged over 65) is lower than in the noncapital regions.

As noted above, the capital region is an economic center that combines the headquarters of key flagship industries and high-tech, knowledge-intensive industries. The division between regular and irregular workers, which arose as a result of labor market reforms after the Asian financial crisis, has become a key axis of socioeconomic conflict in Korea. The proportion of workers under irregular contracts was larger in the capital region than in other regions before the global financial crisis, but this has since reversed. Despite this shift, these statistics indicate that the capital region has many opportunities for individuals to find employment as regular workers.[9]

In terms of the birth rate problem, natural population growth is markedly higher in the capital region than in the noncapital region, even though the two are similar in terms of absolute population size

8 Jeong, "Regional Income Disparities and Risk Sharing in Korea."

9 Nevertheless, the proportion of irregular workers has still been increasing in the capital region since 2014.

(figure 6.3). Natural population growth has steadily declined since the 2000s both in and outside the capital region—low birth rates are a national problem. However, while natural population growth has sharply declined in both regions since 2015, the noncapital region has seen negative growth since 2018. The demographic problems resulting from the low birth rate and an aging population are especially severe outside the capital region.

Net population movement into the capital region has been on the rise since 2015. However, excluding periods of economic crisis, net population movement into the capital region decreased from 1989 to 1997 and from 2002 to 2015. This corresponds to periods in which the system of branch plants in noncapital regions worked well. During periods of economic difficulty, net population movement into the capital region sharply increases due to the relative plentitude of employment opportunities.

Taken together, these regional demographic trends reveal an inflection point in 2015. The data confirm the recent inflow of population into the capital region, indicating that the issues of employment opportunities and demographic challenges have entered a new phase. The concentration of private wealth in the capital region is also becoming a growing problem. It should be noted that the system of branch plants increased individual incomes in certain noncapital regions such as Ulsan—namely, for regular employees working in plants operated by large conglomerates. However, there is a striking regional imbalance in terms of wealth. Around 70 percent of property income is being funneled to the capital region (figure 6.2, panel A).

Housing prices

The most significant socioeconomic issue in Korea today is the explosive rise in housing (apartment) prices in the capital region as a whole and for Seoul in particular. Figure 6.4 compares median real apartment prices in Seoul, the capital region, five major metropolitan areas outside the capital region, and other regions. It also shows trends in the average sale price of apartments over time. Both the median and average (real) sale prices for apartments in Seoul and the capital region began to rise around 2015–16, with existing disparities between other regions widening even further.

The concentration of wealth in the capital region intensified in the 2010s. During this decade, the volume of international trade ceased

FIGURE 6.3 Population in the capital region and labor market changes

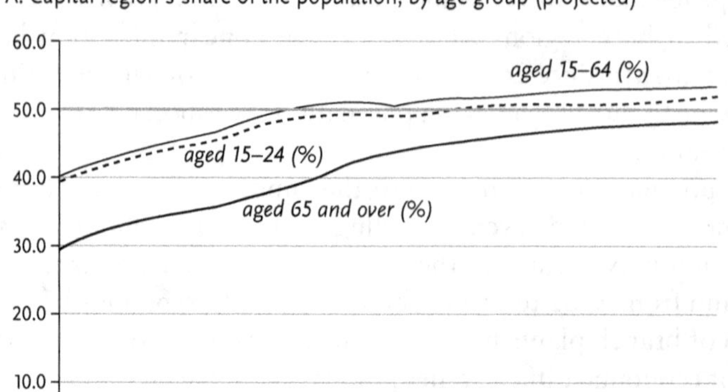

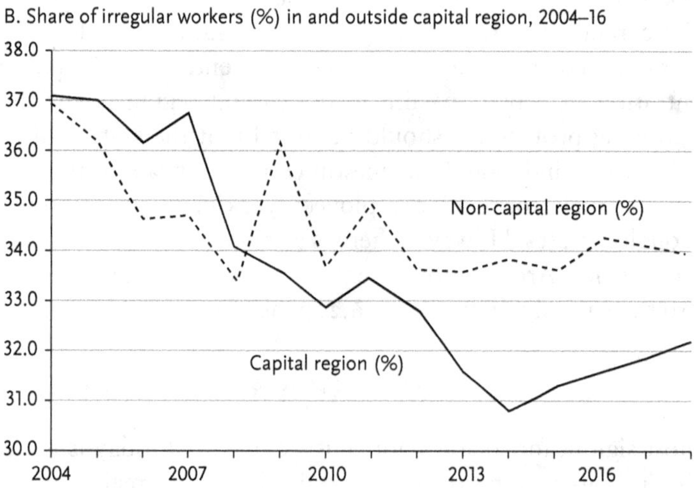

its expansion and Korea entered a period of low economic growth, remaining at an annual rate of around 2 percent. The Park Geun-Hye administration, which began its term in 2013, responded by loosening regulations around the real estate market and injecting massive liquidity into the economy with lower interest rates. As a result, apartment prices in Seoul and the capital region—the heart of Korea's economy—have been rapidly increasing relative to other parts of the country since

C. Natural population growth in and outside capital region, 2000–18

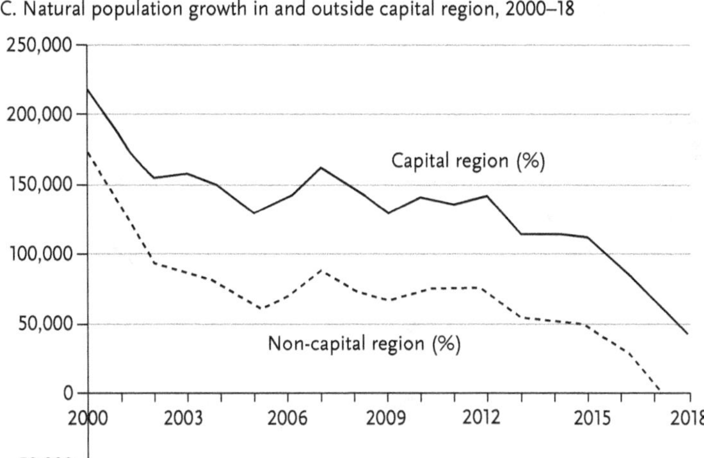

D. Net population movement into capital region, 1985–2018

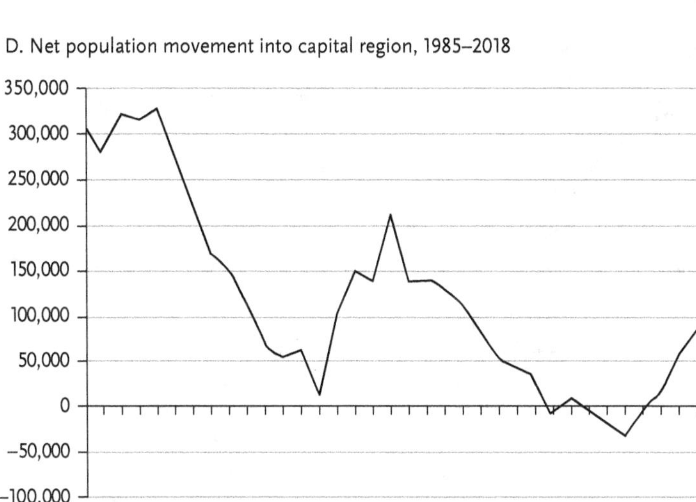

SOURCE: Statistics Korea, http://kosis.kr.

the mid-2010s, with an even more upward movement under the Moon Jae-In administration (figure 6.4). This surge in prices led to increased demand for property located in the capital region among individuals in other parts of the country, since these assets are seen as a form of insurance against income shocks. Overall, this series of economic developments resulted in an increase in GRI for the capital region. The widening wealth imbalance between the capital region and other parts

FIGURE 6.4 Trends in housing prices (capital vs. noncapital regions)

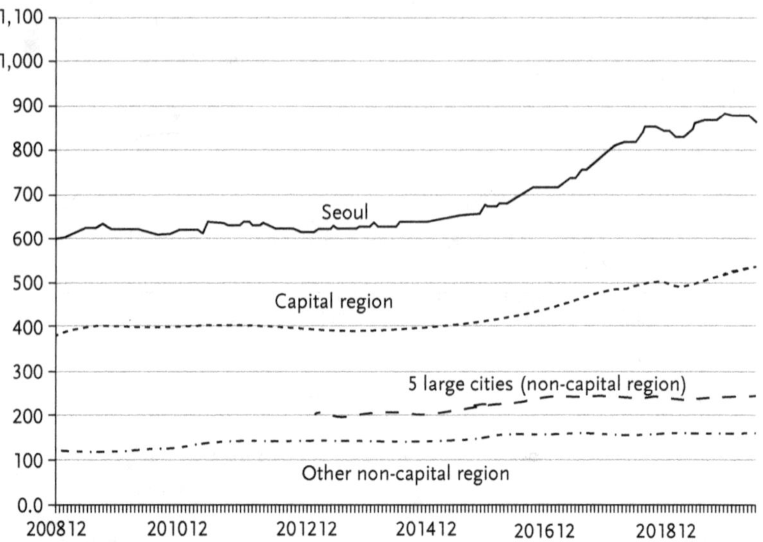

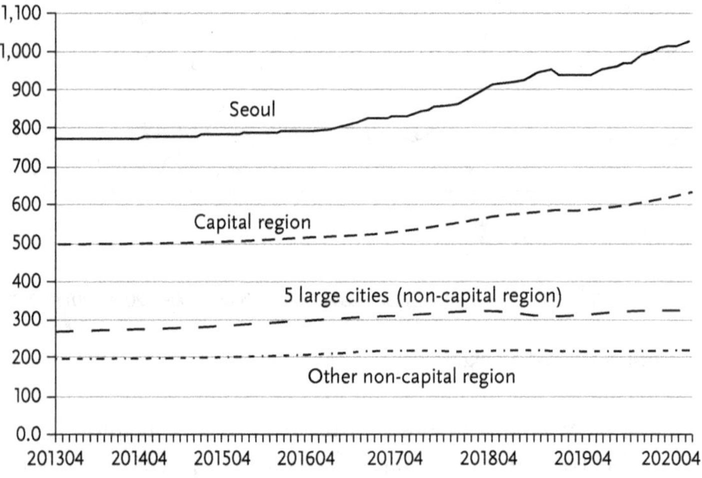

NOTE: Converted to real prices using monthly apartment sale data for each region (January 2019 = 100). There was a change in sample composition for the median apartment price data in January 2019. The data after the change are not directly comparable to the preceding data.

SOURCE: Kookmin Bank, http://kbstar.com.

of the country not only reflects the influence of irrational tendencies on economic behavior, but also indicates the potential emergence of rentier capitalism as a response to low growth in the manufacturing sector.

Political consequences of regional divergence

With the system of branch plants coming under increasing strain since the 2010s, the idea of focusing on the capital region to achieve economic growth has gained traction. This argument is outlined in several ways. First, it is crucial to elevate the capital area's status considering the economic competition between major metropolitan areas across the globe, on the premise that the competitiveness is important for regional development. Second, new sources of economic growth, such as biotechnology and other knowledge-intensive industries, rely on advanced technologies and a highly educated workforce. Thus, it is important to exploit the agglomeration economies of major metropolitan areas as economic hubs in line with market mechanisms. This line of reasoning supports calls for substantial deregulation in the capital region. Lastly, some argue that the boundaries of the "Gangnam area" need to be enlarged to counteract the recent rise in real estate prices in Seoul.[10] By this reasoning, it is necessary to increase the housing supply in localities near the Gangnam area and also to loosen regulations governing redevelopment and reconstruction.[11]

Unlike the capital region, some industrial cities that pursued economic growth through manufacturing have turned into "industrial crisis zones" since the 2010s. These include Geoje, Gunsan, Tongyeong, Yeongam, and Ulsan, which have been suffering from the restructuring of the shipbuilding and automobile industries. There have been previous instances of local industrial decline in Korea; Taebaek, Jeongseon, and Yeongwol in Gangwon Province were affected by the closure of mining facilities. However, the decline of manufacturing regions is unprecedented; a "Rust Belt" could be now emerging in Korea. Key manufacturing areas in the southeastern and southwestern parts of the country will likely be swept by waves of large-scale restructuring due to

10 The "Gangnam area" typically refers to the three districts of Gangnam, Seocho, and Songpa in Seoul. These districts have some of the highest housing prices within Seoul.

11 Park Byeong-Won, "How to Deal with Housing Prices in Gangnam" [in Korean], *Chosun Ilbo*, August 11, 2020.

the U.S.-China trade war, the trade dispute between Korea and Japan, and the rapid technological change accompanying the Fourth Industrial Revolution. In that case, these regions could fall into economic disrepair.

There are also regions of Korea that have been left out of economic growth altogether due to locational disadvantages and regulations. These include areas close to the demilitarized zone, protected natural areas, coastal islands, and various agricultural and fishing communities. These localities are at risk of disappearing entirely due to low birth rates and an aging population, and they have largely fallen into neglect. While certain areas of the country have only recently experienced economic decline after years of growth, these other areas have been excluded from economic growth from the very beginning. Their respective challenges are emerging at the same time.[12]

Regional disparities have emerged as a highly explosive political issue in the United States and Western European countries in recent years. Such inequalities have led to greater electoral support for populist parties and candidates.[13] In regions that have fallen into economic decline or disrepair, voters have turned to political actors who challenge the existing democratic order. The high level of support for President Donald Trump in the Rust Belt of the United States, for example, shows this all too clearly. Those who live in such areas have strongly voiced their discontent in response to economic decline and neglect, and this discontent manifested itself in a geographic form.[14] Even economists at Harvard, for instance, have begun to advocate for "place-based" policies in response to these trends after previously ignoring such policies altogether.[15]

All of the interrelated issues noted above—the restructuring of manufacturing industries in the past decade, the concentration of newly emerging industries in the capital region, sharply rising real estate prices, and demographic problems created by the low birth rate and an

12 Jeong Jun Ho, "Regional Disparities: What Is the Problem, and How to Address It" [in Korean], *Creation and Critique* 47, no. 3 (2019): 71–89.

13 Andrés Rodríguez-Pose, "The Revenge of the Places That Don't Matter (and What to Do about It)," *Cambridge Journal of Regions, Economy and Society* 11, no. 1 (2018): 189–209.

14 Clara Hendrickson, Mark Muro, and William A. Galston, *Countering the Geography of Discontent: Strategies for Left-Behind Places* (Washington, DC: Brookings Institution, 2018).

15 Benjamin A. Austin, Edward L. Glaeser, and Lawrence H. Summers, "Jobs for the Heartland: Place-Based Policies in 21st Century America" (NBER Working Paper No. 24548, National Bureau of Economic Research, Cambridge, MA, 2018), https://www.nber.org/papers/w24548.

aging population—increase the likelihood that both previously underdeveloped regions and areas experiencing a decline in manufacturing will fall into economic neglect or disrepair. The 1987 system was based upon alternating political alliances between the capital region and other regions, such as the Yeongnam (southeastern) and Honam (southwestern) areas. Deepening regional economic inequalities could threaten this system and result in grave consequences for Korea's democracy.

Generational Divergence

Since the 2010s, the question of generational divides has been intensely debated in Korean society. *The 880,000-won Generation*, authored by Woo Seok-Hoon and Park Kwon-Il in 2007, focuses on the generational disparity in income and economic opportunities faced by those born in the 1980s.[16] In this book, the figure of "880,000 won" is calculated by multiplying the average wage of ₩1.19 million for nonregular workers by 0.74, which is the average relative proportion of wages received by workers in their twenties. This book represented the emergence of generational divides as a major topic of public discussion. The issue has since taken center stage in discussions of social divisions in Korea. In particular, Lee Cheol-Seung's *The Unequal Generation* has ignited a fierce debate around the emergence of the so-called 386 Generation as a core element of contemporary Korean society.[17]

The 386 Generation, named after a popular computer model during the information technology boom of the 1990s, refers to the cohort of politicians that currently leads the political left in Korea. In particular, the term refers to individuals who were born in the 1960s, attended college in the 1980s, and entered their thirties in the 1990s. The term had a positive connotation when it first entered popular parlance, but this is no longer the case. Since the 2010s, it has often been used to criticize this generation for becoming the new societal elite.

Lee Cheol-Seung argues that the 386 Generation gained a critical advantage due to two factors: the extensive personal and social networks formed during their involvement in the pro-democracy movement of the 1980s, and the emergence of a dualized, hierarchical labor

16 Woo Seok-Hoon and Park Kwon-Il, *The 880,000 Won Generation: An Economics of Hope in an Age of Despair* [in Korean] (Seoul, Korea: Redian Publishers, 2007).
17 Lee Cheol-Seung, *The Unequal Generation* [in Korean] (Seoul, Korea: Moonji Publishers, 2019).

market after 1997 in line with the forces of globalization. The 386 Generation gained more power than other generations due to this synergistic combination of hierarchy and networks, thereby resulting in greater intergenerational inequalities.[18]

In response, Shin Jin-Wook and Jo Eun-Hye investigate the evolution of the discourse surrounding the 386 Generation and the political usage of the term.[19] They note that a conservative interpretation of generational divides was widely disseminated during the debates surrounding the appointment of Cho Kuk, one of the most prominent public figures of the 386 Generation, as the minister of justice in 2019.[20] Specifically, conservatives exploited the discourse of generational divides to criticize the Moon administration, claiming that the 386 Generation is just another group of privileged elites that opposes reform. Shin and Jo argue that the discourse of the 386 Generation is of no conceptual or practical value, since it is possible to understand and respond to current social and economic problems through other existing discourses on class, gender, and income inequality.

Prior research on generational economic inequality

Are there, in fact, meaningful cohort effects in terms of income and economic opportunities? Yoon Jong-In's empirical analysis notes that intergenerational differences play a large role in present-day income distribution in Korea.[21] According to Yoon, individuals born between

---

18 Lee, *Unequal Generation.*

19 Shin Jin-Wook and Jo Eun-Hye, "Political Genealogy and Semantics of the Discourses on 'Inter-Generational Inequality': A Critical Discourse Analysis of the Structure and Change of the '386' Discourses, 1990–2019" [in Korean] (paper presented at the 2019 Conference of the Korean Sociological Association, December 2019).

20 Cho Kuk was appointed as the minister of justice in 2019 to carry out prosecutorial reform—one of the Moon administration's highest policy priorities. His confirmation hearing at the National Assembly revealed several ethical and legal issues involving him and his family. These included allegations about the falsification of internship certificates submitted with his children's college applications, inappropriate private equity investments, and irregularities at a private school foundation owned by Cho's family. Ministerial appointments are not subject to a binding vote in the National Assembly, and Cho was appointed as the minister of justice, notwithstanding these allegations. He resigned after only a month in office.

21 Yoon Jong-In, "A Study on the Age Effects and the Cohort Effects of Income Distribution in Korea" [in Korean], *Korean Journal of Economic Studies* 66, no. 1 (2018): 81–114.

1945 and 1975 have a higher level of income than the preceding generation even after accounting for the age effects resulting from an aging population. He concludes that the 1945–75 cohort would thus be less vulnerable to economic difficulties in their old age. Furthermore, Lee Gyeong-Hee and Min In-Sik show that children born between 1976 and 1995 faced greater inequalities in economic opportunities compared to children born between 1960 and 1975.[22] In particular, they show that the parents' background holds greater explanatory power in predicting economic outcomes among today's youth, who are similar in age to the children of the baby boomer generation in the United States.[23]

On the other hand, several studies argue that there has not been a recent decline in social mobility, disputing the argument of a generational transmission of socioeconomic status through education.[24] These studies imply that generational divides are of limited use in understanding current social and economic problems in Korea, contrary to the abovementioned empirical studies of cohort effects in the economics literature.

There are also conflicting results regarding cohort effects among studies that focus on the United States and Western European countries. Chauvel notes that intergenerational inequalities are worse among conservative welfare states (e.g., France) than in countries with social democratic (e.g., Sweden) or liberal (e.g., United States) welfare regimes.[25] In conservative welfare states such as France, the initial point of entry into the labor market has a large impact on future incomes, and recent cohorts (youth) are likely to enter the labor market as "outsiders." This

---

22 Lee Gyeong-Hee and Min In-Sik, *A Study of Intergenerational Mobility: Occupations and Income Levels* [in Korean] (Sejong, Korea: Korea Labor Institute, 2016), https://www.kli.re.kr/downloadEngPblFile.do?atchmnflNo=20815.

23 Michael Hout, "Social Mobility," in *Pathways: A Magazine on Poverty, Inequality, and Social Policy,* Special Issue on State of the Union: Millennial Dilemma (Stanford: Stanford Center on Poverty and Inequality, 2019), 29–32.

24 Park Hyeon-Joon, *Changes in Intergenerational Social Mobility: How Open Has Korean Society Become?* [in Korean] (Seoul, Korea: Pakyoungsa, 2021); Kim Chang-Hwan. "Has the Occupational Value of a College Diploma Fallen?" [in Korean] (paper presented at the 7th Symposium of the Korea Inequality Research Network, July 18, 2020); Chung In-Kwan et al., "Intergenerational Social Mobility and Educational Inequality in South Korea: A Comprehensive Review of Empirical Studies since 2000" [in Korean], *Economy and Society* 127 (2020): 12–59.

25 Louis Chauvel, "Welfare Regimes, Cohorts and the Middle Classes," in *Income Inequality: Economic Disparities and the Middle Class in Affluent Countries*, ed. Janet C. Gornick and Markus Jäntti (Stanford: Stanford University Press, 2013), 115–41.

interpretation assumes that the labor market is dualized and that labor market conditions at the time of initial entry have a large effect on income opportunities over an individual's life cycle. Adverse labor market conditions at the time of entry could have long-term, scarring effects among youth.[26] In other words, variation in initial labor market conditions will result in lasting differences in income between cohorts over the entire life cycle.

On the contrary, some argue that cohort effects are not persistent and only appear temporarily as a result of changes in lifestyle.[27] The observed empirical differences could be attributed to the fact that the younger generation finds stable or high-income employment at a later age than the older generation did. For example, individuals may not find full-time employment until their thirties because of lifestyle changes such as marrying at a later age, an increase in double-income couples, greater participation in childrearing, and an increase in college graduates.[28] This interpretation acknowledges the existence of intergenerational disparities, but it does not accept at face value the persistent scarring effects of initial labor market conditions. Rather, it suggests that intergenerational disparities are only temporary and do not last over the entire life cycle. In sum, there is no consensus in the literature regarding intergenerational inequality.

Generational inequalities: Empirical data from Korea

Are there cohort effects in the Korean context? Jeong Jun Ho, Cheon Byung-You, and Jang Jiyeun analyze cohort effects with respect to wages using time-series data from the *Report on Wage Structure Survey* published by the Ministry of Employment and Labor (1988–2018).[29] The results, presented in figure 6.5, show differences in wage oppor-

---

26 Lisa B. Kahn, "The Long-Term Labor Market Consequences of Graduating from College in a Bad Economy," *Labour Economics* 17, no. 2 (2010): 303–16.
27 Liying Luo and James S. Hodges, "The Age-Period-Cohort-Interaction Model for Describing and Investigating Inter-cohort Deviations and Intra-Cohort Life-Course Dynamics," *Sociological Methods & Research* (January 2020), https://doi.org/10.1177/0049124119882451.
28 Hanna Schwander and Silja Hausermann, "Who Is In and Who Is Out?: A Risk-Based Conceptualization of Insiders and Outsiders," *Journal of European Social Policy* 23, no. 3 (2013): 248–69.
29 Jeong Jun Ho, Cheon Byung-You, and Jang Jiyeun, "Cohort Effects of Wage and Jobs in Korea" [in Korean], *Trends and Prospects* 112 (2021): 334–74.

FIGURE 6.5 Age cohort profile of hourly wages

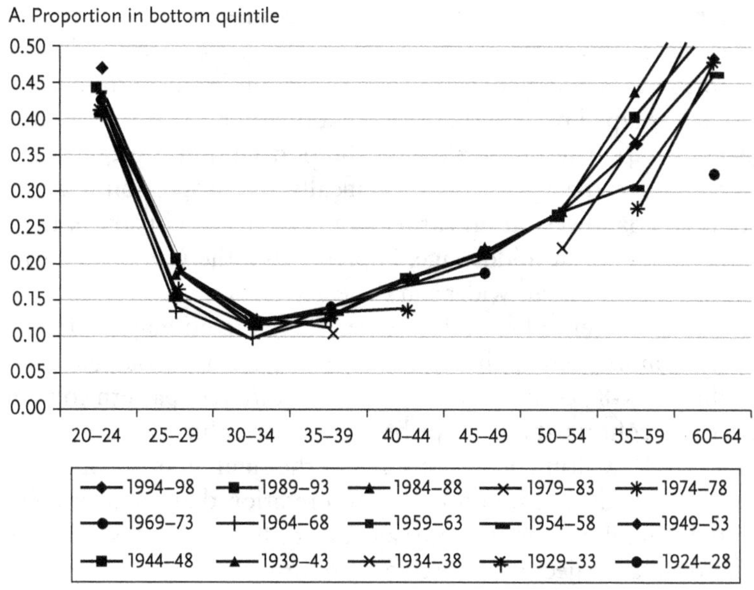

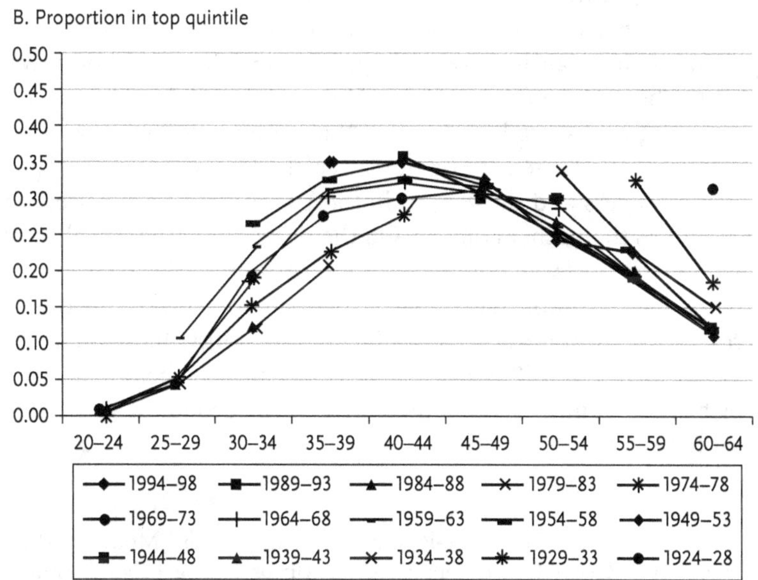

SOURCE: Jeong, Jun Ho, Cheon Byung-You, and Jang Jiyeun, "Cohort Effects of Wage and Jobs in Korea" [in Korean], *Trends and Prospects* 112 (2021): 334–74.

tunities between cohorts over the life cycle by comparing the proportion of individuals in the top and bottom quintiles of the hourly wage distribution. The proportion in the top quintile shows an inverse U-shaped pattern over the life cycle, reaching a peak in the early forties (age 40 to 44). On the contrary, the proportion in the bottom quintile shows a U-shaped pattern that reaches a minimum in the early thirties (age 30 to 34). The proportions in the bottom and top quintiles are different across the age groups. Specifically, the proportion in the bottom quintile is lowest at an earlier age, but the proportion in the top quintile is highest at middle age, implying that the wage gap narrows in the early thirties, but widens in the early forties.

In terms of overall life-cycle pattern, there are no major differences between cohorts across the life cycle. However, the younger cohorts (e.g., the 1979–83 cohort) show a markedly different pattern compared to previous cohorts at ages at or below the early thirties. Although it is difficult to draw firm conclusions due to the small number of observations, the data do not support the interpretation that younger cohorts find stable employment at a later age due to lifestyle changes and then catch up to the trajectory of previous cohorts.[30]

Figure 6.6 shows estimated cohort effects in terms of wage opportunities and wage inequalities. The cohort effects of the top quintile wage opportunity show an inverse U-shaped pattern across cohorts, while that of the bottom quintile display a U-shaped trend. In the former, the highest point is observed for Korea's "baby boomers," who were born between 1955 and 1963.[31] For the latter, the lowest point is recorded for baby boomers and those born in the 1970s, who have better wage opportunities than other cohorts. On the other hand, the so-called millennial generation faces poorer wage opportunities. This suggests that baby boomers are not very likely to belong to the bottom quintile, whereas younger cohorts have a higher probability. Individuals born during or after the 1980s have a higher chance of belonging to the top or bottom quintile. This is indicative of the economic polarization among today's youth.

30 Luo and Hodges, "The Age-Period-Cohort-Interaction Model"; Michael Freedman, "Are Recent Generations Catching Up or Falling Behind? Trends in Inter-Generational Inequality" (Luxembourg Income Study Working Paper Series, no. 689, 2017).

31 The endpoint of the baby boom generation in Korea is sometimes extended to 1974.

FIGURE 6.6 Cohort effects for wage opportunities and inequality, 1929–93

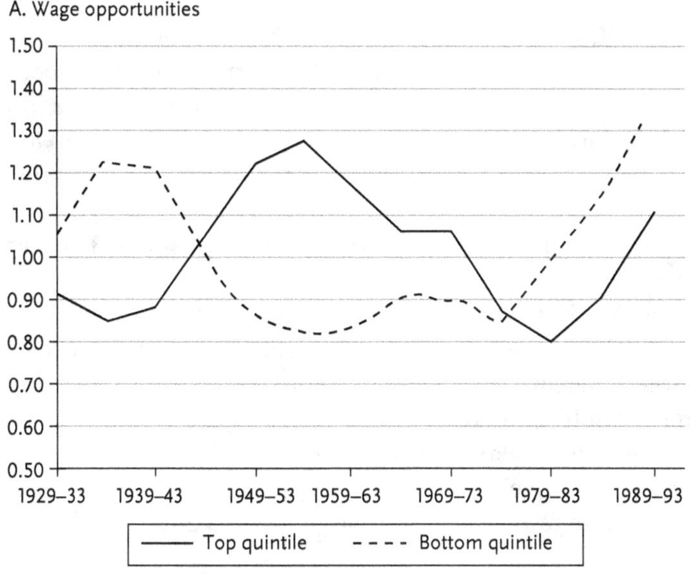

NOTE: Estimated using an APCD (Age-Period-Cohort Detrended) model with control variables including age, cohort, period, level of education, and gender. Dotted lines represent 95 percent confidence intervals. Plotted results show the odds ratio of coefficient estimates from a logistic regression for wage opportunities and coefficient estimates of Gini index from a RIF (recentered impact function) regression for wage inequality.
SOURCE: Jeong, Jun Ho, Cheon Byung-You, and Jang Jiyeun, "Cohort Effects of Wage and Jobs in Korea" [in Korean], *Trends and Prospects* 112 (2021): 334–74.

In figure 6.6, panel B, the value of the Y-axis represents the change in the Gini coefficient. The overall cohort effects of wage inequality show a V-shaped trend across cohorts. Intergenerational wage inequality reaches its lowest value for the first cohort of the so-called 386 Generation, born in 1959–63. Wage inequality between cohorts falls from the pre–baby boom cohorts to the baby boomers. The sign of cohort effects is negative from the baby boomers to the 1974–78 cohort, but after the 1979–83 cohort it becomes positive once again.

With the dualization of the labor market and the expansion of irregular jobs, the younger generation is facing an increasingly uncertain and volatile labor market. Given this context, it is difficult to reasonably interpret intergenerational differences as a temporary cohort effect resulting from delays caused by lifestyle changes. Nevertheless, since there are relatively few observations, caution is warranted when interpreting these results as indicative of lifetime effects.[32]

Sources of generational economic inequality in Korea

IPSOS has published the results of a cross-national survey based on its "Future Optimism Index."[33] This index represents whether the younger generation expects to have a higher standard of living than their parents' generation. The results, shown in figure 6.7, show that youth are most pessimistic in France, with Korea ranking third after Belgium. This indicates that there is higher intergenerational inequality in France than in Sweden or the United States, aligning with Chauvel's analysis.[34] If there is greater labor market flexibility or high welfare spending, there is less intergenerational inequality. The result for Korea suggests that the youth are being affected by generational disparities resulting from a highly dualized labor market and the expansion of irregular jobs.

Figure 6.8 illustrates labor market changes by age group. The share of the elderly population (over age 65) and youth (age 15 to 24) were equal by 2016, and the former has since surpassed the latter. Korea has entered a new phase in its aging problem. Such changes in demographic composition, combined with a seniority-based wage system that enables

32 Luo and Hodges, "The Age-Period-Cohort-Interaction Model."

33 IPSOS, *Global Trends: Fragmentation, Cohesion and Uncertainty* (2017), https://www.ipsos.com/sites/default/files/2017-07/Ipsos%20Global%20Trends%202017%20report.pdf.

34 Chauvel, "Welfare Regimes, Cohorts and the Middle Classes."

FIGURE 6.7 Future Optimism Index (IPSOS), by country

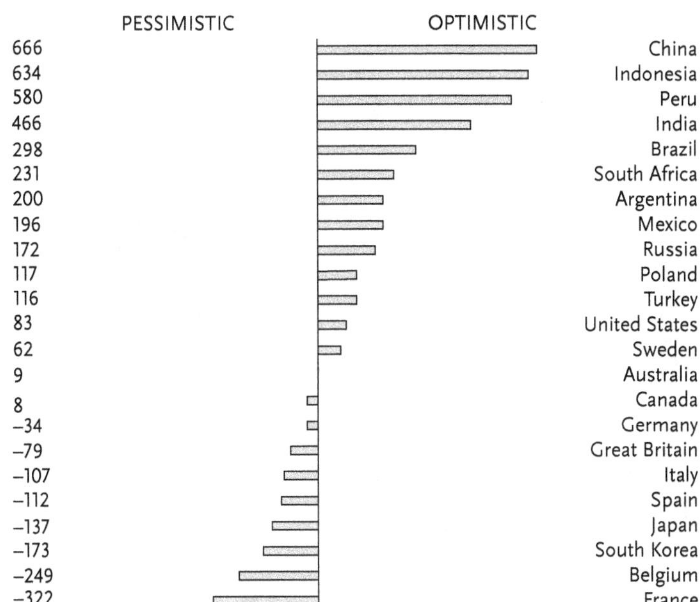

NOTE: The IPSOS Global Trends Survey of 18,180 adults across 22 countries was conducted online from September 12 to October 11, 2016.
SOURCE: IPSOS, *Global Trends: Fragmentation, Cohesion and Uncertainty* (2017), 58, https://www.ipsos.com/sites/default/files/2017-07/Ipsos%20Global%20Trends%202017%20report.pdf.

middle-aged workers to remain in the labor market for a longer duration, are exacerbating the problem of youth unemployment.[35]

Korea's unemployment rate has largely shown an upward trend since 2012. This reflects a slowdown in economic growth, which in turn has brought about economic stagnation. The unemployment rate among youth (ages 15 to 24 or 15 to 29)[36] is around twice as high as the overall unemployment rate, and it has increased since the 2010s.

35 Lee Cheol-Seung, Jeong Jun Ho, and Cheon Byung-You, "Generation, Class, and Hierarchy II: Do Overloaded Baby-Boomers/386-Generation within Firms Lead to More Irregular Workers and Less Youth Employment?" [in Korean], *Korean Journal of Sociology* 54, no. 2 (2020): 1–58.

36 With males in mandatory military service in their early twenties, using two date ranges reveals the difference in unemployment between those in their early twenties and late twenties.

FIGURE 6.8 Unemployment and nonregular workers, by age group

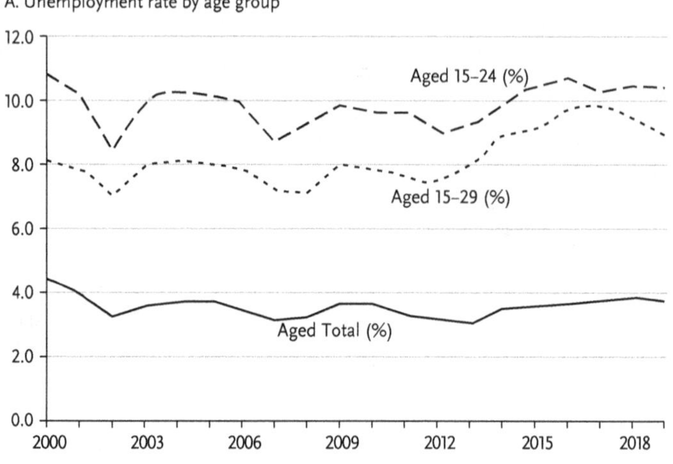

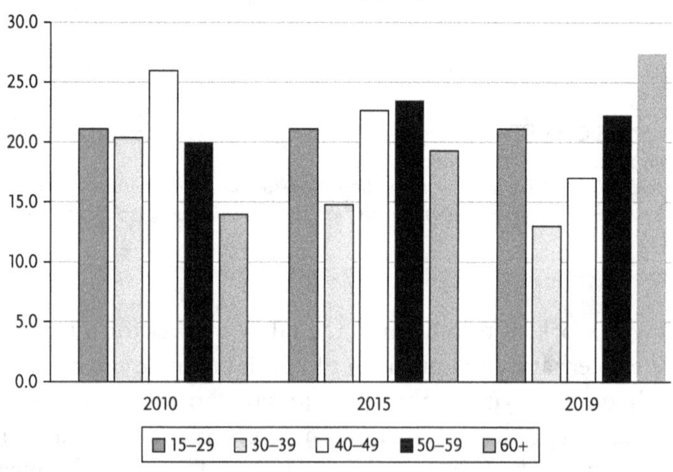

NOTE: In the Local Area Labor Force Survey, nonregular workers include temporary and daily workers.
SOURCE: Statistics Korea, http://kosis.kr.

There has been a recent decline for the 15 to 29 age group, which reflects various short-term policies enacted by the Moon administration to address youth unemployment. These policies include the expansion of public sector jobs, the conversion of irregular jobs into regular jobs, and the provision of various employment-related subsidies.

As seen in the cohort effect analysis of wage opportunities, those born during or after the 1980s have fewer opportunities to climb toward the top of the wage distribution than the baby boom generation or the so-called 386/586 Generation.[37] The unemployment rate among youth continues to increase due to several factors. These are the structural conditions that underlie the political, social, and economic tension and discord between today's youth and older generations in Korea.

As discussed above, there is not only a generational gap between the youth and baby boomers, but also a within-generation gap among youth. As shown in figure 6.8, the proportion of nonregular workers by age group as a fraction of all nonregular workers has increased since the 2010s for the young (age 15 to 29) and the elderly (age 60 or above), with a significant increase in the latter. In recent years, this group of elderly workers has begun to include some baby boomers as well. Korea has the highest elderly poverty rate among Organisation for Economic Co-operation and Development countries due to its weak welfare system. Although Korea's baby boomers have begun to retire, some of them return to their job as nonregular workers because they do not have sufficient economic resources under the current pension system. This implies that the within-generation gap is increasing among the elderly as well as the youth.

Two Divergences and Democracy in Korea

How then do these divergences affect Korean democracy, and what do they imply about the path it might take? In our view, regional and generational divergences have seriously agitated the 1987 system, which was fundamentally built on political mobilization along regional lines. The political right drove this form of regional politics, relying on a "growth alliance" between the capital region and the Yeongnam (southeastern) region—the core of the Korean economy. The progressive Kim Dae-Jung and Roh Moo-Hyun administrations succeeded in achieving a peaceful transfer of power by building a coalition with conservatives in the central region (North and South Chungcheong provinces). In this respect, the noncapital area exerted a meaningful influence on political power. Therefore, attaining balanced economic development between

37 This is an alternative term for the 386 Generation, which accounts for the fact that individuals belonging to that group have now entered their fifties.

the capital region and rest of the country has been a recurring issue under both the conservative and progressive administrations. Socioeconomic problems such as class and labor have been less salient since electoral victories were built around regional competition and partnerships with noncapital areas. This is the limitation of regionalism-based democracy.

Regional divides: The political repercussions of housing prices

Gregory Henderson famously described Korean politics as the "vortex."[38] This paradoxically emphasizes the necessity and significance of a pluralistic democratic system. President Kim Dae-Jung's decisive steps to substantially increase autonomy in local governance across the entire country is one of the most important achievements of the 1987 system. Greater autonomy in local governance provides the institutional apparatus to solidify a pluralized democracy. A balanced regional allocation of population and resources is needed to strengthen a pluralized democracy, but such requirements have not been achieved due to a widening regional divide between the capital region and the rest of the country. The capital region continues to absorb more and more of the country's population and resources. This implies that the spatial scale of Korea's democracy is being narrowed from the entire country to only Seoul or the capital region. In other words, Korea has become an "urban" state.

As noted above, housing prices are a key element of the regional divide in Korea. The sharp rise in housing prices caused by real estate development projects has already had tangible electoral consequences. The best example of this is the New Town Project, a large-scale real estate development project pursued by the conservative Seoul mayors Lee Myung-Bak and Oh Se-Hoon. The eighteenth general election, held in April 2008, was dominated by the construction of the New Town Project as a common campaign pledge of the then ruling Grand National Party candidates. House prices began to fluctuate when this campaign pledge stimulated dreams of homeownership and sparked real estate speculation. Local residents cheered as housing prices rose, and the

38 Gregory Henderson, *Korea: The Politics of the Vortex* (Cambridge: Harvard University Press, 1968).

approval rating of the Grand National Party's candidates rose steeply, resulting in the party's victory in the general election.

The results of the April 2021 by-elections for the mayoral seats in Seoul and Busan, Korea's two largest cities, illustrate the continued political importance of the housing issue. The failure of the Moon administration's real estate policy decisively contributed to the opposition's victory. In the Seoul mayoral by-election, Oh Se-Hoon, the opposition candidate and former mayor, promised private-led redevelopment and deregulation. There was an overall turnout of 58.2 percent for the Seoul mayoral by-election. The turnout in the so-called three "Gangnam area" districts was higher: 61.1 percent in Gangnam district, 64.0 percent in Seocho district, and 61.0 percent in Songpa district. In addition, Oh won 57.5 percent of the votes in Seoul, but 73.6 percent in Gangnam district, 71.0 percent in Seocho district, and 63.9 percent in Songpa district. Among all the districts in Seoul, Oh had the highest level of support in Gangnam district. This is indicative of voters' wishes for a regulatory overhaul.

The rise in housing prices in the capital region since the mid-2010s could alter the political landscape in favor of the conservatives. Ansell reports that high-wealth homeowners in Western countries are less likely to strongly support redistribution.[39] In Korea, Lee Cheol-Seung, Hwang In-Hyee, and Lim Hyun-Ji use data from the late 2000s to the late 2010s to show the weakening support of the universal welfare state through an expansion of the asset-based private welfare system.[40] Their finding suggests that it would be difficult to create a more robust social-democratic welfare system as long as there is regionally segmented asset accumulation. The establishment of a private safety net system through the accumulation of wealth by middle- and high-income earners strengthens the obsession with property and financial asset investment among the middle class, weakening and frustrating the desire for social solidarity. This could ultimately deepen economic inequality after retirement within the middle class and hinder progress toward an inclusive democracy.

39 Ben Ansell, "The Political Economy of Ownership: Housing Markets and the Welfare State," *American Political Science Review* 108, no. 2 (2014): 383–402.

40 Lee Cheol-Seung, Hwang In-Hyee, and Lim Hyun-Ji, "The Socio-Economic Foundations of the Korean Welfare State: Asset Inequality, Insurance Motives, and Social Policy Preferences, 2007–2016" [in Korean], *Korean Political Science Review* 52, no. 5 (2018): 1–30.

Furthermore, a surge in housing prices is likely to heighten a spatial barrier between Seoul and the rest of the country, essentially blocking entry into Seoul. This would strengthen spatial polarization between Seoul (or the capital region) and the rest of the country, which could fuel discontent toward the vested interests of the Seoul metropolitan elite. Place-based identities centered on the housing issue could help mobilize votes in particular geographic regions, since one's location of residence provides a strong basis for the formation of personal identity. This is distinctly different from the growth alliance of the 1987 system. On the other hand, rising housing prices could further marginalize the voices of those who lack stable housing in regions where most residents are homeowners.

With the emergence of industrial rust belts in the noncapital region and the appearance of localities that are at risk of disappearing entirely due to low birth rates and an aging population, some observers believe that regional divides, as in Western Europe and the United States, could lead to more conservative voting behavior in Korea. Also, as the decrease in population growth leads to a smaller number of parliamentary constituencies, the political power of the noncapital region has shrunk. To cope with this situation, politicians and leaders in the southeastern regions of Busan, Ulsan, and South Gyeongsang provinces are scrambling to create a shared vision for pan-regional development based on a strategic "megacity" project that is intended to function as a counterweight to the capital region. Also, Daegu and North Gyeongsang provinces, which are traditional conservative strongholds, and Gwangju and South Jeolla provinces, both progressive bastions, are each discussing the integration of administrative boundaries.

This pursuit of pan-regionalism and administrative mergers shows the urgency of the crisis facing the noncapital region. These political initiatives appear to align with the Moon administration's efforts in its early days to revise the Constitution, including decentralization comparable to a federal state. Implicitly speaking, the merger between Daegu and North Gyeongsang provinces appears to aim at strengthening the solidarity of the conservative base, while the megacity strategy among Busan, Ulsan, and South Gyeongsang provinces seems to focus on making a new breakthrough for the progressives, given the region's current conservative outlook. If this series of political moves fails to produce fruitful results, there could be more conservative voting behavior along the lines of what has been observed in the United States and Western Europe.

Generational divides: Political underrepresentation among youth

The issue of generational divergence gained increasing attention throughout the 2010s, and the conflict between youth and the 386 Generation was amplified during the Moon administration. Whether the intergenerational gap is widening in actuality remains a controversial question. Nevertheless, the youth occupy a relatively high proportion of the bottom end of the labor market. It is also true that the proportion of nonregular workers among the elderly is high, as recent retirees reenter the labor market due to a weak social welfare system. Low growth and fewer job opportunities since the 2010s, greater dualization of the labor market, and the slow exit of baby boomers from the labor market are giving rise to political, social, and economic inequalities between the youth and older generations.

Baby boomers, including the 386 Generation, were historic leaders in establishing the 1987 system. They overcame the oppression of the military regime with resolute determination. These formative experiences, however, seem to have ingrained in them a hierarchical and confrontational approach toward politics.[41] They also served as key organizers of major civic groups that played a significant role in the formation of Korean civil society. The combination of confrontational tactics and organizational skills was critical to democratization and subsequent political developments.

This generation expected the 1987 system to lead to the continued expansion of democracy aimed at integration, not segmentation and cleavages, and into an era of coexistence and competition between progressives and conservatives. However, the Lee Myung-Bak and Park Geun-Hye administrations took steps that undermined Korea's democratic progress. This reinforced the political division between "democratic" and "anti-democratic" forces, with both conservatives and progressives engaging in increasingly confrontational behavior, especially in relation to President Park Geun-Hye's impeachment.

Baby boomers will require substantial resources for a long time due to their enormous population size, depriving today's youth of social and economic opportunities. However, this is not the crux of Korea's generational divergence. The generation gap framework reveals that an

41 See chapter 1 for a more extensive discussion of these issues.

unstable labor market status is prevalent among both young and old people, and the latter is related to the aging problem. In other words, the generational divide is multifaceted, with a combination of both class and demographic issues.

Due to the aging population and a weak social safety net, some baby boomers are facing economic difficulties. Among today's youth, unlike the previous generation, there is a significant within-generation gap in economic opportunities due to an excessive belief in meritocracy and intergenerational transfers of wealth through inheritances and gifts. The concept of generational gaps encompasses not only intergenerational gaps, but also intragenerational gaps. Since the 2010s, low economic growth and a rapidly aging population has resulted in multiple gaps and conflicts between generations, highlighting the political underrepresentation of today's youth.

Conclusion

The Lee Myung-Bak and Park Geun-Hye administrations sought to restore a conservative political order based on the growth alliance of the 1987 system. In particular, the Park administration showed a tendency to rationalize and justify the pre-1987 Park Chung-Hee model. It eventually fell from power as a result of the "Candlelight Revolution" of 2016–17. There was an outpouring of civil resistance, the causes of which could be interpreted in several ways. As a direct cause, one could point to popular resistance against democratic decline and the party and judicial systems that precipitated this decline. The democratic recession during the Lee and Park administrations is sometimes characterized as a shift from a government of "live and let live" to a government that "leaves people to die."[42]

The deepening of regional and generational divergences in the 2010s has led to the emergence of a new group of individuals who strongly feel that they have been "left to die." The Park administration crumbled as it ignored and neglected this new group. Intent on avoiding the path taken by its predecessor, the Moon administration declared "people first" as its slogan as it moved in to fill the power vacuum. However, it has not taken proactive steps to deal with the newly emerging trends

42 Kim Jong-Yeop, *The Regime of Division on the Korean Peninsula and the 1987 System* [in Korean] (Paju, Korea: Changbi Publishers, 2017).

of regional and generational disparities. Instead, the Moon administration focused on class-based issues and redistribution early on in its term—such as increasing the minimum wage, pursuing "income-led growth," and converting irregular jobs to regular jobs—without meaningful results.

The COVID-19 crisis is only exacerbating class divides and regional and generational disparities. Neglecting these widening divergences could result in greater anxiety among the population. In particular, the sharp rise in housing prices in Seoul between 2017 and 2021 has become a source of despair for those outside of Seoul and the younger generation. The political firestorm surrounding the Prosecution Service and judicial policy also shows no signs of abating. Combined with these divisions, Korea's economic divergences could once again throw its democracy into chaos. If it is to achieve economic growth and democratic stability, Korea cannot afford to ignore the vital task of connecting and uniting disparate regions and generations.

Bibliography

Ansell, Ben. "The Political Economy of Ownership: Housing Markets and the Welfare State." *American Political Science Review* 108, no. 2 (2014): 383–402.

Austin, Benjamin A., Edward L. Glaeser, and Lawrence H. Summers. "Jobs for the Heartland: Place-Based Policies in 21st Century America." NBER Working Paper No. 24548, National Bureau of Economic Research, Cambridge, MA, 2018. https://www.nber.org/papers/w24548.

Chauvel, Louis. "Welfare Regimes, Cohorts and the Middle Classes." In *Income Inequality: Economic Disparities and the Middle Class in Affluent Countries*, edited by Janet C. Gornick and Markus Jäntti, 115–41. Stanford: Stanford University Press, 2013.

Choi, Jang-Jip. "Reconsidering the Korean Democracy: Crisis and Alternative." [In Korean.] *Journal of Korean Politics* 29, no. 2 (2020): 1–26.

Chung, In-Kwan et al. "Intergenerational Social Mobility and Educational Inequality in South Korea: A Comprehensive Review of Empirical Studies since 2000." [In Korean.] *Economy and Society* 127 (2020): 12–59.

Freedman, Michael. "Are Recent Generations Catching Up or Falling Behind? Trends in Inter-Generational Inequality." Luxembourg Income Study Working Paper Series, No. 689, 2017.

Henderson, Gregory. *Korea: The Politics of the Vortex*. Cambridge: Harvard University Press, 1968.

Hendrickson, Clara, Mark Muro, and William A. Galston. *Countering the Geography of Discontent: Strategies for Left-Behind Places*. Washington, DC: Brookings Institution, 2018.

Hout, Michael. "Social Mobility." In *Pathways: A Magazine on Poverty, Inequality, and Social Policy*, Special Issue on State of the Union: Millennial Dilemma, 29–32. Stanford: Stanford Center on Poverty and Inequality, 2019.

IPSOS. *Global Trends: Fragmentation, Cohesion & Uncertainty* (2017). https://www.ipsos.com/sites/default/files/2017-07/Ipsos%20Global%20Trends%202017%20report.pdf.

Jeong, Jun Ho. "Regional Income Disparities and Risk Sharing in Korea." [In Korean.] *Space and Environment* 28, no. 2 (2018): 12–44.

———. "Regional Disparities: What Is the Problem, and How to Address It." [In Korean.] *Creation and Critique* 47, no. 3 (2019): 71–89.

Jeong, Jun Ho, Cheon Byung-You, and Jang Jiyeun. "Cohort Effects of Wage and Jobs in Korea." [In Korean.] *Trends and Prospects* 112 (2021): 334–74.

Kahn, Lisa B. "The Long-Term Labor Market Consequences of Graduating from College in a Bad Economy." *Labour Economics* 17, no. 2 (2010): 303–16.

Kim, Chang-Hwan. "Has the Occupational Value of a College Diploma Fallen?" [In Korean.] Paper presented at the 7th Symposium of the Korea Inequality Research Network, July 18, 2020.

Kim, Jong-Yeop. *The Discourses of the 1987 Political Order*. [In Korean.] Paju, Korea: Changbi Publishers, 2009.

———. *The Regime of Division on the Korean Peninsula and the 1987 System*. [In Korean.] Paju, Korea: Changbi Publishers, 2017.

Kookmin Bank. http://kbstar.com.

Lee, Cheol-Seung. *The Unequal Generation*. [In Korean.] Seoul, Korea: Moonji Publishers, 2019.

Lee, Cheol-Seung, Hwang In-Hyee, and Lim Hyun-Ji. "The Socio-Economic Foundations of the Korean Welfare State: Asset Inequality, Insurance Motives, and Social Policy Preferences, 2007–2016." [In Korean.] *Korean Political Science Review* 52, no. 5 (2018): 1–30.

Lee, Cheol-Seung, Jeong Jun Ho, and Cheon Byung-You. "Generation, Class, and Hierarchy II: Do Overloaded Baby-Boomers/386-Generation within Firms Lead to More Irregular Workers and Less Youth Employment?" [In Korean.] *Korean Journal of Sociology* 54, no. 2 (2020): 1–58.

Lee, Gyeong-Hee, and Min In-Sik. *A Study of Intergenerational Mobility: Occupations and Income Levels.* [In Korean.] Sejong, Korea: Korea Labor Institute, 2016. https://www.kli.re.kr/downloadEngPblFile.do?atchmnflNo=20815.

Luo, Liying, and James S. Hodges. "The Age-Period-Cohort-Interaction Model for Describing and Investigating Inter-Cohort Deviations and Intra-Cohort Life-Course Dynamics." *Sociological Methods & Research* (January 2020). https://doi.org/10.1177/0049124119882451.

Massey, Doreen. *Spatial Divisions of Labour: Social Structures and the Geography of Production.* London: Macmillan, 1984.

OECD (Organisation for Economic Co-operation and Development). "OECD Statistics." https://stats.oecd.org/.

Park, Byeong-Won. "How to Deal with Housing Prices in Gangnam." [In Korean.] *Chosun Ilbo*, August 11, 2020.

Park, Hyeon-Joon. *Changes in Intergenerational Social Mobility: How Open Has Korean Society Become?* [In Korean.] Seoul, Korea: Pakyoungsa, 2021.

Rodríguez-Pose, Andrés. "The Revenge of the Places That Don't Matter (and What to Do about It)." *Cambridge Journal of Regions, Economy and Society* 11, no. 1 (2018): 189–209.

Schwander, Hanna, and Silja Hausermann. "Who Is In and Who Is Out?: A Risk-Based Conceptualization of Insiders and Outsiders." *Journal of European Social Policy* 23, no. 3 (2013): 248–69.

Shin, Jin-Wook, and Jo Eun-Hye. "Political Genealogy and Semantics of the Discourses on 'Inter-Generational Inequality': A Critical Discourse Analysis of the Structure and Change of the '386' Discourses, 1990–2019." [In Korean.] Paper presented at the 2019 Conference of the Korean Sociological Association, December 2019.

Statistics Korea. http://kosis.kr.

Woo, Seok-Hoon, and Park Kwon-Il. *The 880,000 Won Generation: An Economics of Hope in an Age of Despair.* [In Korean.] Seoul, Korea: Redian Publishers, 2007.

Yoon, Jong-In. "A Study on the Age Effects and the Cohort Effects of Income Distribution in Korea." [In Korean.] *Korean Journal of Economic Studies* 66, no. 1 (2018): 81–114.

CHAPTER SEVEN

Democracy and the Educational System in Korea

Seongsoo Choi

Perhaps no other issue in Korea garners as much attention or prompts as wide a variety of opinions as education. Many Koreans might claim, based on their experiences as students or parents or educators, to be experts on education policy. Education is frequently blamed for many social problems, and educational reform is often touted as a solution. What such public conceptions of education largely lack, however, is a comparative lens. There have been few systematic analyses comparing the institutional characteristics of Korea's educational system with systems of other countries, present or past. Without a comparative understanding of the institutional origins and characteristics of Korea's educational system, discussions about the future of Korea's education policy will be fruitless, as identifying the system's strengths and weaknesses, and setting policy priorities and visions, will be difficult.

This is particularly true when we consider the political context in which educational institutions are shaped. Democracy and the educational system develop in tandem because education is a nexus that connects the state, market, and civil society. Education also plays an important role in inculcating civic values. The social and political evolution of Korean society, from the repressive authoritarian regime to a mature democratic regime, therefore, must be accounted for to fully explain the past and present institutional characteristics of Korean education.

This chapter aims to take up this task. It begins with an outline of the institutional history of Korea's educational system by examining two phases: its authoritarian origins prior to democratization in

1987, and the changes following democratization. Within this context, I explore the negative and positive aspects of the institutional legacies of the authoritarian era as they remain today, more than thirty years after democratization. This forms the basis for a discussion of possible directions for educational reform, since past and present institutional settings shape the paths that can be taken in the future. I argue that the sociopolitical context of democracy plays a critical role in this regard. I will also shed light on how education can help foster a more mature democracy, focusing on the consequences of policy changes that have been made since the Moon administration.

The Institutional Characteristics of Korea's Educational System

Let me begin by assessing the institutional characteristics of Korea's educational system from an international comparative perspective. The literature of comparative education proposes two major criteria to characterize educational systems with institutional variation: standardization (how an educational system is regulated and coordinated by a national authority) and differentiation (how different educational programs are offered to students, also termed "stratification" when a hierarchy is implied across these programs).[1]

When it comes to standardization, Korea shows a higher degree of it relative to other industrial countries, as seen in the extent to which central or local government standardizes hiring practices and wages for teachers, as well as manages school budgets (figure 7.1, panels A and B). Korea is also highly standardized in terms of having a nationwide, central examination (figure 7.1, panel D). Despite local authorities' relative autonomy in textbook selection and curriculum design (panel C), the fact that most textbooks are government-approved, which are not captured in the comparative data, indicates a high level of standardization. The range of options for textbooks is limited by government guidelines in contrast to many Western countries, which usually have no constraints whatsoever on textbooks. Considering that

1 Herman G. Van de Werfhorst and Jonathan J. B. Mijs, "Achievement Inequality and the Institutional Structure of Educational Systems: A Comparative Perspective," *Annual Review of Sociology* 36, no. 1 (2010): 407–28; Alan C. Kerckhoff, "Education and Social Stratification Processes in Comparative Perspective," *Sociology of Education* 74 (2001): 3–18.

FIGURE 7.1 Standardization indexes of educational systems in industrial countries

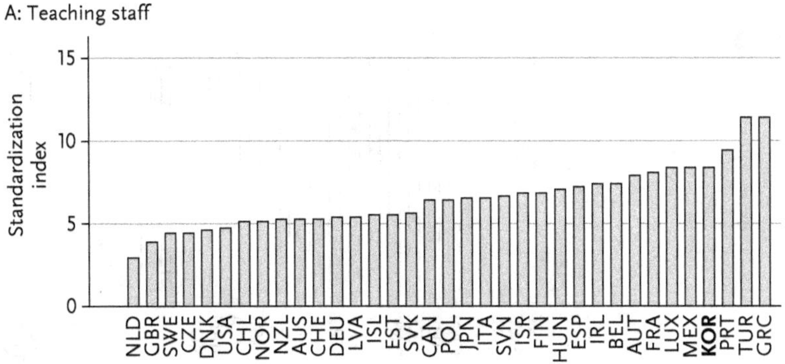

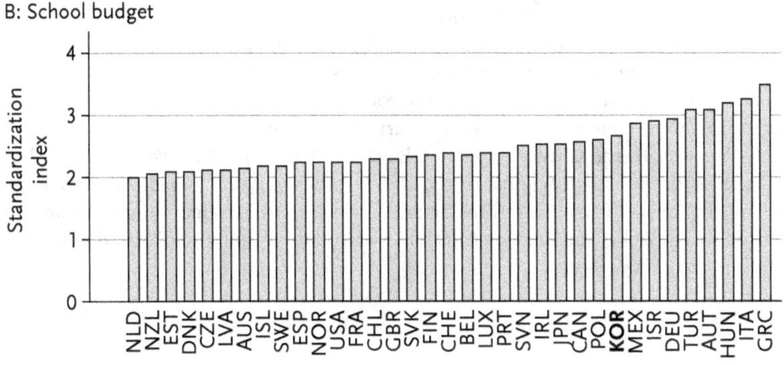

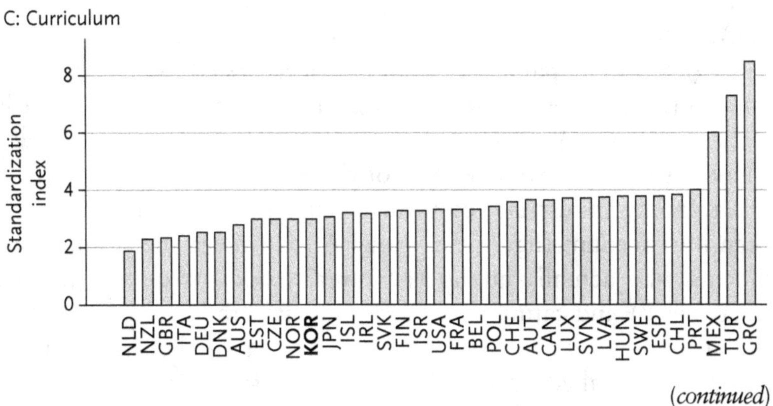

(*continued*)

FIGURE 7.1 *(continued)*

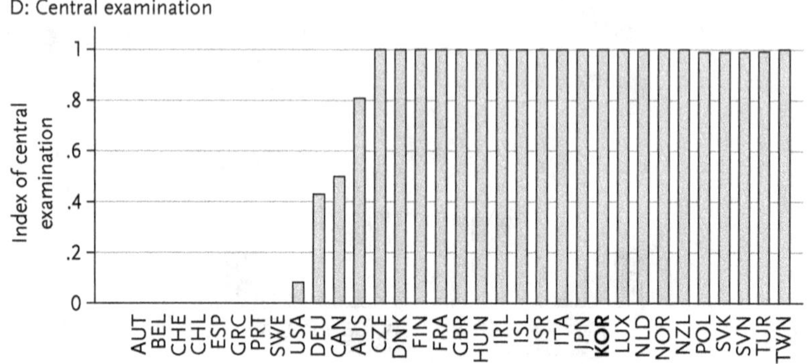

NOTE: The indexes show the sum of the responses to four questions about institutional responsibility (1 = school, 2 = local authority, 3 = central government) for hiring, firing teachers, and establishing their salary scheme (panel A), for formulating and allocating school budgets (panel B), and for choosing textbooks, course content, and courses (panel C). In panel D, countries with a nationwide central examination are coded as 1. Otherwise, the index is zero. Some countries with regional variation have proportional partial scores.
SOURCE: Panels A, B, and C use data from OECD, *PISA 2015 Results (Volume II): Policies and Practices for Successful Schools* (Paris: OECD Publishing, 2016); panel D uses data from Thijs Bol et al., "Curricular Tracking and Central Examinations: Counterbalancing the Impact of Social Background on Student Achievement in 36 Countries," *Social Forces* 92, no. 4 (June 2014): 1545–72.

indices based on the Organisation for Economic Co-operation and Development (OECD) Program for International Student Assessment (PISA) data examine only high schools, the corresponding indices for Korea (figure 7.1, panel C) should be interpreted as a lower-bound estimate (e.g., all elementary school textbooks in Korea are published by the government).

Korea shows an average level of differentiation in secondary education among industrial countries when school tracking structure is taken into account (figure 7.2, panel A). However, the proportion of students who actually attend vocational schools is quite low (figure 7.2, panel B), indicating that most students are being educated in a regular academic curriculum instead of a vocational curriculum. Even within vocational education, there is no dual system that provides students with apprenticeship or internship opportunities that directly tie into the occupational labor market (panel C). Given that the vast majority of upper-secondary students belong to academic tracks despite

FIGURE 7.2 Indexes of educational systems' differentiation and vocational orientation in industrial countries

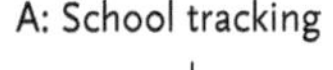

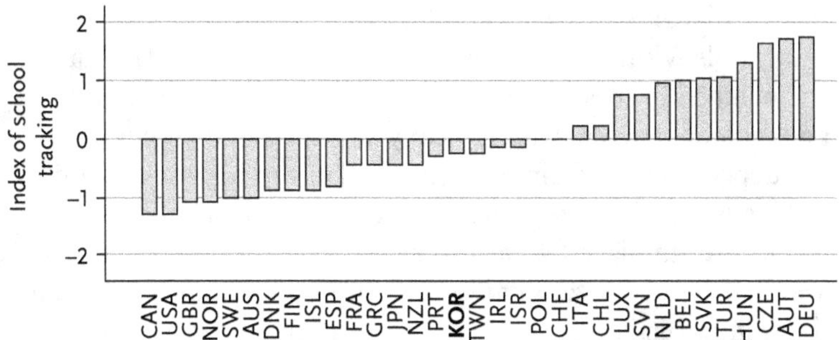

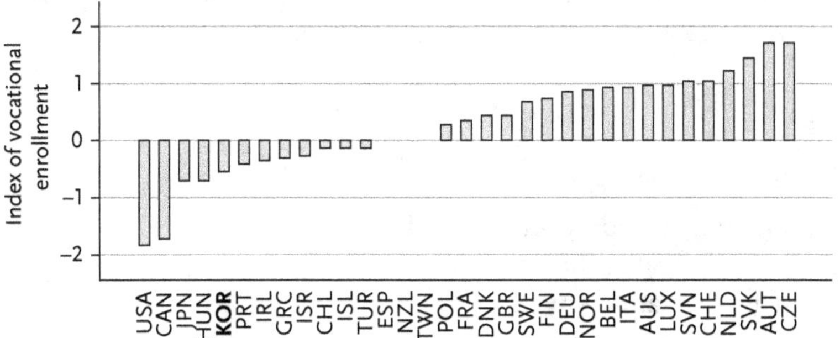

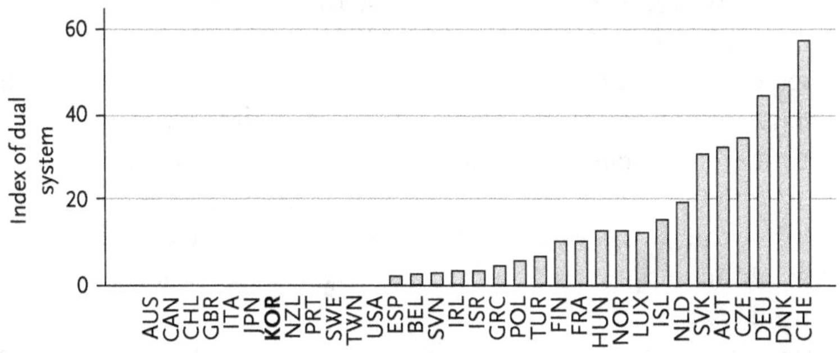

NOTE: In panel A, the index is a score predicted from the factor analysis of three indicators: the age of first tracking selection, the number of curricular tracks available for fifteen-year-olds, and how long the tracked system lasts. In panel B, the index is a score from the principal component analysis of the same indicators but from two different data sources, OECD and UNESCO. In panel C, the index shows the proportion of vocational programs that take place in a dual system (a combination of school-based education and workplace-based training).

SOURCE: Thijs Bol and Herman G. Van de Werfhorst, "Educational Systems and the Trade-Off between Labor Market Allocation and Equality of Educational Opportunity," *Comparative Education Review* 57, no. 2 (May 2013): 285–308.

the country's average level of formal tracking, Korea's educational system displays weak stratification. One could also assess differentiation among schools within the academic track, although this measure is not usually included in cross-country comparative data. For example, in Japan and Taiwan, students are typically stratified in their choice of high schools depending on their performance on the high school entrance exam. This is not the case in Korea, where a high school equalization policy has been in place for most areas of the country since 1976.

Overall, Korea's educational system shows high standardization and low differentiation compared to systems in other countries. Vocational orientation is extremely low. In other words, most students experience a standardized educational environment centered on an academic curriculum with the objective of attending college.

The extent and form of homogenization in Korea's educational system

By combining standardization and differentiation, we can create a useful concept called homogenization. When students learn the same content in the same way from similarly trained teachers in similarly well-equipped school environments (high standardization), and when they mostly attend schools with the same programs regardless of where they live, how well-off they are, or what their learning levels are (low differentiation), their educational experiences are highly homogenized. Homogenization, therefore, measures how much students in a population share similar educational experiences and allows us to assess the role of the educational system in these processes.

Institutionalized education through schools fundamentally acts as a homogenizing force, but how far it goes varies across societies.. Let us now examine the degree of homogenization in students' lives and educational experiences in Korea.

Table 7.1 summarizes, in terms of time, the uniformity of students' lives. On a daily basis, students in Korea spend more time in school than students in other countries. In the past, many high school students in Korea were in school for fifteen hours per day, from 7 a.m. to 10 p.m., due to supplemental classes and night-time self-study sessions on top of regular classes, although this schedule has been somewhat moderated over the past few decades. Saturday classes were abolished only in 2012. It was also common for schools to hold mandatory "supplemental" classes for two to three weeks during summer and winter

TABLE 7.1 Quantitative homogenization of Korea's educational system

Level	Program	Details and Sources
	Regular classes	• Similar to or slightly longer (by 30 minutes to 1 hour for high schools) than that of Western countries.[a]
	Supplemental classes	• 2 additional hours after regular classes in regular high schools • *De facto* extension of regular classes • Official guidelines in the 1990s stipulated that participation was voluntary, but this is rarely observed in practice.[b] • In 1997, all humanities-track high schools in Seoul held supplemental classes after hours.[c] • In 2008, 84% of students in regular high schools in Incheon were forced to take supplemental classes.[d]
Daily schedule	Night self-study	• Most students participate in nightly self-study (9 pm to midnight) after supplemental classes and dinner, unless there are extenuating circumstances. • In 2017, over 80% of high schools nationwide (1,900 out of 2,358) held nightly self-study sessions. Of these schools, 52% held sessions until 10pm, 12% until 11pm, and 12 schools lasted until midnight. In most cases, all students participated.[e] • In 2011, over 90% of high school students in North Chungcheong Province participated in nightly self-study sessions; 75% reported that they were required to do so by the school or by individual teachers.[f]
	"Period 0"	• Students come to school at 7 am, one hour before regular classes start, and participate in self-study or supplementary classes.
	After-school classes	• Held nationwide since 2006. • Similar to supplemental classes, but participation is entirely voluntary. This program is provided in elementary, middle, and high schools, with childcare and extracurricular classes available in elementary and middle schools. • As of 2019, 57% of elementary school students, 29% of middle school students, and 51% of high school students participated; 99% of all schools overall are providing a variety of after-school programs. The overall percentage of students who participate fell from 71% in 2014 to 49% in 2019.[g]
Weekly schedule	Saturday classes	• Saturday morning classes were gradually phased out starting in 2004, and completely eliminated in June 2011. • The elimination of Saturday classes raised concerns about students whose parents could not provide adequate childcare and supervision.[h]
	Regular classes	• 38 weeks across all school levels, equivalent to the OECD average (2018); 190 days in terms of class days, which is slightly above the OECD average of 182–85 days.[i]
Yearly schedule	Supplemental classes (during vacations)	• Until recently, many regular high schools held mandatory sessions for students. • As of 2014, the average rate of participation among 98 regular/special-purpose high schools in Busan was 85%, with classes running for a total of 70 hours (around three weeks, based on 5 hours/day). This was 9 hours shorter than the previous year, as the education authorities prohibited supplemental classes on Saturdays or in the early morning, during "Period 0".[j]
Overall duration	Compulsory education	• As of 2020, compulsory education lasted 9 years (up to middle school). Free education was to be expanded to include high school starting in 2022.

(*continued*)

TABLE 7.1 *(continued)*

Level	Program	Details and Sources
	Compulsory education	• Legal requirements notwithstanding, enrollment in secondary education already surpassed that of OECD and high-income countries in the early 1980s. It passed 90% in the early 1990s and reached near-universal levels in the 2000s (98% as of 2017, relative to OECD average of 89% and high-income country average of 91%).[k]
Overall duration	Early childhood education & care (ECEC)	• As of 2017, close to 95% of children attended an ECEC institution (higher than the OECD average). This is lower than the United Kingdom, France, Denmark, Germany, and New Zealand, and slightly higher than the Netherlands, Sweden, and Japan.[l] • The participation rate in ECEC was below 10% before 1980, but rapidly increased in the 1980s and surpassed the OECD average of 70% in the early 1990s. It reached 87% in the mid-to-late 1990s and has remained stable since. This is the result of a rapid expansion in the number of private preschools through state subsidies in the 1980s.[k] • Free education began in 2012 with the adoption of a standardized preschool curriculum in all ECEC institutions that receive state subsidies. Since the adoption of this curriculum, the enrollment rate increased from 85% in 2010 to 95% in 2017. The OECD average increased from 83% to 87% in the same time period.[l]
Private supplementary education (PSE)		• The total cost of PSE increased forty-fold from 1982 to 2007. The quintile share ratio (top 20% vs. bottom 20%) of spending on PSE decreased from 12 to 5, however. The increase in PSE was led by low-income households.[m] • Between 2007 and 2018, the majority of students (over 80% in elementary, over 70% in middle, and over 50% in high schools) participated in PSE, most for about 10 hours after school.[n] • Over the same time period, the cost of PSE increased along with the participation rate and the total duration of PSE among high school students. This change was driven by lower-middle and middle-income households.[o]

SOURCES: [a] Sohn Min-Ho et al., "A Comparative Study of Primary and Secondary Education Curricula: Focusing on the Organization of Mandatory and Elective Subjects" [in Korean], Ministry of Education, Policy Report 11-1342000-000292-01, December 2017; [b] Chung Eun-Su. "Supplementary Classes for Whom?" [in Korean], *Secondary Education for Us*, February 1995; [c] Lee Han-Ki, "Forced Study Time in the Name of 'Voluntary' Study" [in Korean], *Secondary Education for Us*, September 1997; [d] "83.6% of Students Are Forced to Attend Supplementary Classes" [in Korean], *OhMyNews*, November 11, 2008; [e] Kim Byung-Wook, "[Press Release] Night Voluntary Study Sessions till Midnight in 15 High Schools" [in Korean], October 24, 2017; [f] "75% of Students 'Night Study Session Is Not Voluntary'" [in Korean], *Joongbu Daily*, September 27, 2011; [g] Ministry of Education, "Statistics of Afterschool Classes, 2019" [in Korean], April 30, 2019; [h] Lim Jong-Hwa, "The Educational Implications of the Five School Day System" [in Korean], *Education Review*, December 2011; [i] Ministry of Education. "The Yearly Report of Education Statistics, 2019," August 2019; [j] "High Schools Declare No 0 Period and Saturday Supplementary Classes This Summer" [in Korean], *Busan Daily*, July 22, 2014; [k] World Bank, "World Development Indicators: School enrollment, secondary (% net)," accessed December 1, 2021, https://databank.worldbank.org/; [l] Lee Jeong-Mi, "OECD Statistics on Early Childhood Education and Implications" [in Korean], *National Assembly Research Service: International Statistics - Trends and Analysis* 1 (October 2019): 4–11; [m] Yang Jung-Ho, "Analyzing the Trends of Private Tutoring Expenditure from 1982 to 2017" [in Korean], *Korea Journal of Educational Administration* 31, no. 4 (December 31, 2013): 421–48; [n] Statistics Korea, *Private Education Expenditure Annual Survey*, accessed December 1, 2021, https://kostat.go.kr/portal/korea/kor_nw/1/7/1/index.board; [o] Kim Hyun-Chul, "Time-series of Income-change Effect Eliminated Private Education Expenditure for Each School Level" [in Korean], *Journal of Korean Education* 47, no. 1 (2020): 63–69.

vacations. The duration of compulsory education, currently nine years, is not particularly long in Korea, but the twelve years of primary and secondary schooling is *de facto* universal because almost all students graduate from high school. Furthermore, the degree of participation in early childhood education and care is also far above the average among OECD countries.

Private supplementary education (PSE, or *sa-gyo-yook)* is another institutional factor that can contribute to homogenization in the educational time spent outside of school. PSE is typically understood as a domain that is distinct and separate from public education. However, as indicated by its nickname, "shadow education," PSE is inexorably connected to the public education system. The educational system must be understood not only in terms of school education, but rather as a wider ecosystem that encompasses varieties of PSE. This is especially the case for Korea, where PSE is a highly developed and institutionalized industry. Since it is purchased on the market, PSE is likely to operate as a differentiating force, encompassing a tremendous range of options in terms of individual vs. group classes, the overall size of institutions, medium of delivery (online, in person), intensity, overall duration, continuity, curriculum, and price. At the same time, in Korea, the vast majority of students participate in some forms of PSE, spending considerable proportions of their after-school time in certain PSE classes rather than in other various non-learning activities. This is, therefore, likely a homogenizing force. Whether differentiation or homogenization is more pervasive is an important empirical question in this instance.

As summarized in table 7.1, PSE in Korea leans toward the latter. The commonly used phrase "excessive PSE" not only reflects a concern that PSE imposes a high economic burden on low- and middle-income households, but also implies that it further increases homogenization in a highly homogenized educational system. The homogenization created by PSE (participation rate and time) is especially clear in elementary and middle school.

In sum, Korean children and youth between the ages of four and seventeen are spending a great deal of time studying at school and at PSE institutions after school, and this appears to be particularly true when compared with students in other countries. Arguably, table 7.1 suggests that Korea's education system has already reached the highest level of homogenization plausible, considering the inherent limit in its institutionalizing force of shaping students' private lives in modern democractic societies.

Korea's educational system under authoritarian rule

Why has Korea's educational system reached such an extreme level of homogenization unparalleled in other industrial countries? How did schools and PSE come to be institutionalized in a way that creates such uniformity in the lives of youths? To answer these questions, it is crucial to consider the political context. Korea was ruled by an authoritarian regime that could wield both despotic and infrastructural power.[2] Unlike in a democratic society, where it is difficult to mobilize despotic power, the educational system in Korea's authoritarian regime could brutally suppress the individual lives of children. Comparative education research highlights certain advantages to standardized institutions, but those are largely documented in politically democratized societies.[3] If we extend the story to undemocratic societies, we may see quite a different picture. In an authoritarian context, homogenization, which encompasses standardization and equalization, can be a force to violate students' basic rights and oppress their individuality when combined with the coercive power of a state that uses the educational system to strengthen its political legitimacy. The anti-democratic, anti–human rights aspects of Korea's educational system, as well as the tendency to use education as a means to non-educational ends, are legacies of the authoritarian era in many important ways.

Korea's military dictatorship imposed uniformity on the educational system largely in two ways. First, it used education as a means of repressing civil society. Schools inculcated a totalitarian ideology that emphasized the state over individuality, freedom, and human rights. Students sang the national anthem and recited the pledge of allegiance to the Korean flag as routine school rituals. The Charter for National Education, promulgated in 1968, was printed in textbooks and placed in the classroom, and students were forced to memorize it.[4] This charter stipulated that education was a means to achieve the "revival of the Korean nation." In both its content and how it was taught to students,

2 For a discussion of these concepts, see Michael Mann, "The Autonomous Power of the State: Its Origins, Mechanisms and Results," *European Journal of Sociology* 25, no. 2 (1984): 185–213.

3 Van de Werfhorst and Mijs, "Achievement Inequality and the Institutional Structure of Educational Systems."

4 Yoon-Ki Hong, "Why and How Was the Charter for National Education Made?" [in Korean], *History for Tomorrow* 18 (2004): 111–27.

this charter shows the anti-democratic, anti–human rights origins of homogenization in Korea's educational system.

The Park Chung-Hee regime introduced government-published textbooks after coming to power, replacing the previous system of government-approved textbooks. After the *Yusin* Constitution of 1972, the use of government-published textbooks was extended to all middle schools, while national history and social studies textbooks were standardized even for high schools.[5] The use of harsh corporal punishment and an emphasis on militaristic discipline and absolute obedience (teachers to the principal, students to teachers, and younger students to older students) can also be understood in the same context. Students were required to participate in military-style training at school, and teachers with military backgrounds conducted "militaristic" education. Remnants of this era still remain in Korea's educational system, despite substantial progress in democratizing education.

Second, the government sought to buttress its weak political legitimacy with progress in economic development. In doing so, it subordinated education—along with many other social policies—to the national goal of economic development.[6] It emphasized the role of education in producing the workforce that was required for industrial development. Schools were to produce workers with basic skills who would contribute to the country's drive for economic development. There was little regard for the educational ideals of cultivating modern individuals as citizens. In this vein, school education was considered an instrument for non-educational goals rather than an end. Educational institutions were also more obsessed with selecting talented students and sending them to elite colleges, not only endorsing but emphasizing meritocratic competition for success in achieving a higher status as a prime principle of education. Students also prioritized achieving higher scores in exams in the hopes of attending a good college, finding a good job, and making a fortune, expecting nothing else from schools. The majority of students who were not academically promising were left unattended by schools and teachers.

---

5 Seung-Hoon Kim, "An Analytic Study on Structure and Issues of Textbook Authorization System in Korea" [in Korean], *Journal of Curriculum Studies* 28, no. 2 (2010): 177–204.

6 Joo-Hyoung Ji, "The Shift in the State Form and Mode of Power Exercise in South Korea: From the Authoritarian Developmental State to Neoliberal State Power" [in Korean], *Korean Political Science Review* 43, no. 4 (2009): 175–203.

Schools, therefore, were not a place for educating and developing individuals. They were arenas of competition and survival instead. More importantly, the competition was only about one metric: academic performance. Everyone was ranked based on test scores, regardless of individual talents, interests, and aspirations. The pervasive and narrow meritocratic norm of test scores in Korea's educational system, which holds that hard work will lead to success in an examination that will be the only guaranteed path to lifelong social and economic success, can partly be traced to these modern origins.

In sum, Korea's military dictatorships created an educational system that forcibly imposed uniformity on students without considering their background, abilities, or preferences. The institutions formed during this era did not truly educate students; instead, they treated education as an instrument for achieving national political and economic goals. This gave rise to an educational system and social attitudes in which everyone came to accept that students would compete based solely on academic performance.

Korea's educational system after democratization

Since democratization, how has Korea's educational system changed, and in what ways has it remained the same? The extreme uniformity in school structures that was imposed by the authoritarian regime through militaristic discipline and totalitarian ideology has been weakening since democratization in the sociopolitical domain. This departure from extreme levels of homogenization gave rise to diversification in the way school education was organized. If the surrounding society becomes democratic, the aspects of school education that were enforced with coercive state power lose their legitimacy and can no longer be sustained. In sum, there have been two notable changes: democratization and differentiation.

Two events demonstrate the slow but steady adoption of a more democratic structure for schools. Perhaps the most notable was the formation of the Korean Teachers and Education Workers Union (KTU). Formed in 1989, shortly after democratization, the KTU began to weaken homogenization in the educational system by creating a collective channel for anti-authoritarian voices. The direct election of regional superintendents (*gyo-yook-gam jik-seon-je*), adopted in 2010, was another critical milestone. While it was highly controversial due to concerns about the politicization of educational issues, local education authorities gained independence from the central government as a result of this reform, thus reducing standardization in the system. Since then, regional superintendents have retained authority over the curriculum, school budgets, and hiring of teaching staff. They also have the legal authority to inspect individual schools, including special-purpose high schools (e.g., foreign language high schools, autonomous private high schools), and, if necessary, to revoke the special status of schools within their jurisdictions.

Several important reforms took place amid these democratizing institutional changes. The system of government-published textbooks, which was strengthened under military dictatorships, was changed to one that allowed for a wider range of government-approved or government-authorized textbooks. Schools and teachers now had a wider latitude to choose the required textbooks.[7] Self-study sessions and supplementary classes, which were anything but optional previously, increasingly shifted toward being voluntary. In particular, progressive-leaning superintendents focused on this issue after the introduction of direct local elections in 2010. In a similar vein, in 2016 Gyeonggi Province's superintendent decided to delay the start of classes to 9 a.m.[8]

On the other hand, there have been institutional changes enhancing differentiation and weakening standardization. Changes in the college admissions system are perhaps the most remarkable example. Instead of relying heavily on scores from standardized national exams like the College Scholastic Ability Test (CSAT), admissions standards have been diversified. There is now more of an emphasis on qualitative factors such as school activities and a student's region of residence as an indicator of social disadvantages. As a result, the proportion of admission

---

7 Nevertheless, government guidelines still limit the range of options available as noted earlier in this chapter. Moreover, elementary schools use government-published textbooks. A transition to government-approved and government-authorized textbooks is set to begin in 2022, but only for the upper years of elementary school. There have long been discussions about removing government constraints altogether, but this has not yet been adopted in practice. The Park Geun-Hye administration's anachronistic attempt to bring back a government-published national history textbook, which was made only a few years ago, shows that the legacy of the authoritarian era still runs deep.

8 "Participation in Supplementary Classes and Self-Study Sessions during Winter Break Plummets among High Schools in Busan" [in Korean], *JoongAng Ilbo,* February 13, 2015; "Lee Jae-Jung, Superintendent of Gyeonggi Province, to Abolish Nighttime Self-Study Sessions Starting Next Year" [in Korean], *Hankyoreh,* June 29, 2016.

slots through the CSAT plunged from 71.0 percent in 2002 to 32.5 percent in 2016. Such dramatic changes reflect an effort to foster and appreciate diversity in school education.

Alongside changes to college admissions, there was a corresponding increase in differentiation via diverse school options. The 5.31 Educational Reform of 1995, a major educational reform in the post-democratization era, represents changes in this direction. It highlights growing diversity in students' choices to promote creativity and excellence, and also introduces free market elements in education, especially by deregulating the postsecondary education sector. In this context, a wide variety of special-purpose high schools were introduced, such as foreign-language high schools, international high schools, science high schools, and autonomous public/private high schools. These increased sharply in number after the early 2000s, constituting 10 percent of all high schools in Korea in 2011. In addition, some room for student choice in which general high school to attend was also introduced. The policy was first adopted for schools in Seoul in 2009. The overall policy of high school equalization remains in place, but students' preferences are now partly accounted for.

In this regard, the complete removal of limitations on PSE also deserves attention. In 1980, the Chun Doo-Hwan regime prohibited high-cost PSE, such as individual tutoring, and only allowed low-cost PSE institutions (*hakwon*) to operate. This limited the possibility of differentiation within PSE. The legally permitted form of PSE functioned as an extension of regular school classes and was affordable for even low-income students. The Constitutional Court overturned this policy in 2000, ruling that prohibitions on private tutoring were unconstitutional. A policy that was forcibly implemented by an authoritarian regime was no longer viable in a democratic society. The door was opened to boundless qualitative diversification in PSE, creating yet another path for the educational system to diversify after democratization.

Yet, the institutional features of prioritizing college entrance and ranking students solely by standardized academic achievement for that purpose have persisted, despite the declining significance of the CSAT. These features have even strengthened in some ways, raising concerns that homogenization was reinforced after democratization. Schools, for example, are still an arena of competition for college admissions. The unprecedented rise in college enrollment rates since the mid-1990s, after the 5.31 Reform, has been a key contributing factor. Only a third of high school graduates went on to college in the early 1990s, but college attendance rates rose to 80 percent just ten years after the reform. This suggests that secondary education has been increasingly centered on college admissions. In the past, secondary school education sacrificed the majority of students in favor of a select minority who went to college, while the competition surrounding college admissions was not as intense as it is now. However, after the expansion of college education, college admissions became incredibly important to the vast majority of students.

As discussed above, the loosening of the high school equalization policy brought about greater differentiation among high schools. Ironically, however, such differentiation came with an overall increase in homogenization. Differentiation occurred only among schools on the academic track, and the proportion of students attending vocational high schools has steadily fallen since the mid-1990s (figure 7.3). Furthermore, there has been a rapid increase in the proportion of vocational high school graduates who apply to college instead of seeking employment—by 2010, most of them chose to do so. While this proportion fell in subsequent years, it has begun to rise once again with around half of all vocational high school graduates pursuing a college education. In terms of a focus on preparing for college admissions, therefore, there has essentially been an increase in the homogenization of high schools, regardless of their tracks.

Given these factors, there is now greater pressure on students in terms of college admissions. The societal hierarchy of universities has only been reinforced. After the transition to democracy, the exam-based meritocratic norm has become central to Korea's educational system. A student's score on the CSAT—as well as the university and academic department to which they are accepted—are seen as well-deserved rewards for hard work and individual talent. Several phenomena illustrate this trend clearly. The emphasis on investing in education is widely shared among parents, crossing class divides and geographic regions.[9] University and departmental jackets are becoming popular among youth, especially at elite universities. It appears that the authoritarian-era tendency to subordinate education to college admissions, stressing meritocratic competition as a means of securing a high socioeconomic status, has deepened since democratization.

9 So-Jin Park, "Spatial Stratification Tropes and Making Distinctions: Kangbuk Mothers' Narratives of Their Children's Education" [in Korean], *Korean Cultural Anthropology* 41, no. 1 (2007): 43–81.

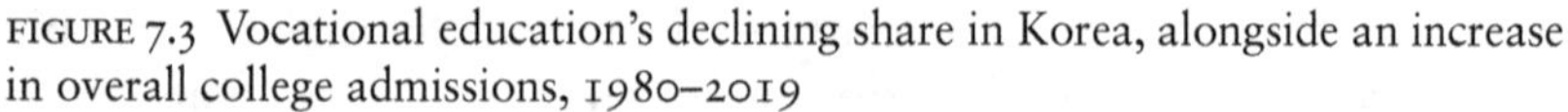

FIGURE 7.3 Vocational education's declining share in Korea, alongside an increase in overall college admissions, 1980–2019

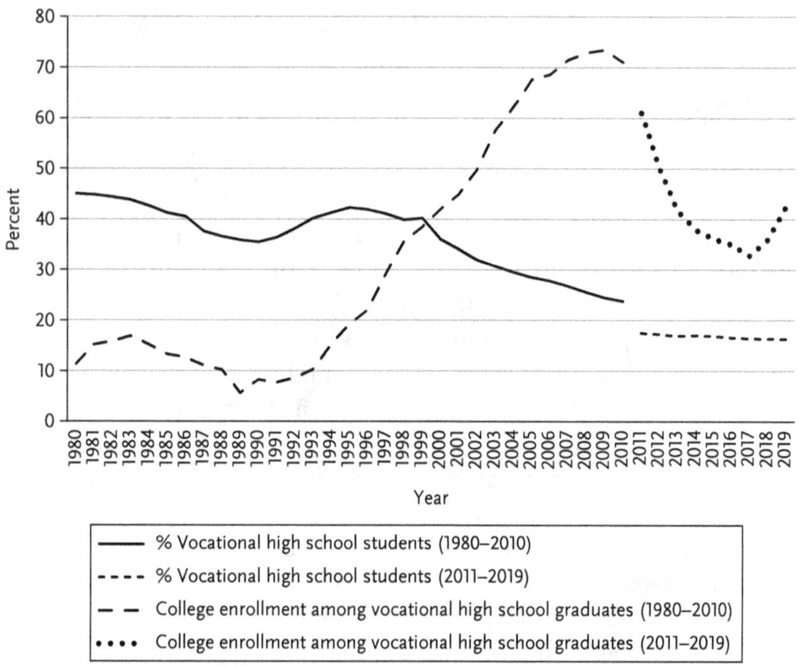

NOTE: The discontinuity in the trends since 2011 is due to a change in the classification of high school types in official statistics.
SOURCE: "Educational Statistics System," Korea Education Development Institute, accessed December 1, 2021, https://kess.kedi.re.kr/index.

The Bright and Dark Sides of Authoritarian Legacies in the Democratic Era

What legacies, positive or negative, do Korea's highly homogenized educational institutions—with their authoritarian origins—have for the educational outcomes of its children and youth and the development of democracy? Comparative educational research suggests that more standardized and less differentiated educational systems, as defined above, are at an advantage in terms of efficiency and equity.[10]

10 Van de Werfhorst and Mijs, "Achievement Inequality and the Institutional Structure of Educational Systems."

Relative to other OECD countries, Korea has achieved the highest level of student academic performance with small variation in overall educational outcomes across individuals and socioeconomic groups.[11] Notwithstanding its authoritarian origin and many individuals' traumatic experiences, the strongly institutionalized force of educational standardization and equalization of the Korean educational system yields comparative advantages in the post-democratization era. Korean schools' weak institutional support for entry into the labor market and the psychological suffering of children are difficult authoritarian legacies that need to be resolved, but societal-level reforms beyond educational reforms, including those concerning markets and families, are arguably more important in meaningfully addressing these problems.

Another critical aspect we need to consider in evaluating the authoritarian legacies of Korea's education system is education's role in the development of democracy. It has been argued that Korea's educational system has been failing in cultivating individuals who are able to exercise free and critical thought and thereby proactively sustain a vibrant democracy, because it instead inculcates hierarchical, authoritarian norms, ignoring students' individualities and voices. This claim seems to assert that the anti-democratic legacy of the authoritarian-era education is still hovering around in the political domain one generation after the democratic transition. For several reasons, this claim fails to withstand logical and empirical scrutiny.

First, even if an educational system has authoritarian characteristics and is extremely homogenized, the primary effect of providing education can still be the creation of a democratic citizenry. Authoritarian education can influence politics in two contrasting ways. On the one hand, schools are a primary institution for state-led socialization, and they discipline children and youth with values, norms, and habits the state intends to instill. As discussed above, students in Korea were forced into militaristic and oppressive rituals and practices in their daily school life in attempts to ingrain anti-democratic values into them. Successful school education under such an anti-democratic regime, therefore, would be expected to produce a population that readily submits to authoritarian rule. On the other hand, education creates social, cultural, and economic conditions in which democratic

11 See, for example, "Education and Training," OECD Statistics, https://stats.oecd.org/; "PISA 2018 Results," OECD, accessed December 1, 2021, https://www.oecd.org/pisa/publications/pisa-2018-results.htm.

citizenship is cultivated. A growing supply of highly educated individuals leads to the formation of a middle class that has diverse desires and heightened expectations of better life outcomes. Indeed, this was a key social force of democratic transition in Korea. Newly educated citizens more readily embraced democratic values. College students were the vanguard of the anti-authoritarian movement in the 1970s and 1980s, culminating in the democratic transition of 1987.

Which tendency is more dominant? Do the anti-democratic features of school education stymie democratic potential? The Korean experience clearly shows that the liberating and pro-democratic effect of education has overwhelmed the oppressive anti-democratic effect. Despite its oppressive, nationalistic, and totalitarian character, the highly homogenized educational system in Korea fostered a democratization movement unparalleled in its persistence and intensity. After democratization in 1987 and many subsequent setbacks, Korean education also produced a mature and robust democratic citizenry that succeeded in impeaching a president through peaceful protests in 2016.

This is quite a paradox. The authoritarian regime pursued economic growth to secure political legitimacy, which led to the expansion of public education and the emergence of a middle class. This eventually provided the political basis for the democratization movement.[12] Education has been documented as "the strongest correlate of civic engagement in all its forms."[13] Korea's recent political history shows that it is the increasing *amount* of education rather than the values that the educational authority tries to instill in students that fosters democratic civic participation. Though we observe a sharp political divide in Korea today, as in many other democratic societies, no political factions, including conservatives who tend to have nostalgic sentiments about the authoritarian past, can deny there is a clear consensus on democracy.

Second, as mentioned before, schools themselves have been transformed during the sociopolitical process of democratization. Schools, which were once elements of a violent, despotic state, have now largely adopted democratic practices. The institutional legacies of

---

12 Michael Seth, "Education Zeal, State Control and Citizenship in South Korea," *Citizenship Studies* 16, no. 1 (2012): 13–28; Myungji Yang, "The Making of the Urban Middle Class in South Korea (1961–1979): Nation-Building, Discipline, and the Birth of the Ideal National Subjects," *Sociological Inquiry* 82, no. 3 (2012): 424–45.

13 Robert D. Putnam, "Tuning In, Tuning Out: The Strange Disappearance of Social Capital in America," *Political Science and Politics* 28, no. 4 (1995): 664–83.

authoritarianism have not vanished entirely, and those remaining legacies have a limited influence in a predominantly democratic context. In addition, both teachers and parents—who are key actors in any educational system—now consist of individuals who came of age during and after democratization.

Third, since the 2000s, Korea has been a highly educated society in which most citizens have at least a high school degree. This is the result of a swift expansion in the provision of public education, and it has crucial political implications. In the past decade, the ascendance of far-right populist forces has precipitated a crisis of democracy in the United States and many European countries. A critical factor behind these political forces is the rapidly widening socioeconomic gap between elites and normal citizens—in particular, low-educated and low-income individuals who have been marginalized amid globalization, financialization, and the advancement of an information technology economy.[14] By contrast, the gap between elites and nonelites is relatively narrow in Korea. Korean elites do not have deep historical roots, on one hand, and the unusually high levels of educational attainment among Korea's citizenry in general play an important role, on the other. In spite of its anti-democratic, anti-educational past, the expansion of Korean education is an important clue for understanding why Korea's democracy has not taken the same path as other Western liberal democracies in recent years.

Nonetheless, there are still reasonable grounds to question whether the current educational system, centered on college admissions and a highly standardized method of evaluation, is truly conducive to cultivating mature democratic values. In Korea, college admissions results, which are based on an individual's performance in high school, are justly considered to be the well-deserved results of meritocratic effort. Moreover, an individual's alma mater is a key factor in shaping significant life chances, such that it is deemed fair to treat people differently based on which college they graduated from. In this instance, Korea's homogenizing educational system cannot foster democratic solidarity among citizens. Instead, education in such a system will act as a persistent engine of inequality that marginalizes particular groups. Frequent

14 Yascha Mounk, *The People vs. Democracy: Why Our Freedom Is in Danger and How to Save It* (Cambridge: Harvard University Press, 2019); Michael J. Sandel, *The Tyranny of Merit: What's Become of the Common Good?* (New York: Farrar, Straus, and Giroux, 2020).

conflicts between regular and irregular workers, as well as the social exclusion of the poor, people with disabilities, refugees, and foreign migrant workers and their children, show that this is already more than just a theoretical concern. The legacies of the authoritarian era have created an unexpected threat to the maturation of democracy.

Education Reform in the Service of Democracy

The legacies of this authoritarian era have provided some unanticipated benefits, but they also present formidable challenges on the path ahead. Discerning the bright and dark sides of these authoritarian legacies is necessary for creating an improved and enhanced educational system. At the same time, educational reform can provide a solid foundation for democratic maturation. I put forward four broad considerations that should be accounted for in discussions about educational reforms in Korea.

First, the highly standardized and equalized institutional character of Korea's educational system should be maintained. While it may not be perfect, the current system has notable strengths. Other countries seek to emulate the high levels of academic achievement present among Korea's students and the fairness of its educational system. There is no reason to discard this advantage. The discussion would be different if these outcomes had come at the expense of opportunities to foster students' creativity or critical thinking. However, there is little evidence to support such concerns. For example, in PISA's problem-solving tests, designed to measure creativity and critical thinking skills, Korea was surpassed only by Finland, suggesting that Korea's standardized, equalized educational system is not particularly suppressing students' creative or critical thinking skills.[15] The institutional capacity that sustains high levels of standardization and equalization is likely to help—not hinder—reforms to Korea's educational system.

It should also be noted that standardized, equalized educational systems are highly resistant to change. Every country's educational system is path dependent and has developed in conjunction with other social institutions. As such, one should be wary of calls to overhaul Korea's educational system and replace it with institutions modeled on those of the United States, European countries, or other developed countries.

15 Hyunjoon Park, *Re-Evaluating Education in Japan and Korea: De-Mystifying Stereotypes* (New York: Routledge, 2013).

For example, the high vocational orientation and differentiation of Germany's educational system can only be maintained in conjunction with the country's strong manufacturing sector, skills-based labor market, and corporatist welfare regime. Similarly, the Korean system, where most children study from early morning until late evening in schools and PSE institutions, is closely related to the country's weak government support for childcare and families, as well as long work hours in the labor market. An educational system does not emerge from a vacuum and does not function in isolation. The complex institutional characteristics of every country's educational system make it extremely difficult to selectively transplant the positive aspects of foreign educational systems.

Second, while maintaining the institutional advantages of the current system, the remaining authoritarian legacies should be replaced and improved in line with the democratic shift that has occurred in Korean society. The most important target of reform is the system's overwhelming emphasis on the use of academic achievement as the only standard with which to rank all students in a fiercely competitive college admissions process. The system prioritizes competition over learning and growth, and students are constantly reminded of their ranking relative to their peers.

The problem is not ranking per se, but rather using the uniform standard of academic grades to do so. Likewise, competition in and of itself is not a problem. The issue is that there is no reasonable alternative for students who are sidelined by this competition. Students should be evaluated based on a wide variety of talents, traits, and experiences, not just academic achievement as measured on a standardized numerical scale. They also should be able to choose to opt out of the competition, if they prefer, without worrying about their future livelihoods and well-being. From this perspective, efforts to diversify the college admissions process by creating tracks that include the comprehensive evaluation of a student's school life records (also referred to as *hakjong*) represent a step in the right direction. Some may be concerned about the risk of rising inequality as a result of greater diversification. However, the institutional capacities underlying standardization and equalization can be important means of mitigating adverse side effects. If it is possible to meaningfully institutionalize diversity within a standardized framework, then this will enable a fair and equitable educational system in which students with diverse talents can learn together and be evaluated according to appropriate standards.

With regard to competition, there needs to be an institutionalized solution to address the majority of students who lose out. One option is to shift the societal focus from producing a small group of high achievers at the top to widening the middle of the distribution. Further improving the skills of high achievers is a challenge, but helping struggling students find stable footing in their studies is an even more formidable task. There must be a policy shift to create institutional and social incentives for schools and teachers to focus on the latter. Korea's success in the battle against the COVID-19 pandemic reveals that the country's strength lies in its high bureaucratic capacity and the voluntary cooperation of its citizenry, not in the excellence of a small group of elites. An education policy that shifts public attention away from the top can be justified not only on a normative basis, but also as an optimal societal strategy. Again, the existing institutional capacities that underlie standardization and equalization can be tremendously useful in this regard.

Third, however, it is important to avoid reforms that further increase standardization and equalization, based on concerns about fairness (*gong-jeong-seong*). For instance, consider the recent controversy surrounding the fairness of college admissions tracks that incorporate evaluations of qualitative factors, such as *hakjong*. Setting aside fundamental disagreements about what constitutes fairness, it is unequivocally wrong to contend that this controversy arose because Korea's educational system is lacking in homogenization. As noted earlier in this chapter, Korea's educational system ranks highly in terms of equality. There is no evidence to indicate that there has been a rise in inequality with regard to access to college education.[16] Further, there is no reason to believe that upper-class households prefer *hakjong*. On the contrary, they appear to prefer the traditional method of using CSAT scores.[17]

16 Seongsoo Choi and Subin Lee, "Has the Inequality of Educational Opportunity Increased in Korea? Cohort Trends in the Inequality of Educational Attainment by Parental Education" [in Korean], *Korean Journal of Sociology* 52, no. 4 (2018): 77–113; Inkwan Chung et al., "Intergenerational Social Mobility and Educational Inequality in South Korea: A Comprehensive Review of Empirical Studies since 2000" [in Korean], *Economy and Society* 127 (2020): 12–59.

17 Chang-Hwan Kim and Heeyoun Shin, "Adaptation Strategy of the Upper Class and Fairness in Elite College Admission" [in Korean], *Korean Journal of Sociology* 54, no. 3 (2020): 35–83; Jeongju Moon and Yool Choi, "College Admission System as a Rule of Exclusion: The Relationship between Social Class and Perception of College Admission System" [in Korean], *Korean Journal of Sociology* 53, no. 3 (2019): 175–215.

Last, such issues of fairness and equality have crucial implications for the role of education in cultivating a mature, democratic citizenry. A meritocratic norm that equates academic grades with merit and accepts unequal rewards based on such a narrow notion of merit can be a double-edged sword when it comes to fostering democratic values.

On the one hand, a sense that everyone belongs to the same meritocratic arena of competition can be a powerful source of homogeneity. The majority of Koreans have a strong trust in meritocratic principles based on standardized assessments, which are believed to be a fair and equitable selection procedure. The strong meritocratic norm reinforces and is reinforced by the country's relatively narrow social and cultural distances across social classes, leading to an unusual combination of atomized individuals and strong social homogeneity. This meritocratic norm, which can be described as a dominant habitus that most Koreans acquire through education, has played an important role in shaping Korea's remarkably dynamic progress toward a consolidated democracy in the past few decades.

On the other hand, meritocracy, while open and democratic in its ideal form, creates social exclusion and reinforces discrimination in the name of "fair competition." Elite and upper-middle-class families seek to form social closure, generating exclusionary cultural and social boundaries as they endeavor to translate their nonmeritocratic privilege into merit-based advantages for their children. A new mode of segregation within and across schools based on neighborhood characteristics (e.g., middle-class children residing in large, high-rise apartment complexes versus lower-class children residing in other forms of housing units) that arose after large-scale urban redevelopment projects in the 2000s and 2010s, popularly known as the "New Town Project," is a quintessential example. When broader and unequal social contexts shaping examination results are ignored in the name of fairness, exam-based merit becomes a source of social exclusion. It perpetuates small, arbitrary, and often insignificant differences in outcome among high-stakes examinations (e.g., CSAT, civil service examinations) in the form of categorically unequal social classes. Recent social backlash in Korea against the conversion of irregular contract employees in public agencies to regular, full-time employees shows how merit is used as an exclusionary institutional mechanism in forming social closure. This exclusionary nature of meritocracy threatens democracy because it erodes social solidarity.

In this regard, strengthening the role of public education in cultivating mature democratic citizens and implementing this is of paramount importance. The necessity of such strengthening has been largely overlooked, particularly due to the long shadow of authoritarian legacies. It is now emerging as a new task for the Korean educational system. As noted above, education enhanced the development of democracy by contributing to economic development and creating a strong middle class. This political effect of education, however, faces a challenge as economic growth slows down and finding a decent job becomes increasingly difficult. Instead, I call for a more direct role of school education as a democratic institution for socialization in cultivating social solidarity.

Successful educational reform should foster more inclusive norms and practices and embrace diversity as a critical social value, while maintaining the dynamic aspects of appreciating achievement and competition. Diversity is a key nexus connecting education and democracy. In school environments where socially, culturally, and economically diverse students study together, students tend to attribute their performance less to their ability and effort, and more to society.[18] Diverse and desegregated schools are, therefore, favorable institutional conditions for education to nurture democratic citizenry and more extensive civic engagement and solidarity. In this regard, again, what was once a negative feature of authoritarian legacy in school education—a highly standardized and equalized system—can be used to help form a new democratic infrastructure.

Legacies of the Moon Administration and Tasks for the New Administration

Finally, I conclude with a discussion about the Moon Jae-In administration's policies and future directions the next administration should take when it comes to education and its role in shaping Korean democracy.

First, the Moon administration increased the proportion of college admissions tracks that are centered on CSAT scores to 40 percent for major universities. This was in response to a sociopolitical controversy over admissions tracks centered on qualitative evaluations (e.g., *hakjong*). This change is questionable in its validity and effectiveness. It is based on an erroneous diagnosis of reforms meant to increase

18 Jonathan J. B. Mijs, "Stratified Failure: Educational Stratification and Students' Attributions of Their Mathematics Performance in 24 Countries," *Sociology of Education* 19, no. 1 (2016): 137–53.

diversity over the past decade, misinterpreting them as undermining fairness and transparency. As noted earlier, this misdiagnosis overrepresents the voices of the upper-middle classes. The government's decision to heighten the importance of the national standardized exam once again in college admissions thus cannot be considered a policy that truly promotes equality of opportunity, which was its nominal intention.

The recent reform of college admissions among U.S. colleges also provides critical evidence against the Moon administration's policy as an avenue toward increased diversity in Korean colleges. Last year, a number of colleges in the United States, including highly selective elite universities, made standardized test scores such as the SAT and ACT optional in response to George Floyd's murder and the COVID-19 crisis. What they found after this change was greater diversity in the body of incoming students, with regard to race and income.[19] It is too early to assess the stratifying impact of the Moon administration's decision, which will not take effect until 2023. It is, therefore, an important task for the new government to mitigate any adverse consequences of this policy in relation to inequality and diversity in education. This will have important implications for the development of Korean democracy.

Second, no reasonable observer can deny that housing policy has been a major failure of the Moon administration. Since 2017, the first year of Moon's presidency, housing prices have increased by 12.2 percent on average, largely driven by the remarkable surge in the price of apartment complexes in Seoul and the surrounding Gyeonggi Province (24.7 percent).[20] The government's failure to stabilize housing prices has many social and political consequences. Here, I would like to specifically discuss their relationship to education and implications for social integration and democracy. The high-rise apartment complex is a typical housing format that most Korean families aspire to live in, since it is a vivid social and cultural marker of upper-middle-class status. One reason why Korean upper- and middle-class families prefer high-rise apartment complexes is their closed structure. The apartment complex is a physical and spatial form that perfectly matches upper-middle-class families' desire to isolate themselves from other social classes. When this type of housing prevails and begins to segregate students from dif-

19 Anemona Hartocollis, "After a Year of Turmoil, Elite Universities Welcome More Diverse Freshman Classes," *New York Times,* April 17, 2021.

20 Monthly statistics of housing prices from the Korea Real Estate Board, accessed December 1, 2021, https://www.reb.or.kr/r-one/main.do.

ferent family backgrounds into different schools, diversity in schools will be eroded. Disadvantaged students will therefore be at greater risk of social exclusion.

The recent surge in housing prices during Moon's presidency is likely to push the entire education system in this direction, which will pose a critical threat to the future of Korean democracy. Children's housing location depends on their parents' economic status and luck. If their place of residence decides their school, this allows them no opportunities to connect and form common experiences with children from other social backgrounds. This could widen social and cultural distances between children from various socioeconomic backgrounds and ultimately undermine prospects for social solidarity. In its social and educational policies, the new administration should focus on countering these detrimental trends.

Bibliography

"75% of Students 'Night Study Session Is Not Voluntary'." [In Korean.] *Joongbu Daily*, September 27, 2011.

"83.6% of Students Are Forced to Attend Supplementary Classes." [In Korean.] *OhMyNews*, November 11, 2008.

Bol, Thijs et al. "Curricular Tracking and Central Examinations: Counterbalancing the Impact of Social Background on Student Achievement in 36 Countries." *Social Forces* 92, no. 4 (June 2014): 1545–72.

Bol, Thijs, and Herman G. Van de Werfhorst. "Educational Systems and the Trade-Off between Labor Market Allocation and Equality of Educational Opportunity." *Comparative Education Review* 57, no. 2 (May 2013): 285–308.

Choi, Seongsoo, and Subin Lee. "Has the Inequality of Educational Opportunity Increased in Korea? Cohort Trends in the Inequality of Educational Attainment by Parental Education." [In Korean.] *Korean Journal of Sociology* 52, no. 4 (2018): 77–113.

Chung, Eun-Su. "Supplementary Classes for Whom?" [In Korean.] *Secondary Education for Us* (February 1995).

Chung, Inkwan et al. "Intergenerational Social Mobility and Educational Inequality in South Korea: A Comprehensive Review of Empirical Studies since 2000." [In Korean.] *Economy and Society* 127 (2020): 12–59.

Hartocollis, Anemona. "After a Year of Turmoil, Elite Universities Welcome More Diverse Freshman Classes." *New York Times,* April 17, 2021.

"High Schools Declare No 0 Period and Saturday Supplementary Classes This Summer." [In Korean.] *Busan Daily,* July 22, 2014.

Hong, Yoon-Ki. "Why and How Was the Charter for National Education Made?" [In Korean.] *History for Tomorrow* 18 (2004): 111–27.

Ji, Joo-Hyoung. "The Shift in the State Form and Mode of Power Exercise in South Korea: From the Authoritarian Developmental State to Neoliberal State Power." [In Korean.] *Korean Political Science Review* 43, no. 4 (2009): 175–203.

Kerckhoff, Alan C. "Education and Social Stratification Processes in Comparative Perspective." *Sociology of Education* 74 (2001): 3–18.

Kim, Byung-Wook. "Night Voluntary Study Sessions till Midnight in 15 High Schools." [In Korean.] Press release, October 24, 2017.

Kim, Chang-Hwan, and Heeyoun Shin. "Adaptation Strategy of the Upper Class and Fairness in Elite College Admission." [In Korean.] *Korean Journal of Sociology* 54, no. 3 (2020): 35–83.

Kim, Hyun-Chul. "Time-Series of Income-Change Effect Eliminated Private Education Expenditure for Each School Level." [In Korean.] *Journal of Korean Education* 47, no. 1 (2020): 63–69.

Kim, Seung-Hoon. "An Analytic Study on Structure and Issues of Textbook Authorization System in Korea." [In Korean.] *Journal of Curriculum Studies* 28, no. 2 (2010): 177–204.

Korea Education Development Institute. "Educational Statistics System." Accessed December 1, 2021. https://kess.kedi.re.kr/index.

Korea Real Estate Board. "Monthly Statistics of Housing Prices." [In Korean.] Accessed December 1, 2021. https://www.reb.or.kr/r-one/main.do.

Lee, Han-Ki. "Forced Study Time in the Name of 'Voluntary' Study." [In Korean.] *Secondary Education for Us* (September 1997).

"Lee Jae-Jung, Superintendent of Gyeonggi Province, to Abolish Nighttime Self-Study Sessions Starting Next Year." [In Korean.] *Hankyoreh,* June 29, 2016.

Lee, Jeong-Mi. "OECD Statistics on Early Childhood Education and Implications." [In Korean.] *National Assembly Research Service: International Statistics—Trends and Analysis* 1 (October 2019): 4–11.

Lim, Jong-Hwa. "The Educational Implications of the Five School Day System." [In Korean.] *Education Review* (December 2011).

Mann, Michael. "The Autonomous Power of the State: Its Origins, Mechanisms and Results." *European Journal of Sociology* 25, no. 2 (1984): 185–213.

Mijs, Jonathan J. B. "Stratified Failure: Educational Stratification and Students' Attributions of Their Mathematics Performance in 24 Countries." *Sociology of Education* 19, no. 1 (2016): 137–53.

Ministry of Education. "Statistics of Afterschool Classes, 2019." [In Korean.] April 30, 2019.

Moon, Jeongju, and Yool Choi. "College Admission System as a Rule of Exclusion: The Relationship between Social Class and Perception of College Admission System." [In Korean.] *Korean Journal of Sociology* 53, no. 3 (2019): 175–215.

Mounk, Yascha. *The People vs. Democracy: Why Our Freedom Is in Danger and How to Save It.* Cambridge: Harvard University Press, 2019.

OECD (Organisation for Economic Co-operation and Development). *PISA 2015 Results (Volume II): Policies and Practices for Successful Schools.* Paris: OECD Publishing, 2016.

———. "PISA 2018 Results." Accessed December 1, 2021. https://www.oecd.org/pisa/publications/pisa-2018-results.htm.

OECD Statistics. "Education and Training." https://stats.oecd.org/.

Park, Hyunjoon. *Re-Evaluating Education in Japan and Korea: De-Mystifying Stereotypes.* New York: Routledge, 2013.

Park, So-Jin. "Spatial Stratification Tropes and Making Distinctions: Kangbuk Mothers' Narratives of Their Children's Education." [In Korean.] *Korean Cultural Anthropology* 41, no. 1 (2007): 43–81

"Participation in Supplementary Classes and Self-Study Sessions during Winter Break Plummets among High Schools in Busan." [In Korean.] *JoongAng Ilbo,* February 13, 2015.

Putnam, Robert D. "Tuning In, Tuning Out: The Strange Disappearance of Social Capital in America." *Political Science and Politics* 28, no 4 (1995): 664–83.

Sandel, Michael J. *The Tyranny of Merit: What's Become of the Common Good?* New York: Farrar, Straus and Giroux, 2020.

Seth, Michael. "Education Zeal, State Control and Citizenship in South Korea." *Citizenship Studies* 16, no. 1 (2012): 13–28.

Sohn, Min-Ho et al. "A Comparative Study of Primary and Secondary Education Curricula: Focusing on the Organization of Mandatory and Elective Subjects." [In Korean.] Ministry of Education, Policy Report 11-1342000-000292-01, December 2017.

Statistics Korea. *Private Education Expenditure Annual Survey.* Accessed December 1, 2021. https://kostat.go.kr/portal/korea/kor_nw/1/7/1/index.board.

Van de Werfhorst, Herman G., and Jonathan J. B. Mijs. "Achievement Inequality and the Institutional Structure of Educational Systems: A Comparative Perspective." *Annual Review of Sociology* 36, no. 1 (2010): 407–28.

World Bank. "World Development Indicators: School Enrollment, Secondary (% Net)." Accessed December 1, 2021. https://databank.worldbank.org/.

Yang, Jung-Ho. "Analyzing the Trends of Private Tutoring Expenditure from 1982 to 2017." [In Korean.] *Korea Journal of Educational Administration* 31, no. 4 (December 31, 2013): 421–48.

Yang, Myungji. "The Making of the Urban Middle Class in South Korea (1961–1979): Nation-Building, Discipline, and the Birth of the Ideal National Subjects." *Sociological Inquiry* 82, no. 3 (2012): 424–45.

CHAPTER EIGHT

Social Media and the Salience of Polarization in Korea

Yong Suk Lee

Protests are ubiquitous in Seoul. Both progressives and conservatives take to the streets for various political and social causes, and protestors from opposing camps sometimes hold rallies side by side. In late 2019, when news erupted that Cho Kuk's daughter had received preferential treatment in college admissions and that Cho's wife fabricated documents to beef up her daughter's résumé, for weeks Seoul saw large protests opposing his nomination as justice minister, with simultaneous counterprotests. To the casual bystander, these protests show an increasingly polarized Korea. The antagonism between conservatives and progressives is on full display online, whether through mainstream news media outlets such as *Chosun Ilbo* and *Hankyoreh*, which have become increasingly polarized,[1] or numerous online communities. If one reads the online news and people's *daetgeul* (comments and replies to news articles or online posts), it appears that people have become increasingly caustic and sensational on the internet, and less accepting of opposing viewpoints.

Has South Korea (Korea) truly become more polarized? Or does it just appear to be so, while the true extent of polarization remains unchanged? Korean history is laden with examples of political rivalry and factionalism. Purging of royal lineages or scholars based on faction was common during the latter part of the Joseon dynasty, primarily as a means to secure power. Ideological schisms continued during Japan's

1 Gi-Wook Shin, *One Alliance, Two Lenses: U.S.-Korea Relations in a New Era* (Stanford: Stanford University Press, 2010).

colonial rule.[2] As Aram Hur explains in chapter 2, clashes between conservatives and progressives were common during Korea's postcolonial democratic transition and into the latter decades of the twentieth century. During Korea's transition from authoritarian rule in the 1980s, students protested against the old guard almost every day.[3] The recent candlelight protests that occurred during the impeachment of President Park Geun-Hye encapsulate the dynamic evolution of political ideology in Korea. It may well be that Korea has long had factions or parties with opposing views, and perhaps the discord between opposing parties is no less severe today than it was before.

However, what makes today's political environment different is the media. The media landscape, once dominated by television and newspapers, has been evolving rapidly with the advent of internet technology and social media. News outlets have become disaggregated, and the modes by which people access news have become diverse. Internet news and social media lower the barrier to entry, and nearly anyone who is willing can create and disseminate news. This easy access to and distribution of news through social media raises several concerns.

First is the proliferation of so-called fake news. News without factual confirmation can easily spread to thousands and millions of people in a matter of days.[4] Another is the so-called echo-chamber effect. People with like-minded views use the same news outlets and thereby hear and see only the content that aligns with their beliefs.[5] Because of these features, there is much speculation that social media increases polarization.[6] However, this issue is still being debated because of empirical difficulties in precisely identifying the causal impact of social media. The relationship between social media and polarization may be

---

2 Michael Robinson, "Ideological Schism in the Korean Nationalist Movement, 1920–1930: Cultural Nationalism and the Radical Critique," *Journal of Korean Studies* 4 (1982): 241–68.

3 Gi-Wook Shin and Paul Y. Chang, eds., *South Korean Social Movements: From Democracy to Civil Society* (London and New York: Routledge, 2011).

4 Souroush Vousoughi, Deb Roy, and Sinan Aral, "The Spread of True and False News Online," *Science* 359, no. 6380 (2018): 1146–51.

5 Cass Sunstein, *Echo Chambers: Bush v. Gore, Impeachment, and Beyond* (Princeton: Princeton University Press, 2001); Eytan Bakshy, Solomon Messing, and Lada A. Adamic, "Exposure to Ideologically Diverse News and Opinion on Facebook," *Science* 348, no. 6239 (2015): 1130–32.

6 "Political Polarization in the American Public," Pew Research Center, June 12, 2014, https://www.pewresearch.org/politics/2014/06/12/political-polarization-in-the-american-public/.

driven by people with particularly polarized views using social media, rather than social media meaningfully affecting people's ideologies. At the very least, it is now widely accepted that social media is increasingly being used by people as a news source, and that news from social media can shape peoples' view of the world.

In this chapter, I examine how social media interacts with today's polarized society and discuss the implications for polarization in Korea and for Korea's democracy. I break down the analysis into the following sections. First, I examine polarization patterns across various Organisation for Economic Co-operation and Development (OECD) countries, and how polarization has evolved in Korea. The empirical evidence does not lend itself to simple conclusions. It suggests that overall polarization has been at the same level for a long time, though there may have been an increase in recent years. Cross-country evidence indicates that Korea is not unique. There are countries where polarization has increased, but also countries where polarization has remained steady or even decreased. In the next section, I argue that it may not be polarization that has been increasing in Korea, but rather the salience of polarization. The salience of polarization has increased both online and offline, especially in the form of political protests. I argue that new online media technologies, especially social media, drive this trend.

I next examine this point using original survey data from Korea. The survey assessed social media use, political ideology, and protest participation in relation to the impeachment of President Park Geun-Hye. I find that users of social media, compared to those who rely on other sources for their news, hold more extreme ideological views and are more likely to participate in protests. The relationship between extreme views and protest participation is especially robust among social media users. In the last section, I discuss three channels through which the salience of extreme and polarized political viewpoints on social and online media can affect democracy by influencing public opinion. The way that specific users and political parties interact with social media can exacerbate division in modern societies. I conclude with suggestions about how to minimize the potential harms of polarization in today's disaggregated media environment.

Polarization Patterns in OECD Countries and Korea

The political animosity between Republicans and Democrats in the United States has been creating a deeper rift between the two parties.

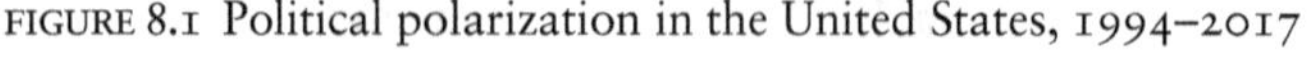

FIGURE 8.1 Political polarization in the United States, 1994–2017

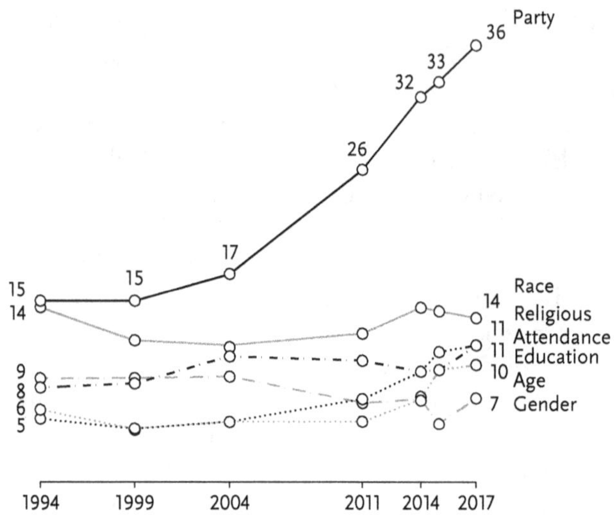

NOTE: The vertical axis indicates the percentage point gap between different groups.
SOURCE: Pew Research Center, "The Partisan Divide on Political Values Grows Even Wider." October 5, 2017.

Since 1994, the Pew Research Center has regularly surveyed Americans on ten questions related to political values, such as whether the government should do more to help the needy, whether immigrants strengthen the country or are a burden, whether diplomacy or military strength is the best way to ensure peace, and perceptions of homosexuality and abortion. The partisan divide on these issues has steadily grown since 1994. Recently, partisan differences on fundamental political values grew drastically under the Trump administration. Figure 8.1 indicates the average gap between the share of two groups taking the conservative position across the ten questions. The average gap between Democrats and Republicans increased from 15 percentage points in 1994 to 36 percentage points in 2017. On the other hand, gaps based on race, religious attendance, education, age, and gender remained relatively stable.[7]

7 "The Partisan Divide on Political Values Grows Even Wider," Pew Research Center, October 5, 2017, https://www.pewresearch.org/politics/2017/10/05/the-partisan-divide-on-political-values-grows-even-wider/.

Political polarization is not unique to the United States. Brexit has created deep political rifts in the United Kingdom. Far-right groups are emerging in many European countries, and the clash between conservatives and progressives on issues such as immigration and globalization is intensifying.[8] However, what we see in the news does not necessarily imply that polarization is increasing in the general population, since the news selectively highlights events and often showcases the loudest voices. Moreover, generalizing trends in polarization across multiple countries is difficult because of data challenges. Unlike economic measures such as gross domestic product growth, unemployment rate, or inflation, political values are not consistently documented and are difficult to quantify. Though several cross-country surveys ask questions about political values, the survey questions are usually not uniform across countries or over time, making cross-country comparisons unreliable.

In a recent paper, Boxell, Gentzkow, and Shapiro analyze trends in polarization across several OECD countries.[9] They compile multiple data sources and construct measures of affective polarization. Affective polarization is the degree to which people feel more negatively toward other political parties than toward their own. Affective polarization has increased dramatically in the United States in recent years. A party member rated a same-party member 27 points higher than an out-party member in 1978; by 2016, that difference had increased to 45.9 points. As a 2017 Pew Research Center report indicates, the partisan divide increased even more under the Trump administration and during the COVID-19 pandemic.[10] The increase in affective polarization in the United States is the largest among all countries in the sample.

The same report also finds that affective polarization increased in Canada, New Zealand, and Switzerland, but that it decreased in Australia, Britain, Norway, Sweden, and Germany since the 1980s. However, after 2000, affective polarization increased in all countries except for

---

8 "In Western Europe, Populist Parties Tap Anti-Establishment Frustration but Have Little Appeal across Ideological Divide," Pew Research Center, July 12, 2018, https://www.pewresearch.org/global/2018/07/12/in-western-europe-populist-parties-tap-anti-establishment-frustration-but-have-little-appeal-across-ideological-divide/.

9 Levi Boxell, Matthew Gentzkow, and Jesse M. Shapiro, "Cross-Country Trends in Affective Polarization" (NBER Working Paper no. 26669, National Bureau of Economic Research, Cambridge, MA, 2020), https://www.nber.org/papers/w26669.

10 "The Partisan Divide on Political Values Grows Even Wider," Pew Research Center.

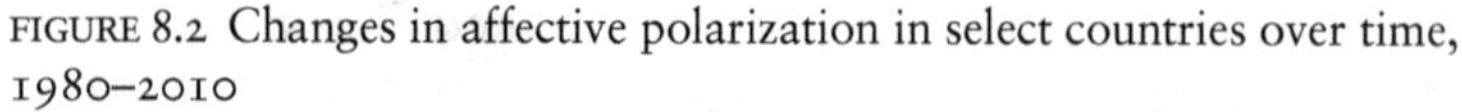

FIGURE 8.2 Changes in affective polarization in select countries over time, 1980–2010

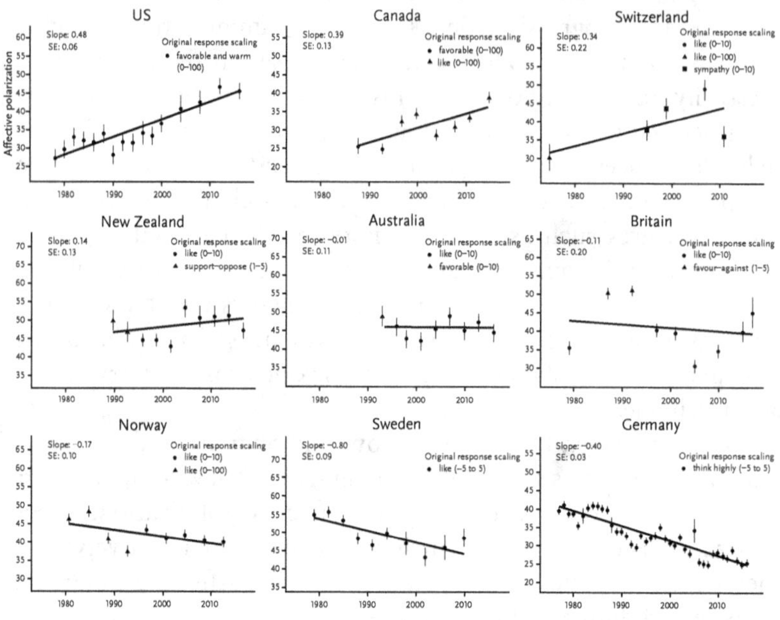

SOURCE: Levi Boxell, Matthew Gentzkow, and Jesse M. Shapiro, "Cross-Country Trends in Affective Polarization," NBER Working Paper no. 26669 (2020), https://www.nber.org/papers/w26669.

Germany, Norway, and Switzerland (figure 8.2). The authors do not attribute these trends to increasing inequality or immigration, since these patterns have been similar in most countries in the sample. Instead, the authors point to the rise of cable news as a potential explanation. Cable news channels have been expanding in all of these countries. These channels cater to specific audiences, leading to audience segmentation.

Polarization patterns in Korea: Descriptive survey data

Despite the widespread belief that polarization is rising in the West,[11] the pattern across OECD countries is varied. Countries that had high

11 Mohamed A. El-Erian, "How Political Polarisation Is Crippling Western Democracies," World Economic Forum, May 12, 2015, https://www.weforum.org/agenda/2015/05/how-political-polarisation-is-crippling-western-democracies/.

levels of affective polarization in the 1980s have generally seen a decline over the long run, with a recent increase in only some. Countries that had relatively low levels of affective polarization have experienced an increase.

Examining polarization trends in Korea is more challenging than in other OECD countries due to the sparsity of relevant public opinion surveys. Though various government surveys are conducted using a representative sample of the Korean population, they generally do not ask about political beliefs, ideology, or values.

However, a recent report by the Korea Development Institute uses two surveys to provide some insight into how polarization has evolved in Korea.[12] One is the World Value Survey (WVS), conducted in multiple countries since 1981. The WVS is a nationally representative survey that examines people's values and beliefs and allows for comparison over time and across countries. It asks about people's political values along the liberal-conservative spectrum; beliefs regarding democracy, elections and leadership, economic inequality, and redistribution; and thoughts on social issues including immigration, gender inequality, homosexuality, and environmental protection. The survey has been conducted in Korea since 1982, with the most recent one being in 2010. This is a limitation of the WVS—it has been unable to capture the dramatic political changes of the past decade, especially with the emergence of social media. The Korea General Social Survey (KGSS) is another survey that the report uses to shed light on polarization patterns in Korea. The KGSS has been conducted annually since 2003 and hence offers a window into trends in ideological beliefs in more recent years. One key limitation is that, unlike the WVS, the questions in the KGSS frequently change over the years, and only a few can be used to analyze political polarization. Nonetheless, examining the responses from the WVS and KGSS sheds light on how political polarization may have evolved in Korea in recent years.

According to the WVS, the share of the population who identify themselves as conservative or progressive remained quite steady until 2010. About 20 percent of the population identified as conservative, 60 percent as moderate, and another 20 percent as progressive across several iterations of the survey. The WVS only has data up to 2010, but according to the KGSS the share of individuals who identify as

12 Lim Won-Hyuk et al., *Opinion Polarization in Korea: Its Characteristics and Drivers*, KDI Report 2019-03, 2019.

progressives has considerably increased in recent years, as discussed below. Also, the WVS indicates that the gap in beliefs on key social-economic issues between conservatives and progressives has remained relatively steady, though there are indications of a slight divergence in recent years on some issues.[13]

Figure 8.3, panel A, shows how progressives, moderates, and conservatives responded when asked whether people's income should differ based on effort in a 10-point scale; 1 refers to the progressive view that income should be more equitable, and 10 represents the conservative view that income should differ based on effort. Conservatives' views are about 1 point higher on average, and this gap is relatively stable across the different survey rounds. (Round 2 was conducted in 1990, and round 6 was conducted in 2010.) Figure 8.3, panel B, shows how each group responded to the statement that men should have priority over women when jobs are scarce, with 1 indicating disagreement and 3 indicating agreement. Other than the second round, the gap between conservatives and progressives is quite stable. Figure 8.3, panel C, represents viewpoints on whether economic growth or environmental protection is more important (1 favors economic growth and 2, environmental protection). Progressives consider environmental protection to be relatively more important, and the gap between the progressives and conservatives has been widening in recent years. Overall, the analysis finds that the gap between liberals and conservatives is relatively stable on economic issues, while it may have slightly increased on social and environmental issues.[14]

When one examines the most recent iterations of the KGSS, it becomes more evident that the gap between liberals and conservatives has increased, albeit only for the few questions related to economic issues that are available over multiple years. According to the KGSS, there has been an increase in the share of people who identify themselves as progressive and a steady decrease in the share of people who identify themselves as conservative, especially in recent years. Figure 8.4, panel A, illustrates respondents' belief on whether the government should play an active role in reducing income inequality. There was no difference between conservatives and progressives in 2003, but the gap has steadily widened. A similar pattern can be observed when we examine people's trust in labor unions (figure 8.4, panel B) or conglomerates

13 Lim, *Opinion Polarization in Korea.*
14 Lim, *Opinion Polarization in Korea.*

FIGURE 8.3 Partisan gaps in Korean political beliefs, as indicated by the World Values Survey, 1990–2010

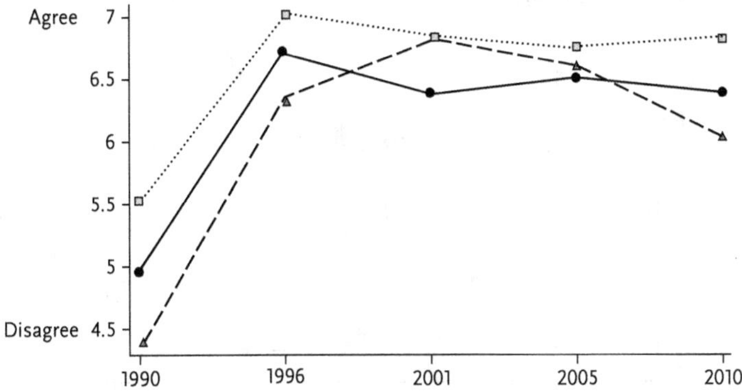

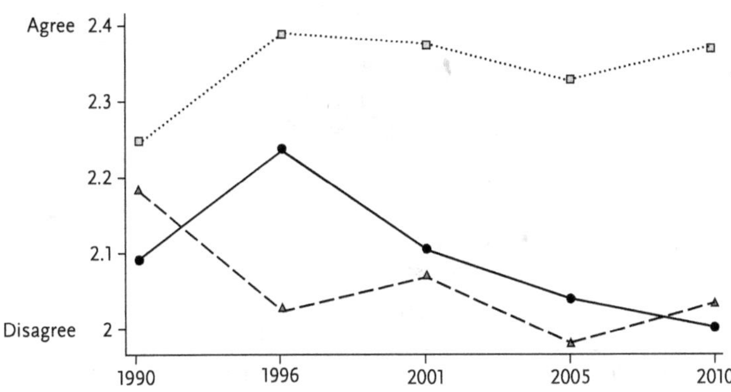

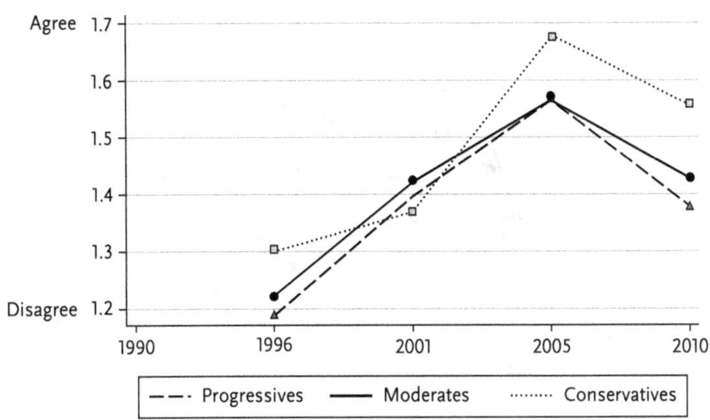

SOURCE: Lim Won-Hyuk et al., *Opinion Polarization in Korea: Its Characteristics and Drivers* [in Korean], KDI Report 2019-03 (2019).

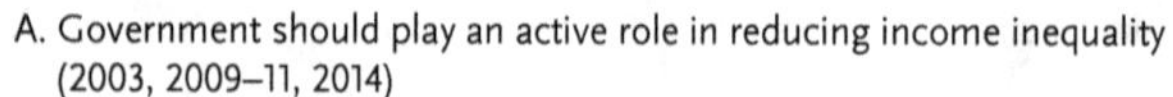
FIGURE 8.4 Partisan gaps in Korean political beliefs, as indicated by the Korea General Social Survey, various years

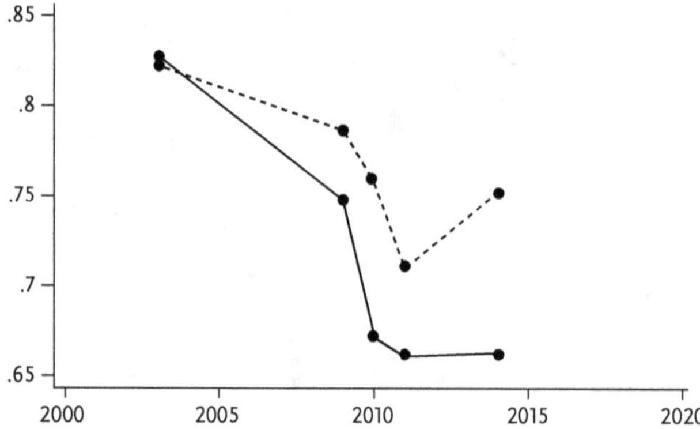

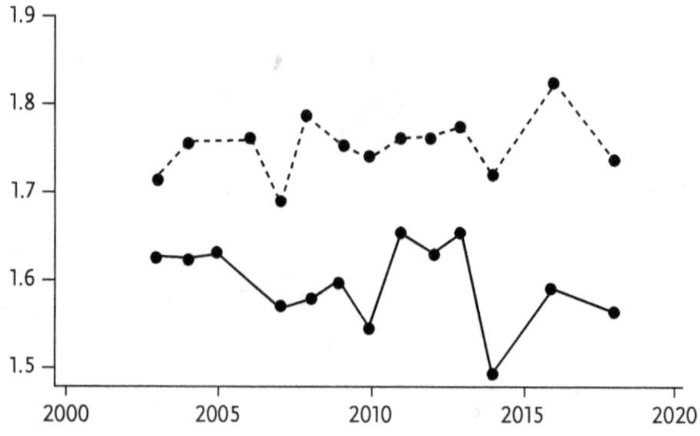

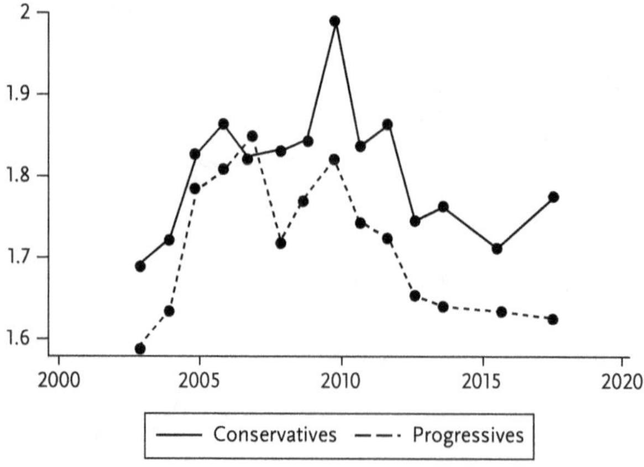

SOURCE: Lim Won-Hyuk et al., *Opinion Polarization in Korea: Its Characteristics and Drivers*, KDI Report 2019-03 (2019).

(figure 8.4, panel C). However, the gap between how progressives and conservatives perceive issues related to North Korea has remained relatively stable.[15]

Overall, the WVS and the KGSS indicate that political polarization in Korea was relatively steady until 2010, but partisan gaps gradually increased with respect to certain issues, especially in recent years. Nevertheless, the magnitude of the partisan gap on ideological issues in Korea is still relatively low, and political polarization is not as acrimonious as in the United States.[16] There are, however, limits to what can be captured in these metrics. Other scholars, including Aram Hur in chapter 2, paint a more contentious picture of Korean politics, where illiberal tactics have been frequently deployed by both conservative and progressive governments.

The Salience of Polarization

The descriptive evidence from survey data may not fully capture the degree of polarization in Korea. Statistics represent averages, and averages change relatively slowly over time. However, on issues like polarization, outliers may have larger influences than the average. A 2018 analysis by Pennycook, Cannon, and Rand finds that increased exposure to fake news increases people's tendency to believe in such news,[17] while Vosoughi, Roy, and Aral conclude that false information travels faster than truthful information on social media.[18] Taken together, these tendencies may amplify extreme voices much more than moderate ones. What may matter most is peoples' perception that society is increasingly polarized. When individuals are consistently exposed to extreme views, they may perceive that polarization is increasing, regardless of the degree to which polarization has actually changed. Such a perception could be due to the increasing salience of extreme viewpoints both online and on the streets. Factors contributing to this include online media, and in particular social media.

---

15 Lim, *Opinion Polarization in Korea.*

16 Lim, *Opinion Polarization in Korea.*

17 Gordon Pennycook, Tyrone D. Cannon, and David G. Rand, "Prior Exposure Increases Perceived Accuracy of Fake News," *Journal of Experimental Psychology: General* 147, no. 12 (2018): 1865–80.

18 Vousoughi, Roy, and Aral, "The Spread of True and False News Online."

Social media differs from traditional offline media in terms of its low barriers to entry and its reliance on user-generated content.[19] Individuals can easily create and distribute news on social media, without being fact-checked. Major social media companies like Facebook and Twitter do not consider themselves to be media companies, but platforms where users can connect and share information. Hence, whether they are obliged to fact-check and censor fake news remains a controversial issue. Nonetheless, news with little to no factual basis has been proliferating online.[20] Moreover, social media enables people to easily share news with like-minded individuals, potentially creating an echo-chamber effect.[21] It thus promotes the salience of news that conforms to one's prior beliefs while offering a buffer of silence against opposing viewpoints. Content that criticizes conservative views will be salient to a progressive, and vice versa. If content that represents moderate views is buried among the more extreme voices on social media, online consumers may perceive society as being more polarized than it actually is.

I argue that social media facilitates the salience of polarization, regardless of whether it causally increases polarization. This has important implications for democracy. Whether social media causally increases actual polarization continues to be debated in academia. In fact, Boxell et al. find that growth in ideological polarization in recent years was more pronounced among those who were least likely to use social media.[22] Social media exposes people to content that reinforces

19 Ekaterina Zhuravskaya, Maria Petrova, and Ruben Enikolopov, "Political Effects of the Internet and Social Media," *Annual Review of Economics* 12 (August 2020): 415–38.

20 Hunt Allcott and Matthew Gentzkow. "Social Media and Fake News in the 2016 Election," *Journal of Economic Perspectives* 31, no. 2 (Spring 2017): 211–36; Samantha Bradshaw and Philip N. Howard. "Troops, Trolls and Troublemakers: A Global Inventory of Organized Social Media Manipulation" (Working Paper no. 2017.12, Computational Propaganda Research Project, University of Oxford, 2017; David M. J. Lazer et al., "The Science of Fake News," *Science* 359, no. 6380 (2018): 1094–96.

21 "Political Polarization in the American Public," Pew Research Center; Bakshy, Messing, and Adamic, "Exposure to Ideologically Diverse News and Opinion on Facebook."

22 Levi Boxell, Matthew Gentzkow, and Jesse M. Shapiro, "Greater Internet Use Is Not Associated with Faster Growth in Political Polarization among US Demographic Groups," *Proceedings of the National Academy of Sciences* 114, no. 4 (2017): 10612–17.

their prior beliefs, but whether this echo-chamber effect increases political polarization is still unclear.

Another channel by which social media can influence polarization is through on-the-ground protests. Acemoglu, Hassan, and Tahoun find that the number of Twitter posts related to Tahrir Square was predictive of protest participation during the Arab Spring in Egypt.[23] Fergusson and Molina find a positive association between Facebook releases and protests across countries.[24] Furthermore, Enikolopov, Makarin, and Petrova show that social media penetration increased political protests in Russia.[25]

The main channel by which social media facilitates political protests is by reducing the cost of coordinating collective action. Consider how protests were conducted in the late twentieth century in South Korea. Back then, college students would gather in club rooms, cafes, and bars, avoiding the eyes of plainclothes policemen and sidestepping curfews to plan protests. Once a plan of action was in place, they would carefully disseminate the time and place of the protest. This process was difficult and risky. Today, one can simply share an anonymous post about a protest initiative on social media. In a matter of hours, that post can reach thousands of people of all ages, gender, education levels, and occupations. Such posts would be shared more widely among individuals who sympathize with the initiative. Social media thereby facilitates a larger number of protests, and these protests collectively represent a greater diversity of views.

In part due to the influence of social media, Seoul is now flooded with concurrent protests that represent opposing views. Moreover, the size of these protests can easily balloon. If it were not for social media's efficiency in mobilizing people, there most likely would not have been a crowd of more than a million people on the streets of Seoul demanding the impeachment of Park Geun-Hye, nor the large number of middle-aged citizens and seniors congregated in support of Park Geun-Hye. This stark contrast of two opposing groups protesting side by side

---

23 Daron Acemoglu, Tarek A. Hassan, and Ahmed Tahoun, "The Power of the Street: Evidence from Egypt's Arab Spring," *Review of Financial Studies* 31, no. 1 (2018): 1–42.

24 Leopoldo Fergusson and Carlos Molina, "Facebook Causes Protests" (CEDE Working Paper no. 2019-41, University of the Andes, 2019).

25 Ruben Enikolopov, Alexey Makarin, and Maria Petrova, "Social Media and Protest Participation: Evidence from Russia," *Econometrica* 88, no. 4 (July 2020): 1479–514.

increases the perception that society has become more polarized. Thus, social media increases the salience of polarization both online and on the ground.

Responses from the KGSS reveal some general patterns related to political participation in relation to political views. The survey finds that both self-identified progressives and conservatives, compared to moderates, are more likely to have shared election-related posts online. Though the patterns for posting comments (*daetgeul*) on news articles are not as clear-cut, progressives tend to be more proactive. This could be attributed to the fact that progressives tend to be younger in Korea, and the younger generation is more accustomed to posting comments online. Again, progressives and conservatives are more active in making donations compared to moderates. Most of these are online donations and can be considered a form of online political participation. Finally, progressives and conservatives are more likely to participate in protests, which was the case in both 2014 and 2018. The drastic increase in participation among progressives in 2018 was likely due to the events surrounding the impeachment of Park Geun-Hye.

Though the KGSS offers a snapshot of some online political activities and protest participation of respondents by ideology, the survey data do not allow for an analysis of the relationship between ideological preferences and protest participation of social media users. To examine this relationship, I conducted an original survey focusing on a highly significant event that captured the attention of the Korean public: the impeachment of President Park Geun-Hye. The next section draws on that survey and the research article that analyzes the survey and its findings that are relevant to this chapter.[26]

Social Media, Protests, and the Salience of Polarization

Park was impeached mainly due to revelations that her longtime friend, Choi Soon-Sil, exercised improper influence over state affairs despite having no official position in government. In September 2016, several news outlets reported that Choi had access to classified government documents and had provided feedback on presidential addresses. Furthermore, Choi was alleged to have established several foundations,

26 Yong-Suk Lee, "Social Media and Rigid Beliefs: Evidence from Impeachment of the President" (Keough School of Global Affairs Working Paper, 2021).

and, taking advantage of her close ties with Park, had requested donations from major conglomerates to fund the foundations' activities, as well as buy horses and fund her daughter's equestrian activities. Park was accused of being involved, as she had met with many CEOs of these conglomerates around the same time. Choi also used her influence to send her daughter to a prestigious women's university and then reprimanded a professor who gave her daughter low grades due to poor attendance and performance. The public was shocked to learn that someone with no official government position could wield so much political and financial power. In late October 2016, Park publicly acknowledged her close ties with Choi, and her approval ratings fell to an all-time low of 5 percent.[27]

The public took to the streets. On October 29, 2016, the first candlelight protest demanding Park's resignation was held in downtown Seoul. These protests became weekly events and grew larger as time passed, with crowd estimates ranging from 0.5 to 1.5 million by late November.[28] The protests continued into December, when the opposition party brought an impeachment resolution before the National Assembly for violations of the Constitution and the law. After the National Assembly voted 234 to 56 to impeach President Park, the Constitutional Court had six months to issue a ruling.

However, it was not only the progressives who mobilized these street protests—conservatives and pro-Park supporters rallied against the candlelight protests. The counterprotests—the so-called *Taegukgi* protests—argued that Park was not guilty as she had not taken any bribes. Though she had made bad judgments regarding Choi, they argued that her actions were not a cause for impeachment and that there was a lack of evidence for the accusations made against Park.

Shortly before the Constitutional Court's ruling on the impeachment trial on March 10, 2017, I conducted an online survey to examine how media use relates to polarization and protest participation by hiring an online survey company. Excluding respondents who did not complete either survey or completed it in a time too short to be considered reliable, the survey yielded 2,749 respondents. Approximately 46 percent

27 Justin Fendos, "The History of a Scandal: How South Korea's President Was Impeached," *The Diplomat*, January 24, 2017, http://thediplomat.com/2017/01/the-history-of-a-scandal-how-south-koreas-president-was-impeached/.
28 Charlie Campbell, "Huge Numbers Demand the Ouster of South Korea's President in a Fifth Week of Protests," *TIME*, November 28, 2016, http://time.com/4583033/south-korea-protest-demonstration-seoul-park-geun-hye-choi-soon-sil/.

were in their twenties due to an oversampling of college students, and the remaining 54 percent was relatively evenly split across respondents in their thirties, forties, and fifties. The gender split was almost even, with about 50.5 percent of the respondents being female. I collected information related to primary news sources, political leanings and worldviews, personal characteristics, and protest participation.[29]

Key variables

This section outlines the key variables of interest that were measured in the survey.

IDEOLOGICAL CONSISTENCY AND EXTREME IDEOLOGICAL BELIEFS

Many individuals have a mix of progressive and conservative viewpoints on different issues. However, there are also those who have consistently liberal or conservative views across multiple issues, and such people tend to be more involved in the political process.[30] The increase in the number of people with consistent ideological views reflects the recent rise in political polarization.[31]

I measured the respondents' ideological consistency by asking the extent to which they agreed with four questions that gauged their ideological worldview in the South Korean context, shown in table 8.1. Using a scale of 1 to 10, a "1" indicates complete agreement with the progressive statement, while a "10" indicates the same for a conservative view.

I constructed a measure of ideological consistency by adding the responses across the four questions, normalizing so that the midpoint was equal to zero, and then taking the absolute value. This measure would be higher for respondents with higher levels of ideological consistency. I also constructed a measure of extreme ideological beliefs by summing the instances in which each individual responded to the above questions with a 1 or 10. Though more than 65 percent did not choose the most extreme views on any of the questions, approximately 5 percent chose an extreme response to all four—mostly the most progressive response.

---

29 Lee, "Social Media and Rigid Beliefs."

30 "Political Polarization in the American Public," Pew Research Center.

31 Mathew Gentzkow, "Polarization in 2016" (white paper, Toulouse Network for Information Technology, 2016).

TABLE 8.1 Survey questions

	Progressive view	Conservative view
1	"Luck and connections determine success"	"If you work hard, you will eventually live a good life."
2	"Income should be more equal"	"Income inequality is necessary to motivate people."
3	"The government should guarantee the people's livelihood"	"Each individual should support himself/herself."
4	"Small and medium enterprises will drive future growth"	"Conglomerates will drive future growth."

NOTE: Respondents were asked to agree or disagree with statements on a scale of 1 to 10, with "1" representing the progressive view, and "10" representing the conservative view.
SOURCE: Author.

PROTEST PARTICIPATION

I also asked whether respondents had participated in the candlelight protests and, if so, how often. Over 31 percent of the respondents had participated in the candlelight protests: 18 percent participated once, 6.3 percent participated twice, 3.7 percent participated three times, 0.7 percent participated four times, and 2.6 percent participated five or more times. I also asked about participation in the pro-Park *Taegukgi* protests, and 2.6 percent indicated that they had taken part. Because the survey oversampled younger individuals, the true participation rate in the candlelight protests among the entire population would likely be lower than indicated by this survey and higher for the *Taegukgi* protests. The younger population tends to be more progressive and the older population more conservative in Korea, especially on social issues and redistributions.

PRIMARY NEWS SOURCE

Respondents primarily received their news from television (41.6 percent) and online websites (41 percent). Social media (e.g., Facebook, Instagram, Twitter, Kakaostory, Band) was the primary source of news for 8.7 percent of the respondents. Furthermore, 5.5 percent primarily got their news from friends and family, 2.36 percent from print media, and 0.8 percent from the radio. The survey also asked how much the participants believed in their primary news source. Those who chose TV had the highest level of trust at 55 percent, while those who chose social media had the lowest at 40 percent.

Results

Figure 8.5 illustrates how ideological views, the political spectrum, and protest participation varied by primary news source. The circles indicate the mean and the bands indicate the 95 percent confidence interval.[32] The results show that social media users are more consistent in their ideological views and are more likely to hold extreme ideological views. Overall, they identified as more progressive compared to users of other news sources. They were more likely to participate in (more) protests, and this was the case for both the candlelight protests and the pro-Park protests. Despite pro-Park supporters being considerably older, social media is significantly related to their protest participation.

Figure 8.6 further illustrates basic individual characteristics—age, gender, education, income, region, risk tolerance, and personality traits—by primary news source. Social media users tend to be younger. In terms of gender, there is a fairly even split. College students are more likely to use social media as their primary source of news. There are no distinguishing features of social media users in terms of education level, income level, or location of residence.

Finally, figure 8.7 examines the relationship between protest participation and ideological consistency by social media use. The black dots indicate social media users, the gray dots indicate other media users, and the lines indicate the best linear fit for each group. As the different slopes suggest, protest participation among social media users was more strongly associated with greater ideological consistency and more extreme ideological views.

As I show elsewhere, the descriptive patterns noted above are statistically meaningful in a regression framework. Moreover, I find that the relationship between social media and protest participation is unique to social media and not exhibited among other media sources, which confirms social media's unique ability to facilitate coordination among like-minded people. Overall, the findings from the original survey indicate that social media users indeed are more extreme in their viewpoints and more polarized as measured by their ideological consistency. People who hold extreme views are more likely to participate

32 The news sources were listed in the order of the number of people using each news source. Hence, the confidence intervals are smaller for TV and websites and wider for print and radio.

FIGURE 8.5 Position on the political spectrum, by primary type of news source

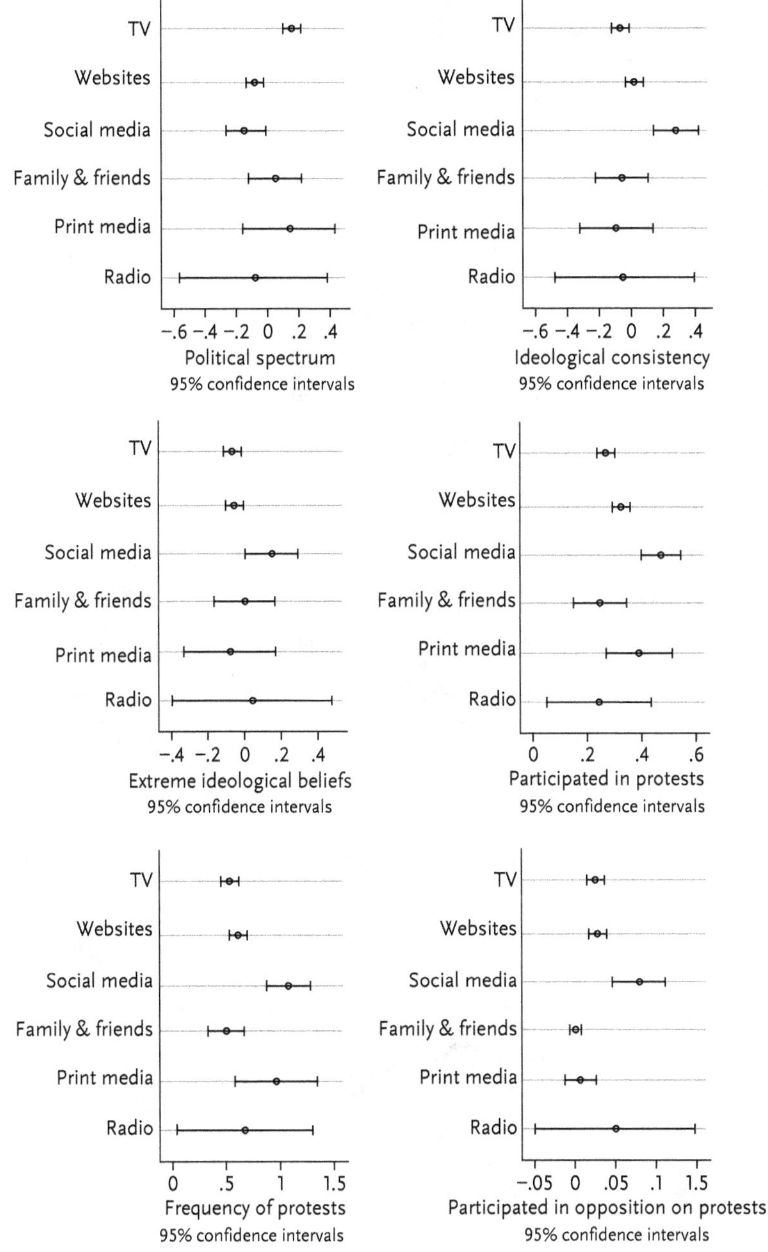

NOTE: Circles indicate means, and bands indicate 95 percent confidence intervals.
SOURCE: Yong-Suk Lee, "Social Media and Rigid Beliefs: Evidence from Impeachment of the President" (Keough School of Global Affairs Working Paper, 2021).

FIGURE 8.6 Demographic characteristics, by type of primary news source

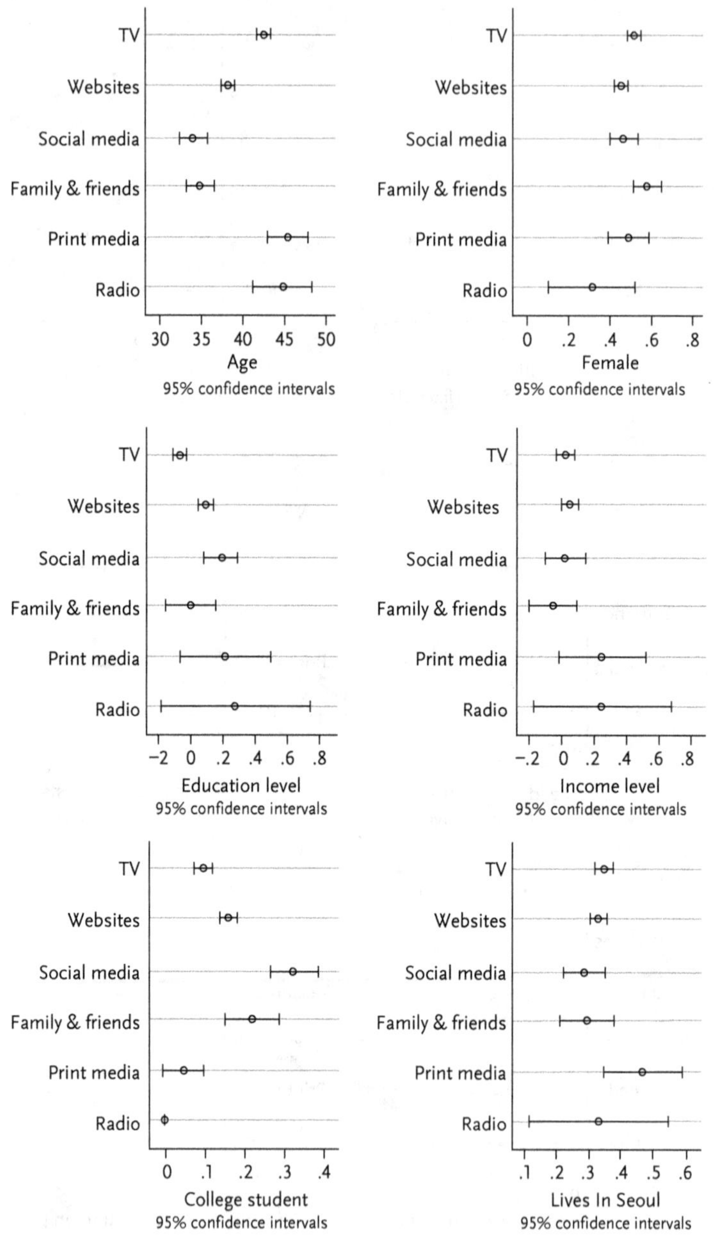

NOTE: Circles indicate means, and bands indicate 95 percent confidence intervals.
SOURCE: Yong-Suk Lee, "Social Media and Rigid Beliefs: Evidence from Impeachment of the President" (Keough School of Global Affairs Working Paper, 2021).

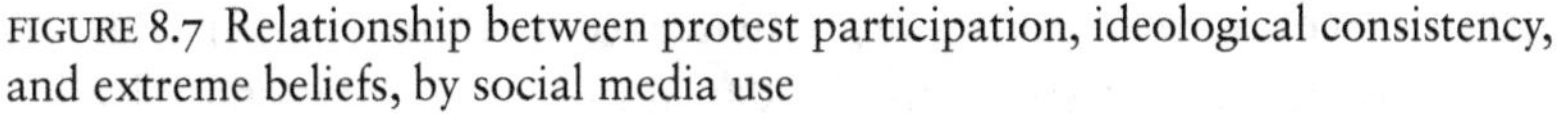

FIGURE 8.7 Relationship between protest participation, ideological consistency, and extreme beliefs, by social media use

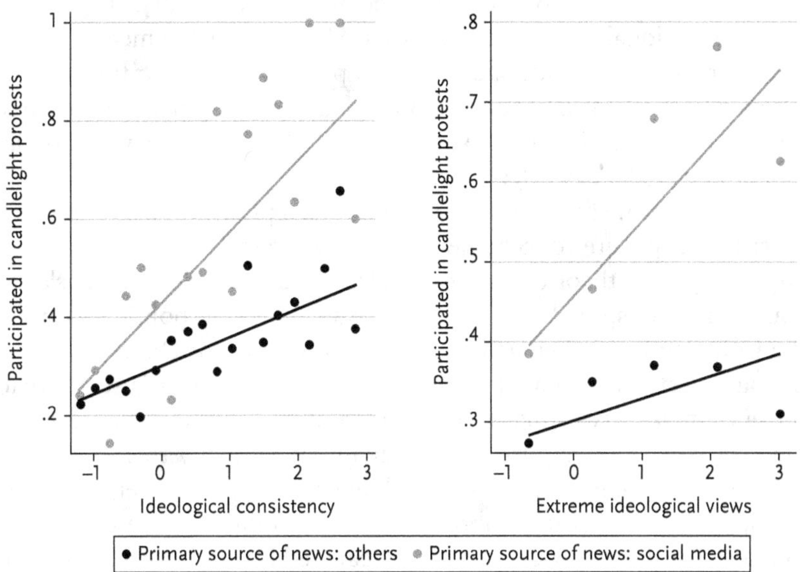

NOTE: Dots represent a binned scatter plot where each dot represents the mean value at each bin. Black dots indicate social media users; gray dots indicate users of other media, including TV, websites, family and friends, print media, and radio. The lines indicate the best linear fit for each group.

SOURCE: Yong-Suk Lee, "Social Media and Rigid Beliefs: Evidence from Impeachment of the President" (Keough School of Global Affairs Working Paper, 2021).

in protests, and this tendency is considerably stronger for individuals who rely on social media as their primary news source.

It is unclear whether these findings also apply to other contexts. The number of respondents who used social media as their primary news source was relatively small, and the survey was conducted at an unprecedented moment in Korea's political history. Nonetheless, the survey underscores how the balkanized media environment brought about by social media can increase activities that sow the images of increasing polarization both online and offline.

Discussion and Conclusion

Social media facilitated the nationwide candlelight protests that led to the impeachment of Park Geun-Hye, and Moon Jae-In's electoral victory. However, the increasing salience of extreme and polarized political viewpoints on social media can undermine democracy by influencing public opinion and also encouraging political participation among individuals with extreme views. Moreover, social media may be intentionally used by specific users and political parties to further sow division in modern societies for political gain.[33] There are at least three distinct ways in which the rise of extreme and polarized views on social and online media can affect a democracy.

First, social media can alter peoples' perception of reality through persistent exposure to extreme or polarized views, or even fake news and conspiracy theories. For example, the effectiveness of masks in containing the spread of COVID-19 was a divisive political issue in the United States. When a White House or Center for Disease Control official tweeted that masks are not effective, social media users spread those views by retweeting the message thousands of times, which muddied the truth and enabled some individuals to justify their refusal to wear masks. The fact that countries like Korea, which better contained the spread of the virus, embraced masks to minimize the contagion, or the scientific evidence that masks can reduce the spread of the virus, became irrelevant to this segment of the population. What is more disconcerting is that political parties can deliberately take advantage of extreme viewpoints on social media and use these to their advantage, knowing that doing so could increase attention and approval from their constituents, while further influencing political moderates to swing to their side.

Second, social media lowers the cost of mobilizing protests. These protests have a tangible impact on shaping public opinion and the policymaking process. In addition to academic research that finds a causal impact of protests on public opinion,[34] the mass protests that eventually led to the impeachment of Park Geun-Hye or the Arab Spring in Egypt speak directly to this phenomenon. A relatively small number of people can more effectively mobilize political protests with social media as compared to the level of organization and manpower that were needed

33 Christopher Mims, "Why Social Media Is So Good at Polarizing Us," *Wall Street Journal*, October 19, 2020, https://www.wsj.com/articles/why-social-media-is-so-good-at-polarizing-us-11603105204.

34 Andreas Madestam et al., "Do Political Protests Matter? Evidence from the Tea Party Movement," *Quarterly Journal of Economics* 128, no. 4 (2013): 1633–85.

to plan protests historically. If people with extreme and polarized beliefs actively use social media to mobilize like-minded individuals, it may enable them to have a disproportionately large social and political impact. The unprecedented attack on the U.S. capitol building on January 6, 2021, illustrates this all too clearly.

Finally, social and online media can interact with cable news to have an outsized impact on public opinion. This is a relatively recent trend that deserves close attention. Boxell, Gentzkow, and Shapiro suggest cable news as another factor contributing to polarization today, since it reaches a large number of viewers who may have a small online or social media footprint.[35] This likely applies to Korea as well. Cable news can pick up a viral social media post that caters to its polarized audiences and this dynamic can further exacerbate the salience of polarization and alter the public's perception of society. This could explain how social media may indirectly polarize older individuals who do not rely on social media or online news.

Moreover, such a cycle is not limited to social media and cable news. Today's fragmented media landscape encompasses traditional outlets such as TV, news, and radio to more recent outlets such as online news, podcasts, and YouTube channels. The list only keeps expanding, and the augmentation of media sources based on political viewpoints may further deepen ideological divisions. The emergence of media platforms in Korea that appeal to subgroups of the population—such as Naver (moderates), Daum (liberals), Facebook (men in their forties and fifties), Instagram (women in their twenties), and YouTube (otherwise "marginalized" opinions or older conservatives)—will likely continue to divide the population. Furthermore, cable news channels (*jongpyeon*) such as JTBC, Channel A, TV Chosun, and MBN have become powerful sources of news in Korea, influencing the political preferences of different subgroups of the population.

What can be done to minimize the potential harms of polarization by social media and the like? The current disaggregated media environment will likely continue. Online platforms like TikTok or Instagram, which currently do not primarily function as sources of news, could eventually incorporate aspects of news media as well. In democracies, including Korea, people have the freedom to choose their news media

35 Boxwell, Gentzkow, and Shapiro, "Cross-Country Trends in Affective Polarization."

and freedom of speech. However, if such online platforms are to serve as news media, they should endeavor to abide by traditional journalistic values, such as fact-checking and objectivity, or at minimum to not distort facts or distribute fake news. However, voluntary endeavors by technology companies will not be sufficient. Facebook itself is having trouble identifying fake news on its platform, despite using state-of-the-art artificial intelligence algorithms. When something is hard to detect, it becomes even more challenging to regulate.

Another strategy could be to create an agency that assesses the factual accuracy of the news being distributed by each news media and continuously informs the public on how well each outlet is doing. It would be something akin to a credit rating agency or organization that assesses the quality of nongovernmental organizations, but for online and social media news platforms. Such efforts could be complemented with an extensive program of media literacy education at schools and universities. Alternatively, online media platforms could altogether ban political ads and posts, as Snapchat has done, or ban political posts during election periods, as Twitter and Facebook did during the U.S. presidential elections.

Lastly, mainstream news organizations could step up to the occasion. As the disaggregated media environment persists and sensational news from small news agencies circulates through social media and the internet, the yearning for independent, objective news sources will increase. If traditional news agencies can play a more active role, unswayed by political ideology and committed to upholding a free and vibrant press that is essential to any democracy, they could serve as a lighthouse among the sea of misinformation. Although there are considerable hurdles to achieving this goal, every effort should be made to foster a media environment that is conducive to the dissemination of independent, objective information.

The appropriate solution will differ based on the institutions and the state of the media and online platforms of each country. Though these platforms helped the Moon administration come to power through the candlelight protests, they have also been widely used for political gain by the opposition during President Moon's term. Finding an effective way to minimize the potential harms and polarization arising from social media will undoubtedly require a process of trial and error. Efforts to formulate and implement possible solutions should begin in Korea without delay. The state of the media environment will have significant implications for the future of Korean democracy.

Bibliography

Acemoglu, Daron, Tarek A. Hassan, and Ahmed Tahoun. "The Power of the Street: Evidence from Egypt's Arab Spring." *Review of Financial Studies* 31, no. 1 (2018): 1–42.

Allcott, Hunt, and Matthew Gentzkow. "Social Media and Fake News in the 2016 Election." *Journal of Economic Perspectives* 31, no. 2 (Spring 2017): 211–36.

Bakshy, Eytan, Solomon Messing, and Lada A. Adamic. "Exposure to Ideologically Diverse News and Opinion on Facebook." *Science* 348, no. 6239 (2015): 1130–32.

Boxell, Levi, Matthew Gentzkow, and Jesse M. Shapiro. "Greater Internet Use Is Not Associated with Faster Growth in Political Polarization among US Demographic Groups." *Proceedings of the National Academy of Sciences* 114, no. 4 (2017): 10612–17.

———. "Cross-Country Trends in Affective Polarization." NBER Working Paper no. 26669, National Bureau of Economic Research, Cambridge, MA, 2020. https://www.nber.org/papers/w26669.

Bradshaw, Samantha, and Philip N. Howard. "Troops, Trolls and Troublemakers: A Global Inventory of Organized Social Media Manipulation." Working Paper no. 2017.12, Computational Propaganda Research Project, University of Oxford, 2017.

Campbell, Charlie. "Huge Numbers Demand the Ouster of South Korea's President in a Fifth Week of Protests." *TIME*, November 28, 2016. http://time.com/4583033/south-korea-protest-demonstration-seoul-park-geun-hye-choi-soon-sil/.

Enikolopov, Ruben, Alexey Makarin, and Maria Petrova. "Social Media and Protest Participation: Evidence from Russia." *Econometrica* 88, no. 4 (July 2020): 1479–514.

Fendos, Justin. "The History of a Scandal: How South Korea's President Was Impeached." *The Diplomat*, January 24, 2017. http://thediplomat.com/2017/01/the-history-of-a-scandal-how-south-koreas-president-was-impeached/.

Fergusson, Leopoldo, and Carlos Molina. "Facebook Causes Protests." CEDE Working Paper no. 2019-41, University of the Andes, 2019.

Gentzkow, Mathew. "Polarization in 2016." Toulouse Network for Information Technology whitepaper. 2016.

Lazer, David. M. J. et al. "The Science of Fake News." *Science* 359, no. 6380 (2018): 1094–96.

Lim, Won-Hyuk et al. *Opinion Polarization in Korea: Its Characteristics and Drivers*. KDI Report 2019-03, 2019.

Lee, Yong Suk. "Social Media and Rigid Beliefs: Evidence from Impeachment of the President." Keough School of Global Affairs working paper, 2021.

Madestam, Andreas et al. "Do Political Protests Matter? Evidence from the Tea Party Movement." *Quarterly Journal of Economics* 128, no. 4 (2013): 1633–85.

Mims, Christopher. "Why Social Media Is So Good at Polarizing Us." *Wall Street Journal*, October 19, 2020. https://www.wsj.com/articles/why-social-media-is-so-good-at-polarizing-us-11603105204.

Pennycook, Gordon, Tyrone D. Cannon, and David G. Rand. "Prior Exposure Increases Perceived Accuracy of Fake News." *Journal of Experimental Psychology: General* 147, no. 12 (2018): 1865–80.

Pew Research Center. "Political Polarization in the American Public." June 12, 2014. https://www.pewresearch.org/politics/2014/06/12/political-polarization-in-the-american-public/.

———. "The Partisan Divide on Political Values Grows Even Wider." October 5, 2017. https://www.pewresearch.org/politics/2017/10/05/the-partisan-divide-on-political-values-grows-even-wider/.

———. "In Western Europe, Populist Parties Tap Anti-Establishment Frustration but Have Little Appeal across Ideological Divide." July 12, 2018. https://www.pewresearch.org/global/2018/07/12/in-western-europe-populist-parties-tap-anti-establishment-frustration-but-have-little-appeal-across-ideological-divide/.

Robinson, Michael. "Ideological Schism in the Korean Nationalist Movement, 1920–1930: Cultural Nationalism and the Radical Critique." *Journal of Korean Studies* 4 (1982): 241–68.

Shin, Gi-Wook. *One Alliance, Two Lenses: U.S.-Korea Relations in a New Era*. Stanford: Stanford University Press, 2010.

Shin, Gi-Wook, and Paul Y. Chang, eds. *South Korean Social Movements: From Democracy to Civil Society*. London and New York: Routledge, 2011.

Sunstein, Cass. *Echo Chambers: Bush v. Gore, Impeachment, and Beyond*. Princeton: Princeton University Press, 2001.

Vousoughi, Soroush, Deb Roy, and Sinan Aral. "The Spread of True and False News Online." *Science* 359, no. 6380 (2018): 1146–51.
Zhuravskaya, Ekaterina, Maria Petrova, and Ruben Enikolopov. "Political Effects of the Internet and Social Media." *Annual Review of Economics* 12 (August 2020): 415–38.

CHAPTER NINE

Illiberalism in Korean Foreign Policy

Victor Cha

There is widespread discussion in political science and in public policy circles about the decline of democracy. If Samuel Huntington's "Third Wave" of democratization carried through the end of the Cold War, "declinists" date the erosion of democracy to around 2006, from when measurements of political freedom experienced a secular decline.

The decline of democracy arguably has reached Korea as well. Once a shining example of peaceful democratic transition, some scholars have argued that South Korea's (hereafter Korea, or ROK) polarized environment, demonization of political opponents, and erosion of checks and balances, have moved the country in an illiberal direction. While other scholars in this volume study the impact on domestic politics and society, this chapter analyzes how the erosion of democracy is externalized in foreign policy. I derive some basic propositions about how illiberalism affects a state's foreign policy and then apply these to the case of Korea. I find that elements of illiberal foreign policy—in its objectives, tactics, and execution—ring truer than most would recognize. The argument is not that this backsliding is permanent. Instead, this erosion, even if it is temporary, could have secondary and tertiary effects on the resilience of the U.S.-Korea alliance and long-lasting impacts on Korea's international reputation.

The author thanks Andy Lim, Dana Kim, Seiyeon Ji, and Rebecca Spencer for research assistance.

Illiberalism in Korean Foreign Policy

Korea is among the most successful cases of peaceful democratic transition in world history. The resilience of the country's democratic system was on full display from 2016 to 2017, when mass civic activism and protest, coupled with institutions that called for leadership accountability, resulted in the peaceful impeachment of one leader and the election of another. Mass populism did not degenerate into chaos, and the leadership conceded power according to the rule of law.

But as Gi-Wook Shin has written, Korea is not safe from democratic erosion.[1] While its democratic institutions may be robust, norms are being undermined. The Moon Jae-In government wraps itself in the cloth of populism, given its origins in the Candlelight Movement, but the actions that it takes in the name of the people blatantly violate democratic norms. The government holds all the levers of power in the executive, legislative, and judicial branches and carries out "cleansing" campaigns designed to root out political "evils" of the past. While there has always been a history of political revenge in Korean politics, the current campaign has not only jailed two former conservative presidents, but also targeted lower-level professional bureaucrats with charges of political disloyalty.[2] Deep, preexisting ideological divides between the left and right fuel an almost manic effort by the incumbent to demonize everything done by the opponent, with no sense of compromise or consensus building. Society is left badly polarized as a result. The loss of social cohesion, combined with perceptions of a dim economic future—as President Moon Jae-In's wage and work policies have not spurred growth or higher employment—pose serious threats to the Korean democracy's resiliency.[3]

Democratic erosion in Korea is visible in the country's foreign policy in four basic ways: (1) values-based diplomacy, (2) consensus-based diplomacy, (3) polarized foreign policy, and (4) overreach. I offer four basic propositions to explain how illiberalism manifests itself in how Korea deals with other countries. There are both short- and long-term

1 Gi-Wook Shin, "South Korea's Democratic Decay," *Journal of Democracy* 31, no. 3 (July 2020): 100–14.

2 Shin, "South Korea's Democratic Decay," 103.

3 Adam Przeworski, *Crises of Democracy* (Cambridge: Cambridge University Press, 2019).

consequences of illiberal foreign policy, not just for Korea, but for its relations with allies and its standing in the region.

Values-Based Diplomacy: Deprioritizing Human Rights

The first proposition about the relationship between democratic erosion and foreign policy relates to the way the government deprioritizes political freedom, civil liberties, and transparency in its diplomatic goals. This runs against what is sometimes known as "democracy promotion policy," of which there may be "high policy" (set by the government) or "low policy" (put forward by nongovernmental organizations, NGOs). The United States saw an unadulterated decline in "high policy" democracy promotion under the four years of the Trump administration, while "low policy" promotion continued. As Tom Carothers and Frances Brown have observed, when the United States' official policy reflects a devaluing of democracy as a goal—be this in the form of silence in the face of democratic offenses at home or abroad—this invariably hurts the perceived legitimacy and effectiveness of democracy promotion at the level of low policy.[4]

Korea has devalued democracy and human rights in its foreign policy under the Moon administration, evident in its silence regarding the repression of rights around the world. Notably, the Moon administration has not taken a public position condemning China's national security law in Hong Kong. Moon reportedly did not oppose, but "noted well" Chinese leader Xi Jinping's démarche in December 2019 that the protests in Hong Kong were a matter of internal sovereignty for China. By contrast, Japan's prime minister, Shinzo Abe, told Xi at the same venue that Hong Kong should remain "free and open" and that Beijing should exercise restraint.[5] This put Korea out of step with fellow

4 Thomas Carothers and Frances Z. Brown, "Can U.S. Democracy Policy Survive Trump?," Carnegie Endowment for International Peace, October 1, 2018, https://carnegieendowment.org/2018/10/01/can-u.s.-democracy-policy-survive-trump-pub-77381.

5 Kingling Lo, "South Korea Rejects China's Version of President Moon's Hong Kong Remarks," *Korea Times,* December 26, 2019, https://www.koreatimes.co.kr/www/world/2019/12/672_280890.html; Tae-Jung Kang, "On Hong Kong South Korea Is Caught between China and US," *The Diplomat,* May 29, 2020, https://thediplomat.com/2020/05/on-hong-kong-south-korea-is-caught-between-china-and-us/.

democracies like the United States, Australia, Canada, the United Kingdom, the European Union, New Zealand, and Japan, which have criticized the security law in Hong Kong as a blatant violation of Beijing's international commitments to preserve the principality's semiautonomous system.[6]

Seoul has also been conspicuously silent with regard to China's detention of Uighurs in Xinjiang. In the same December 2019 meeting, Moon reportedly said nothing in response to Xi's explanation of the situation in Xinjiang, which the Chinese foreign ministry reported as Seoul's agreement to this being China's internal affair. Korea disputed the latter characterization,[7] but it was missing from the list of thirty-nine countries that condemned human rights abuses in Xinjiang at the United Nations.[8] Indeed, China was so confident of Korea's reticence that the Chinese ambassador in Seoul stated publicly that he was "certain" Korea would understand China's position once representatives were debriefed on it.[9] This was an extraordinary statement that speaks to how democratic values have dropped off the radar screen of foreign policy.

---

6 U.S. Department of State, "Joint Statement on Hong Kong," November 18, 2020, https://hk.usconsulate.gov/n-2020111801/; Council of the European Union, "Declaration of the High Representative on Behalf of the European Union on the Adoption by China's National People's Congress of a National Security Legislation on Hong Kong," July 1, 2020, https://europa.eu/!Dw76JV.

7 The Korean government stated that Moon "listened well" to Xi's explanation. "S. Korea Conveys to China Moon's Correct Comments on Hong Kong, Xinjiang," Yonhap News Agency, December 29, 2019, https://en.yna.co.kr/view/AEN20191229003900320. See the Chinese Ministry of Foreign Affairs' press conference statement at: Ministry of Foreign Affairs of the People's Republic of China, "Foreign Ministry Spokesperson Geng Shuang's Regular Press Conference on December 23, 2019," December 23, 2019, https://www.fmprc.gov.cn/mfa_eng/xwfw_665399/s2510_665401/2511_665403/t1727131.shtml.

8 Zachary Basu, "More Countries Join Condemnation of China over Xinjiang Abuses," *Axios*, October 8, 2020, https://www.axios.com/un-statement-china-uighurs-xinjiang-6b29dbf5-b93c-4c70-bd4c-333e1c23471f.html.

9 Xing said, "我们将积极向韩国朋友介绍有关涉香港安全立法的背景，相信韩国朋友能够理解和给予充分的支持," which translates to "We will actively introduce the background of Hong Kong National Security Law to our Korean friends, and believe that our Korean friends will understand and give full support." See "Ambassador Xing Haiming Participates in CCTV News Live Discussion" [in Chinese], Embassy of the People's Republic of China in the Republic of Korea, May 27, 2020, http://kr.china-embassy.org/chn/sghd/t1783294.htm.

This deprioritizing of democratic values has been evident not just off the peninsula but also closer to home, where the Moon government has sought to roll back the NGO community in Korea.

North Korea is one of the world's worst human rights abusers. In Freedom House's *2020 Freedom in the World Report*, it received a score of 3 out of 100 ("not free"), ranking the fifth worst out of the 210 countries and territories rated.[10] In February 2014, the UN Commission of Inquiry on human rights abuses in North Korea recommended that the regime's leadership be internationally reprimanded. In a letter addressed to Kim Jong-un, which was included in the commission's report, the commissioners noted that it will "recommend that the United Nations refer the situation in the DPRK to the International Criminal Court to render accountable all those, including possibly yourself, who may be responsible for the crimes against humanity referred to in this letter and in the Commission's report."[11]

For successive Korean governments, whether progressive or conservative, that were inclined to seek engagement with North Korea, the human rights issue has posed awkward policy predicaments. On the one hand, Koreans are repulsed by the regime's treatment of its people, its detainment of Korean citizens, and Pyongyang's uncooperativeness in facilitating reunions of separated families on either side of the Demilitarized Zone. On the other, they know that pressing on human rights as a policy will result in two suboptimal outcomes. First, it will complicate—if not impede—efforts at engagement with the North, since Pyongyang angrily rejects all human rights demands by external actors as hypocritical and hostile. Second, it will fail to effect any tangible improvements in the North's human rights' record. For this reason, progressive Korean governments have maintained a policy of "benign neglect" of human rights. Though hailing from the political spectrum that fought for democracy and human rights in the South, these progressives are loath to press this issue with the North, and have instead focused on broader engagement initiatives that might

---

10 See the North Korea section in Freedom House, "Freedom in the World 2020," https://freedomhouse.org/country/north-korea/freedom-world/2020, accessed November 30, 2021.

11 See Annex I of UN Human Rights Council, *Report of the Detailed Findings of the Commission of Inquiry on Human Rights in the Democratic People's Republic of Korea*, A/HRC/25/63 (February 7, 2014), https://www.ohchr.org/en/hrbodies/hrc/coidprk/pages/reportofthecommissionofinquirydprk.aspx.

create an environment to open a discussion on human rights further down the road.

The Moon government has also quietly instituted a policy of rollback, aggressively targeting the activities and funding of the human rights community in the South. As one NGO leader described, the campaign is tantamount to a "purge" and the level of pressure is "unprecedented."[12] The policy became evident in the aftermath of Kim Jong-un's sister Kim Yo-Jong's public complaints in May 2020 about humanitarian balloon launches by Korean NGOs from Ganghwa Island that carried bibles, money, DVDs, and USB drives with information about the outside world into North Korea.[13] A key interlocutor for inter-Korean engagement, Kim Yo-Jong denounced the North Korean defectors who had launched the balloons as "human scum little short of wild animals who betrayed their own homeland," and warned that Korea "will be forced to pay a dear price if they let this situation go on," including "the possibility of the complete withdrawal of the already desolate Kaesong Industrial Park following the stop to tour of Mt. Kumgang, or shutdown of the north-south joint liaison office whose existence only adds to trouble, or the scrapping of the north-south agreement in military field which is hardly of any value."[14]

The information campaigns are spearheaded by two groups: Fighters for a Free North Korea, which is led by North Korean defector Park Sang-Hak, who has been sending balloons into the North since 2004; and Keunsaem, headed by his younger brother Park Jong-Oh, who uses plastic bottles to carry information across the West Sea. The older Park has survived two failed assassination attempts by the North. Aside from threats and criticisms from the North Korean government, the activists have also faced pressures from the South Korean government to stop their campaigns. In a *Washington Post* op-ed in 2020, Park listed a litany of actions taken by the South Korean government to stop their activities. These included pressing charges against their groups for violating inter-Korean exchanges and cooperation law by sending unauthorized materials (balloons/leaflets and bottles) into the

---

12 Email correspondence with North Korean human rights NGO leader, August 4, 2020.

13 "Kim Yo Jong Rebukes S. Korean Authorities for Conniving at Anti-DPRK Hostile Act of 'Defectors from North'," KCNA, June 4, 2020, https://kcnawatch.org/newstream/1591219896-544350772/kim-yo-jong-rebukes-s-korean-authorities-for-conniving-at-anti-dprk-hostile-act-of-defectors-from-north/.

14 "Kim Yo Jong Rebukes S. Korean Authorities."

North, revoking their corporate permits, and rescinding their right to hold charity fundraisers. Their offices have been raided by the police, and they are under criminal investigation for complaints filed by both the Ministry of Unification and local governments, who argued that their balloon campaigns threatened the safety of local residents by triggering retaliation from the North.[15] In December 2020, the Korean government passed a law criminalizing these balloon launches as punishable by fines and imprisonment, despite widespread opposition from domestic and international human rights communities.[16]

The Moon government has also taken unprecedented steps in dealing with defector cases on both sides of the border. In November 2019, Seoul returned two North Korean defectors who had sought political asylum in the South. The two defectors, North Korean fishermen, were arrested by Korean authorities after crossing the maritime border. They confessed to the killings of their captain—for harsh treatment—and fifteen crewmen, expressing their wish to defect to the South. Less than a week later, they were deported by Korean authorities through Panmunjom back to the North, without access to lawyers, a court hearing, or a chance to appeal their deportation.[17] The two men were almost certainly executed on their return. The government initially tried to do this quietly to avoid controversy. However, once the story was leaked to the press, the government issued a statement that the detainees were "atrocious criminals" who "lacked sincerity" in their desire to defect, and therefore were not eligible for asylum, which had long been the

15 Park Sang-Hak, "We Send Food and Information into North Korea. Why Is Seoul Trying to Stop Us?," *Washington Post,* July 13, 2020, https://www.washingtonpost.com/opinions/2020/07/13/we-send-food-information-into-north-korea-why-is-seoul-trying-stop-us/; Ahn Sung-Mi, "Seoul to Press Charges against Defector Groups Sending Anti-Pyongyang Leaflets," *The Korea Herald*, June 10, 2020, http://www.koreaherald.com/view.php?ud=20200610000933; Shim Kyu-Seok, "Gov't Moves to Revoke Defector Groups' Permits," *Korea JoongAng Daily,* June 29, 2020, https://koreajoongangdaily.joins.com/2020/06/29/national/northKorea/leaflets-defectors-unification-ministry/20200629192200341.html.

16 Josh Rogin, "South Korea's New Anti-Leaflet Law Sparks Backlash in Washington," *Washington Post,* December 17, 2020, https://www.washingtonpost.com/opinions/2020/12/17/south-koreas-new-anti-leaflet-law-sparks-backlash-washington/.

17 Choe Sang-Hun, "2 North Koreans Tried to Defect. Did Seoul Send Them to Their Deaths?," *New York Times,* December 18, 2019, https://www.nytimes.com/2019/12/18/world/asia/north-korea-fishermen-defectors.html; "North Korean Fishermen 'Killed 16 Colleagues' before Fleeing to South," BBC News, November 7, 2019, https://www.bbc.com/news/world-asia-50329588.

standard practice for all defectors. This decision was roundly criticized by human rights groups, who sent a joint statement signed by sixty-seven NGOs and groups to President Moon.[18] In another case in September 2020, a South Korean government official attempted to defect by jumping off a ship and swimming into North Korean waters. North Korean security forces shot the individual and then doused the body in gasoline and burned him alive.[19] The Moon government's reaction was muted, with some critical statements but no concrete actions. These actions (or lack thereof) signaled a new policy that is hostile toward defection and defied the constitutional mandate of awarding citizenship to any defectors from the North.

The Moon government's rollback policy toward human rights is also manifest in its campaign to defund NGOs. One example is the "The North Korean Defectors' Camaraderie" (*talbukja dongjihoe*), an organization founded by the late Hwang Jang-Yop, one of the highest-ranking North Korean defectors to date. Though previous progressive governments did not agree with the agenda of this conservative human rights' organization, they continued to quietly provide it with some funding. By contrast, the Moon government completely cut off funding to this organization and many others. This open hostility toward the defector community is political in nature, since these groups often associate themselves with the political right in Korea. It does not reflect any appreciation of liberal values and human rights.[20]

In another unprecedented act in the fall of 2020, the Unification Ministry took unilateral action against the Database Center for North Korean Human Rights (NKDB), an NGO dedicated to interviewing North Korean defectors at the Hanawon resettlement facility. The primary purpose of these interviews was to gather data about human rights abuses, and NKDB was the single-largest source of this information based on the testimonials of recent defectors. The ministry suspended NKDB's access to Hanawon, giving no reason other than to say

18 See joint letter sent to President Moon Jae-In, "Letter to President Moon Jae-in RE: ROK's Stance on Human Rights in North Korea," Human Rights Watch, December 16, 2019, https://www.hrw.org/news/2019/12/16/letter-president-moon-jae-re-roks-stance-human-rights-north-korea.

19 Hyung-Jin Kim, "Seoul: North Korea Kills S. Korean Official, Burns His Body," Associated Press, September 24, 2020, https://apnews.com/article/international-news-south-korea-north-korea-seoul-05385eedb0b036cd1b1b09184a8d7184.

20 Email correspondence with North Korean human rights NGO leader, August 4, 2020.

that a similar project existed within the Korean government, which was technically true, but the government made none of those data public for NGOs to use.[21] NKDB explained this measure on Twitter not just as an act against the organization, but as a wider blow to democracy: "This is not just an NKDB issue, it is the suppression of invaluable civil society activity. Keeping records of North Korean human rights abuses paves the way for transitional justice and a peaceful Korean future."[22]

The government has justified these policies in ways that narrow the definition of acceptable human rights conversations to only those that align with the government's policy objectives. In July 2020, when announcing the cancellation of licenses of two groups involved in sending outside information into North Korea, the Ministry of Unification stated that the NGOs were endangering the lives of local citizens with their activities, adding that they "seriously hindered" the government's policy of unification and impeded the government's "efforts to promote unification."[23] The following month, the ministry announced that it would audit all human rights and defector resettlement NGOs to ensure that their activities did not violate government agreements with the North or the spirit of inter-Korean reconciliation.[24] It also suggested that the broadcasts of international organizations like Radio Free Asia or Voice of America into North Korea were not beyond investigation.[25]

This is not to say that Korea has given up on democracy. The government continues to pursue democracy promotion and humanitarian work through agencies such as the Korea International Cooperation Agency. However, the devaluing of human rights, as evident in its high-profile policies related to North Korea and China, undercuts

---

21 "Unification Ministry Suspends Investigations into Human Rights in N. Korea," *Dong-A Ilbo,* September 16, 2020, https://www.donga.com/en/article/all/20200916/2182823/1.

22 See https://twitter.com/twtNKDB/status/1311553042525741056. Thanks to Sheena Chestnut Greitens for discussions on this issue and directing me to this thread.

23 Elizabeth Shim, "South Korea Rescinds Defectors Permits after Leaflet Dispute," UPI, July 17, 2020, https://www.upi.com/Top_News/World-News/2020/07/17/South-Korea-rescinds-defectors-permits-after-leaflet-dispute/3871594987256/.

24 Jeongmin Kim, "South Korea's Unification Ministry to Inspect Non-Profit Groups in Mid-August," *NK News*, July 24, 2020, https://www.nknews.org/2020/07/south-koreas-unification-ministry-to-inspect-non-profit-groups-in-mid-august/.

25 Chad O'Carroll, "Seoul Won't Rule Out Action against Radio Stations Broadcasting into North Korea," *NK News*, August 11, 2020, https://www.nknews.org/2020/08/seoul-wont-rule-out-action-against-radio-stations-broadcasting-into-north-korea/.

the efficacy and credibility of Korea's efforts further from home. As Carothers notes, the efficacy of "low policy" democracy promotion is limited unless reinforced by high policy.

Consensus-Based Diplomacy: Precipitating Perception Gaps

The second core proposition for how illiberalism manifests itself in foreign policy relates to a decline in consensus-based policy. If one of the indicators of democratic erosion in a society is polarization, then one of the parallel signs in foreign policy is a growing disconnect between public opinion and government policy. A government is typically expected to lead and to build consensus on foreign affairs where none might have previously existed. Political leaders do not follow populist whims on foreign affairs, but make policy based on core values and the national interest, which may stand apart from parochial interests of pressure groups or public opinion. They rely on foreign policy professionals, diplomats, and experts to help fill the gap through a process of dialogue and consensus building. However, when professional diplomats are excluded from the policy process, gaps between policy and the public start to grow. Evidence of these gaps and the absence of efforts on the part of the government to build consensus suggests the democratic erosion of foreign policy.

Korea's policy toward China increasingly manifests attributes of such erosion. Of ten policies in the last seven years in which the United States and China held opposite positions, Korea has effectively chosen to take China's side on six of these.[26] Seoul's affinity for Beijing was not specific to one political party, as both conservative and progressive governments chose China. In 2015, for example, Park Geun-Hye went against the Obama administration's recommendations and accepted an invitation from Xi Jinping to attend the Victory Day celebrations as the only U.S.-allied leader on the viewing stand with Xi and Putin. In November 2013, when China declared an Air Defense Identification Zone in the East China Sea, Korea tried unsuccessfully to cut a secret deal with China to remove one Korean-claimed island from the zone before it sided with the United States and Japan in op-

26 For a full list of these policies, see Victor Cha, "Allied Decoupling in an Era of US-China Strategic Competition," *Chinese Journal of International Politics* 13, no. 4 (Winter 2020): 509–38.

posing it.[27] Moon has practiced similar policy stances toward China. The government has hesitated to join Western initiatives like the Economic Prosperity Network, designed to diversify supply chains out of China.[28] Seoul has remained silent on U.S. initiatives like the Blue Dot Network and the Clean Network, intended to counter China's 5G and debt trap diplomacy.[29] As noted above, Seoul has not joined U.S. opposition to Chinese actions in Hong Kong and Xinjiang. When the United States asked Seoul in 2019 to support the Free and Open Indo-Pacific (FOIP) strategy, the Moon Jae-In government stopped short of doing so, for fear of alienating China.[30]

Of course, these rejections of U.S. entreaties do not spell disaster for the alliance. Allies often disagree, and these disagreements do not affect the core of the alliance. Nevertheless, the contrast with another democratic U.S. ally, Australia, is striking.[31] Of ten policies where Canberra faced competing demands from Washington and Beijing, it sided with the United States on eight of them.[32] In contrast to Seoul, Canberra offered full-throated support for the U.S. FOIP strategy, and opposed China's militarization of islands in the South China Sea. When the Trump administration called for decoupling next-generation wireless networks from China, Australia acted first—even before the United States—to exclude the Chinese company Huawei from its 5G network. The Korean government, on the other hand, tried to distance itself from the issue, only saying that LG Uplus's decision to use Huawei

27 Victor Cha, "Korea's Mistake on China's ADIZ Controversy," CSIS Korea Chair Platform, December 2, 2013, https://www.csis.org/analysis/korea%E2%80%99s-mistake-china%E2%80%99s-adiz-controversy.

28 Kim So-Youn, "US Directly Asks S. Korea to Join Economic Coalition that Excludes China," *Hankyoreh*, June 8, 2020, http://english.hani.co.kr/arti/english_edition/e_national/948417.html.

29 Kim Seung-Yeon, "U.S. Renews Calls on S. Korea to Join Economic Security Campaign against China," Yonhap News Agency, October 14, 2020, http://yna.kr/AEN20201014008400325.

30 Moon acknowledged the U.S. strategy but never explicitly supported it. "Remarks by President Trump and President Moon of the Republic of Korea in Joint Press Conference," The White House, June 30, 2019, https://www.whitehouse.gov/briefings-statements/remarks-president-trump-president-moon-republic-korea-joint-press-conference/.

31 Victor Cha, "Leading by Example: Two Different Responses to China's Rise," *The Interpreter,* November 11, 2020, https://www.lowyinstitute.org/the-interpreter/leading-example-two-different-responses-chinas-rise.

32 Cha, "Leading by Example."

technology and components was a private sector matter.[33] Australia also joined the United States, the United Kingdom, and Canada in harshly criticizing Beijing's repression of political freedoms in Hong Kong and Xinjiang, as well as China's opacity regarding the origins of the COVID-19 pandemic.

The point of highlighting the different responses to China is not to say that Australia or Korea should blindly follow the United States. On the contrary, Canberra's decision to side with Washington was based on a sovereign and independent calculation of its national interests, just as Seoul's decision to side with China was based on the government's calculation of what it believes is best for Korea.

However, a range of actions and decisions across conservative and progressive governments in Korea suggest a compromising of democratic values, rule of law, and right to privacy in order to accommodate Chinese policies. Korea's reasons for accommodating China relate largely to gaining Beijing's strategic understanding regarding North Korea.[34] While each government is entitled to its own policy priorities, the manner in which these policies are carried out is what is at issue. In most cases, these decisions were taken in secret, without consensus building across the government and without input from key stakeholders.

The result has been an ever-widening gap between public perceptions and the government's policy. Seoul's leaning toward its continental neighbor does not appear to be the sentiment of the country. In a Center for Strategic and International Studies (CSIS) report, *Mapping the Future of US-China Policy*, that surveyed policy experts and the general public, only 4 percent of Koreans replied that the country should prioritize cooperation with China over the United States. Only 17 percent of respondents advocated "neutrality" between its neighbor and its patron ally.[35] According to a Pew Research Center Survey released in October 2020, 83 percent of Korean respondents had little or no confidence that Xi Jinping "would do the right thing regarding

---

33 Kim Seung-Yeon, "U.S. Renews Calls on S. Korea to Join Economic Security Campaign against China."

34 For Korea's "North Korea dilemma" in dealing with China, see Ellen Kim and Victor Cha, "Between a Rock and a Hard Place: South Korea's Strategic Dilemmas with China and the United States," *Asia Policy* 21 (January 2016): 101–21.

35 For the full text of the report, see CSIS, *Mapping the Future of U.S. China Policy: Views of U.S. Thought Leaders, the U.S. Public, and U.S. Allies and Partners* (Washington, DC: CSIS, 2020), https://chinasurvey.csis.org/.

world affairs," which represented a nine-point increase over the previous year and was a higher percentage than that of Australia and the United States. Only 24 percent of Koreans had a "favorable" or "somewhat favorable" view of China.[36] Moreover, in the CSIS survey mentioned above, Koreans aligned with the general consensus among other allies and partners in calling for a tougher line against China's growing assertiveness. Regarding policy on Huawei, for example, 76 percent of economic and national security experts in Korea favored blocking Huawei from the country's 5G network. On COVID-19, more Koreans (79 percent) than Australians (73 percent) believe that China has done a bad job of handling the pandemic. In Korea, the gap between the public's thinking and the government's foreign policy remains unusually wide.

It is important to note that a similar gap between public opinion and government policy did not exist in previous administrations. During the Roh Moo-Hyun administration, public opinion regarding China was more balanced, with just under 50 percent identifying China as a major threat in 2004–06.[37] This was more or less in line with the government's hedging policy, which did not suggest strong alignments with China, but acknowledged that sometimes Seoul would not blindly follow the United States. Roh's successor, Lee Myung-Bak, took a relatively tougher stance toward China as relations worsened over a series of issues. Public opinion polls followed suit, with an increase in the number of Koreans in 2012 who saw China as a threat (57 percent).[38] Lee's successor, Park Geun-Hye, undertook a policy of strategic engagement toward China and worked to build a personal rapport with Xi Jinping. This new attitude tracked along with an improvement in the public's perceptions of China. In 2013, 51 percent of Koreans had a favorable view of Xi and China, compared to 87 percent now who

---

36 Laura Silver, Kat Devlin, and Christine Huang, "Unfavorable Views of China Reach Historic Highs in Many Countries," Pew Research Center, October 6, 2020, https://www.pewresearch.org/global/2020/10/06/unfavorable-views-of-china-reach-historic-highs-in-many-countries/.

37 "Joint EAT-CCGA Survey of Views toward Seven Countries in East Asia and the Pacific: The World as It Is Viewed by Koreans" [in Korean], East Asia Institute, March 4, 2008, http://www.eai.or.kr/data/bbs/kor_report/200906081158573 2.pdf.

38 Kim Chang-Won, "[Joint Survey of Public Opinion] 88 Percent in South Korea, 90 Percent in China, and 61 Percent in Japan Say 'History Issues Not Yet Resolved'" [in Korean], *Dong-A Ilbo*, January 6, 2012, https://www.donga.com/news/Inter/article/all/20120106/43121061/1.

have an unfavorable view.[39] Thus, the gaps between public opinion and government policy on China remained fairly narrow during both previous progressive and conservative Korean governments, but this has grown into a chasm under the current government.

Polarized Foreign Policy: Demonization of the Other

Steven Levitsky and Daniel Ziblatt argue that democracies die when norms of toleration, restraint, and compromise give way to polarization and fight-to-the-death partisan conflict, where winning the battle is more important than the public interest.[40] Thus, the third proposition about illiberalism and foreign policy is that the inability to externalize democratic norms of compromise and negotiation result in inflexible, zero-sum diplomacy and demonization of foreign interlocutors. This trait has been especially evident in Korea's policy toward Japan.

Many scholars have noted the overdetermined nature of conflict in Japan-Korea relations due to a multitude of variables related to history, attitudes, economics, right-wing politics, media, and court rulings.[41] A full discussion of these variables is beyond the scope of this chapter. What deserves attention is the nadir that the relationship has plummeted to under the Moon administration, and how policy positions on the Korean side have become uncompromising and nonnegotiable.

The Moon administration continues to claim that it does not recognize the 1965 Japan-Korea normalization treaty's scope related to reparations for historical injustices. Though the agreement took the form of an international legal document signed by two sovereign governments

39 "Favorability Rating of Political Leaders in Neighboring Countries" [in Korean], Gallup Korea, September 26, 2013, https://www.gallup.co.kr/gallupdb/reportContent.asp?seqNo=477.

40 Steven Levitsky and Daniel Ziblatt, "This Is How Democracies Die," *The Guardian,* January 21, 2018, https://www.theguardian.com/us-news/commentisfree/2018/jan/21/this-is-how-democracies-die.

41 See Victor Cha, *Alignment Despite Antagonism* (Stanford: Stanford University Press, 1999); Chong-Sik Lee, *Japan and Korea: The Political Dimension* (Stanford: Hoover Institution Press, 1985); Katrin Fraser Katz, "Domestic Interest Configuration and Island Disputes: Cyclical Surges of Nationalist and Internationalist Influence in Northeast Asia" (PhD dissertation, Northwestern University, 2017), https://arch.library.northwestern.edu/concern/generic_works/5x21tf562; Jennifer Lind, *Apologies in International Politics* (Ithaca: Cornell University Press, 2008).

and ratified by their respective legislatures, the Moon administration has invalidated the treaty on the grounds that it was negotiated on the Korean side by an illegitimate and nondemocratic government, and that it did not resolve all colonial reparations on the part of the people. As the deputy national security advisor, Kim Hyun-Chong, stated,

> The ROK government has consistently maintained the position that the crimes against humanity in which the Japanese state organs including the government and the military had participated cannot be deemed as resolved by the 1965 Claims Agreement and thus the individual rights of the forced labor victims to claim reparations are very much alive.[42]

The Moon government also refused to recognize an agreement negotiated by its predecessor with Japan on the issue of "comfort women." Putting aside whether the agreement met Korean demands (Japan conceded on acknowledging government complicity, and provided government funding for the compensation fund), Seoul rejected the agreement because Park Geun-Hye had negotiated it and said that it did not reflect the will of the people.[43]

The Moon government also threatened to end a trilateral intelligence-sharing agreement involving Korea, the United States, and Japan. The agreement serves the security interests of all three countries with regard to North Korean contingencies. Seoul announced it would terminate the security arrangement if Japan did not make concessions on an export control measure. It did not consult with the United States, even as it drew U.S. security interests into the dispute

---

42 "Opening Remarks by Deputy National Security Advisor Hyun Chong Kim at Press Briefing," Cheong Wa Dae, August 28, 2019, https://english1.president.go.kr/BriefingSpeeches/Briefings/451.

43 President Moon was quoted as saying: "The negotiations over the 'comfort women' issue between Seoul and Tokyo violated universal principles established by the international community in settling historic issues, and above all it was a political agreement that excluded the directly-related party and citizens. The unopened deal, which was later confirmed to be existent, greatly disappointed the citizens. Though on the surface the deal approached an agreement between the two governments, as well as the citizens, I, as president, make it clear again that the 'comfort women' issue cannot be settled through such a manner. Truth is what matters most in history. We need to face our painful history, although we may want to avoid it. I hope that both Korea and Japan can overcome their unfortunate history and become true-hearted friends." See "Truth Is What Matters Most in History: President Moon," Cheong Wa Dae, December 29, 2017, https://english1.president.go.kr/Media/News/225.

with Japan and even though severing these intelligence ties would be harmful to the alliance.[44]

There are two effects of this posture on society and foreign policy. First, the way in which the government has approached the disputes with Japan has contributed to intense division and polarization of the Korean body politic. As Gi-Wook Shin writes, "It is truly shameful to watch high-level officials dividing the public into 'pro- or anti-Japanese' and 'patriots or traitors'. . . . This is unbecoming of a country that prides itself on having become a member of the G20 after achieving both industrialization and democratization."[45] By using the Japan issue to create "winners" and "losers" in the body politic, the government leaves no room for domestic compromise or consensus building, which would be a prerequisite to any serious attempt at reconciliation with Japan.

The second effect of this democratic erosion in foreign policy relates to the damage done to the alliance with the United States. In pursuing a zero-sum policy toward Japan, the Moon administration sought to hold hostage U.S. alliance equities by threatening to end the trilateral intelligence sharing agreement. U.S. officials were not consulted about this action; if they had been, they would have opposed it. They perceived it as a strong-arm attempt by Seoul to force Washington to take its side on the dispute with Japan in order to preserve critical intelligence sharing vis-à-vis North Korean missile threats. The tactic prompted a trip by National Security Advisor John Bolton to Seoul and Tokyo. U.S. disgust at Korean actions was not only damaging to the reservoir of trust and goodwill in the alliance, but also reinforced the perception that Seoul was not executing alliance policy in a transparent and consultative fashion.[46]

---

44 Kim Seung-Yeon, "S. Korea Warns Japan of Rolling Back Decision to Suspend GSOMIA's Termination," Yonhap News Agency, January 9, 2020, http://yna.kr/AEN20200109003200325.

45 Gi-Wook Shin, "The Perils of Populism," APARC Commentary, September 2019, https://fsi-live.s3.us-west-1.amazonaws.com/s3fs-public/shin_perils_of_populist_nationalism.pdf.

46 For Bolton's trip to Korea, see "U.S. Adviser Bolton Travels to Japan, South Korea amid Trade Dispute," Reuters, July 20, 2019, https://reut.rs/2SqTrHL; Joyce Lee, "U.S. Security Adviser Bolton Meets South Korean Officials, Seeks Stronger Ties," Reuters, July 23, 2019, https://reut.rs/2Y1O6wr. It should be noted that Seoul was not the only party acting in atypical terms. On other issues, like the Special Measures Agreement, the United States had taken unprecedented, nontransparent actions that hurt the alliance as well.

Overreach

All governments would like experts and public policy commentators to speak positively of their policies. While ideal, universal "good press" is impossible in the world of politics. Nevertheless, representatives of liberal governments remain undeterred in positively "spinning" domestic and international audiences about the merits of their policies. This leads to the fourth proposition about illiberal foreign policy practice: governments go beyond political "spin" and practice "overreach"—trying to coerce support or dampen down public criticism. Officials may sometimes walk right up to this line between political spin and overreach by subtly "favoring" certain think tanks or individuals in the public policy debate, offering events with visiting high-level officials, or providing funding for projects. When this line is crossed, however, it reflects an undemocratic way of carrying out foreign policy. This practice was evident with regard to the Korean government's actions against a U.S.-based research institute in 2018.

The Korean government demanded that the U.S.-Korea Institute (USKI) at Johns Hopkins University in Washington, DC, remove its director, a conservative Korean affairs expert. When the institute rejected this directive, the government cut off funding for the institute, leading to its closing in May 2018. Robert Gallucci, the chairman of USKI, stated, "It's utterly inappropriate for a foreign government, and an ally by the way, to threaten an American academic institution this way. It's just incredibly and wildly inappropriate."[47] The government claimed that its decision to defund the annual $1.87 million contribution through the government-affiliated Korea Institute for International Economic Policy (KIEP) was due to inadequate financial accounting, and "insufficient transparency in selecting visiting scholars," but it also mentioned the "excessively long tenure of the director."[48] Gallucci confirmed that Korean officials could provide no evidence of financial mismanagement

47 Anna Fifield, "Korea Think-Tank at U.S. University to Close after Seoul Withdraws Funding," *Washington Post,* April 11, 2018, https://www.washingtonpost.com/world/asia_pacific/korea-think-tank-at-us-university-to-close-after-seoul-withdraws-funding/2018/04/11/87adc3a8-3d64-11e8-912d-16c9e9b37800_story.html.

48 Elizabeth Redden, "US-Korea Institute Closes after Alleged Meddling," *Inside Higher Ed,* April 11, 2018, https://www.insidehighered.com/quicktakes/2018/04/11/us-korea-institute-close-after-alleged-meddling.

and added that the threats were far from subtle: "I have been directly pressured, in writing and orally, to fire [the director] and was told that if I did not, all funding would be cut off."[49]

Many saw this as an incredibly ham-fisted attempt to intervene in and shape the activities of independent Korea-related research activities in Washington, DC. This author said, "There are no imaginable circumstances in which an educational institution should have its academic freedoms trampled upon."[50] The government tried to distance itself from the controversy by designating KIEP, which provided the annual funding to USKI, as the chief interlocutor acting on instructions from the National Assembly audit committee. However, the head of KIEP served on an advisory panel for the Moon administration, and KIEP's vice president admitted that it had briefed the Blue House on the situation regarding USKI.

The action was unprecedented in that no Korean government in recent memory had undertaken such a blatant act of coercion to suppress policy commentary in the United States. Yet the action came in the context of intervention into academic independence at home, as the Moon government was in the midst of replacing the heads of all government-affiliated think tanks.[51] Two individuals familiar with the government's actions said the Moon administration "wanted to run the institute like a [state-run] think tank."[52]

These illiberal measures against USKI represented more than a bilateral dispute between the two protagonists, because they had a negative impact on the alliance. Though not documented on paper, White House officials were angered by the Moon administration's actions against an American educational institution. The fact that the threats were leveled at Gallucci, a retired, well-respected, and well-liked national security expert in both Democratic and Republican circles, added to the anger. Senior officials of the National Security Council issued a stern

49 Fifield, "Korea Think-Tank"; Matthew Pennington, "US Think Tank on North Korea to Close as South Korea Cuts Funds," Associated Press, April 9, 2018, https://www.businessinsider.com/ap-us-think-tank-on-korea-to-close-as-skorea-cuts-funds-2018-4.

50 Fifield, "Korea Think-Tank."

51 The four government-affiliated think tanks related to foreign policy and defense are the Korea National Diplomatic Academy, the Korea Institute for Defense Analyses, the Korea Institute for National Unification, and the Institute for National Security Strategy.

52 Fifield, "Korea Think-Tank."

démarche to the Korean ambassador in Washington about the inappropriateness of such behavior. The USKI incident fueled an already negative view held by Trump officials of the Moon administration's ideological leanings and the alliance overall. When compared with support from other allies like Japan and Australia in dealing with China's rise and North Korea, the Moon government's pro-engagement stance toward North Korea and hedging on China had already relegated them to a second-tier ally in the Trump administration's calculations. The USKI incident only cemented that negative attitude.

The Effects of Illiberal Korean Foreign Policy

What are the consequences of a democratic erosion of Korea's foreign policy? There are certainly short-term effects, as described in this chapter, as when other states express disappointment or offer critical comments about Korea's silence on Hong Kong, the defunding of human rights' groups at home, or the continued dysfunction of Japan-Korea relations. Proponents of the government's policies probably estimate that they can weather this storm and tolerate temporary discomfort in foreign policy. However, there are arguably longer-term and more corrosive effects for Korea's external relations. These relate to Korea's growing isolation in coalitional politics among like-minded countries in the region.

Figure 9.1 illustrates the density of ties among the five major Asian democracies related to nine recent coalitional initiatives. These initiatives address topics from security to supply chains to development assistance. Admittedly, some of these do not involve Korea, such as the U.S.-Japan-Australia trilaterals. However, Korea's absence is—as discussed below—not due to intentional exclusion by the democratic parties. If Korea had wanted to participate in the trilateral, then it would have been invited to do so.

What emerges is a picture of Korea that is increasingly isolated from its democratic partners in the region, leaving it vulnerable to Chinese influence and coercion. Table 9.1 is another representation of several recent security and trade multilateral initiatives in the region. Some of these coalitional groupings have been well established over the past decade, while others are fairly new. Many of them involve like-minded democracies as core members. All of them are motivated by a desire to shape a regional order in which rules are transparent, equitable, and followed by all concerned.

FIGURE 9.1 Density of ties among Asia's democracies in coalitional initiatives (2021)

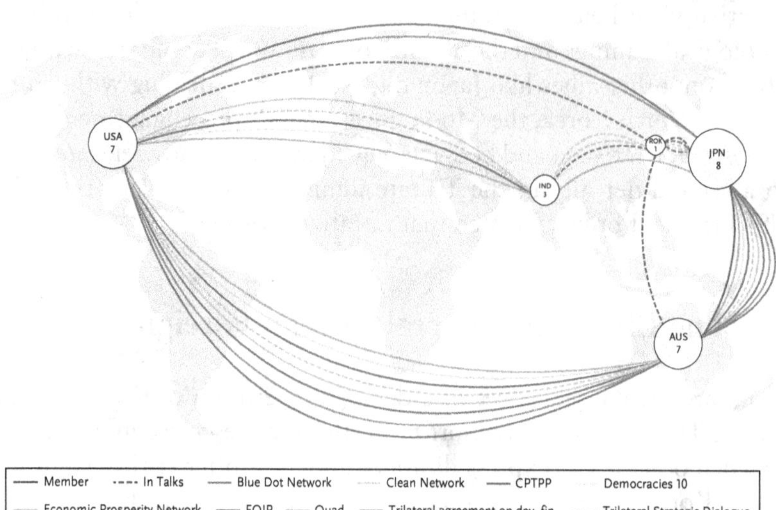

SOURCE: Author, based on publicly available data.

As table 9.1 summarizes, what is most concerning about these initiatives is that Korea has, by choice or by omission, been left out of nearly all of them: the Trilateral Strategic Dialogue, the U.S.-Australia-Japan Development Assistance Trilateral, the Comprehensive and Progressive Agreement for Trans-Pacific Partnership, the Blue Dot Network, the Economic Prosperity Network, the Quadrilateral Security Dialogue, Quad-Plus, Free and Open Indo-Pacific, and Democracy 10. This troubling trend indicates that the organizers of these initiatives do not see Korea as sharing similar values, or that Seoul does not see itself as playing a role in shaping the rules-based international liberal order.

One of the most obvious manifestations of this trend are changes in Japan's perceptions of Korea. In official ministry documents, the Government of Japan has, until recently, always referred to Korea as a country with which it shares democratic values and strategic interests, making it Japan's "most important neighbor" (table 9.2).

But from 2018, the Japanese Foreign Ministry's diplomatic Blue Book removed this reference to Korea, signaling a changed perception of the country. The reference returned two years later, but in diluted language suggesting a weakened perception of Korea as the most

TABLE 9.1 Coalitional diplomacy and Korea, 2008–20

Diplomatic initiative and status		
Purpose	**Signals from Korea**	**Membership status**
Trilateral Strategic Dialogue (established 2008)		
August 1, 2019: Trilateral Strategic Dialogue Joint Ministerial Statement reiterates commitment to working proactively together to (1) Maintain and promote a free, open, prosperous and inclusive Indo-Pacific region, and (2) Reaffirm a commitment to work with other countries to uphold a rules-based order.[a]	**No official government commentary from the ROK.**	**Korea not a member.** Members: United States, Australia, Japan
US-Australia-Japan Development Assistance Trilateral (announced July 30, 2018)[b]		
To invest in infrastructure projects in the Indo-Pacific region that build infrastructure, address key development challenges, increase connectivity, and promote economic growth.	**No official government commentary from the ROK.**	**Korea not a member.** Members: United States, Japan, Australia
Comprehensive and Progressive Agreement for Trans-Pacific Partnership (CPTPP) (signed on March 8, 2018; entered into force on December 30, 2018)		
The CPTPP binds its members, which represent about 13.5 percent of global merchandise trade, to 30 chapters providing for freer trade and investment access.[c] The rights and obligations under the CPTPP fall into two categories: **Rules**: for example, on how countries should make new food safety regulations or whether they can ban the transfer of data to other CPTPP members. **Market access**: how far each CPTPP member will cut its tariffs, open its services markets, liberalize visa conditions for business, etc. The CPTPP provides for almost complete liberalization of tariffs among participants.	**June 15, 2018**: Deputy Prime Minister Kim Dong-Yeon states ROK is considering joining CPTPP talks.[d] **December 13, 2018**: Deputy Prime Minister Hong Nam-Ki presides over 202nd Ministerial Meeting on International Economic Affairs, and states that the ROK is committed to RCEP along with CPTPP.[e] Reiterates this in February 2019[f] and December 2020.[g] **November 15, 2020**: ROK signs RCEP trade pact with 14 nations (10 members of ASEAN as well as South Korea, China, Japan, Australia, and New Zealand)[h]	**Korea not a member (but has expressed an interest to join).** Current members: Australia, Brunei, Canada, Chile, Japan, Malaysia, Mexico, New Zealand, Peru, Singapore, Vietnam.

(continued)

TABLE 9.1 *(continued)*

Diplomatic initiative and status		
Purpose	**Signals from Korea**	**Membership status**
	Blue Dot Network (announced November 4, 2019)	
Initiated by the U.S. State Department, the network seeks to bring together governments, the private sector, and civil society under "shared standards for global infrastructure development." Aims include to certify and attract infrastructure projects that demonstrate and uphold global infrastructure principles among developing and emerging economies.[i] The Blue Dot Network is often seen as functioning in opposition to the Chinese-led Belt and Road Initiative.[k]	Korean media has reported the country as being a part of the Blue Dot Network, but there is little to no record of press releases from the government itself.[j] While the initial U.S. government press release had no mention of the ROK, the Overseas Private Investment Corporation (a U.S. government agency) cited the Blue Dot Network as being a joint venture with Korea. **2019:** "The 'Blue Dot Network' project is a joint project between Korea, Japan International Cooperation Bank (JBIC) and Australian Ministry of Foreign Affairs (DFAT)." (U.S. Overseas Private Investment Corporation [OPIC])[k]	**Korean membership unclear.** Members: United States, Japan, Australia
	Economic Prosperity Network (discussions began March 2020; not yet formally established)	
Initiated by the United States, the network is to be made up of "countries, companies, and civil society organizations that are anchored in trust and that operate by a set of trust principles. Entities that respect those values are natural partners and likely to prosper. Those that don't are likely unreliable as partners and pose a threat to stability."[m]	**June 5, 2020:** The EPN is explained to Second Vice Foreign Minister Lee Tae-Ho by U.S. Under Secretary of State Krach. Both sides agreed to continue to discuss these issues in the future.[n] Little additional commentary.	**Korea is not currently a member and has not expressed explicit interest in joining.** Countries envisioned to join by the United States include Australia, India, Japan, New Zealand, Korea, and Vietnam. On June 25, 2020, Undersecretary Krach stated: "Countries that currently do not abide by those trust principles will be excluded from membership."[o]

Diplomatic initiative and status		
Purpose	**Signals from Korea**	**Membership status**
	Clean Network (launched August 5, 2020)	
Initiated by the United States, "The Clean Network program is the Trump Administration's comprehensive approach to safeguarding the nation's assets including citizens' privacy and companies' most sensitive information from aggressive intrusions by malign actors, such as the Chinese Communist Party."[p] There are five branches to the network: Clean Carrier, Clean Store, Clean Apps, Clean Cloud, and Clean Cable.[p]	**October 14, 2020**: The United States raised the topic of its Clean Network at the Fifth Senior Economic Dialogue. Vice Foreign Minister Lee said Korea made it clear that "whether a private telecom company uses the equipment of a specific enterprise is up to that company to decide...but regarding the general security risks posed by the 5G technology in the telecommunication market," they agreed to work closely with the U.S. and cooperate on technological issues.[q]	**Korea not a member, but in discussions.** According to the United States, as of December 2020, more than 50 countries and 170 telecommunications operators (including SK and KT of Korea) had joined the network, including but not limited to: United Kingdom, Czech Republic, Poland, Sweden, Estonia, Romania, Denmark, and Latvia.[q]
	Quadrilateral Security Dialogue (initiated 2007–08, revived 2017 [ASEAN Summit]; Quad Plus [tentative next step])	
Operates as a meeting format for senior officials to discuss regional security issues and as the basis for naval exercises and tabletop exercises. Meant as an "Asian Arc of Democracy," envisioned to ultimately include countries in central Asia, Mongolia, the Korean Peninsula, and Southeast Asia—"virtually all the countries on China's periphery, except for China itself."[r]	**September 29, 2020**: a MOFA spokesperson emphasized in response to questions on joining a Quad Plus "the position that the Korean government attaches great importance to the principles of openness, transparency, inclusion, and compliance with international norms in regional cooperation"[s] **November 13, 2020**: Deputy Director of Blue House national security office said there had been no "formal request" made by the U.S. government to the ROK government to join the Quad, suggesting an informal one was made and rejected by the ROK.[t]	**Korea not a member.** Members: United States, Japan, Australia, India. Other possible future members: New Zealand, Brazil, Israel, Vietnam.[u]

(*continued*)

TABLE 9.1 (*continued*)

Diplomatic initiative and status		
Purpose	**Signals from Korea**	**Membership status**
	Free and Open Indo Pacific (FOIP) (U.S. State Department adopted and formalized FOIP strategy in 2017)	
The U.S. and participating nations' Indo-Pacific strategies all focus on rules-based order, economic prosperity, and greater connectivity across (sub)regions.	**November 2017**: ROK reaction to Trump's request regarding FOIP is reportedly negative: (1) Moon advisor rejected the idea as largely instigated by Japan; (2) when asked about FOIP, Blue House gave a non-answer but later confirmed to press that ROK did not agree to join FOIP.[v] **August 2019**: At the Shangri- la Dialogue, ROK Defense Minister makes news for being unable to use the term "FOIP" in public statements.[w] **November 2019**: Instead of FOIP, Moon proposes NAPCOR (the Northeast Asia Plus Community of Responsibility). U.S. State Department and MOFA put out a fact sheet at the East Asia Summit in Bangkok about similarities between FOIP and NAPCOR.[x]	**Korea has been slow to adopt similar FOIP language for other participating nations, and only embraces economic aspects as they relate to ROK's Southern Diplomacy (policy toward Southeast Asia).**[y] Members (as cited by the U.S.): Japan, India, Australia, Korea, Taiwan.
	Democracy 10 (tentative)	
First proposed by the UK prime minister Boris Johnson in May 2019 as a group to coordinate telecommunications policy and develop an alternative to China's Huawei.[z]	**No official government commentary from the ROK.**	**Korea has not made any positive overtures toward the idea of Democracy 10.** Prospective members: United States, United Kingdom, Japan, France, Germany, Canada, Italy, Korea, India, Australia. (Korea later joins the expanded Summit for Democracies in Dec. 2021, which had over 100 participant countries.

SOURCES:

[a] "Trilateral Strategic Dialogue Joint Ministerial Statement, August 1, 2019," U.S. Department of State, August 2, 2019, https://2017-2021.state.gov/trilateral-strategic-dialogue-joint-ministerial-statement-august-1-2019/index.html.

[b] "The U.S., Australia and Japan Announce Trilateral Partnership on Infrastructure Investment in the Indo-Pacific," U.S. Embassy in Canberra, July 31, 2018, https://au.usembassy.gov/the-u-s-australia-and-japan-announce-trilateral-partnership-on-infrastructure-investment-in-the-indopacific/.
[c] Jack Caporal, "The CPTPP: (Almost) One Year Later," CSIS, November 5, 2019, https://www.csis.org/analysis/cptpp-almost-one-year-later.
[d] "199th Ministerial Meeting on International Economic Affairs," ROK Ministry of Economy and Finance, June 1, 2018, https://english.moef.go.kr/pc/selectTbPressCenterDtl.do?boardCd=N0001&seq=4498.
[e] "202nd Ministerial Meeting on International Economic Affairs," ROK Ministry of Economy and Finance, December 13, 2018, https://english.moef.go.kr/pc/selectTbPressCenterDtl.do?boardCd=N0001&seq=4598.
[f] "203rd Ministerial Meeting on International Economic Affairs," ROK Ministry of Economy and Finance, February 14, 2019, https://english.moef.go.kr/pc/selectTbPressCenterDtl.do?boardCd=N0001&seq=4627.
[g] "2021 Economic Policies," ROK Ministry of Economy and Finance, December 17, 2020, https://english.moef.go.kr/pc/selectTbPressCenterDtl.do?boardCd=N0001&seq=5033.
[h] Chi-Dong Lee, "S. Korea signs RCEP trade pact after summit with 14 partner nations," Yonhap News Agency, November 15, 2020, https://en.yna.co.kr/view/AEN20201115001754315?section=search.
[i] "Blue Dot Network," U.S. State Department, accessed November 30, 2021, https://2017-2021.state.gov/blue-dot-network/index.html.
[j] Cho Gwi-Dong, "The U.S. promotes 'Blue Dot Network' against China's 'Belt and Road' Initiative" [in Korean], *Chosun Ilbo*, November 6, 2019, https://www.chosun.com/site/data/html_dir/2019/11/06/2019110603583.html.
[k] Mercy A. Kuo, "Blue Dot Network: The Belt and Road Alternative: Insights from Matthew P. Goodman," *The Diplomat*, April 7, 2020, https://thediplomat.com/2020/04/blue-dot-network-the-belt-and-road-alternative/.
[l] "Special Briefing with Keith Krach, Under Secretary of State for Economic Growth, Energy, and the Environment; Cordell Hull, Acting Under Secretary of Commerce for Industry and Security; Dr. Christopher Ford, Assistant Secretary of State for International Security and Nonproliferation; and Ian Steff, Assistant Secretary of Commerce for Global Markets," U.S. Department of State, May 20, 2020, https://2017-2021.state.gov/special-briefing-with-keith-krach-under-secretary-of-state-for-economic-growth-energy-and-the-environment-cordell-hull-acting-under-secretary-of-commerce-for-industry-and-security-dr-christophe/index.html.
[m] "Special Briefing with Keith Krach, Under Secretary of State for Economic Growth, Energy, and the Environment; Cordell Hull, Acting Under Secretary of Commerce for Industry and Security; Dr. Christopher Ford, Assistant Secretary of State for International Security and Nonproliferation; and Ian Steff, Assistant Secretary of Commerce for Global Markets," U.S. Department of State, May 20, 2020, https://2017-2021.state.gov/special-briefing-with-keith-krach-under-secretary-of-state-for-economic-growth-energy-and-the-environment-cordell-hull-acting-under-secretary-of-commerce-for-industry-and-security-dr-christophe/index.html.
[n] "Second Vice Foreign Minister Lee Tae-Ho and U.S. State Department Economic Undersecretary Krach's Phone Call" [in Korean], June 5, 2020, https://www.korea.kr/news/pressReleaseView.do?newsId=156394148&pageIndex=1.
[o] "Under Secretary Keith Krach Briefs the Press on Huawei and Clean Telcos," U.S. State Department, June 25, 2020, https://2017-2021.state.gov/telephonic-briefing-with-keith-krach-under-secretary-for-economic-growth-energy-and-the-environment/index.html.
[p] "The Clean Network," U.S. State Department, accessed November 30, 2021, https://2017-2021.state.gov/the-clean-network/index.html.

(*continued*)

TABLE 9.1 (*continued*)

[q] Seung-Yeon Kim, "U.S. Renews Calls on S. Korea to Join Economic Security Campaign Against China," Yonhap News Agency, October 14, 2020, https://en.yna.co.kr/view/AEN20201014008400325.
[r] Frank Ching, "Asian Arc of Democracy," *Korea Times*, February 24, 2008, https://www.koreatimes.co.kr/www/opinion/2020/09/638_19480.html.
[s] "Ministry of Foreign Affairs Daily Briefing" [in Korean], September 29, 2020, https://www.korea.kr/news/policyBriefingView.do?newsId=156413737.
[t] "No Formal Request from U.S. over 'Quad' Coalition, Cheong Wa Dae Official Says," Yonhap News Agency, November 13, 2020, https://en.yna.co.kr/view/AEN20201113006800315?input=2106m.
[u] Jagannath P. Panda, "India, the Blue Dot Network, and the "Quad Plus" Calculus," *Journal of Indo-Pacific Affairs* (Fall 2020): 4–22.
[v] Jaechun Kim, "South Korea's Free and Open Indo-Pacific Dilemma," *The Diplomat*, April 27, 2018, https://thediplomat.com/2018/05/south-koreas-free-and-open-indo-pacific-dilemma/.
[w] Ramon Pacheco Pardo, "South Korea Holds the Key to the Indo-Pacific," *The Hill*, August 18, 2019, https://thehill.com/opinion/international/457542-south-korea-holds-the-key-to-the-indo-pacific.
[x] "U.S. & ROK Issue a Joint Factsheet on their Regional Cooperation Efforts," U.S. Embassy & Consulate in the Republic of Korea, November 2, 2019, https://kr.usembassy.gov/110219-joint-fact-sheet-by-the-united-states-and-the-republic-of-korea-on-cooperation-between-the-new-southern-policy-and-the-indo-pacific-strategy/.
[y] Andrew Yeo, "South Korea and the Free and Open Indo-Pacific Strategy," CSIS, July 20, 2020, https://www.csis.org/analysis/south-korea-and-free-and-open-indo-pacific-strategy.
[z] Hirsh Chitkara, "How the UK's Proposed 'D10 Club' Telecom Strategy Would Fare Against Huawei," *Business Insider*, June 1, 2020, https://www.businessinsider.com/how-uk-proposed-telecom-coalition-could-counter-huawei-2020-6.

important like-minded country in the region. This is significant for two reasons. First, Japan is a core leader of every initiative in the region involving a coalition of like-minded liberal democracies. If Tokyo reflects a different view of Korea, then this will naturally affect Seoul's inclusion in other such groupings. Second, this is problematic not just for Japan-Korea relations, but also for the U.S.-Korea alliance as a Biden presidency disposes of the unilateralism of its predecessor and initiates multilateral diplomacy in all regions of the world including Asia, with Japan as its core partner. President Biden has clearly signaled his predilection for coalitional movements among like-minded states to build a rules-based liberal order, from which Korea might be excluded if current trends persist. It would be a tragic irony if democratic erosion in Korea, a model of peaceful democratic transition in Asia, leads to weaker ties with an America under a Biden administration that trumpets democratic values both at home and abroad.

TABLE 9.2 Japanese designations of Korea in the Blue Book, 2015–20

Year	Designation
2015[a]	"The ROK is Japan's **most important neighbor** and good Japan-ROK relations are essential in ensuring the peace and stability of the Asia-Pacific region."
2016[b]	"The year 2015 was the milestone year of the 50th anniversary of the normalization of Japan-ROK relations. The ROK is Japan's **most important neighbor** that shares strategic interests, and good Japan-ROK relations are essential in ensuring peace and stability of the Asia-Pacific region."
2017[c]	"The ROK is Japan's **most important neighbor** which shares strategic interests, and the partnership and cooperation of Japan-ROK are essential in ensuring peace and stability of the Asia-Pacific region."
2018[d]	"The partnership and cooperation between Japan and the ROK are essential in ensuring the peace and stability of the Asia-Pacific region."
2019[e]	"In 2018, the relations between Japan and the ROK faced an extremely severe situation amid a series of negative moves by the ROK. . . . Meanwhile, three Japan-ROK Summit Meetings and eight Japan-ROK Foreign Ministers' Meetings were held. Based on its consistent position, Japan continued to urge the ROK to take appropriate measures to address the difficult issues between the two countries, and confirmed with the ROK that Japan-ROK and Japan-ROK-U.S. would work closely on the issues of North Korea."
2020[e]	"The Republic of Korea (ROK) is **an important neighboring country** for Japan. . . . In spite of the above, in 2019, following on from 2018, the relations between Japan and the ROK continued to face difficult situations amid unending negative moves by the ROK. . ."

SOURCE: [a] "Diplomatic Bluebook 2015," Ministry of Foreign Affairs Japan, 2015, https://www.mofa.go.jp/policy/other/bluebook/2015/html/chapter2/c020101.html.
[b] "Diplomatic Bluebook 2016," Ministry of Foreign Affairs Japan, 2016, https://www.mofa.go.jp/policy/other/bluebook/2016/html/chapter2/c020101.html.
[c] "Diplomatic Bluebook 2017," Ministry of Foreign Affairs Japan, 2017, https://www.mofa.go.jp/policy/other/bluebook/2017/html/chapter2/c020101.html.
[d] "Diplomatic Bluebook 2018," Ministry of Foreign Affairs Japan, 2018, https://www.mofa.go.jp/policy/other/bluebook/2018/html/chapter2/c020101.html.
[e] "Diplomatic Bluebook 2019," Ministry of Foreign Affairs Japan, 2019, https://www.mofa.go.jp/policy/other/bluebook/2019/html/chapter2/c020102.html.
[f] "Diplomatic Bluebook 2020," Ministry of Foreign Affairs Japan, 2020, https://www.mofa.go.jp/policy/other/bluebook/2020/html/chapter2/c020102.html.

Conclusion

Democratic erosion is evident in foreign policy when a state no longer privileges such values in its diplomacy. The state does not externalize norms of compromise and negotiation in its relations with other states. Moreover, the state allows gaps to develop between its policy and the public's support, and it engages in "overreach" to dampen criticism of its policies. In Korea's case, deep internal polarization has led to the erosion of civil norms of governance, and this has become externalized in the goals and execution of foreign policy. The changing character of this foreign policy is not entirely Korea's fault. It has been facilitated by four years of American leadership that failed to uphold democratic values and adopted a highly transactional approach to foreign relations. Nonetheless, the costs of an illiberal foreign policy are felt not just at home, but in valued relationships with key allies and partners. And the deleterious effects can be long term, as Korea runs the risk of suffering increasing isolation from coalitional initiatives among like-minded democracies in the region. Being left out of such multilateral efforts, which value rule abidance, transparency, and equity, would be damaging not just to Korea's international prestige, but also to its strategic position vis-à-vis a powerful illiberal neighbor.

Bibliography

Ahn, Sung-Mi. "Seoul to Press Charges against Defector Groups Sending Anti-Pyongyang Leaflets." *Korea Herald*, June 10, 2020. http://www.koreaherald.com/view.php?ud=20200610000933.

Basu, Zachary. "More Countries Join Condemnation of China over Xinjiang Abuses." *Axios*, October 8, 2020. https://www.axios.com/un-statement-china-uighurs-xinjiang-6b29dbf5-b93c-4c70-bd4c-333e1c23471f.html.

Caporal, Jack. "The CPTPP: (Almost) One Year Later." CSIS, November 5, 2019. https://www.csis.org/analysis/cptpp-almost-one-year-later.

Carothers, Thomas, and Frances Z. Brown. "Can U.S. Democracy Policy Survive Trump?" Carnegie Endowment for International Peace, October 1, 2018. https://carnegieendowment.org/2018/10/01/can-u.s.-democracy-policy-survive-trump-pub-77381.

Cha, Victor. *Alignment despite Antagonism.* Stanford: Stanford University Press, 1999.

———. "Korea's Mistake on China's ADIZ Controversy." CSIS Korea Chair Platform, December 2, 2013. https://www.csis.org/analysis/korea%E2%80%99s-mistake-china%E2%80%99s-adiz-controversy.

———. "Leading by Example: Two Different Responses to China's Rise." *The Interpreter*, November 11, 2020. https://www.lowyinstitute.org/the-interpreter/leading-example-two-different-responses-chinas-rise.

———. "Allied Decoupling in an Era of US-China Strategic Competition." *Chinese Journal of International Politics* 13, no. 4 (Winter 2020): 509–38.

Cheong Wa Dae. "Truth Is What Matters Most in History: President Moon." December 29, 2017. https://english1.president.go.kr/Media/News/225.

———. "Opening Remarks by Deputy National Security Advisor Hyun Chong Kim at Press Briefing." August 28, 2019. https://english1.president.go.kr/BriefingSpeeches/Briefings/451.

Ching, Frank. "Asian Arc of Democracy." *Korea Times*, February 24, 2008. https://www.koreatimes.co.kr/www/opinion/2020/09/638_19480.html.

Chitkara, Hirsh. "How the UK's Proposed 'D10 Club' Telecom Strategy Would Fare against Huawei." *Business Insider*, June 1, 2020. https://www.businessinsider.com/how-uk-proposed-telecom-coalition-could-counter-huawei-2020-6.

Cho, Gwi-Dong. "The U.S. Promotes 'Blue Dot Network' against China's 'Belt and Road' Initiative." [In Korean.] *Chosun Ilbo*, November 6, 2019. https://www.chosun.com/site/data/html_dir/2019/11/06/2019110603583.html.

Choe, Sang-Hun. "2 North Koreans Tried to Defect. Did Seoul Send Them to Their Deaths?" *New York Times*, December 18, 2019.

Council of the European Union. "Declaration of the High Representative on Behalf of the European Union on the Adoption by China's National People's Congress of a National Security Legislation on Hong Kong." July 1, 2020. https://europa.eu/!Dw76JV .

East Asia Institute. "Joint EAT-CCGA Survey of Views toward Seven Countries in East Asia and the Pacific: The World as It Is Viewed by Koreans." [In Korean.] March 4, 2008. http://www.eai.or.kr/data/bbs/kor_report/2009060811585732.pdf.

Embassy of the People's Republic of China in the Republic of Korea. "Ambassador Xing Haiming Participates in CCTV News Live Discussion." [In Chinese.] May 27, 2020. http://kr.china-embassy.org/chn/sghd/t1783294.htm.

Fifield, Anna. "Korea Think-Tank at U.S. University to Close after Seoul Withdraws Funding." *Washington Post*, April 11, 2018.

Freedom House. "Freedom in the World 2020." Accessed November 30, 2021. https://freedomhouse.org/country/north-korea/freedom-world/2020.

Gallup Korea. "Favorability Rating of Political Leaders in Neighboring Countries." [In Korean.] September 26, 2013. https://www.gallup.co.kr/gallupdb/reportContent.asp?seqNo=477.

Human Rights Watch. "Letter to President Moon Jae-in RE: ROK's Stance on Human Rights in North Korea." December 16, 2019. https://www.hrw.org/news/2019/12/16/letter-president-moon-jae-re-roks-stance-human-rights-north-korea.

Kang, Tae-Jung. "On Hong Kong South Korea Is Caught between China and US." *The Diplomat*, May 29, 2020. https://thediplomat.com/2020/05/on-hong-kong-south-korea-is-caught-between-china-and-us/.

Katz, Katrin Fraser. "Domestic Interest Configuration and Island Disputes: Cyclical Surges of Nationalist and Internationalist Influence in Northeast Asia." PhD dissertation, Northwestern University, 2017. https://arch.library.northwestern.edu/concern/generic_works/5x21tf562?locale=en.

Kim, Chang-Won. "[Joint Survey of Public Opinion] 88 Percent in South Korea, 90 Percent in China, and 61 Percent in Japan Say 'History Issues Not Yet Resolved'." [In Korean.] *Dong-A Ilbo*, January 6, 2012. https://www.donga.com/news/Inter/article/all/20120106/43121061/1.

Kim, Ellen, and Victor Cha. "Between a Rock and a Hard Place: South Korea's Strategic Dilemmas with China and the United States." *Asia Policy* 21 (January 2016): 101–21.

Kim, Hyung-Jin. "Seoul: North Korea Kills S. Korean Official, Burns His Body." Associated Press, September 24, 2020. https://apnews.com/article/international-news-south-korea-north-korea-seoul-05385eedb0b036cd1b1b09184a8d7184.

Kim, Jaechun. "South Korea's Free and Open Indo-Pacific Dilemma." *The Diplomat*, April 27, 2018. https://thediplomat.com/2018/05/south-koreas-free-and-open-indo-pacific-dilemma/.

Kim, Jeongmin. "South Korea's Unification Ministry to Inspect Non-Profit Groups in Mid-August." *NK News*, July 24, 2020. https://www.nknews.org/2020/07/south-koreas-unification-ministry-to-inspect-non-profit-groups-in-mid-august/.

Kim, Seung-Yeon. "S. Korea Warns Japan of Rolling Back Decision to Suspend GSOMIA's Termination." Yonhap News Agency, January 9, 2020. http://yna.kr/AEN20200109003200325.

———. "U.S. Renews Calls on S. Korea to Join Economic Security Campaign against China." Yonhap News Agency, October 14, 2020. http://yna.kr/AEN20201014008400325.

Kim, So-Youn. "US Directly Asks S. Korea to Join Economic Coalition that Excludes China." *Hankyoreh*, June 8, 2020. http://english.hani.co.kr/arti/english_edition/e_national/948417.html.

"Kim Yo Jong Rebukes S. Korean Authorities for Conniving at Anti-DPRK Hostile Act of 'Defectors from North'." KCNA, June 4, 2020. https://kcnawatch.org/newstream/1591219896-544350772/kim-yo-jong-rebukes-s-korean-authorities-for-conniving-at-anti-dprk-hostile-act-of-defectors-from-north/.

Kuo, Mercy A. "Blue Dot Network: The Belt and Road Alternative: Insights from Matthew P. Goodman." *The Diplomat*, April 7, 2020. https://thediplomat.com/2020/04/blue-dot-network-the-belt-and-road-alternative/.

Lee, Chi-Dong. "S. Korea Signs RCEP Trade Pact after Summit with 14 Partner Nations." Yonhap News Agency, November 15, 2020. http://yna.kr/AEN20201115001754315.

Lee, Chong-Sik. *Japan and Korea: The Political Dimension.* Stanford: Hoover Institution Press, 1985.

Lee, Joyce. "U.S. Security Adviser Bolton Meets South Korean Officials, Seeks Stronger Ties." Reuters, July 23, 2019. https://reut.rs/2Y1O6wr.

Levitsky, Steven, and Daniel Ziblatt. "This Is How Democracies Die." *The Guardian*, January 21, 2018. https://www.theguardian.com/us-news/commentisfree/2018/jan/21/this-is-how-democracies-die.

Lind, Jennifer. *Apologies in International Politics.* Ithaca: Cornell University Press, 2008.

Lo, Kingling. "South Korea Rejects China's Version of President Moon's Hong Kong Remarks." *Korea Times*, December 26, 2019. https://www.koreatimes.co.kr/www/world/2019/12/672_280890.html.

"Ministry of Foreign Affairs Daily Briefing." [In Korean.] September 29, 2020. https://www.korea.kr/news/policyBriefingView.do?newsId=156413737.

Ministry of Foreign Affairs of Japan. *Diplomatic Bluebook 2015.* Tokyo: Ministry of Foreign Affairs, 2015. https://www.mofa.go.jp/policy/other/bluebook/2015/html/chapter2/c020101.html.

———. *Diplomatic Bluebook 2016*. Tokyo: Ministry of Foreign Affairs, 2016. https://www.mofa.go.jp/policy/other/bluebook/2016/html/chapter2/c020101.html.

———. *Diplomatic Bluebook 2017*. Tokyo: Ministry of Foreign Affairs, 2017. https://www.mofa.go.jp/policy/other/bluebook/2017/html/chapter2/c020101.html.

———. *Diplomatic Bluebook 2018*. Tokyo: Ministry of Foreign Affairs, 2018. https://www.mofa.go.jp/policy/other/bluebook/2018/html/chapter2/c020101.html.

———. *Diplomatic Bluebook 2019*. Tokyo: Ministry of Foreign Affairs, 2019. https://www.mofa.go.jp/policy/other/bluebook/2019/html/chapter2/c020102.html.

———. *Diplomatic Bluebook 2020*. Tokyo: Ministry of Foreign Affairs, 2020. https://www.mofa.go.jp/policy/other/bluebook/2020/html/chapter2/c020102.html.

Ministry of Foreign Affairs of the People's Republic of China. "Foreign Ministry Spokesperson Geng Shuang's Regular Press Conference on December 23, 2019." December 23, 2019. https://www.fmprc.gov.cn/mfa_eng/xwfw_665399/s2510_665401/2511_665403/t1727131.shtml.

"No Formal Request from U.S. over 'Quad' Coalition, Cheong Wa Dae Official Says." Yonhap News Agency, November 13, 2020. http://yna.kr/AEN20201113006800315.

"North Korean Fishermen 'Killed 16 Colleagues' before Fleeing to South." BBC News, November 7, 2019. https://www.bbc.com/news/world-asia-50329588.

O'Carroll, Chad. "Seoul Won't Rule Out Action against Radio Stations Broadcasting into North Korea." *NK News*, August 11, 2020. https://www.nknews.org/2020/08/seoul-wont-rule-out-action-against-radio-stations-broadcasting-into-north-korea/.

Panda, Jagannath P. "India, the Blue Dot Network, and the "Quad Plus" Calculus." *Journal of Indo-Pacific Affairs* (Fall 2020): 4–22.

Pardo, Ramon Pacheco. "South Korea Holds the Key to the Indo-Pacific." *The Hill*, August 18, 2019. https://thehill.com/opinion/international/457542-south-korea-holds-the-key-to-the-indo-pacific.

Park, Sang-Hak. "We Send Food and Information into North Korea. Why Is Seoul Trying to Stop Us?" *Washington Post*, July 13, 2020.

Pennington, Matthew. "US Think Tank on North Korea to Close as South Korea Cuts Funds." Associated Press, April 9, 2018. https://

www.businessinsider.com/ap-us-think-tank-on-korea-to-close-as-skorea-cuts-funds-2018-4.

Przeworski, Adam. *Crises of Democracy.* Cambridge: Cambridge University Press, 2019.

Redden, Elizabeth. "US-Korea Institute Closes after Alleged Meddling." *Inside Higher Ed*, April 11, 2018. https://www.insidehighered.com/quicktakes/2018/04/11/us-korea-institute-close-after-alleged-meddling.

Rogin, Josh. "South Korea's New Anti-Leaflet Law Sparks Backlash in Washington." *Washington Post*, December 17, 2020.

ROK Ministry of Economy and Finance. "199th Ministerial Meeting on International Economic Affairs." June 1, 2018. https://english.moef.go.kr/pc/selectTbPressCenterDtl.do?boardCd=N0001&seq=4498.

———. "202nd Ministerial Meeting on International Economic Affairs." December 13, 2018. https://english.moef.go.kr/pc/selectTbPressCenterDtl.do?boardCd=N0001&seq=4598.

———. "203rd Ministerial Meeting on International Economic Affairs." February 14, 2019. https://english.moef.go.kr/pc/selectTbPressCenterDtl.do?boardCd=N0001&seq=4627.

———. "2021 Economic Policies." December 17, 2020. https://english.moef.go.kr/pc/selectTbPressCenterDtl.do?boardCd=N0001&seq=5033.

"S. Korea Conveys to China Moon's Correct Comments on Hong Kong, Xinjiang." Yonhap News Agency, December 29, 2019. https://en.yna.co.kr/view/AEN20191229003900320.

"Second Vice Foreign Minister Lee Tae-Ho and U.S. State Department Economic Undersecretary Krach's Phone Call." [In Korean.] June 5, 2020. https://www.korea.kr/news/pressReleaseView.do?newsId=156394148&pageIndex=1.

Shim, Elizabeth. "South Korea Rescinds Defectors Permits after Leaflet Dispute." UPI, July 17, 2020. https://www.upi.com/Top_News/World-News/2020/07/17/South-Korea-rescinds-defectors-permits-after-leaflet-dispute/3871594987256/.

Shim, Kyu-Seok. "Gov't Moves to Revoke Defector Groups' Permits." *Korea JoongAng Daily*, June 29, 2020. https://koreajoongangdaily.joins.com/2020/06/29/national/northKorea/leaflets-defectors-unification-ministry/20200629192200341.html.

Shin, Gi-Wook. "The Perils of Populism." APARC Commentary, September 2019. https://fsi-live.s3.us-west-1.amazonaws.com/s3fs-public/shin_perils_of_populist_nationalism.pdf.

———. "South Korea's Democratic Decay." *Journal of Democracy* 31, no. 3 (July 2020): 100–14.

Silver, Laura, Kat Devlin, and Christine Huang. "Unfavorable Views of China Reach Historic Highs in Many Countries." Pew Research Center, October 6, 2020. https://www.pewresearch.org/global/2020/10/06/unfavorable-views-of-china-reach-historic-highs-in-many-countries/.

UN Human Rights Council. *Report of the Detailed Findings of the Commission of Inquiry on Human Rights in the Democratic People's Republic of Korea*. A/HRC/25/63. February 7, 2014. https://www.ohchr.org/en/hrbodies/hrc/coidprk/pages/reportofthecommissionofinquirydprk.aspx.

"Unification Ministry Suspends Investigations into Human Rights in N. Korea." *Dong-A Ilbo*, September 16, 2020. https://www.donga.com/en/article/all/20200916/2182823/1.

"U.S. Adviser Bolton Travels to Japan, South Korea amid Trade Dispute." Reuters, July 20, 2019. https://reut.rs/2SqTrHL.

U.S. Department of State. "Trilateral Strategic Dialogue Joint Ministerial Statement, August 1, 2019." August 2, 2019. https://2017-2021.state.gov/trilateral-strategic-dialogue-joint-ministerial-statement-august-1-2019/index.html.

———. "Special Briefing with Keith Krach, Under Secretary of State for Economic Growth, Energy, and the Environment; Cordell Hull, Acting Under Secretary of Commerce for Industry and Security; Dr. Christopher Ford, Assistant Secretary of State for International Security and Nonproliferation; and Ian Steff, Assistant Secretary of Commerce for Global Markets." May 20, 2020. https://2017-2021.state.gov/special-briefing-with-keith-krach-under-secretary-of-state-for-economic-growth-energy-and-the-environment-cordell-hull-acting-under-secretary-of-commerce-for-industry-and-security-dr-christophe/index.html.

———. "Under Secretary Keith Krach Briefs the Press on Huawei and Clean Telcos." June 25, 2020. https://2017-2021.state.gov/telephonic-briefing-with-keith-krach-under-secretary-for-economic-growth-energy-and-the-environment/index.html.

———. "Joint Statement on Hong Kong." November 18, 2020. https://hk.usconsulate.gov/n-2020111801/.

———. "Blue Dot Network." Accessed November 30, 2021. https://2017-2021.state.gov/blue-dot-network/index.html.

———. "The Clean Network." Accessed November 30, 2021. https://2017-2021.state.gov/the-clean-network/index.html.

U.S. Embassy and Consulate in the Republic of Korea. "U.S. & ROK Issue a Joint Factsheet on Their Regional Cooperation Efforts." November 2, 2019. https://kr.usembassy.gov/110219-joint-fact-sheet-by-the-united-states-and-the-republic-of-korea-on-cooperation-between-the-new-southern-policy-and-the-indo-pacific-strategy/.

U.S. Embassy in Canberra. "The U.S., Australia and Japan Announce Trilateral Partnership on Infrastructure Investment in the Indo-Pacific." July 31, 2018. https://au.usembassy.gov/the-u-s-australia-and-japan-announce-trilateral-partnership-on-infrastructure-ivestment-in-the-indopacific/.

The White House. "Remarks by President Trump and President Moon of the Republic of Korea in Joint Press Conference." June 30, 2019. https://www.whitehouse.gov/briefings-statements/remarks-president-trump-president-moon-republic-korea-joint-press-conference/.

Yeo, Andrew. "South Korea and the Free and Open Indo-Pacific Strategy." CSIS, July 20, 2020. https://www.csis.org/analysis/south-korea-and-free-and-open-indo-pacific-strategy.

CHAPTER TEN

The Democratic Recession

A Global and Comparative Perspective

Larry Diamond

The democratic travails and challenges documented in this book are hardly unique to Korea. Over the past fifteen years, the world has slid into an increasingly visible and persistent democratic recession.[1] Until recently, this was a mild and even ambiguous phenomenon, so much so that distinguished scholars challenged the notion that it was happening at all.[2] However, in recent years the global trend has gathered unsettling momentum.

This chapter traces the trends of accelerating democratic recession in the world, which seem to be morphing into a "third reverse wave" of democratic failures, in the framework of Samuel Huntington's model of democratic and authoritarian waves over the past two decades.[3] First, I review the statistical trends since 2006 of steadily declining freedom and a rising pace of democratic breakdowns. Then I describe in narrative terms some of the instances and elements of this decay, which have been eroding or destroying democracy in a number of large and strategically important states. Next, I analyze the causes of this trend. These include both domestic factors (political values, political institutions, and the craft of political leaders) and external factors, including geopolitical developments, socioeconomic trends, and the changing balance of global power with the rise of China and the resurgence of

1 Larry Diamond, *The Spirit of Democracy: The Struggle to Build Free Societies throughout the World* (New York: Times Books, 2008), 56–87.
2 Steven Levitsky and Lucan Way, "The Myth of Democratic Recession," *Journal of Democracy* 26, no. 1 (January 2015): 45–58.
3 Samuel P. Huntington, *The Third Wave: Democratization in the Late Twentieth Century* (Norman: University of Oklahoma Press, 1991).

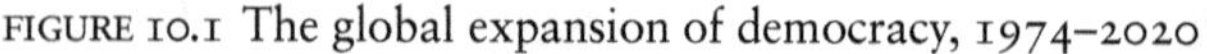

FIGURE 10.1 The global expansion of democracy, 1974–2020

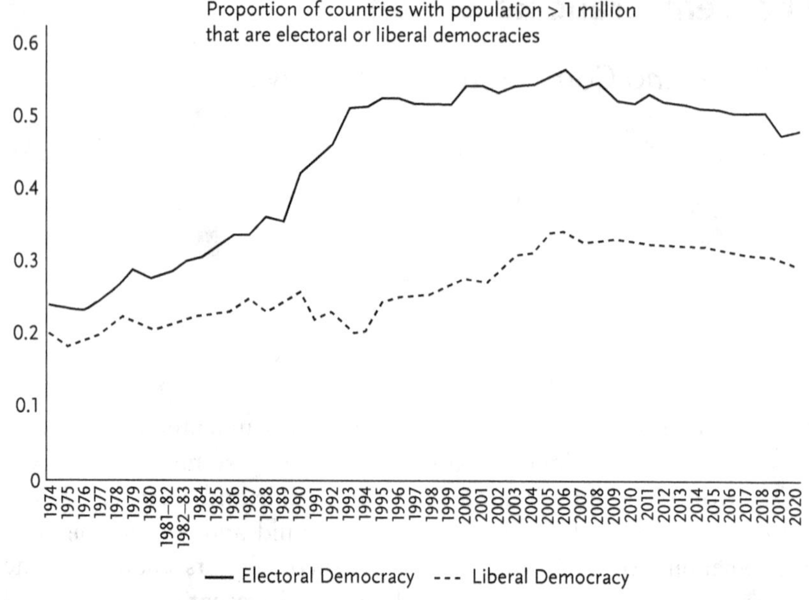

SOURCE: Author's calculations based on annual Freedom House scores.

Russia as authoritarian global powers. In conclusion, I consider lessons from around the world on how to reverse democratic backsliding, and how Korea might learn from and adapt them.

The Global Democratic Recession

The earliest sign of trouble was that democracy simply stopped expanding. In fact, 2006 was the high-water mark for democracy in the world, with the percentage of democracies peaking at 61 percent among all states and 57 percent among states with a population of over one million (figure 10.1). Since then, the proportion of democracies in the world has gradually declined to 55 percent of all states and 48 percent of states with a population of over one million in 2020. The percentage of people living in democracies declined from 55 percent in 2006 to 47 percent in 2020.[4] The year 2019 marked the first time since the end

4 Each of these is a measurement at the end of the calendar year.

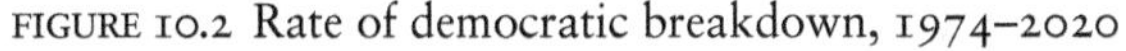

FIGURE 10.2 Rate of democratic breakdown, 1974–2020

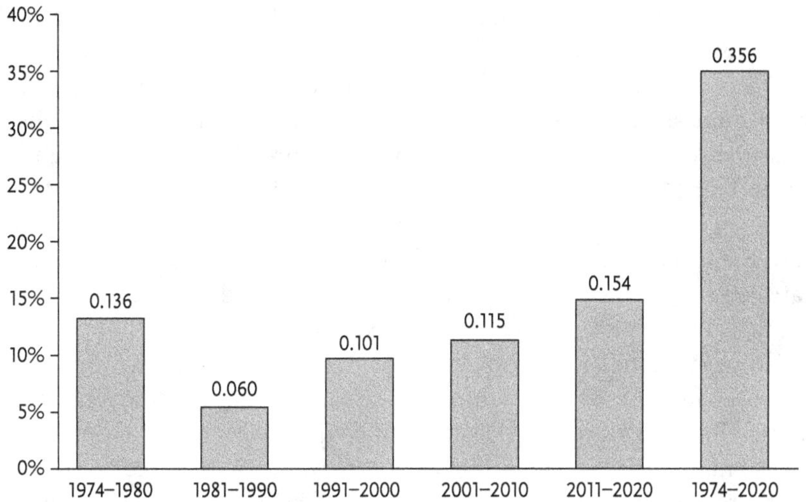

SOURCE: Author's calculations based on annual Freedom House scores.

of the Cold War that a majority of states with a population of over one million were not democratic, and also the first time that a majority of the world's people did not live in a democracy.

The decline in the proportion of democratic states has entailed two statistical trends. First, since the peak of the "Third Wave" of global democratization in the 1990s, the rate of transitions to democracy has been declining. In the 1990s, 43 percent of all existing authoritarian regimes gave way to democratic forms of government. That rate of democratic transition then declined to 20 percent in the 2000s and 17.3 percent in the 2010s. At the same time—and perhaps more concerning for the purposes of this volume—the rate of democratic breakdown steadily increased. The percentage of democratic regimes that failed by one means or another (whether by military coup, executive coup, or incremental backsliding) increased from a mere 6 percent in the 1980s to 10 percent in the 1990s, 11.5 percent in the 2000s, and 15.4 percent in the most recent decade (2011–20) (figure 10.2). The latter half of the 2010s (2015–19) was the first five-year period since the beginning of the Third Wave in 1974 when more countries abandoned democracy (twelve) than transited to it (seven).

Beginning in 2006, levels of freedom also started to recede across the world. Based on data from Freedom House, the ratio of countries gaining in freedom to the number declining in freedom fell to about parity in 2006 and has remained between 50 and 70 percent ever since.[5] This is the reverse of the pattern during the fifteen years (1991–2005) following the demise of the Soviet Union.

According to Freedom House, the erosion in freedom in Korea has been modest: from 86 in 2012 to 83 in 2020, with 100 as the highest possible score for any country. However, Korea has fallen far behind other Third Wave democracy pacesetters like Taiwan (94 in 2020) and Chile (93). Moreover, if we disaggregate the Freedom House scores into the three elements of political rights, civil liberties, and the rule of law, we see that Korea's decline in rule of law and transparency measures has been particularly pronounced (figure 10.3).

To be sure, the impact on aggregate freedom scores in the world has still been modest. Between 2006 and 2019, average global scores on the 100-point scale of political rights and civil liberties fell by 6.2 percent. These numbers do not tell the whole story, however. Since the democratic recession began in 2006, democracy has been failing in a number of large and strategically important states, such as Bangladesh, Thailand, Turkey, the Philippines, and for the first time in a member state of the European Union (EU)—Hungary.[6] These instances followed the executive-led strangulation (in the early years of the new century) of an emerging democracy in Russia and of a long-standing but deeply troubled democracy in Venezuela. Other states, like Sri Lanka and Nepal, have moved back and forth or hovered on the precipice. And many democracies have been deteriorating in quality, including the world's four largest—the United States, India, Indonesia, and Brazil—and the largest democracy in Central and Eastern Europe, Poland.[7] In fact, there has been substantial democratic backsliding in many prominent established and Third Wave democracies. From 2012 to 2020, Hungary declined by 19 points on the Freedom House 100-point scale,

5 Sarah Repucci, "Freedom in the World 2020: A Leaderless Struggle for Democracy," Freedom House, accessed November 30, 2021, https://freedomhouse.org/report/freedom-world/2020/leaderless-struggle-democracy.

6 Jacques Rupnik, "Hungary's Illiberal Turn: How Things Went Wrong," *Journal of Democracy* 23, no. 3 (July 2012): 132–37; Miklós Bankuti, Gábor Halmai, and Kim Lane Scheppele, "Hungary's Illiberal Turn: Disabling the Constitution," *Journal of Democracy* 23, no. 3 (July 2012): 138–46.

7 Joanna Fomina and Jack Kucharczyk, "The Specter Haunting Europe: Populism and Protest in Poland," *Journal of Democracy* 27, no. 4 (October 2016): 58–68.

FIGURE 10.3 Trends in Korea's Freedom House scores, 2005–20

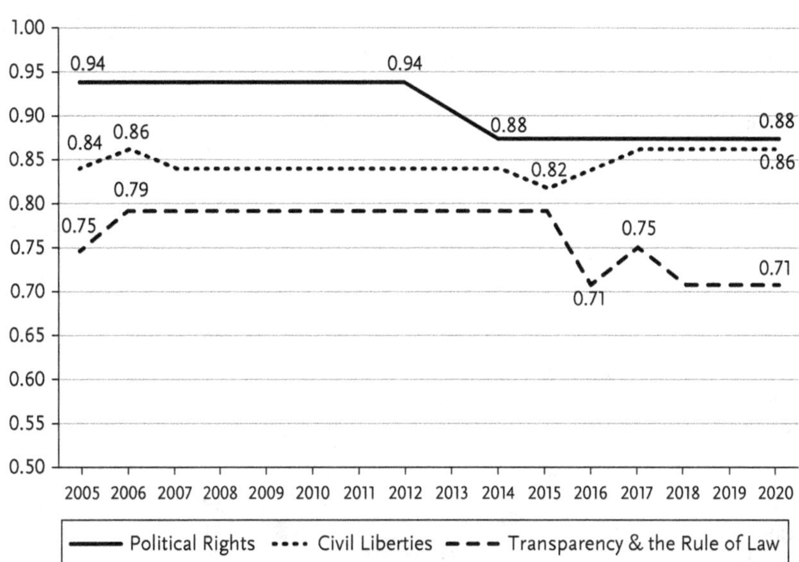

SOURCE: Freedom House annual reports.

Poland by 11, the United States by 10, India and Indonesia by 9, Brazil by 7, Mexico by 4, and Korea by 3.

We can group the countries with the most geopolitical weight—the nineteen members of the G20 (which also includes the European Union as a twentieth member), and ten others that are among the twenty most populous countries in the world—into three categories, based on their standing in 2005, the year before the onset of the global democratic recession: advanced industrial democracies, emerging market (and mainly illiberal) democracies, and autocracies. Between 2005 and 2020, twenty of these twenty-nine countries suffered a meaningful decline (of at least three points) on the 100-point Freedom House scale, and only one improved meaningfully. Among the nine advanced democracies (all of them liberal), five declined by at least three points, and only one—Japan—improved by at least that much. Among the ten emerging market democracies, eight declined by at least three points and none improved by at least that much. Thailand and Turkey suffered catastrophic implosions. Mexico joined Bangladesh and the Philippines in registering double-digit declines, and India and South Africa dropped

TABLE 10.1 Freedom House scores for G-20 and other populous countries (2005–20)

Country	2005	2012	2020	Change from 2005 to 2020
Advanced democracies				
Australia	96	97	97	+1
Canada	98	98	98	0
France	93	95	90	–3
Germany	97	96	94	–3
Italy	92	88	90	–2
Japan	88	88	96	+8
South Korea	87	86	83	–4
United Kingdom	96	97	93	–3
United States	93	93	83	–10
Emerging market democracies				
Argentina	84	80	84	0
Bangladesh	53	56	39	–14
Brazil	77	81	74	–3
India	76	76	67	–9
Indonesia	65	68	59	–6
Mexico	80	65	61	–19
Philippines	72	63	56	–16
South Africa	88	81	79	–9
Thailand	67	53	30	–37
Turkey	65	61	32	–33
Authoritarian regimes				
China	17	17	9	–8
Dem. Republic of Congo	20	20	20	0
Egypt	30	41	18	–12
Ethiopia	36	18	22	-–14
Iran	24	18	16	–8
Nigeria	48	46	45	–3
Pakistan	35	42	37	+2
Russia	35	27	20	–15
Saudi Arabia	12	10	7	–5
Vietnam	19	19	19	0

NOTE: Scored on a scale of 0 to 100, 100 indicating most free.
SOURCE: Freedom House, *Freedom in the World* reports, 2005, 2012, 2020.

by nine points. Among the ten large autocracies, such as China, Russia, and Egypt, seven suffered declines of at least three points, and none gained by that margin (table 10.1).

The downward trend has been especially striking in Asia. While Japan and Taiwan stand out as resilient liberal democracies that have improved over the past decade, the Moon Jae-In administration in South Korea has been "going the other way, exacerbating polarization, eroding democratic norms, and appealing to chauvinistic nationalism" in a process of creeping political hegemony that is poorly understood outside the country and has yet to register in international democracy ratings.[8] Beyond the death squads and relentless assaults on independent institutions and critics in the Philippines, corruption is on the rise as the rule of law deteriorates.[9] India—by far the most populous democracy not only in Asia but the world—has witnessed an escalating assault on civil liberties, rule of law, and religious tolerance under Narendra Modi's populist Bharatiya Janata Party (BJP) government.[10] Indonesia has also experienced a significant decline in civil liberties and democratic integrity. Bangladesh is mired in polarization and personalistic, one-party domination. The military rules from behind the curtain in Pakistan and China are becoming ever-more authoritarian and belligerent. Beyond these regional powers, Malaysia and Singapore both began and ended this period around the midpoint of the 100-point scale. Burma has suffered a brutal military coup against a fragile and military-dominated semidemocracy, while Thailand is stuck in a military-dominated hybrid regime. As this volume shows, Korea has been moving in an illiberal direction under a ruling party with hegemonic pretensions.[11]

Globally, an overwhelming majority of the largest, most powerful, and influential countries have been regressing politically over the past decade and a half. Including Korea, many advanced liberal democracies have become less liberal—notably the most powerful liberal country, the United States. Numerous electoral democracies have slid down the path of creeping authoritarianism, with less protection of civil liberties, weaker accountability and rule of law, and more intense political polarization, undermining the functionality of democratic institutions and the normative commitments that sustain them. A growing number of other electoral democracies have been breaking down. Competitive authoritarian regimes, such as Kenya, Tanzania, Uganda, and Cambodia,

8 Gi-Wook Shin, "South Korea's Democratic Decay," *Journal of Democracy* 31, no. 3 (July 2020): 101.

9 Panos Mourdoukoutas, "Duterte Is Turning Philippines into a More Corrupt and Less Democratic State," *Forbes*, January 24, 2020, https://www.forbes.com/sites/panosmourdoukoutas/2020/01/24/duterte-is-turning-philippines-into-a-more-corrupt-and-less-democratic-state/?sh=6b4aec912768.

10 Sumit Ganguly, "An Illiberal India?," *Journal of Democracy* 31, no. 1 (January 2020): 193–202.

11 Shin, "South Korea's Democratic Decay."

have been squeezing out their competition, to the point that the latter three are virtual one-party states.[12] Regimes that were already deeply authoritarian have become much more so.

The picture has been further darkened by the rise and fall (or at least stalling) of numerous hopes for democratic transition. When Malaysia's ruling Barisan Nasional coalition was defeated in the May 2018 parliamentary elections for the first time in the country's history, hopes for a transition to democracy were euphoric, and not entirely unrealistic.[13] However, political divisions and opportunism within the opposition coalition have stalled this transition and may now be unraveling it.[14] A similar fate fell upon Nigeria in 2015, when an incumbent president was defeated in an election for the first time in the country's fifty-five-year history, but the country became only marginally more democratic.[15] Among the twenty countries where mass public protests or an "electoral earthquake" might have brought a transition to democracy in the last fifteen years, only two have actually achieved democracy (Tunisia and Ukraine).[16]

Explaining the Democratic Recession

What accounts for this protracted global democratic recession? In most instances of democratic regression or failure, we find familiar agents of destruction: elected political leaders, greedy for power and wealth, who knock away various constraints on their power and enlarge and entrench it in undemocratic ways. Less common these days are military leaders who seize upon civilian incompetence, corruption, or polarization and dysfunction to take power directly. Military intervention still happens occasionally, for example, in Thailand, Egypt, and, most recently and brutally, Burma. But for the most part, this has been an era

12 Lee Morgenbesser, "Cambodia's Transition to Hegemonic Authoritarianism," *Journal of Democracy* 30, no. 1 (January 2019): 158–71.

13 Sophie Lemière, "The Downfall of Malaysia's Ruling Party," *Journal of Democracy* 29, no. 4 (October 2018): 114–28.

14 Brian Wong, "Democracy in Crisis," *The Diplomat*, February 27, 2020, https://thediplomat.com/2020/02/democracy-in-crisis-where-does-malaysia-go-from-here/.

15 Wole Soyinka, "Lessons from Nigeria's Militarized Experiment," *New York Times*, October 9, 2019, https://www.nytimes.com/2019/10/09/opinion/nigeria-militarized-democratic-experiment.html.

16 Larry Diamond, "Democratic Regression in Comparative Perspective: Scope, Methods, and Causes," *Democratization* 28, no. 1 (2020): 22–42.

FIGURE 10.4 Country trends in Freedom House aggregate scores, 2005–20

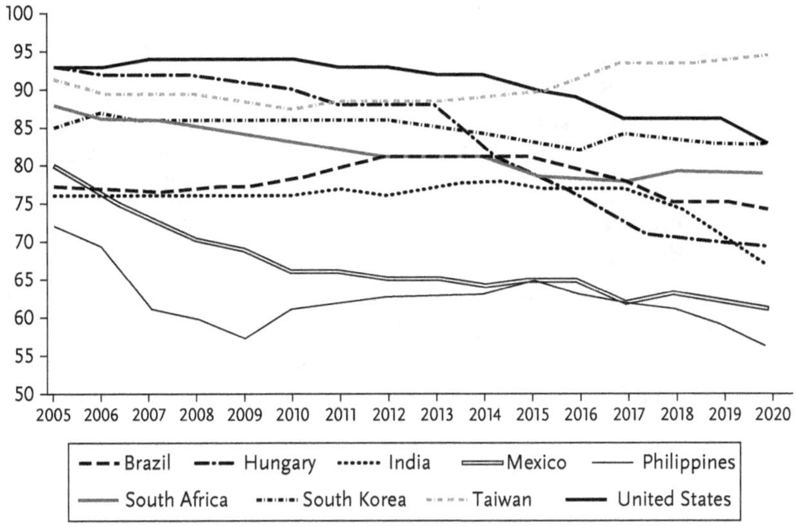

SOURCE: Freedom House annual reports.

of civilian assaults on democracy. Polarized parties and politicians still figure prominently in democratic breakdowns.[17] However, in this era, the authoritarian politician—Hugo Chávez and then Nicolás Maduro in Venezuela, Recep Tayyip Erdoğan in Turkey, Viktor Orbán in Hungary, Jaroslaw Kaczynski and the Law and Justice Party (PiS) in Poland, Rodrigo Duterte in the Philippines, and now Narendra Modi in India, Jair Bolsonaro in Brazil, and Nayib Bukele in El Salvador—is more the instigator of the polarization than the product. In all these cases, populist politicians rose to power by inflaming divisions and mobilizing the good, deserving "people" against corrupt elites—the professional or "deep" state and their effete, educated handmaidens in the other (liberal) political parties—and also against a host of external threats, such as international institutions, refugees and migrants, and "undeserving" minorities who do not truly "belong" in the country.

17 Jennifer McCoy and Murat Somer, "Toward a Theory of Pernicious Polarization and How It Harms Democracies: Comparative Evidence and Possible Remedies," *Annals of the American Academy of Political and Social Science* 681 (2019): 234–71.

Political values and norms

Within countries, culture and institutions determine whether potential autocrats are elected to office, and if they are, whether they are effectively constrained from realizing their ambitions. Strong prevailing norms of commitment to democracy; rejection of authoritarian options; mutual tolerance, trust, and restraint; and a willingness to compromise thus play a crucial role in inoculating democracy against authoritarian attacks.

In East and Southeast Asia, particularly in the Philippines and Mongolia, the populist assault on democracy has been facilitated by a decline in public commitment to democratic values and norms, as revealed by data from the Asian Barometer Survey over the past two decades.

Looking at the seven East Asian countries with significant democratic experience over the past two decades (Japan, Korea, Taiwan,

FIGURE 10.5 Trends in satisfaction with democracy

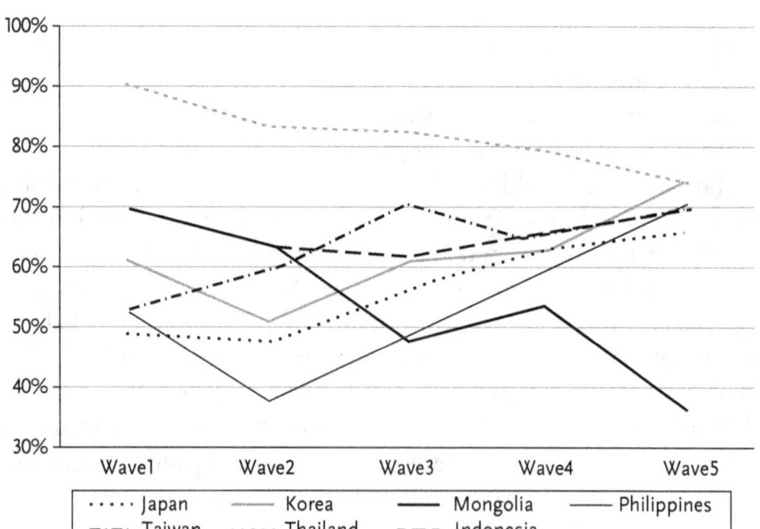

NOTE: Surveys were conducted at different times for each country. Wave 1 conducted 2001–03, Wave 2 in 2005–07, Wave 3 in 2010 and 2011, Wave 4 in 2014–16, and Wave 5 in 2018 and 2019.
SOURCE: Asian Barometer Surveys.

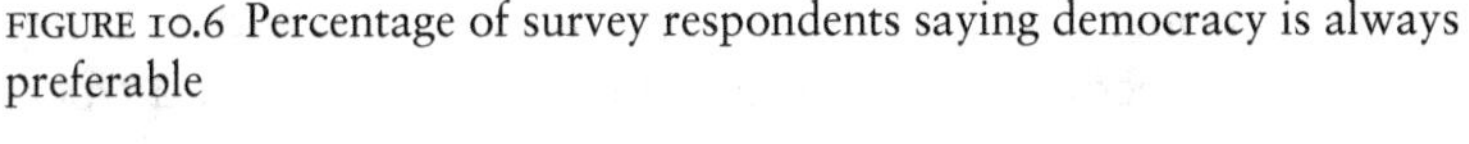

FIGURE 10.6 Percentage of survey respondents saying democracy is always preferable

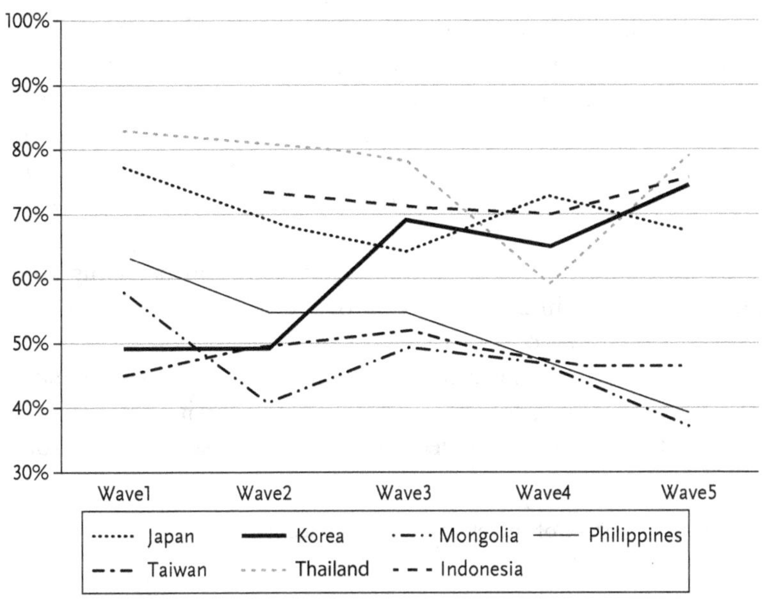

NOTE: Surveys were conducted at different times for each country. Wave 1 conducted 2001–03, Wave 2 in 2005–07, Wave 3 in 2010 and 2011, Wave 4 in 2014–16, and Wave 5 in 2018 and 2019.
SOURCE: Asian Barometer Surveys.

Mongolia, the Philippines, Thailand, and Indonesia), satisfaction with democracy declined precipitously in Mongolia, from 64 percent during Wave 2 of the survey (2006) to 37 percent most recently (around 2019). By contrast, satisfaction with democracy in Korea steadily rose during that period from 51 to 74 percent (figure 10.5). The Philippines also stands out for its declining support to democracy, as measured by the percentage agreeing with the statement "democracy is always preferable": from the Wave 1 survey (2001–03) to the Wave 5 survey (2019–20), this level of support declined from 64 percent to 40 percent. By contrast, agreement that "democracy is always best" steadily rose from 49 to 75 percent in Korea and remained above two-thirds in Japan and Indonesia (figure 10.6).

Most revealing has been the significant drop in the percentage of public in the Philippines and Mongolia rejecting all three conventional authoritarian options: one-party rule, strongman rule, and military rule. This robust rejection of authoritarianism dropped from 47 percent around 2002 to 31 percent most recently in Mongolia, and from 40 to 31 percent in the Philippines. By contrast, the three advanced industrial democracies of East Asia—Japan, Korea, and Taiwan—have exhibited consistently strong rejection (above two-thirds of the public) of all three authoritarian options. Somewhat concerning, however, has been the trend in Korea. While in Japan and Taiwan rejection of authoritarianism has steadily grown—from about 70 percent near the turn of this century to over 80 percent in 2019—Korea has moved in the opposite direction, with authoritarian rejection declining from a peak of 83 percent in 2006 (the year of the Wave 2 survey) to 70 percent in 2019 (figure 10.7).

Part of the reason, as is evident in figure 10.8, has been the increase (to 22 percent) in the proportion of Koreans endorsing the proposal to "Get rid of parliament and elections and have a strong leader decide

FIGURE 10.7 Percentage of survey respondents rejecting all authoritarian options

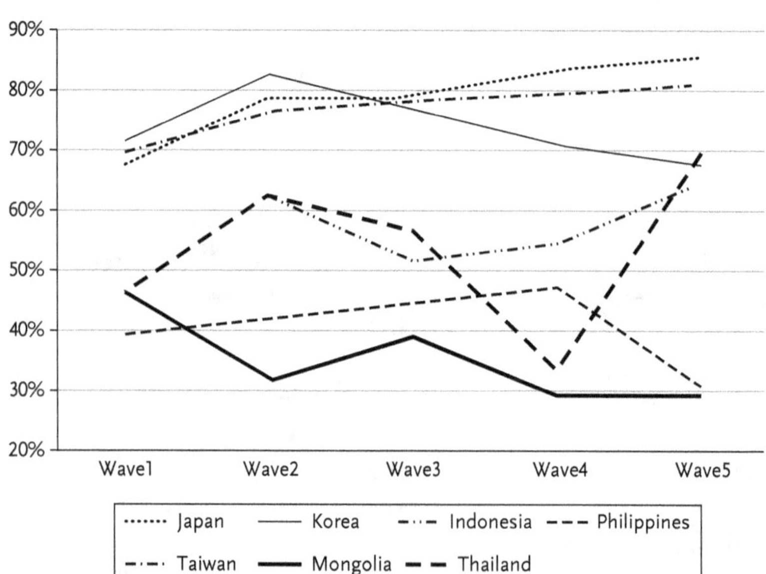

NOTE: Surveys were conducted at different times for each country. Wave 1 conducted 2001–2003, Wave 2 in 2005–2007, Wave 3 in 2010 and 2011, Wave 4 in 2014–2016, and Wave 5 in 2018 and 2019.
SOURCE: Asian Barometer Surveys.

FIGURE 10.8 Trends in support for authoritarian strong leaders

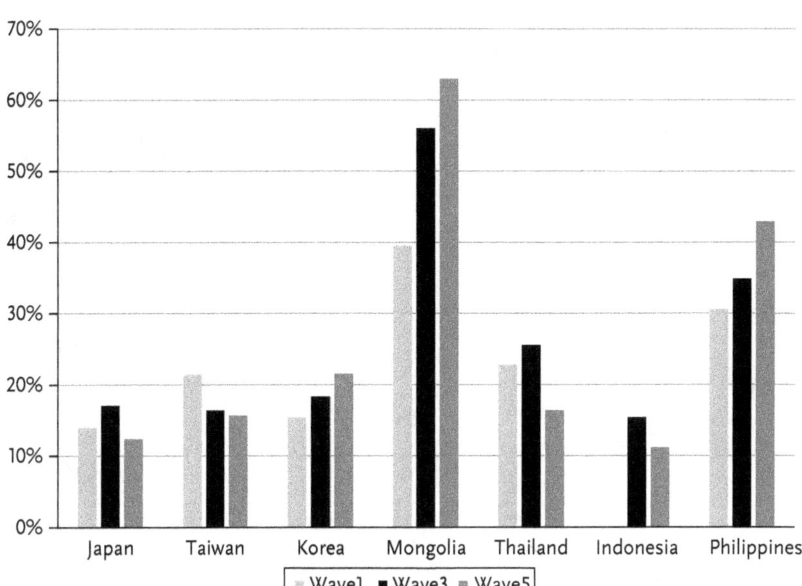

NOTE: Surveys were conducted at different times for each country. Wave 1 conducted 2001–03, Wave 3 in 2010 and 2011, and Wave 5 in 2018 and 2019.
SOURCE: Asian Barometer Surveys.

things." This exceeds the levels of support for this proposition even in the weaker democracies of Thailand and Indonesia. Support for this proposition has spiked to a shocking level in Mongolia (63 percent) and to a high level in the Philippines (43 percent) as well (figure 10.8).

More encouraging, in Korea there has been a steady decline in support for authoritarian values, such as whether the government should decide which ideas should be discussed in society, whether judges should defer to the executive in important cases, and whether the public should simply let "morally upright" leaders decide everything. In Japan, Taiwan, and Korea, average levels of support for a battery of seven such authoritarian values steadily fell over nearly two decades of the five surveys. This decline in average support for authoritarian values was especially dramatic in Korea, from 44 percent in 2003 to 29 percent in 2019. By contrast, the average levels of support for authoritarian values remained around or above 60 percent in the other four countries and increased in recent years in the Philippines (figure 10.9).

FIGURE 10.9 Trends in support for authoritarian values

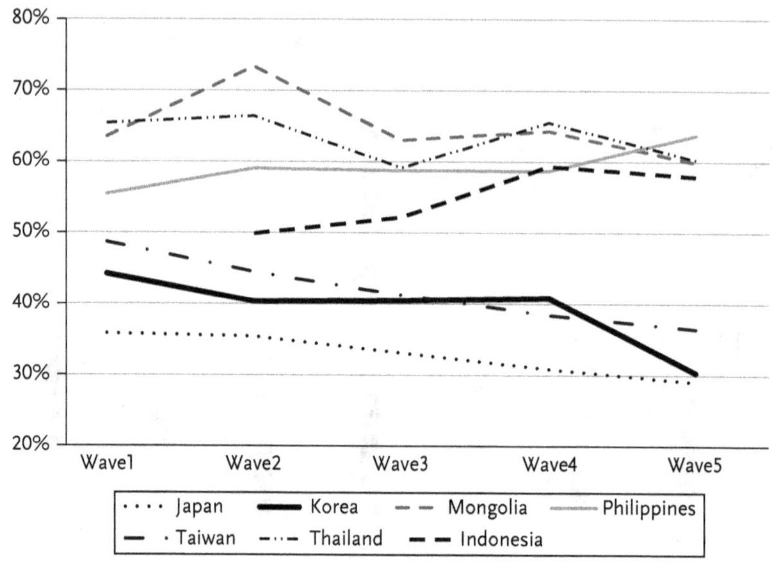

NOTE: Surveys were conducted at different times for each country. Wave 1 conducted 2001–2003, Wave 2 in 2005–2007, Wave 3 in 2010 and 2011, Wave 4 in 2014–2016, and Wave 5 in 2018 and 2019.
SOURCE: Asian Barometer Surveys.

Political and civic institutions

The second factor that can inhibit democratic backsliding is political institutions: whether the system has strong, institutionalized parties and agents of horizontal accountability (independent legislatures, courts, countercorruption agencies, regulatory bodies, election commissions, and other entities) that monitor, circumscribe, and constrain the power of elected executives. Strong political parties with institutionalized linkages to voters also limit the scope for populists to forge direct, personalistic ties to mass constituencies.[18] The strength of the legislature also has an independent effect in inhibiting authoritarian encroachment. Where legislatures are weak and compliant, unable to monitor and restrain an overbearing executive, checks and balances

18 Paul D. Kenney, *Populism and Patronage: Why Populists Win Elections in India, Asia, and Beyond* (Oxford: Oxford University Press, 2017).

and civil liberties tend to erode, while corruption thrives.[19] This is true for other agencies of horizontal accountability as well, like the courts and countercorruption bodies. The third factor is civil society, as independent nongovernmental organizations and mass media become essential supplements and reinforcements for agencies of horizontal accountability. If a country has high levels of education and income, along with a strong private sector independent of the state, it is more likely to have these elements of culture, civil society, and political institutions. Nevertheless, reasonably high economic development does not guarantee these elements, and low levels of development do not necessarily condemn a country to authoritarianism.[20]

There is some statistical evidence to suggest that weak rule of law is a "leading indicator" of trouble for democracy. As noted earlier, virtually all of the democracies that broke down during this most recent period (or any other) have been "illiberal," which is to say that competitive, democratic elections have coexisted with high levels of corruption and weak rule-of-law institutions. In addition, countries in every region typically perform worse on transparency and the rule of law than they do on political rights and civil liberties.

Political craft

Political craft—or, one could say, skill in authoritarian aggrandizement of power—has also been a relevant factor. There are basically three types of political leaders in a democracy: those who respect democratic norms and would not think to violate them; those who lack strong commitment to democracy but also lack the nerve or skill to dismantle it; and those who have both the ambition and the skill to bury democracy. The weaker the democratic institutions and other societal and external constraints, the less leadership skill is needed to dismantle democracy.

What are the skills of authoritarian populism? Populists gain and enlarge their power by manipulating fear of and hostility to established elites and outsiders (both "enemies of the people"), often through charismatic appeal to emotions, such as fear and anger. Populism may

19 Stephan Haggard and Robert Kaufman, *Backsliding: Democratic Regress in the Contemporary World* (Cambridge: Cambridge University Press, 2021).

20 For a more detailed overview, see Larry Diamond, *Ill Winds: Saving Democracy from Russian Rage, Chinese Ambition, and American Complacency* (New York: Penguin Press, 2019), 15–39.

appeal to rational interests, but it also creates images of threat, corruption, and cultural pollution with a strong nonrational or even irrational component. Populist leaders bypass mediating institutions and forge a direct relationship with "the people." They negate pluralism by insisting they are the only legitimate representatives of the people.[21] All of this requires considerable strategic and rhetorical skill, as well as mastery of both the conventional mass media and social media in the modern era.

Then there is the strategy and skill needed to demolish democratic institutions. Again, if the constraints in the constitutional system and civil society are weak, then the aspiring autocrat may be able to move swiftly to capture or undermine the institutional pillars of democracy. The hollowing out of democracy in Hungary, an EU member state, without the government being expelled from the European Union or seriously sanctioned, took consummate skill on the part of Viktor Orbán. Erdoğan in Turkey, Duterte in the Philippines, Kaczynski (head of the ruling PiS) in Poland, and Modi in India have all exhibited classic features of successful authoritarian populist leadership: charismatic mobilization of an intensely loyal mass following, cynical demonization of opponents and independent monitors, and a shrewd strategic nose for how to delegitimize and marginalize established elites and vulnerable minorities while promoting an ultra-majoritarian vision of democracy. One reason for concern about Korean democracy is that President Moon Jae-In has shown these characteristics too.[22] The fact that Poland and India are still (for now, just barely) electoral democracies, and that democracy persists in Korea testifies not to the limited skill and ambition of their populist leaders but to the strength of countervailing norms and institutions, and also to their leaders' lack of sufficient support in parliament to amend the constitution.

Each of these populist leaders does the work of eroding democracy through a sequence of incremental encroachments that I call "the autocrats' twelve-step program."[23] While the exact pace and sequence varies from one case to the next, the substance is strikingly common across widely varying cases. The early steps seek to weaken and disable checks

---

21 Jan-Werner Müller, *What Is Populism?* (Philadelphia: University of Pennsylvania Press, 2016); William A. Galston, *Anti-Pluralism: The Populist Threat to Liberal Democracy* (New Haven: Yale University Press, 2018).

22 Shin, "Korea's Democratic Decay."

23 Diamond, *Ill Winds*, 64–65.

on the power of the ruler. The opposition is relentlessly portrayed as corrupt and disloyal, and therefore illegitimate. The media is attacked as "fake news" and unpatriotic, part of the broader network of corrupt elites who disdain the real people. Thus, it must gradually be cowed and conquered. The courts are denounced as elitist and undemocratic, standing in the way of the "will of the people" as expressed at the ballot box. Therefore, they must be purged and stacked with politically loyal judges.

Then the authoritarian project attacks the foundations of the "deep state"—the civil service, the security apparatus, the agencies of horizontal accountability—purging them of "disloyal" elements and bending them to the will of the ruler and his or her party. Gradually, the executive, though democratically elected, knocks away the guardrails of liberal democratic restraint. Public broadcasting is taken over and made a mouthpiece of the ruling party. Stricter control is asserted over what can be conveyed on the internet—if it is critical of the government and ruling party. The business community is harnessed to the mission of partisan domination, with threats of tax and regulatory retribution for enterprises that do not "get with the program." Consequently, opposition parties are starved of funding. A new class of crony capitalists—slavishly loyal to the ruling party—is enriched through state contracts and licenses. These business cronies and servants of the ruling party then fund its campaigns and buy up what remains of the independent media.

As checks on the elected ruler and his or her party fall away, the emboldened autocrats turn their focus to the last remaining instruments of scrutiny and accountability in civil society. Independent civic associations, think tanks, universities, student groups, human rights organizations, writers, artists, and intellectuals are stigmatized as arrogant, snobbish, selfish elites who have betrayed "the people" and the country. Some are prosecuted and jailed so that others will get the message that resistance is futile. Finally, elections come again, but in a system where political pluralism and contestation have been reduced to faint whispers of their prior strength. To make matters worse, the ruling party gradually extends its control over electoral administration, rigging the rules to ensure that no "accidents" happen on the road to reelection. In this way, political competition and representation are formally preserved, but their democratic content is hollowed out. Gradually, the system morphs from an electoral democracy—with its uncertain outcomes—into a "competitive authoritarian" regime, in which fear governs civic life, the opposition lacks resources or legal protections, and state institutions praise and empower the autocrat.

International context

Given the limitations of human nature, there was always ample danger of this kind of regression and reversion. The biggest difference between the Third Wave (1975–2005) and the democratic recession (2006 to the present) has been the international context. During the last quarter of the twentieth century, the United States pursued an increasingly forthright and explicit foreign policy on behalf of democracy and human rights. It was never consistent or free of *realpolitik* deals with friendly autocrats, but at critical junctures in places like Argentina, the Philippines, Korea, Chile, and South Africa, the United States increasingly sided with the popular democratic opposition against unpopular authoritarian incumbents.[24] On top of the public messages and private warnings of American diplomacy, U.S. foreign assistance transferred resources, knowledge, and skills to help democratic parties, civil society groups, and institutional actors prevail over authoritarian alternatives.[25] Europe followed suit, both in diplomacy and in aid.[26]

We can break down the past forty-five years of global politics into three distinct fifteen-year segments. During the final period of the Cold War, from 1975 to 1990, freedom and democracy gradually expanded as the United States and Europe swung more energetically behind movements for human rights, civic space, and democratization. The number of democracies in the world increased from forty-six to seventy-four, and the percentage of all states that were democracies rose from 29 to 45 percent. From 1990 to 2005, the world experienced what the late Charles Krauthammer famously called a "unipolar moment."[27] The

24 George P. Shultz, *Turmoil and Triumph: My Years as Secretary of State* (New York: Charles Scribner's Sons, 1993), 608–42; Huntington, *The Third Wave*; Diamond, *The Spirit of Democracy*, 111–16.

25 Thomas Carothers, *Aiding Democracy Abroad: The Learning Curve* (Washington, DC: Carnegie Endowment for International Peace, 1999); Thomas Carothers, *Critical Mission: Essays on Democracy Promotion* (Washington, DC: Carnegie Endowment for International Peace, 2004).

26 Diamond, *The Spirit of Democracy*, 136–42.

27 Charles Krauthammer, "The Unipolar Moment," *Foreign Affairs* 70, no. 1 (1991): 23–33.

other superpower, the Soviet Union, had collapsed. China was still far from being able to pose a global economic, military, or geopolitical challenge. The United States stood alone as the "one first-rate power," with "no prospect in the immediate future of any power to rival it." Krauthammer underestimated the importance of Europe's economic influence and political conditionality, but we can identify this period as one of global democratic hegemony, during which the number of democracies peaked in 2005 at 117 and the percentage of democracies at 61 percent.

By then, the world was transitioning to a third period of democratic recession. Beginning around 2006, a powerful set of global changes converged to take the breath out of the Third Wave of global democratization. The most obvious factor was the disastrous U.S. decision to invade and occupy Iraq, which marked the end of America's "unipolar" hegemony and of its appetite for "democracy promotion."[28] In both Europe and the United States, this term came to be associated with the use of force and costly efforts to combat insurgencies and impose democracies in Afghanistan and Iraq. A new, or renewed, "pessimistic view of democracy promotion" took hold,[29] in part due to the rising salience of counterterrorism in the hierarchy of America's foreign policy priorities. The United States seemed increasingly willing to trade off democracy and human rights concerns for security cooperation in the Global War on Terror.

Global socioeconomic trends

The first decade of the twenty-first century also saw the acceleration of four deep and interrelated social and economic trends with important implications for democracy. First, was the rise of the internet, social media, and digital technology. These were powerful tools for organizing mass, decentralized protests against dictatorships, but they were less successful in facilitating the transformation of these protests into organized, coordinated, politically led movements for democratic change.

28 Larry Diamond, *Squandered Victory: The American Occupation and the Bungled Effort to Bring Democracy to Iraq* (New York: Henry Holt, 2005).
29 Thomas Carothers, "Is the U.S. Giving Up on Supporting Democracy Abroad?," *Foreign Policy*, September 8, 2016, https://carnegieendowment.org/2016/09/08/is-united-states-giving-up-on-supporting-democracy-abroad-pub-64516.

The failure of most Arab Spring protests to secure lasting democratic reform, for example, was due in no small measure to this limitation.[30] With the digital revolution came extraordinary new means for promoting disinformation, group hatred, and political polarization, which have facilitated the rise of illiberal and authoritarian populism.

Second, was the shift from manufacturing to finance and technology/knowledge production as dominant sources of wealth generation, which has been a major contributing factor to increasing income inequality, including in Korea. A growing share of national income and wealth has been captured by the top 10 percent, the top 1 percent, and especially the top tenth of the 1 percent of income earners.

Third, was the acceleration of globalization, with China joining the World Trade Organization in 2001, and rising levels of immigration into advanced economies. This displaced labor in the United States and some other advanced industrial economies, further aggravating social and economic insecurities and resentments. Fourth, was the long-term impact of the neoliberal revolution in economic policy, with its emphasis on deregulation and more scope for the free functioning of markets. In the United States, this freed up financial markets to engage in ever riskier and more speculative lending and financial transactions. This potent mixture—deregulation, digitization, financialization, globalization—resulted in the 2008 financial crash, which, since it originated in the United States, further damaged the reputation of democracy, as well as the resources and political self-confidence of the United States and other advanced democracies.

Initially, the effect on democracy of the financial and economic crises that erupted in 2008 seemed to be defeats for incumbents rather than the overthrow of democracies.[31] However, the longer-term impact has been more damaging, giving rise to substantial anxiety and social conflict and providing fertile soil for the rise of populist, nativist, anti-immigrant politics, with illiberal and even blatantly authoritarian undertones.

It is difficult to disentangle the multiple effects of changes in the international geopolitical and normative environment. Yet, a backlash has been gathering for some time against these intertwined shocks

30 Marc Lynch, "After the Arab Spring: How the Media Trashed the Transitions," *Journal of Democracy* 26, no. 4 (October 2015): 90–99.

31 Larry Diamond, "The Impact of Economic Crisis: Why Democracies Survive," *Journal of Democracy* 22, no. 1 (January 2011): 17–30.

and dislocations that made many ordinary people, particularly in less densely populated smaller towns and rural areas, feel threatened and marginalized, falling in status and economic prospects. At the same time they felt they were losing control of their country (to the European Union and other supranational institutions), their democracy (to unelected experts, civil servants, and judges), and their culture and society (to immigration and to "progressive values" favoring diversity, inclusion, and racial and gender equality).[32]

Russian rage and Chinese ambition

The last major element in the transformed global environment was "Russian rage and Chinese ambition,"[33] which in different ways have damaged and eroded the post–World War II, and especially the post–Cold War, hegemony of liberal values and institutions. To bend global norms, expectations, and institutions away from democracy, each of these authoritarian projects has relied principally on a form of influence known as "sharp power," because of the razor-like precision with which it cuts into the fabric of other societies.[34] In contrast to soft power, which seeks to inspire and persuade transparently though attraction and the power of example, sharp power operates in the shadows to compromise institutions through methods that are "covert, coercive, or corrupting."[35] Its coercion stops short of military force, economic sanctions, or other "hard power" means of compelling compliance, but it represents an insidious form of global power projection.

Russia's principal instrument of sharp power has been a kind of asymmetric warfare—a vast state-sponsored campaign to sow division and doubt in Western democracies and to aid the electoral fortunes of right-wing (and occasionally left-wing) illiberal populists who are sympathetic to Russia and dismissive of international liberal alliances

32 On the latter point, and the finding for a "cultural backlash" driving the illiberal populist wave, see Pippa Norris and Ronald F. Inglehart, *Cultural Backlash: Trump, Brexit, and Authoritarian Populism* (Cambridge: Cambridge University Press, 2019).

33 Diamond, *Ill Winds*.

34 Christopher Walker, "What Is Sharp Power?," *Journal of Democracy* 29, no. 3 (July 2018): 9–23; Juan Pablo Cardenal et al., *Sharp Power: Rising Authoritarian Influence* (Washington, DC: National Endowment for Democracy, 2017).

35 Larry Diamond and Orville Schell, *China's Influence and America's Interests: Promoting Constructive Vigilance* (Stanford: Hoover Institution, 2019), 5.

like NATO, the European Union, the G7, and other forms of democratic solidarity, integration, and cooperation. Russia sent financial aid to some right-wing populist European parties like the National Front in France, but its most damaging offensive was its social media disinformation efforts to aid the 2016 Brexit campaign and the 2016 presidential campaign of Donald Trump.

Far more consequential has been the rise of China to superpower status, powered by thirty years of 8–10 percent annual economic growth, a rapidly expanding military and global propaganda apparatus, and tens of billions of dollars in annual funding for a Belt and Road Initiative to construct infrastructure and telecommunications networks that assist economic development, while also binding countries to China's influence.[36] With a much larger budget at its disposal than Russia, China has been pumping resources (overtly and covertly) into associations, parties, politicians, media, think tanks, and universities in democracies and other societies abroad. The goal is not necessarily to destabilize individual democracies (save for Taiwan), but rather to stifle public criticism of China, preempt foreign and defense policies that could hinder China's rise to global dominance, and thus create "a world safe for autocracy." As China becomes the dominant source of global funding for the construction of highways, bridges, ports, and other physical infrastructure, and as it builds the digital highways that carry—and likely capture—the conversations and data of a growing number of societies, China displaces Western influence and promotes the idea that it has a superior, more functional model of governance. It relentlessly advances this notion by propagandizing through its sprawling global media empire,[37] infusing Chinese content into various forms of reporting, as well as training journalists in the Chinese Communist Party's manner of organizing and operating mass media. As with Russia's sharp power efforts, China's global campaign is generating a significant backlash.[38] The hard press of sharp power may leave countries

36 Minxin Pei, "A Play for Global Leadership," *Journal of Democracy* 29, no. 2 (April 2018): 37–51.

37 Louisa Lim and Julia Bergin, "Inside China's Audacious Global Propaganda Campaign," *The Guardian*, December 7, 2018, https://www.theguardian.com/news/2018/dec/07/china-plan-for-global-media-dominance-propaganda-xi-jinping.

38 Yaroslav Trofimov, "Europe's Face-Off with China," *Wall Street Journal*, February 28, 2020, https://www.wsj.com/articles/europes-face-off-with-china-11582905438; Steven Erlanger, "Global Backlash Build against China over Corona-

feeling coerced and conflicted, rather than attracted and inspired, but it is nevertheless a form of power with immense potential.

As president of the United States, Donald Trump accelerated the global power shift to autocracies, even as he began to counter China's projection of sharp power. Trump embraced autocrats around the world, including North Korea's Kim Jong-Un, while spurning democratic allies. By weakening America's standing and democratic alliances in the world, Trump played directly into the Russian and Chinese depictions of Western democracies as decadent and inefficacious.

Then came COVID-19. Although the pandemic originated in China and spread globally as a result of the embedded fear, rigidity, and opacity of the Chinese communist system, the Chinese state quickly brought it under control at home. The virus then surged out of control first in much of Europe and then in two of the four largest democracies in the world, the United States and Brazil, with India experiencing a crisis later as well. In reality, there appeared to be no clear relationship between regime type and the effective management of the pandemic. Democracies like Taiwan and Korea that acted early, vigorously, and transparently to coordinate a response, put public health officials at the forefront, and prioritized testing, tracing, and mask wearing enjoyed success in controlling the virus. However, the image of the United States, with its incompetent elected leaders completely unable to contain the virus, did further reputational damage to democracy. The pandemic proved to be a gift to political leaders—both of autocracies and democracies—who were interested in aggrandizing their power. From Hungary and Bangladesh to the Philippines and India, rulers exploited the opportunity to arrest critics, journalists, health workers, human rights activists, opposition leaders, and anyone else threatening "public order."[39]

Conclusion: Implications for Korea and Other Democracies

The democratic recession that began as a slow and quite uneven ebbing of progress fifteen years ago has now morphed into a widespread

virus," *New York Times*, May 3, 2020, https://www.nytimes.com/2020/05/03/world/europe/backlash-china-coronavirus.html.

39 Larry Diamond, "Democracy Versus the Pandemic: The Coronavirus Is Emboldening Autocrats the World Over," *Foreign Affairs*, June 13, 2020, https://www.foreignaffairs.com/articles/world/2020-06-13/democracy-versus-pandemic.

and substantial regression of freedom and democracy across the world. One of the most sobering aspects of this regression has been the decay—or at least decline in quality—of many long-established democracies that have been presumed to be "consolidated" and stable. Most prominently, this includes the United States, which has registered the largest decline in the Freedom House score of any advanced industrial democracy. It also includes India and many "Third Wave" democracies like Korea, Brazil, and Poland that are now more than three decades past their democratic transitions.

The chapters in this volume document a disturbing trend of deepening polarization and erosion of democratic norms and restraints that may not have begun with the Moon Jae-In administration but has certainly accelerated under it. As Gi-Wook Shin and Ho-Ki Kim note in their introduction, the context for this descent of Korean democracy has been the rise of populist politics, posing an existential cleavage between the pure, deserving people and a corrupt, exploitative—indeed, "evil"—political establishment. As a political system that is uniquely dependent on the need for mutual tolerance, forbearance, compromise, and restraint, democracy cannot long survive a political struggle that is pitched as an existential battle between good and evil—how is it possible to tolerate and compromise with an "evil" opposing force that threatens transcendent values? If the other side is indeed evil, then a struggle to eradicate it is the logical and morally necessary course.

The global democratic recession has featured a tragic succession of cases in which the populist framing of the opposition as evil, selfish, and corrupt—preying on the suffering majority—has justified creeping assaults on freedom, checks and balances, and the rule of law, along with the personalization of political power. This has been the core narrative that has justified illiberal assaults on the independence of the media, the prosecutors, the judiciary, and the state bureaucracy, and on the civil liberties of political opponents and critics, in such diverse countries as Venezuela under Chávez, Turkey under Erdoğan, Hungary under Orbán, Poland under the Law and Justice Party, and the Philippines under Duterte.

The deterioration of democracy is not nearly as far along in Korea, but it is following the same trajectory. Fortunately, that trajectory is not irreversible. Populist assaults brought democracy to the brink of failure in Bolivia, Ecuador, Colombia, South Africa, and elsewhere, before electoral alternation arrested and at least partially reversed the authoritarian trends. Electoral pushbacks against the divisive, zero-sum populist politics of polarization have also made inroads against authoritarianism in Turkey and Hungary and have substantially restored the health of democracy in Greece. The struggle is now ongoing in the United States, where one of the two major political parties has been substantially captured by an illiberal, populist mentality that is hostile to democratic procedures and norms. What lessons can Korea learn from these cases?

First, it is important to separate the contest over ideology and programs from the contest over democratic norms and procedures. One reason for hope about the future of democracy in Korea is that some prominent progressive intellectuals, such as Choi Jang-Jip and some of the contributors to this volume, have spoken up forthrightly against the authoritarian actions of the Moon administration, even though these individuals may sympathize with many of the administration's social and economic policy goals. Populists pursue a hegemonic project, attempting to aggrandize executive power and permanently marginalize the "evil" and "corrupt" opposition in the pursuit of what they claim to be an existential moral cause. This project puts democratic institutions and principles on the defensive. The struggle to resist this push must become a broad front that welcomes principled individuals from a wide variety of political ideologies and backgrounds, united by a single common purpose: to resist creeping authoritarianism and restore democracy to good health.

Second, as Ginsburg and Huq stress in their analysis of how some democracies have managed to free themselves from the downward spiral of creeping authoritarianism, it is crucial to preserve and reawaken the neutrality of key state institutions. As the current political drama in the United States attests, no such institution is more important than "neutral electoral machinery staffed by officials able to resist political capture." More broadly, in cases of what Ginsburg and Huq call democracy's "near misses," the system held together because in other sectors, such as the security apparatus and the civilian bureaucracy, "a large number of unelected elite actors committed themselves to democracy."[40]

Defending the independence and rallying the professional spirit of nonpartisan state actors require a very broad coalition that transcends traditional social and ideological divides—and that even unites

40 Tom Ginsburg and Aziz Huq, "Democracy's 'Near Misses'," *Journal of Democracy* 29, no. 4 (October 2018): 28.

"erstwhile political opponents."[41] This is the third lesson from countries that have turned back or begun to make progress in reversing democratic backsliding. Those who are committed to democracy—whether they come from the left, right, or center, or from no previous political posture at all—must methodically and impartially document the incumbent administration's transgressions against democratic principles and norms. They must appeal to judicial, accountability, security, and bureaucratic actors in the state to perform their duties without fear or favor and rise to defend such conscientious actors against political retribution. Then, a broad civic coalition must craft an agenda for reform that fixes the systemic vulnerabilities exploited by the overreaching executive and repairs institutional damage. In Korea, the reform agenda would need to include legislation to strengthen judicial autonomy and electoral reforms to reduce partisan polarization as well as the potential for domination of the National Assembly by the executive. Let us consider them in reverse order.

The relationship between the executive and the legislature presents an intrinsic dilemma for presidential democracies. If the legislature is too fragmented, or even if the ruling party simply lacks a legislative majority, then democracy faces the danger of deadlock and stagnation, and even recurrent efforts to impeach elected presidents—as has happened in Brazil and Peru. The combination of presidentialism and proportional representation, yielding a parliament of multiple parties, has been a difficult and often destabilizing one for Brazil and other Latin American countries.[42] Yet recently, it has perhaps saved Brazilian democracy by denying its authoritarian populist president, Jair Bolsonaro, the legislative backing he needed to transform the system. Legislative majorities that were utterly deferential to the executive have been critical to the success of authoritarian populist projects in countries like Venezuela, Hungary, and Turkey.[43] Thus, an electoral system that gives rise to a moderate multiparty system, anchored by two preeminent but not exclusively dominant parties, may represent the best balance for Korea. Switching to a parliamentary system would probably be better for Korean democracy, but that option would offer no immunity against a descent into populist author-

41 Ginsburg and Huq, "Democracy's 'Near Misses'."
42 Scott Mainwaring, "Presidentialism, Multipartyism, and Democracy: The Difficult Combination," *Comparative Political Studies* 26 (July 1993): 198–227.
43 Haggard and Kaufman, *Backsliding*.

itarianism, as the cases of Turkey, Hungary, Bangladesh, and India show.

Korea today has a substantially majoritarian electoral system for its unicameral National Assembly, with 84 percent of its three hundred seats filled through first-past-the-post elections in single-member districts. Notwithstanding the recent manipulation of the proportional representation rules that was advantageous to the larger parties in filling the remaining forty-seven seats, this is an electoral system likely to give rise to a two-party-dominant system, and hence to polarization between competing parties of the left and right—even if their names and leaders keep changing. Given the paralyzing nature of political polarization in Korea, and the way it has served and intertwined with illiberal populism, it may be time for the country to consider a more fundamental reform of its electoral system: designing a more balanced mixed-member proportional system that would fill up to half the National Assembly seats through proportional representation.

For example, Korea could opt to fill only half (or 60 percent) of the three hundred seats in single-member constituencies and elect the remainder from national party lists, without requiring the calculating gamesmanship of the recent rule change that has given rise to "satellite" parties of the ruling parties. Alternatively, it could keep the current 253 geographic constituencies (or slightly reduce them to 200) and enlarge the National Assembly by adding on a more serious and substantial proportional representation component of perhaps 200 seats, with a modest threshold of 2–5 percent for entry into parliament.[44] Doing this would likely serve the worthy goal suggested by Kwanhu Lee in chapter 3 of increasing the diversity of political representation. In fact, if Korea also required parties to list women in at least every other position on their ranked party lists, it could significantly increase the proportion of women in its parliament (currently 17 percent), which is quite low by the standards of today's advanced industrial democracies.[45]

44 The Korean Constitution only establishes a floor (of two hundred seats) for the National Assembly, and otherwise leaves it to that body to set the number of members. Many advanced democracies with populations in the tens of millions have parliaments with four hundred members or more, including Britain, Germany, France, Italy, and Japan.

45 Most European democracies have more than 30 percent women in the lower house of parliament, and some now approach 50 percent. The United States lags at 24 percent, precisely because it does not have a proportional representation component to its electoral system.

Filling a substantial number of seats through proportional representation might also enable the rise of a "third force" in Korean politics, coming from the more pragmatic center, which may not be able to prevail in many single-seat constituencies but could win enough of the vote to keep the National Assembly from being dominated by either of the two dominant parties. Proportional representation might also enable other new parties to form and win some seats as well. This could require a future Korean president to pursue a more flexible and accommodating pattern of bargaining in order to accomplish their goals—and make it more difficult for a president to pursue undemocratic legislation, or to depict the political landscape as a zero-sum struggle between good and evil. Shifting the single-seat constituencies to ranked-choice voting could also serve these goals, giving voters more choice and smaller parties and independents a meaningful chance to contest constituency-level races.

When electoral alternation comes in Korea, there will be a natural temptation by the right to retaliate in kind and deliver "payback" to the former governing left. This turning of the tables could be used to justify further aggrandizement of executive power and politicization of state and judicial functions. For Korean democracy to thrive, this cycle must be broken. Prosecutions of former officials should be exceptional and pursued by wholly independent prosecutors. Executive power must be restrained, and a new civic force must emerge in the mass media, universities, and civil society dedicated principally to the defense of democracy.

To address the concern of Seongwook Heo in chapter 5 about the politicization of the judiciary, Korea could consider lengthening the terms of constitutional and supreme court justices. A six-year term for court justices enables a Korean president to appoint too many of them during their five-year presidential term. Appointments to the U.S. constitutional court are too long (for life), but Korea's are too short. Some American reformers, including this author, have called for eighteen-year terms for the nine U.S. Supreme Court justices, with appointments staggered every two years so that a U.S. president could appoint a new justice in the first and third year of each presidential term. Korea could devise a similar arrangement, with perhaps a ten- to fifteen-year term for justices. For example, if Constitutional Court justices served fifteen-year terms, a rhythm could eventually be established whereby a Korean president would appoint one new justice in the first, third, and fifth years of their term, appointing one-third of the nine-member court by the end of the term. A similar rhythm could be established for Korea's fourteen-member Supreme Court, perhaps by enlarging the court to fifteen justices and having a president appoint one justice per year to fifteen-year terms. Longer terms tend to depoliticize the court and free justices from short-term considerations.

What Korean democracy most needs now is a reform coalition drawn from disaffected elements of the political right and left and civil society thinkers, activists, and organizations who see the need to break the downward spiral of zero-sum, self-righteous politics and hyper-politicization of the judiciary, the state, and society. If such a coalition can achieve institutional reforms to reduce polarization, this will take some of the toxicity out of the political culture, and both developments in turn will make Korean democracy more functional and less embittered. That could begin to turn the tide on illiberal populism and the politics of vengeance, crisis, and decay. So could a different electoral strategy by the party or coalition out of power, one which seeks to transcend the politics of polarization and personal destruction with a politics of inclusion, pragmatism, and even—to borrow the campaign theme of the opposition in Turkey, which lifted it to victory over Erdoğan's party in recent municipal elections—"radical love."[46]

In the end, only so much can be accomplished through legal and institutional reforms. What can be done by democratic reform legislation can be undone by a future populist president with hegemonic pretensions—so long as he or she has majority support in the National Assembly, and especially if the populist has a special majority to amend the constitution. In the end, democracy can only be sustained by a broad normative commitment at both the elite and mass levels. This requires not just a formal commitment to winning power through electoral competition, but also recognition of the need for truly free and fair elections and for ongoing respect for the political and civil rights of opposition and minority groups. The question of how to build a new culture of commitment to democratic norms of tolerance and mutual respect and restraint among diverse political forces should be a leading one in Korean society today.

---

46 Michael Wuthrich and Melvin Inglesby, "The Pushback against Populism: Running on 'Radical Love' in Turkey," *Journal of Democracy* 31, no. 2 (April 2020): 24–40.

Bibliography

Bankuti, Miklós, Gábor Halmai, and Kim Lane Scheppele. "Hungary's Illiberal Turn: Disabling the Constitution." *Journal of Democracy* 23, no. 3 (July 2012): 138–46.

Cardenal, Juan Pablo et al. *Sharp Power: Rising Authoritarian Influence*. Washington, DC: National Endowment for Democracy, 2017.

Carothers, Thomas. *Aiding Democracy Abroad: The Learning Curve*. Washington, DC: Carnegie Endowment for International Peace, 1999.

———. *Critical Mission: Essays on Democracy Promotion*. Washington, DC: Carnegie Endowment for International Peace, 2004.

———. "Is the United States Giving Up on Supporting Democracy Abroad?" *Foreign Policy*, September 8, 2016. https://carnegieendowment.org/2016/09/08/is-united-states-giving-up-on-supporting-democracy-abroad-pub-64516.

Diamond, Larry. *Developing Democracy: Toward Consolidation*. Baltimore: Johns Hopkins University Press, 1999.

———. *Squandered Victory: The American Occupation and the Bungled Effort to Bring Democracy to Iraq*. New York: Henry Holt, 2005.

———. *The Spirit of Democracy: The Struggle to Build Free Societies throughout the World*. New York: Times Books, 2008.

———. "The Impact of the Economic Crisis: Why Democracies Survive." *Journal of Democracy* 22, no. 1 (January 2011): 17–30.

———. *Ill Winds: Saving Democracy from Russian Rage, Chinese Ambition, and American Complacency.* New York: Penguin Press, 2019.

———. "Democracy Versus the Pandemic: The Coronavirus Is Emboldening Autocrats the World Over." *Foreign Affairs*, June 13, 2020. https://www.foreignaffairs.com/articles/world/2020-06-13/democracy-versus-pandemic.

———. "Democratic Regression in Comparative Perspective: Scope, Methods, and Causes." *Democratization* 28, no. 1 (2020): 22–42.

Diamond, Larry, and Orville Schell. *China's Influence and America's Interests: Promoting Constructive Vigilance*. Stanford: Hoover Institution, 2019.

Erlanger, Steven. "Global Backlash Builds against China over Coronavirus." *New York Times*, May 3, 2020. https://www.nytimes.com/2020/05/03/world/europe/backlash-china-coronavirus.html.

Fomina, Joanna, and Jack Kucharczyk. "The Specter Haunting Europe: Populism and Protest in Poland." *Journal of Democracy* 27, no. 4 (October 2016): 58–68.

Galston, William A. *Anti-Pluralism: The Populist Threat to Liberal Democracy*. New Haven: Yale University Press, 2018.

Ganguly, Sumit. "An Illiberal India?" *Journal of Democracy* 31, no. 1 (January 2020): 193–202.

Ginsburg, Tom, and Aziz Huq. "Democracy's 'Near Misses'." *Journal of Democracy* 29, no. 4 (October 2018): 16–30.

Haggard, Stephan, and Robert Kaufman. *Backsliding: Democratic Regress in the Contemporary World*. Cambridge: Cambridge University Press, 2021.

Huntington, Samuel P. *The Third Wave: Democratization in the Late Twentieth Century*. Norman: University of Oklahoma Press, 1991.

Kenney, Paul D. *Populism and Patronage: Why Populists Win Elections in India, Asia, and Beyond*. Oxford: Oxford University Press, 2017.

Krauthammer, Charles. "The Unipolar Moment." *Foreign Affairs* 70, no. 1 (1991): 23–33.

Lynch, Marc. "After the Arab Spring: How the Media Trashed the Transitions." *Journal of Democracy* 26, no. 4 (October 2015): 90–99.

Lemière, Sophie. "The Downfall of Malaysia's Ruling Party." *Journal of Democracy* 29, no. 4 (October 2018): 114–28.

Levitsky, Steven, and Lucan Way. "The Myth of Democratic Recession." *Journal of Democracy* 26, no. 1 (January 2015): 45–58.

Lim, Louisa, and Julia Bergin. "Inside China's Audacious Global Propaganda Campaign." *The Guardian*, December 7, 2018. https://www.theguardian.com/news/2018/dec/07/china-plan-for-global-media-dominance-propaganda-xi-jinping.

Mainwaring, Scott. "Presidentialism, Multipartyism, and Democracy: The Difficult Combination." *Comparative Political Studies* 26 (July 1993): 198–227.

McCoy, Jennifer, and Murat Somer. "Toward a Theory of Pernicious Polarization and How It Harms Democracies: Comparative Evidence and Possible Remedies." *Annals of the American Academy of Political and Social Science* 681 (2019): 234–71.

Morgenbesser, Lee. "Cambodia's Transition to Hegemonic Authoritarianism." *Journal of Democracy* 30, no. 1 (January 2019): 158–71.

Mourdoukoutas, Panos. "Duterte Is Turning Philippines into a More Corrupt and Less Democratic State." *Forbes*, January 24, 2020. https://www.forbes.com/sites/panosmourdoukoutas/2020/01/24/duterte-is-turning-philippines-into-a-more-corrupt-and-less-democratic-state/?sh=6b4aec912768.

Müller, Jan-Werner. *What Is Populism?* Philadelphia: University of Pennsylvania Press, 2016.

Norris, Pippa, and Ronald F. Inglehart. *Cultural Backlash: Trump, Brexit, and Authoritarian Populism*. Cambridge: Cambridge University Press, 2019.

Obe, Ayo. "Aspirations and Realities in Africa: Nigeria's Emerging Two-Party System?" *Journal of Democracy* 30, no. 3 (July 2019): 109–23.

Pei, Minxin. "A Play for Global Leadership." *Journal of Democracy* 29, no. 2 (April 2018): 37–51.

Repucci, Sarah. "Freedom in the World 2020: A Leaderless Struggle for Democracy." Freedom House. Accessed November 30, 2021. https://freedomhouse.org/report/freedom-world/2020/leaderless-struggle-democracy.

Rupnik, Jacques. "Hungary's Illiberal Turn: How Things Went Wrong." *Journal of Democracy* 23, no. 3 (July 2012): 132–37.

Shin, Gi-Wook. "South Korea's Democratic Decay." *Journal of Democracy* 31, no. 3 (July 2020): 100–14.

Shultz, George P. *Turmoil and Triumph: My Years as Secretary of State*. New York: Charles Scribner's Sons, 1993.

Soyinka, Wole. "Lessons from Nigeria's Militarized Experiment." *New York Times*, October 9, 2019. https://www.nytimes.com/2019/10/09/opinion/nigeria-militarized-democratic-experiment.html.

Trofimov, Yaroslav. "Europe's Face-Off with China." *Wall Street Journal*, February 28, 2020. https://www.wsj.com/articles/europes-face-off-with-china-11582905438.

Walker, Christopher. "What Is Sharp Power?" *Journal of Democracy* 29, no. 3 (July 2018): 9–23.

Wong, Brian. "Democracy in Crisis: Where Does Malaysia Go from Here?" *The Diplomat*, February 27, 2020. https://thediplomat.com/2020/02/democracy-in-crisis-where-does-malaysia-go-from-here/.

Wuthrich, Michael, and Melvin Inglesby. "The Pushback against Populism: Running on 'Radical Love' in Turkey." *Journal of Democracy* 31, no. 2 (April 2020): 24–40.

EPILOGUE

Korea's 2022 Presidential Election

Populism in the Post-Truth Era

Ho-Ki Kim and Gi-Wook Shin

The conference on which this book is based was held in November 2020. As the conference papers were being revised and prepared for publication, a presidential election was well underway in Korea. The ruling Democratic Party chose its candidate, Lee Jae-Myung, in October 2021, and the People Power Party—the main opposition party—selected its candidate, Yoon Seok-Youl, the following month. Sim Sang-Jeong of the Justice Party and Ahn Cheol-Soo of the People's Party were also vying for the presidency.

When this book is published, a new president will have been elected in Korea. The intent of this epilogue is not to speculate about who might enter the Blue House in May 2022, but rather to assess the current state and future of Korea's democracy by closely examining how the presidential election has unfolded thus far (as of January 2022) against the backdrop of the Moon administration's challenging legacy that has been discussed in the chapters of this book.

Korea was a guiding light for democracies in Asia from the late 1980s, but clouds have been gathering over Korean democracy since the 2010s. The Park Geun-Hye administration, which began in 2013, regressed to an authoritarian mode of governance reminiscent of the Park Chung-Hee era, in tension with Korea's democratic and pluralistic civil society. These tensions erupted in the candlelight protests of 2016 and 2017, ultimately leading to the impeachment of Park—a watershed moment in Korea's political history. As noted in this book, Korea's democratization was led not by the political elite, but instead by civil society and social movements. Through the candlelight protests, Korea's civil society essentially rejected and ousted an authoritarian state once again. Political scientist Yascha Mounk praised the candlelight protests for successfully defending Korea's liberal democracy.[1]

The Moon Jae-In administration (2017–22), which came to power in the aftermath of popular protests and presidential impeachment, had a golden opportunity to correct the undemocratic practices of the previous government and to advance Korea's democracy. The administration instead took the opposite course, resorting to zero-sum politics in which opponents were demonized, democratic norms eroded, and political life grew ever more polarized. The Moon administration's illiberal nature was most clearly exhibited in its campaign to "eradicate deep-rooted evils," which demonized and punished political opponents according to the Manichean logic of good and evil, endangering Korea's liberalism and pluralism. Mutual tolerance and forbearance in today's Korean politics are scant.

It is under these circumstances that the current presidential contest began. Korean society is highly polarized, and both the ruling and main opposition parties have engaged in extensive negative campaigns against each other. Many say that this is the most uninspiring presidential election since democratization in 1987—one that is not about choosing the most appealing candidate, but instead about avoiding the worst. Still, it is worth considering the sociopolitical implications of the ongoing presidential race for Korean democracy.

Three aspects merit close attention in understanding the features of the current election as well as its implications for the future of Korean democracy: the personal profiles of the candidates, the populist nature of the race, and the emergence of a "post-truth" era.

First, the two leading contenders share important personal characteristics, despite representing opposing political forces. Both Lee and Yoon have no legislative experience in the National Assembly, a first in Korean history after democratization. Lee has served as the mayor of Seongnam City and the governor of Gyeonggi Province, and his administrative record in local government has earned relatively high marks. Yoon Seok-Youl, a former prosecutor, became widely known for his role in leading the Moon administration's campaign to "eradicate deep-rooted evils." He became all but a household name during his term as prosecutor general, when he withstood political pressure from

1 Yascha Mounk, *The People vs. Democracy: Why Our Freedom Is in Danger and How to Save It* (Cambridge: Harvard University Press, 2018).

the ruling bloc to be lenient toward their own people under criminal investigation.

How did individuals with no legislative experience become presidential candidates of Korea's two leading political parties, and what do their candidacies say about Korean politics? In the Democratic Party primaries, Lee Jae-Myung defeated Lee Nak-Yeon, who had served as the first prime minister during the Moon administration and then the head of the ruling Democratic Party. Similarly, Yoon Seok-Youl won out against Hong Joon-Pyo, an experienced politician with a wide-ranging political career that spans over two decades. This outcome reflects a deep and broad mistrust of politicians among a wide swath of the Korean public. The people voiced their dissatisfaction by rejecting the political establishment and seeking new leaders beyond the halls of power in Yeouido, Korea's Beltway. Yoon's candidacy is highly unusual, even compared to that of Lee. Though Yoon was appointed by President Moon as prosecutor general, he is now the candidate of the conservative opposition party. He draws his political clout from two sources: he is regarded as a stalwart reformer for his high-profile role in the campaign to "eradicate deep-rooted evils," and he is also seen as a victim of the Moon administration's political oppression. Therefore, the supporters of the opposition party, whose utmost goal is to reclaim the Blue House, found their candidate in Yoon—someone they see as a reformer who unjustly suffered at the hands of the ruling party.

Lee and Yoon may be far apart in ideological terms, but they bear resemblance to the prevailing mode of contemporary political leadership across the world. As can be seen from former president Donald Trump and President Xi Jinping, "strongmen" have taken center stage in global politics in the twenty-first century. This type of leader stresses decisiveness and forceful action over rational deliberation and compromise. Strongmen draw their support from the people, not necessarily from within established political parties. These characteristics are typical of populist leaders, and thus Lee Jae-Myung and Yoon Seok-Youl indicate that contemporary Korean politics is also being driven by populist strongmen.

Second, the manner in which the presidential race has unfolded has unmistakably populist characteristics. Populism in the twenty-first century greatly differs from populism in the twentieth century, which sought to appeal to public sentiment. Jan-Werner Müller argues that twenty-first-century populism has two defining features: anti-elitism and anti-pluralism.[2] The former attacks the elite, while the latter rejects coexistence with other political forces. Anti-elitism manifests as hatred for party politics, while anti-pluralism reveals itself in the demonization of other political actors. A culture of direct dealing between populist leaders and their supporters, enabled by advances in information technology, is the third defining characteristic. Trumpism in the United States is the archetype of twenty-first-century populism.

Korea has entered a populist era too, and democratization no longer operates as a "master frame" as in past elections. Democracy vs. authoritarianism is no longer a central campaign issue, and democratic activist experience does not confer much political capital. While many Koreans in their forties and fifties still look upon the generation of former activists as a force that confronted and resisted the military dictatorship, most in their twenties and thirties simply regard this generation as Korea's new establishment elite. The pro-democracy activists' power and influence rested on their moral superiority over the preceding generation, which had prioritized economic development above all else, but that moral ground has been lost. The scandal surrounding the appointment of Cho Kuk as justice minister in the Moon administration illustrated this fall from grace in no uncertain terms.

In this populist era, both conservatives and progressives are seeking to garner support by accentuating the divide between the elite and the people. In the Korean context, progressives attack the generation of conservatives who led successful industrialization as the old elite, while conservatives now charge the generation of progressive pro-democracy activists of being the new elite. They have engaged in extensive negative campaigns, not hesitating to make personal attacks, including attacks on each other's families, and directed their political messaging almost entirely at their own supporters. In such a polarized and divisive atmosphere, the qualities and capabilities of each candidate become a peripheral concern, as the two sides lock in an ever-intensifying struggle to seize political power with little chance for rational discussion of key policy issues.

Third, in today's newly emerging "post-truth" era, appealing to subjective beliefs, instead of relying on objective facts, decisively sways public opinion. Beliefs and emotions replace facts and rationality. Overwhelmed with a deluge of information, individuals are heavily inclined

2 Jan-Werner Müller, *What Is Populism?* (Philadelphia: University of Pennsylvania Press, 2016).

to see and listen only to the news that appeals to them. This further reinforces political and social "tribalism" in the public sphere and in civil society. Anti-elitism, anti-pluralism, and a culture of direct contact between populist leaders and ordinary people are all strengthened by the political tribalism of a post-truth society. Politics then descends into a brutal struggle for power between competing "tribes," each held together by an unshakable commitment to commonly held beliefs and sentiments.

This political tribalism is spurring a "culture war" in many places around the world, and Korea is no exception. James Hunter, who defined a "culture war" within the U.S. context, argued that American society was split into two opposing camps based on "hot-button" issues such as abortion, separation of church and state, privacy, homosexuality, and gun rights.[3] A culture war constrains the space for mutual tolerance and societal consensus building, which is crucial to sustaining liberal democracy. In particular, the 2020 presidential election marked a new height in America's culture war. It almost appeared as if American society had split into two entirely separate countries, delineated by support for or opposition to Donald Trump.

In Korea, ever since the democratic era, there has been a fierce culture war between conservatives and progressives on issues like the legacy of authoritarian leaders (Syngman Rhee and Park Chung-Hee) and views of North Korea and Japan. Today, the traditional divide between the rich and the poor intersects with new, twenty-first-century divides around gender and age. It is impossible to understand the political identities of Korea's youth without simultaneously considering the multiple dimensions of wealth, generation, and gender. The political institution of a single, five-year presidential term has an amplifying effect. Since a new individual must be elected as president every five years, a ferocious ideological war repeats itself with every election. Thus, Korea's culture war continues to grow in intensity.

The concept of a culture war can account for identity politics in Korea. Identity refers to the thoughts, emotions, and ideologies that provide an individual with a sense of self and influence one's actions as much as economic and material interests. The previous mode of politics is being replaced by identity politics, which expresses resentment and resistance toward a status quo that disregards or rejects elements of

3 James D. Hunter, *Culture Wars: The Struggle to Define America* (New York: Basic Books, 1991).

one's identity, be it religion, race, nationality, or gender. Identity politics can easily lead to "political fandoms," in which supporters only see and listen to content that reinforces their political attitudes. As is the case in the United States, prospects for tolerance, coexistence, and compromise are becoming increasingly dim in Korea.

Whither Korea's democracy? Unfortunately, what we have observed so far in this election does not provide a definite or reassuring view of the road ahead. In retrospect, Korea has certainly been an exemplar of democracy across Asia for the past four decades. The way in which it constructively combined economic development (industrialization) and political progress (democratization) has served as a promising model for other countries. Yet, what were once just preliminary signs of democratic backsliding are now undeniable marks of democratic decay in Korea. As this presidential election will be the first held in the era of post-truth and populism, it is critical to safeguard democracy and social integration. Korea's preexisting inequalities and societal conflicts make this task all the more urgent.

It is our sincere hope that the new administration will choose democracy over populism, pursue social integration over "eradicating deep-rooted evils," and emphasize the truth instead of resorting to post-truth. Democracy and social integration, which draw their strength from a public sphere based on truth and the dynamism of civil society, are the most prudent means by which to address and alleviate inequality and societal conflict.

Only time will tell if these aspirations are realized. We hope that this volume will be of assistance to all those in Korea who seek to restore, protect, and advance its democracy.

Bibliography

Hunter, James D. *Culture Wars: The Struggle to Define America*. New York: Basic Books, 1991.

Mounk, Yascha. *The People vs. Democracy: Why Our Freedom Is in Danger and How to Save It*. Cambridge: Harvard University Press, 2018.

Müller, Jan-Werner. *What Is Populism?* Philadelphia: University of Pennsylvania Press, 2016.

Index

The authorized representative in the EU for product safety and compliance is:
Mare Nostrum Group
B.V Doelen 72
4831 GR Breda
The Netherlands

www.ingramcontent.com/pod-product-compliance
Lightning Source LLC
Chambersburg PA
CBHW061001280326
41935CB00009B/783

* 9 7 8 1 5 3 8 1 7 7 8 1 5 *